THE UPANISHADS

TEXTS, TRANSLATIONS AND COMMENTARIES

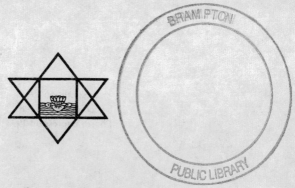

Sri Aurobindo

The Upanishads

TEXTS, TRANSLATIONS AND COMMENTARIES

Sri Aurobindo Ashram

Pondicherry

First edition 1971
Second edition 1981
Fourth impression 1992

(PB) ISBN 81-7058-003-X
(HB) ISBN 81-7058-280-6

Published by Sri Aurobindo Ashram Publication Department
Printed at Sri Aurobindo Ashram Press, Pondicherry
PRINTED IN INDIA

EDITORS' NOTE

The present volume comprises Sri Aurobindo's final translations of and commentaries on every Upanishad or other Vedantic text he worked on. Sri Aurobindo began translating and writing on the Upanishads around 1900 – several years before he took up yoga – and he continued this work for more than two decades. During this period his interpretation of these ancient writings underwent considerable development. For this reason translations and commentaries done before 1910 (the year Sri Aurobindo settled in Pondicherry and devoted himself exclusively to yoga) and those he did afterwards have been placed in separate sections of this book. A third section contains incomplete and fragmentary work from both periods. Since the organising principle of the volume has been the degree of perfection to which Sri Aurobindo carried his work on each text he took up, the traditional order of the Upanishads has not been followed.

NOTE TO THE SECOND PRINTING

In this printing a translation of most of Chapter One, Section 3 of the Chhandogya Upanishad has been added. The rest of the book is unchanged.

Contents

"The Katha Upanishad of the Black Yajurveda"

The First Cycle; First Chapter.

1. Vajasravasa, desiring, gave all he had. Now Vajasravasa had a son named Nachiketas.

2. As the gifts were led past, faith took possession of him who was yet a boy unwed and he pondered:

3. "Cattle that have drunk their water, eaten their grass, yielded their milk, worn out their organs, of undelight are the worlds to which he goes who gives such as these."

4. He said to his father, "Me, O my father, to whom wilt thou give?" A second time and a third he said it, and he replied, "To Death I give thee."

5. "Among many I walk the first, among many I walk the midmost; something Death means to do which today by me he will accomplish."

6. "Look back and see, even as were the men of old, — look round — even as are they that have come after. Mortal man withers like the fruits of the field and like the fruits of the field he is born again."

His attendants say to Yama.

7. "Fire is the Brahmin who enters as a guest the houses of men; him thus they appease. O Son of Vivasvan, the maker of the gods...

8. That man of little understanding, in whose house a Brahmin dwells fasting, all his hope and his expectation, and what he has gained and the good and truth that he has spoken and the wells he has dug and the sacrifices he has offered and all his sons and his cattle are torn from him by that guest unhonoured.

9. "Because for three nights thou hast sat in my house, O Brahmin, a guest worthy of reverence, — salutation to thee, O Brahmin, on me let there be the weal, — therefore three boons do thou choose, for each night a boon."

10. "Tranquillised in his mind and thought, since of heart be the Gautama, my father, let his passion for me pass away from him; assured in heart let him greet me from thee, from death delivered; this boon, the first of those I choose, the first of those."

11. "Even as before assured in heart and by me released shall he be, Auddalaka Aruni, thy father; at ease shall he sleep through the nights with his passion passed away from thee, having seen thee from death's jaws delivered."

12. "In heaven fear is not at all, in heaven thou art not, nor old age and its terrors; crossing over hunger and thirst as over two rivers, leaving sorrow behind the soul in heaven rejoices."

13. "Therefore that heavenly Flame which thou, O Death, expound unto me, for I believe. They who win heaven for their portion have immortality. This for the second boon I have chosen."

14. "Hearken to me and understand, O Nachiketas, I declare to thee that heavenly flame, for I know it. Know this to be the possession of infinite being and the foundation that is established in the secret cave of our being."

First page of Sri Aurobindo's translation of *Katha Upanishad*.

tion, formation and growth which are the very substance of life; but the visible principle of life can only emerge when the necessary material conditions have been prepared which will permit it to organise itself in Matter. So also Life is instinct with the stuff of Mind, abounds with an unconscious * sensation, will, intelligence, but the visible principle of Mind can only emerge when the necessary vital conditions have been prepared which will permit it to organise itself in living Matter. Mind too is instinct with the stuff of supermind—sympathies, unities, intuitions, emergences of preexistent knowledge, inherent self-effectivities of will which disguise themselves in a mental form; but the visible principle of supermind can only emerge when the necessary mental conditions are prepared which will permit it to organise itself in man, the mental living creature.

This necessary preparation is proceeding in human development as the corresponding preparations were developed in the lower stages of the evolution,—with the same gradations, retardations, inequalities; but still it is more enlightened, increasingly self-conscious, nearer to a conscious sureness. And the very fact that this progress is attended by less in detail, less timidity of error, a less conservative attachment to the step gained the hope and almost the assurance that when the new principle emerges it will not be by the creation of a new and quite different type which will leave the rest of mankind in the same position to it as are the animals to man, but by the elevation of humanity as a whole to a higher level, for Man, first among Nature's children, has shown the capacity to change himself by his own effort and the conscious aspiration to transcend.

These considerations justify to the reason the idea of a Mind beyond our mind, but only as a final evolution out of Matter. The Upanishad, however, enthrones it as the already existing creator and ruler of Mind; it is a secret

---

* I use the language of the materialist Haeckel in spite of its paradoxical form.

Page of the *Arya* with Sri Aurobindo's alterations and additions.

INTRODUCTION

Introduction

THE Upanishads are the supreme work of the Indian mind, and that it should be so, that the highest self-expression of its genius, its sublimest poetry, its greatest creation of the thought and word should be not a literary or poetical masterpiece of the ordinary kind, but a large flood of spiritual revelation of this direct and profound character, is a significant fact, evidence of a unique mentality and unusual turn of spirit. The Upanishads are at once profound religious scriptures, — for they are a record of the deepest spiritual experiences, — documents of revelatory and intuitive philosophy of an inexhaustible light, power and largeness and, whether written in verse or cadenced prose, spiritual poems of an absolute, an unfailing inspiration inevitable in phrase, wonderful in rhythm and expression. It is the expression of a mind in which philosophy and religion and poetry are made one, because this religion does not end with a cult nor is limited to a religio-ethical aspiration, but rises to an infinite discovery of God, of Self, of our highest and whole reality of spirit and being and speaks out of an ecstasy of luminous knowledge and an ecstasy of moved and fulfilled experience, this philosophy is not an abstract intellectual speculation about Truth or a structure of the logical intelligence, but Truth seen, felt, lived, held by the inmost mind and soul in the joy of utterance of an assured discovery and possession, and this poetry is the work of the aesthetic mind lifted up beyond its ordinary field to express the wonder and beauty of the rarest spiritual self-vision and the profoundest illumined truth of self and God and universe. Here the intuitive mind and intimate psychological experience of the Vedic seers passes into a supreme culmination in which the Spirit, as is said in a phrase of the Katha Upanishad, discloses its own very body, reveals the very word of its self-expression and discovers to the mind the vibration of rhythms which repeating themselves within in the spiritual hearing seem to build up the soul and set it satisfied and complete on the heights of self-knowledge.

This character of the Upanishads needs to be insisted upon
with a strong emphasis, because it is ignored by foreign trans-
lators who seek to bring out the intellectual sense without feeling
the life of thought-vision and the ecstasy of spiritual experience
which made the ancient verses appear then and still make them
to those who can enter into the element in which these utterances
move, a revelation not to the intellect alone, but to the soul and
the whole being, make of them in the old expressive word not
intellectual thought and phrase, but *śruti*, spiritual audience, an
inspired Scripture. The philosophical substance of the Upanishads demands at this day no farther stress of appreciation of its
value; for even if the amplest acknowledgement by the greatest
minds were wanting, the whole history of philosophy would be
there to offer its evidence. The Upanishads have been the acknowledged source of numerous profound philosophies and religions that flowed from it in India like her great rivers from their
Himalayan cradle fertilising the mind and life of the people and
kept its soul alive through the long procession of the centuries,
constantly returned to for light, never failing to give fresh illumination, a fountain of inexhaustible life-giving waters. Buddhism with all its developments was only a restatement, although
from a new standpoint and with fresh terms of intellectual definition and reasoning, of one side of its experience and it carried
it thus changed in form but hardly in substance over all Asia and
westward towards Europe. The ideas of the Upanishads can be
rediscovered in much of the thought of Pythagoras and Plato and
form the profoundest part of Neo-Platonism and Gnosticism
with all their considerable consequences to the philosophical
thinking of the West, and Sufism only repeats them in another
religious language. The larger part of German metaphysics is
little more in substance than an intellectual development of great
realities more spiritually seen in this ancient teaching, and
modern thought is rapidly absorbing them with a closer, more
living and intense receptiveness which promises a revolution both
in philosophical and in religious thinking; here they are filtering
in through many indirect influences, there slowly pouring through
direct and open channels. There is hardly a main philosophical
idea which cannot find an authority or a seed or indication in

these antique writings — the speculations, according to a certain view, of thinkers who had no better past or background to their thought than a crude, barbaric, naturalistic and animistic ignorance. And even the larger generalisations of Science are constantly found to apply to the truth of physical Nature formulas already discovered by the Indian sages in their original, their largest meaning in the deeper truth of the spirit.

And yet these works are not philosophical speculations of the intellectual kind, a metaphysical analysis which labours to define notions, to select ideas and discriminate those that are true, to logicise truth or else to support the mind in its intellectual preferences by dialectical reasoning and is content to put forward an exclusive solution of existence in the light of this or that idea of the reason and see all things from that viewpoint, in that focus and determining perspective. The Upanishads could not have had so undying a vitality, exercised so unfailing an influence, produced such results or seen now their affirmations independently justified in other spheres of inquiry and by quite opposite methods, if they had been of that character. It is because these seers saw Truth rather than merely thought it, clothed it indeed with a strong body of intuitive idea and disclosing image, but a body of ideal transparency through which we look into the illimitable, because they fathomed things in the light of self-existence and saw them with the eye of the Infinite, that their words remain always alive and immortal, of an inexhaustible significance, an inevitable authenticity, a satisfying finality that is at the same time an infinite commencement of truth, to which all our lines of investigation when they go through to their end arrive again and to which humanity constantly returns in its minds and its ages of greatest vision. The Upanishads are Vedanta, a book of knowledge in a higher degree even than the Vedas, but knowledge in the profounder Indian sense of the word, *jñāna*. Not a mere thinking and considering by the intelligence, the pursuit and grasping of a mental form of truth by the intellectual mind, but a seeing of it with the soul and a total living in it with the power of the inner being, a spiritual seizing by a kind of identification with the object of knowledge is *jñāna*. And because it is only by an integral knowing of the self that this kind of direct knowledge can be made complete, it was the self that the Vedantic sages sought to know, to live in and to be one with it by identity. And through this endeavour they came easily to see that the self in us is one with the universal self of all things and that this self again is the same as God and Brahman, a transcendent Being or Existence, and they beheld, felt, lived in the inmost truth of all things in the universe and the inmost truth of man's inner and outer existence by the light of this one and unifying vision. The Upanishads are epic hymns of self-knowledge and world-knowledge and God-knowledge. The great formulations of philosophic truth with which they abound are not abstract intellectual generalisations, things that may shine and enlighten the mind but do not live and move the soul to ascension, but are ardours as well as lights of an intuitive and revelatory illumination, reachings as well as seeings of the one Existence, the transcendent Godhead, the divine and universal Self and discoveries of his relation with things and creatures in this great cosmic manifestation. Chants of inspired knowledge, they breathe like all hymns a tone of religious aspiration and ecstasy, not of the narrowly intense kind proper to a lesser religious feeling, but raised beyond cult and special forms of devotion to the universal Ananda of the Divine which comes to us by approach to and oneness with the self-existent and universal Spirit. And though mainly concerned with an inner vision and not directly with outward human action, all the highest ethics of Buddhism and later Hinduism are still emergences of the very life and significance of the truths to which they give expressive form and force, —and there is something greater than any ethical precept and mental rule of virtue, the supreme ideal of a spiritual action founded on oneness with God and all living beings. Therefore even when the life of the forms of the Vedic cult had passed away, the Upanishads still remained alive and creative and could generate the great devotional religions and motive the persistent Indian idea of the Dharma.

The Upanishads are the creation of a revelatory and intuitive mind and its illumined experience, and all their substance, structure, phrase, imagery, movement are determined by and stamped with this original character. These supreme and all-embracing truths, these visions of oneness and self and a universal divine being are cast into brief and monumental phrases which bring them at once before the soul's eye and make them real and imperative to its aspiration and experience or are couched in poetic sentences full of revealing power and suggestive thought-colour that discover a whole infinite through a finite image. The One is there revealed, but also disclosed the many aspects, and each is given its whole significance by the amplitude of the expression and finds as if in a spontaneous self-discovery its place and its connection by the illumining justness of each word and all the phrase. The largest metaphysical truths and the subtlest subtleties of psychological experience are taken up into the inspired movement and made at once precise to the seeing mind and loaded with unending suggestion to the discovering spirit. There are separate phrases, single couplets, brief passages which contain each in itself the substance of a vast philosophy and yet each is only thrown out as a side, an aspect, a portion of the infinite self-knowledge. All here is a packed and pregnant and yet perfectly lucid and luminous brevity and an immeasurable completeness. A thought of this kind cannot follow the tardy, careful and diffuse development of the logical intelligence. The passage, the sentence, the couplet, the line, even the half line follows the one that precedes with a certain interval full of an unexpressed thought, an echoing silence between them, a thought which is carried in the total suggestion and implied in the step itself, but which the mind is left to work out for its own profit, and these intervals of pregnant silence are large, the steps of this thought are like the paces of a Titan striding from rock to distant rock across infinite waters. There is a perfect totality, a comprehensive connection of harmonious parts in the structure of each Upanishad; but it is done in the way of a mind that sees masses of truth at a time and stops to bring only the needed word out of a filled silence. The rhythm in verse or cadenced prose corresponds to the sculpture of the thought and the phrase. The metrical forms of the Upanishads are made up of four half lines each clearly cut, the lines mostly complete in themselves and integral in sense, the half lines presenting two thoughts or distinct parts of a thought that are wedded to and complete each other, and the sound movement follows a corresponding principle, each step brief and marked off by the distinctness of its pause, full of echoing cadences that remain long vibrating in the inner hearing: each is as if a wave of the infinite that carries in it the whole voice and rumour of the ocean. It is a kind of poetry — word of vision, rhythm of the spirit, — that has not been written before or after.

The imagery of the Upanishads is in large part developed from the type of imagery of the Veda and though very ordinarily it prefers an unveiled clarity of directly illuminative image, not unoften also it uses the same symbols in a way that is closely akin to the spirit and to the less technical part of the method of the older symbolism. It is to a great extent this element no longer seizable by our way of thinking that has baffled certain western scholars and made them cry out that these scriptures are a mixture of the sublimest philosophical speculations with the first awkward stammerings of the child mind of humanity. The Upanishads are not a revolutionary departure from the Vedic mind and its temperament and fundamental ideas, but a continuation and development and to a certain extent an enlarging transformation in the sense of bringing out into open expression all that was held covered in the symbolic Vedic speech as a mystery and a secret. It begins by taking up the imagery and the ritual symbols of the Veda and the Brahmanas and turning them in such a way as to bring out an inner and a mystic sense which will serve as a sort of psychical starting-point for its own more highly evolved and more purely spiritual philosophy. There are a number of passages especially in the prose Upanishads which are entirely of this kind and deal, in a manner recondite, obscure and even unintelligible to the modern understanding, with the psychic sense of ideas then current in the Vedic religious mind, the distinction between the three kinds of Veda, the three worlds and other similar subjects; but, leading as they do in the thought of the Upanishads to deepest spiritual truths, these passages cannot be dismissed as childish aberrations of the intelligence void of sense or of any discoverable bearing on the higher thought in which they culminate. On the contrary we find that they have a deep enough significance once we can get inside their symbolic meaning. That appears in a psycho-physical passing upward into a psycho-spiritual knowledge for which we would now use more intellectual, less concrete and imaged terms, but which is still valid for those who practise Yoga and rediscover the secrets of our psycho-physical and psycho-spiritual being. Typical passages of this kind of peculiar expression of psychic truths are Ajatashatru's explanation of sleep and dream or the passages of the Prashna Upanishad on the vital principle and its motions, or those in which the Vedic idea of the struggle between the Gods and the demons is taken up and given its spiritual significance and the Vedic godheads more openly than in Rik and Saman characterised and invoked in their inner function and spiritual power.

I may cite as an example of this development of Vedic idea and image a passage of the Taittiriya in which Indra plainly appears as the power and godhead of the divine mind:

"He who is the Bull of the Vedas of the universal form, he who was born in the sacred rhythms from the Immortal, — may Indra satisfy me through the intelligence. O God, may I become a vessel of the Immortal. May my body be full of vision and my tongue of sweetness, may I hear the much and vast with my ears. For thou art the sheath of Brahman covered over and hidden by the intelligence."

And a kindred passage may also be cited from the Isha in which Surya the Sun-God is invoked as the godhead of knowledge whose supreme form of effulgence is the oneness of the Spirit and his rays dispersed here on the mental level are the shining diffusion of the thought mind and conceal his own infinite supramental truth, the body and self of this Sun, the truth of the spirit and the Eternal:

"The face of the Truth is covered with a golden lid: O fostering Sun, that uncover for the law of the truth, for sight. O fosterer, O sole Rishi, O controlling Yama, O Surya, O son of the Father of creatures, marshal and mass thy rays: the Lustre that is thy most blessed form of all, that I see, He who is this, this Purusha, He am I."

The kinship in difference of these passages with the imagery and style of the Veda is evident and the last indeed paraphrases or translates into a later and more open style a Vedic verse of the Atris:

"Hidden by your truth is the Truth that is constant for ever where they unyoke the horses of the Sun. There the ten thousands stand together, That is the One: I have seen the supreme Godhead of the embodied gods."

This Vedic and Vedantic imagery is foreign to our present mentality which does not believe in the living truth of the symbol, because the revealing imagination intimidated by the intellect has no longer the courage to accept, identify itself with and boldly embody a psychic and spiritual vision; but it is certainly very far from being a childish or a primitive and barbarous mysticism; this vivid, living, luminously poetic intuitive language is rather the natural expression of a highly evolved spiritual culture.

The intuitive thought of the Upanishads starts from this concrete imagery and these symbols, first to the Vedic Rishis secret seer words wholly expressive to the mind of the seer but veils of their deepest sense to the ordinary intelligence, link them to a less covertly expressive language and pass beyond them to another magnificently open and sublime imagery and diction which at once reveals the spiritual truth in all its splendour. The prose Upanishads show us this process of the early mind of India at its work using the symbol and then passing beyond it to the overt expression of the spiritual significance. A passage of the Prashna Upanishad on the power and significance of the mystic syllable AUM illustrates the earlier stage of the process:

"This syllable OM, O Satyakama, it is the supreme and it is the lower Brahman. Therefore the man of knowledge passes by this house of the Brahman to the one or the other. And if one meditate on the single letter, he gets by it knowledge and soon he attains on the earth. And him the

Riks lead to the world of men and there perfected in Tapas and Brahmacharya and faith he experiences the greatness of the spirit. Now if by the double letter he is accomplished in the mind, then is he led up by the Yajus to the middle world, to the moon-world of Soma. He in the world of Soma experiences the majesty of the spirit and returns again. And he who by the triple letter again, even this syllable OM, shall meditate on the highest Purusha, is perfected in the light that is the Sun. As a snake puts off its skin, even so is he released from sin and evil and is led by the Samans to the world of Brahman. He from this dense of living souls sees the higher than the highest Purusha who lies in this mansion. The three letters are afflicted by death, but now they are used undivided and united to each other, then are the inner and the outer and the middle action of the spirit made whole in their perfect using and the spirit knows and is not shaken. This world by the Riks, the middle world by the Yajus and by the Samans that which the seers make known to us. The man of knowledge passes to Him by OM, his house, even to the supreme spirit that is calm and ageless and fearless and immortal."

The symbols here are still obscure to our intelligence, but indications are given which show beyond doubt that they are representations of a psychical experience leading to different states of spiritual realisation and we can see that these are three outward, mental and supramental, and as the result of the last a supreme perfection, a complete and integral action of the whole being in the tranquil eternity of the immortal Spirit. And later in the Mandukya Upanishad the other symbols are cast aside and we are admitted to the unveiled significance. Then there emerges a knowledge to which modern thought is returning through its own very different intellectual, rational and scientific method, the knowledge that behind the operations of our outward physical consciousness are working the operations of another, subliminal, — another and yet the same, — of which our waking mind is a surface action, and above — perhaps, we still say — is a spiritual superconscience in which can be found, it may well be, the high-

est state and the whole secret of our being. We shall see, when
we look closely at the passage of the Prashna Upanishad, that
this knowledge is already there, and I think we can very rationally
conclude that these and similar utterances of the ancient sages,
however perplexing their form to the rational mind, cannot be
dismissed as a childish mysticism, but are the imaged expression,
natural to the mentality of the time, of what the reason itself by
its own processes is now showing us to be true and a very profound truth and real reality of knowledge.

The metrical Upanishads continue this highly charged symbolism but carry it more lightly and in the bulk of their verses
pass beyond this kind of image to the overt expression. The Self,
the Spirit, the Godhead in man and creatures and Nature and all
this world and in other worlds and beyond all cosmos, the
Immortal, the One, the Infinite is hymned without veils in the
splendour of his eternal transcendence and his manifold self-
revelation. A few passages from the teachings of Yama, lord of
the Law and of Death, to Nachiketas, will be enough to illustrate
something of their character:

"Om is this syllable. This syllable is the Brahman, this
syllable is the Supreme. He who knows the imperishable
Om, whatso he wills, it is his. This support is the best, this
support is the highest; and when a man knows it, he is great-
ened in the world of Brahman. The omniscient is not born,
nor dies, nor has he come into being from anywhere, nor is
he anyone. He is unborn, he is constant and eternal, he is
the Ancient of Days who is not slain in the slaying of the
body....

He is seated and journeys far, and lying still he goes to
every side. Who other than I should know this ecstatic Godhead? The wise man comes to know the great Lord and Self
established and bodiless in these bodies that pass and has
grief no longer. This Self is not to be won by teaching nor by
brain-power nor by much learning: he whom the Spirit
chooses, by him alone it can be won, and to him this Spirit
discloses its own very body. One who has not ceased from ill-
doing, one who is not concentrated and calm, one whose

mind is not tranquil, shall not get him by the brain's wisdom. He of whom warriors and sages are the food and death is the spice of his banquet, who knows where is He?...

The Self-born has cloven his doors outward, therefore man sees outward and not in the inner self: only a wise man here and there turns his eyes inward, desiring immortality, and looks on the Self face to face. The child minds follow after surface desires and fall into the net of death which is spread wide for us; but the wise know of immortality and ask not from things inconstant that which is constant. One knows by this Self form and taste and odour and touch and its pleasures and what then is here left over? The wise man comes to know the great Lord and Self by whom one sees all that is in the soul that wakes and all that is in the soul that dreams and has grief no longer. He who knows the Self, the eater of sweetness close to the living being, the lord of what was and what will be, shrinks thereafter from nothing that is. He knows him who is that which was born of old from Tapas and who was born of old from the waters and has entered in and stands in the secret cavern of being with all these creatures. He knows her who is born by the life force, the infinite Mother with all the gods in her, her who has entered in and stands in the secret cavern of being with all these creatures. This is the Fire that has the knowledge and it is hidden in the two tinders as the embryo is borne in pregnant women; this is the Fire that must be adored by men watching sleeplessly and bringing to him the offering. He is that from which the Sun rises and that in which it sets: and in him all the gods are founded and none can pass beyond him. What is here, even that is in other worlds, and what is there, even according to that is all that is here. He goes from death to death who sees here only difference. A Purusha no bigger than a thumb stands in man's central self and is the lord of what was and what shall be, and knowing him thenceforth one shrinks from nothing that is. A Purusha no bigger than a man's thumb and he is like a light without smoke; he is the Lord of what

was and what shall be; it is he that is today and it is he that
shall be tomorrow."

The Upanishads abound with passages which are at once
poetry and spiritual philosophy, of an absolute clarity and
beauty, but no translation empty of the suggestions and the grave
and subtle and luminous sense echoes of the original words and
rhythms can give any idea of their power and perfection. There
are others in which the subtlest psychological and philosophical
truths are expressed with an entire sufficiency without falling
short of a perfect beauty of poetical expression and always so as
to live to the mind and soul and not merely be presented to the
understanding intelligence. There is in some of the prose Upanishads another element of vivid narrative and tradition which
restores for us though only in brief glimpses the picture of that
extraordinary stir and movement of spiritual enquiry and passion
for the highest knowledge which made the Upanishads possible.
The scenes of the old world live before us in a few pages, the sages
sitting in their groves ready to test and teach the comer, princes
and learned Brahmins and great landed nobles going about in
search of knowledge, the king's son in his chariot and the illegitimate son of the servant-girl, seeking any man who might carry
in himself the thought of light and the word of revelation, the
typical figures and personalities, Janaka and the subtle mind of
Ajatashatru, Raikwa of the cart, Yajnavalkya militant for truth,
calm and ironic, taking to himself with both hands without attachment worldly possessions and spiritual riches and casting at last
all his wealth behind to wander forth as a houseless ascetic,
Krishna son of Devaki who heard a single word of the Rishi
Ghora and knew at once the Eternal, the Ashramas, the courts
of kings who were also spiritual discoverers and thinkers, the
great sacrificial assemblies where the sages met and compared
their knowledge. And we see how the soul of India was born and
how arose this great birth-song in which it soared from its earth
into the supreme empyrean of the spirit. The Vedas and the
Upanishads are not only the sufficient fountain-head of Indian
philosophy and religion, but of all Indian art, poetry and literature. It was the soul, the temperament, the ideal mind formed

and expressed in them which later carved out the great philosophies, built the structure of the Dharma, recorded its heroic youth in the Mahabharata and Ramayana, intellectualised indefatigably in the classical times of the ripeness of its manhood, threw out so many original intuitions in science, created so rich a glow of aesthetic and vital and sensuous experience, renewed its spiritual and psychic experience in Tantra and Purana, flung itself into grandeur and beauty of line and colour, hewed and cast its thought and vision in stone and bronze, poured itself into new channels of self-expression in the later tongues and now after eclipse re-emerges always the same in difference and ready for a new life and a new creation.

SECTION ONE

Translations and Commentaries Done after 1910

ISHA UPANISHAD

Isha Upanishad

ईशा वास्यमिदꣳ सर्वं यत् किञ्च जगत्यां जगत् ।
तेन त्यक्तेन भुञ्जीथा मा गृधः कस्य स्विद्धनम् ॥१॥

1. All this is for habitation[1] by the Lord, whatsoever is individual universe of movement in the universal motion.
   By that renounced thou shouldst enjoy; lust not after
   any man's possession.

कुर्वन्नेवेह कर्माणि जिजीविषेच्छतꣳ समाः ।
एवं त्वयि नान्यथेतोऽस्ति न कर्म लिप्यते नरे ॥२॥

2. Doing verily[2] works in this world one should wish to live
   a hundred years. Thus it is in thee and not otherwise than
   this; action cleaves not to a man.[3]

असूर्या नाम ते लोका अन्धेन तमसावृताः ।
ताꣳस्ते प्रेत्याभिगच्छन्ति ये के चात्महनो जनाः ॥३॥

---

[1] There are three possible senses of *vāsyam*, "to be clothed", "to be worn as a garment"
and "to be inhabited". The first is the ordinarily accepted meaning. Shankara explains it in
this significance, that we must lose the sense of this unreal objective universe in the sole perception of the pure Brahman. So explained the first line becomes a contradiction of the whole
thought of the Upanishad which teaches the reconciliation, by the perception of essential
Unity, of the apparently incompatible opposites, God and the World, Renunciation and
Enjoyment, Action and internal Freedom, the One and the Many, Being and its Becomings,
the passive divine Impersonality and the active divine Personality, the Knowledge and the
Ignorance, the Becoming and the Not-Becoming, Life on earth and beyond and the supreme
Immortality. The image is of the world either as a garment or as a dwelling-place for the
informing and governing Spirit. The latter significance agrees better with the thought of the
Upanishad.

[2] *Kurvanneva*. The stress of the word *eva* gives the force, "doing works indeed, and not
refraining from them".

[3] Shankara reads the line, "Thus in thee — it is not otherwise than thus — action cleaves
not to a man." He interprets *karmāṇi* in the first line in the sense of Vedic sacrifices which
are permitted to the ignorant as a means of escaping from evil actions and their results and
attaining to heaven, but the second *karma* in exactly the opposite sense, "evil action". The
verse, he tells us, represents a concession to the ignorant; the enlightened soul abandons
works and the world and goes to the forest. The whole expression and construction in this
rendering become forced and unnatural. The rendering I give seems to me the simple and
straightforward sense of the Upanishad.

3. Sunless[1] are those worlds and enveloped in blind gloom
    whereto all they in their passing hence resort who are
    slayers of their souls.

अनेजदेकं मनसो जवीयो नैनद्देवा आप्नुवन् पूर्वमर्षत् ।
तद्धावतोऽन्यानत्येति तिष्ठत् तस्मिन्नपो मातरिश्वा दधाति ॥४॥

4. One unmoving that is swifter than Mind, That the Gods
    reach not, for It progresses ever in front. That, standing,
    passes beyond others as they run. In That the Master of
    Life[2] establishes the Waters.[3]

तदेजति तन्नैजति तद् दूरे तद्वन्तिके ।
तदन्तरस्य सर्वस्य तदु सर्वस्यास्य बाह्यतः ॥५॥

5. That moves and That moves not; That is far and the same
    is near; That is within all this and That also is outside all
    this.

---

[1] We have two readings, *asūryāḥ*, sunless, and *asuryāḥ*, Titanic or undivine. The third
verse is, in the thought structure of the Upanishad, the starting-point for the final movement in the last four verses. Its suggestions are there taken up and worked out. The prayer
to the Sun refers back in thought to the sunless worlds and their blind gloom, which are
recalled in the ninth and twelfth verses. The sun and his rays are intimately connected in
other Upanishads also with the worlds of Light and their natural opposite is the dark and
sunless, not the Titanic worlds.

[2] *Mātariśvan* seems to mean "he who extends himself in the Mother or the container"
whether that be the containing mother element, Ether, or the material energy called Earth in
the Veda and spoken of there as the Mother. It is a Vedic epithet of the God Vayu, who,
representing the divine principle in the Life-energy, Prana, extends himself in Matter and
vivifies its forms. Here it signifies the divine Life-power that presides in all forms of cosmic
activity.

[3] *Apas*, as it is accentuated in the version of the White Yajurveda, can mean only
"waters". If this accentuation is disregarded, we may take it as the singular *apas*, work,
action. Shankara, however, renders it by the plural, works. The difficulty only arises because
the true Vedic sense of the word had been forgotten and it came to be taken as referring
to the fourth of the five elemental states of Matter, the liquid. Such a reference would be
entirely irrelevant to the context. But the Waters, otherwise called the seven streams or the
seven fostering Cows, are the Vedic symbol for the seven cosmic principles and their activities,
three inferior, the physical, vital and mental, four superior, the divine Truth, the divine Bliss,
the divine Will and Consciousness, and the divine Being. On this conception also is founded
the ancient idea of the seven worlds in each of which the seven principles are separately active
by their various harmonies. This is, obviously, the right significance of the word in the
Upanishad.

यस्तु सर्वाणि भूतानि आत्मन्येवानुपश्यति ।
सर्वभूतेषु चात्मानं ततो न विजुगुप्सते ॥६॥

6. But he who sees everywhere the Self in all existences and all existences in the Self, shrinks not thereafter from aught.

यस्मिन् सर्वाणि भूतानि आत्मैवाभूद् विजानतः ।
तत्र को मोहः कः शोक एकत्वमनुपश्यतः ॥७॥

7. He in whom it is the Self-Being that has become all existences that are Becomings,[1] for he has the perfect knowledge, how shall he be deluded, whence shall he have grief who sees everywhere oneness?

स पर्यगाच्छुक्रमकायमव्रणमस्नाविरं शुद्धमपापविद्धम् ।
कविर्मनीषी परिभूः स्वयम्भूर्याथातथ्यतोऽर्थान् व्यदधाच्छाश्वतीभ्यः समाभ्यः ॥८॥

8. It is He that has gone abroad — That which is bright, bodiless, without scar of imperfection, without sinews, pure, unpierced by evil. The Seer, the Thinker,[2] the One who becomes everywhere, the Self-existent has ordered objects perfectly according to their nature from years sempiternal.

अन्धं तमः प्रविशन्ति येऽविद्यामुपासते ।
ततो भूय इव ते तमो य उ विद्यायाश् रताः ॥९॥

9. Into a blind darkness they enter who follow after the Ignorance, they as if into a greater darkness who devote themselves to the Knowledge alone.

---

[1] The words *sarvāṇi bhūtāni* literally, "all things that have become", is opposed to Atman, self-existent and immutable being. The phrase means ordinarily "all creatures", but its literal sense is evidently insisted on in the expression *bhūtāni abhūt* "became the Becomings". The idea is the acquisition in man of the supreme consciousness by which the one Self in him extends itself to embrace all creatures and realises the eternal act by which that One manifests itself in the multiple forms of the universal motion.

[2] There is a clear distinction in Vedic thought between *kavi*, the seer and *manīṣī*, the thinker. The former indicates the divine supra-intellectual Knowledge which by direct vision and illumination sees the reality, the principles and the forms of things in their true relations, the latter, the labouring mentality, which works from the divided consciousness through the possibilities of things downward to the actual manifestation in form and upward to their reality in the self-existent Brahman.

अन्यदेवाहुर्विद्ययाऽन्यदाहुरविद्यया ।
इति शुश्रुम धीराणां ये नस्तद्विचचक्षिरे ॥१०॥

10. Other, verily,[1] it is said, is that which comes by the Know-
    ledge, other that which comes by the Ignorance; this is the
    lore we have received from the wise who revealed That to our
    understanding.

विद्याञ्चाविद्याञ्च यस्तद्वेदोभयꣳ सह ।
अविद्यया मृत्युं तीर्त्वा विद्ययामृतमश्नुते ॥११॥

11. He who knows That as both in one, the Knowledge and the
    Ignorance, by the Ignorance crosses beyond death and by
    the Knowledge enjoys Immortality.

अन्धं तमः प्रविशन्ति येऽसम्भूतिमुपासते ।
ततो भूय इव ते तमो य उ सम्भूत्याꣳ रताः ॥१२॥

12. Into a blind darkness they enter who follow after the Non-
    Birth, they as if into a greater darkness who devote them-
    selves to the Birth alone.

अन्यदेवाहुः सम्भवादन्यदाहुरसम्भवात् ।
इति शुश्रुम धीराणां ये नस्तद्विचचक्षिरे ॥१३॥

13. Other, verily, it is said, is that which comes by the Birth,
    other that which comes by the Non-Birth; this is the lore we
    have received from the wise who revealed That to our
    understanding.

सम्भूतिञ्च विनाशञ्च यस्तद्वेदोभयꣳ सह ।
विनाशेन मृत्युं तीर्त्वा सम्भूत्याऽमृतमश्नुते ॥१४॥

14. He who knows That as both in one, the Birth and the dis-

---

[1] *Anyadeva — eva* here gives to *anyad* the force, "Quite other than the result described in
the preceding verse is that to which lead the Knowledge and the Ignorance." We have the
explanation of *anyad* in the verse that follows. The ordinary rendering, "Knowledge has one
result, Ignorance another", would be an obvious commonplace announced with an exaggerated
pompousness, adding nothing to the thought and without any place in the sequence of the
ideas.

solution of Birth, by the dissolution crosses beyond death
and by the Birth enjoys Immortality.

हिरण्मयेन पात्रेण सत्यस्यापिहितं मुखम् ।
तत् त्वं पूषन्नपावृणु सत्यधर्माय दृष्टये ॥१५॥

15. The face of Truth is covered with a brilliant golden lid; that
do thou remove, O Fosterer,[1] for the law of the Truth,
for sight.

पूषन्नेकर्षे यम सूर्य प्राजापत्य व्यूह रश्मीन् समूह ।
तेजो यत् ते रूपं कल्याणतमं तत्ते पश्यामि
योऽसावसौ पुरुषः सोऽहमस्मि ॥१६॥

16. O Fosterer, O sole Seer, O Ordainer, O illumining Sun,
O power of the Father of creatures, marshal thy rays, draw
together thy light; the Lustre which is thy most blessed form
of all, that in Thee I behold. The Purusha there and there,
He am I.

वायुरनिलममृतमथेदं भस्मान्तꣳ शरीरम् ।
ॐ क्रतो स्मर कृतꣳ स्मर क्रतो स्मर कृतꣳ स्मर ॥१७॥

17. The Breath of things[2] is an immortal Life, but of this body

---

[1] In the inner sense of the Veda Surya, the Sun-God, represents the divine Illumination
of the Kavi which exceeds mind and forms the pure self-luminous Truth of things. His principal power is self-revelatory knowledge, termed in the Veda "Sight". His realm is described
as the Truth, the Law, the Vast. He is the Fosterer or Increaser, for he enlarges and opens
man's dark and limited being into a luminous and infinite consciousness. He is the sole Seer,
Seer of Oneness and Knower of the Self, and leads him to the highest Sight. He is Yama,
Controller or Ordainer, for he governs man's action and manifested being by the direct Law
of the Truth, *satyadharma,* and therefore by the right principle of our nature, *yāthātathyataḥ,*
a luminous power proceeding from the Father of all existence, he reveals in himself the divine
Purusha of whom all beings are the manifestations. His rays are the thoughts that proceed
luminously from the Truth, the Vast, but become deflected and distorted, broken up and
disordered in the reflecting and dividing principle, Mind. They form there the golden lid
which covers the face of the Truth. The Seer prays to Surya to cast them into right order and
relation and then draw them together into the unity of revealed truth. The result of this
inner process is the perception of the oneness of all beings in the divine Soul of the Universe.

[2] Vayu, called elsewhere Matarishwan, the Life Energy in the universe. In the light of
Surya he reveals himself as an immortal principle of existence of which birth and death and
life in the body are only particular and external processes.

ashes are the end. OM! O Will,[1] remember, that which was done remember! O Will, remember, that which was done remember.

अग्ने नय सुपथा राये अस्मान् विश्वानि देव वयुनानि विद्वान् ।
युयोध्यस्मज्जुहुराणमेनो भूयिष्ठां ते नमउक्ति विधेम ॥१८॥

18. O god Agni, knowing all things that are manifested, lead us by the good path to the felicity; remove from us the devious attraction of sin.[2] To thee completest speech of submission we would dispose.[3]

---

[1] The Vedic term *kratu* means sometimes the action itself, sometimes the effective power behind action represented in mental consciousness by the will. Agni is this power. He is divine force which manifests first in matter as heat and light and material energy and then, taking different forms in the other principles of man's consciousness, leads him by a progressive manifestation upwards to the Truth and the Bliss.

[2] Sin, in the conception of the Veda, from which this verse is taken bodily, is that which excites and hurries the faculties into deviation from the good path. There is a straight road or road of naturally increasing light and truth, *rjuḥ panthāḥ, ṛtasya panthāḥ*, leading over infinite levels and towards infinite vistas, *vītāni pṛṣṭhāni*, by which the law of our nature should normally take us towards our fulfilment. Sin compels it instead to travel with stumblings amid uneven and limited tracts and along crooked windings (*duritāni, vṛjināni*).

[3] The word *vidhema* is used of the ordering of the sacrifice, the disposal of the offerings to the God and, generally, of the sacrifice or worship itself. The Vedic *namas*, internal and external obeisance, is the symbol of submission to the divine Being in ourselves and in the world. Here the offering is that of completest submission and the self-surrender of all the faculties of the lower egoistic human nature to the divine Will-force, Agni, so that, free from internal opposition, it may lead the soul of man through the truth towards a felicity full of the spiritual riches, *rāye*. That state of beatitude is the intended self-content in the principle of pure Love and Joy, which the Vedic initiates regarded as the source of the divine existence in the universe and the foundation of the divine life in the human being. It is the deformation of this principle by egoism which appears as desire and the lust of possession in the lower worlds.

ANALYSIS

Plan of the Upanishad

THE Upanishads, being vehicles of illumination and not of instruction, composed for seekers who had already a general familiarity with the ideas of the Vedic and Vedantic seers and even some personal experience of the truths on which they were founded, dispense in their style with expressed transitions of thought and the development of implied or subordinate notions.

Every verse in the Isha Upanishad reposes on a number of ideas implicit in the text but nowhere set forth explicitly; the reasoning also that supports its conclusions is suggested by the words, not expressly conveyed to the intelligence. The reader, or rather the hearer, was supposed to proceed from light to light, confirming his intuitions and verifying by his experience, not submitting the ideas to the judgment of the logical reason.

To the modern mind this method is invalid and inapplicable; it is necessary to present the ideas of the Upanishad in their completeness, underline the suggestions, supply the necessary transitions and bring out the suppressed but always implicit reasoning.

The central idea of the Upanishad, which is a reconciliation and harmony of fundamental opposites, is worked out symmetrically in four successive movements of thought.

FIRST MOVEMENT

In the first, a basis is laid down by the idea of the one and stable Spirit inhabiting and governing a universe of movement and of the forms of movement. (*Verse 1, line 1*)

On this conception the rule of a divine life for man is founded, — enjoyment of all by renunciation of all through the exclusion of desire. (*Verse 1, line 2*)

There is then declared the justification of works and of the physical life on the basis of an inalienable freedom of the soul, one with the Lord, amidst all the activity of the multiple movement. (*Verse 2*)

Finally, the result of an ignorant interference with the right manifestation of the One in the multiplicity is declared to be an involution in states of blind obscurity after death. (*Verse 3*)

SECOND MOVEMENT

In the second movement the ideas of the first verse are resumed and amplified.

The one stable Lord and the multiple movement are identified as one <u>Brahman</u> of whom, however, the unity and stability are the higher truth and who contains all as well as inhabits all. (*Verses 4,5*)

The basis and fulfilment of the rule of life are found in the experience of unity by which man identifies himself with the cosmic and transcendental Self and is identified in the Self, but with an entire freedom from grief and illusion, with all its becomings. (*Verses 6,7*)

THIRD MOVEMENT

In the third movement there is a return to the justification of life and works (the subject of *Verse 2*) and an indication of their divine fulfilment.

The degrees of the Lord's self-manifestation in the universe of motion and in the becomings of the one Being are set forth and the inner law of all existences declared to be by His conception and determination. (*Verse 8*)

Vidya and Avidya, Becoming and Non-becoming are reconciled by their mutual utility to the progressive self-realisation which proceeds from the state of mortality to the state of Immortality. (*Verses 9-14*)

FOURTH MOVEMENT

The fourth movement returns to the idea of the worlds and under the figures of Surya and Agni the relations of the Supreme Truth and Immortality (*Verses 15,16*), the activities of this life (*Verse 17*), and the state after death (*Verse 18*) are symbolically indicated.

THE INHABITING GODHEAD:
LIFE AND ACTION

Verses 1 - 3*

THE BASIS OF COSMIC EXISTENCE

God and the world, Spirit and formative Nature are confronted and their relations fixed.

COSMOS

All world is a movement of the Spirit in itself and is mutable and transient in all its formations and appearances; its only eternity is an eternity of recurrence, its only stability a semblance caused by certain apparent fixities of relation and grouping.

Every separate object in the universe is, in truth, itself the whole universe presenting a certain front or outward appearance of its movement. The microcosm is one with the macrocosm.

Yet in their relation of principle of movement and result of movement they are continent and contained, world in world, movement in movement. The individual therefore partakes of the nature of the universal, refers back to it for its source of activity, is, as we say, subject to its laws and part of cosmic Nature.

SPIRIT

Spirit is lord of its movement, one, immutable, free, stable and eternal.

The Movement with all its formed objects has been created in order to provide a habitation for the Spirit who, being One,

*1 All this is for habitation by the Lord, whatsoever is individual universe of movement in the universal motion. By that renounced thou shouldst enjoy; lust not after any man's possession.

2 Doing verily works in this world one should wish to live a hundred years. Thus it is in thee and not otherwise than this; action cleaves not to a man.

3 Sunless are those worlds and enveloped in blind gloom whereto all they in their passing hence resort who are slayers of their souls.

yet dwells multitudinously in the multiplicity of His mansions.

It is the same Lord who dwells in the sum and the part, in the Cosmos as a whole and in each being, force or object in the Cosmos.

Since He is one and indivisible, the Spirit in all is one and their multiplicity is a play of His cosmic consciousness.

Therefore each human being is in his essence one with all others, free, eternal, immutable, lord of Nature.

TRANSITIONAL THOUGHT

AVIDYA

The object of habitation is enjoyment and possession; the object of the Spirit in Cosmos is, therefore, the possession and enjoyment of the universe. Yet, being thus in his essence one, divine and free, man seems to be limited, divided from others, subject to Nature and even its creation and sport, enslaved to death, ignorance and sorrow. His object in manifestation being possession and enjoyment of his world, he is unable to enjoy because of his limitation. This contrary result comes about by Avidya, the Ignorance of oneness: and the knot of the Ignorance is egoism.

EGO

The cause of ego is that while by Its double power of Vidya and Avidya the Spirit dwells at once in the consciousness of multiplicity and relativity and in the consciousness of unity and identity and is therefore not bound by the Ignorance, yet It can, in mind, identify Itself with the object in the movement, absorbingly, to the apparent exclusion of the Knowledge which remains behind, veiled at the back of the mentality. The movement of Mind in Nature is thus able to conceive of the object as the reality and the Inhabitant as limited and determined by the appearances of the object. It conceives of the object, not as the universe in one of its frontal appearances, but as itself a separate existence standing out from the Cosmos and different in being from all the rest of it. It conceives similarly of the Inhabitant. This is the illusion of ignorance which falsifies all realities. The illusion is called *ahaṁkāra*, the separative ego-sense which makes each being conceive of itself as an independent personality.

The result of the separation is the inability to enter into harmony and oneness with the universe and a consequent inability to possess and enjoy it. But the desire to possess and enjoy is the master impulse of the Ego which knows itself obscurely to be the Lord, although owing to the limitations of its relativity, it is unable to realise its true existence. The result is discord with others and oneself, mental and physical suffering, the sense of weakness and inability, the sense of obscuration, the straining of energy in passion and in desire towards self-fulfilment, the recoil of energy exhausted or disappointed towards death and disintegration.

Desire is the badge of subjection with its attendant discord and suffering. That which is free, one and lord, does not desire, but inalienably contains, possesses and enjoys.

THE RULE OF THE DIVINE LIFE

Enjoyment of the universe and all it contains is the object of world-existence, but renunciation of all in desire is the condition of the free enjoyment of all.

The renunciation demanded is not a moral constraint of self-denial or a physical rejection, but an entire liberation of the spirit from any craving after the forms of things.

The terms of this liberation are freedom from egoism and, consequently, freedom from personal desire. Practically, this renunciation implies that one should not regard anything in the universe as a necessary object of possession, nor as possessed by another and not by oneself, nor as an object of greed in the heart or the senses.

This attitude is founded on the perception of unity. For it has already been said that all souls are one possessing Self, the Lord; and although the Lord inhabits each object as if separately, yet all objects exist in that Self and not outside it.

Therefore by transcending Ego and realising the one Self, we possess the whole universe in the one cosmic consciousness and do not need to possess physically.

Having by oneness with the Lord the possibility of an infinite free delight in all things, we do not need to desire.

Being one with all beings, we possess, in their enjoyment, in ours and in the cosmic Being's, delight of universal self-expression. It is only by this Ananda at once transcendent and universal that man can be free in his soul and yet live in the world with the full active Life of the Lord in His universe of movement.

THE JUSTIFICATION OF WORKS

This freedom does not depend upon inaction, nor is this possession limited to the enjoyment of the inactive Soul that only witnesses without taking part in the movement.

On the contrary, the doing of works in this material world and a full acceptance of the term of physical life are part of its completeness.   *ParaAtma*

For the active Brahman fulfils Itself in the world by works and man also is in the body for self-fulfilment by action. He cannot do otherwise, for even his inertia acts and produces effects in the cosmic movement. Being in this body or any kind of body, it is idle to think of refraining from action or escaping the physical life. The idea that this in itself can be a means of liberation, is part of the Ignorance which supposes the soul to be a separate entity in the Brahman.

Action is shunned because it is thought to be inconsistent with freedom. The man when he acts, is supposed to be necessarily entangled in the desire behind the action, in subjection to the formal energy that drives the action and in the results of the action. These things are true in appearance, not in reality.

Desire is only a mode of the emotional mind which by ignorance seeks its delight in the object of desire and not in the Brahman who expresses Himself in the object. By destroying that ignorance one can do action without entanglement in desire.

The Energy that drives is itself subject to the Lord, who expresses Himself in it with perfect freedom. By getting behind Nature to the Lord of Nature, merging the individual in the Cosmic Will, one can act with the divine freedom. Our actions are given up to the Lord and our personal responsibility ceases in His liberty.

The chain of Karma only binds the movement of Nature and not the soul which, by knowing itself, ceases even to appear to be bound by the result of its works.

Therefore the way of freedom is not inaction, but to cease from identifying oneself with the movement and recover instead our true identity in the Self of things who is their Lord.

THE OTHER WORLDS

By departing from the physical life one does not disappear out of the Movement, but only passes into some other general state of consciousness than the material universe.

These states are either obscure or illuminated, some dark or sunless.

By persisting in gross forms of ignorance, by coercing perversely the soul in its self-fulfilment or by a wrong dissolution of its becoming in the Movement, one enters into states of blind darkness, not into the worlds of light and of liberated and blissful being.

1. BRAHMAN:
ONENESS OF GOD AND THE WORLD

Verses 4-5*

BRAHMAN — THE UNITY

The Lord and the world, even when they seem to be distinct, are not really different from each other; they are one Brahman.

"ONE UNMOVING"

God is the one stable and eternal Reality. He is One because there is nothing else, since all existence and non-existence are He. He is stable or unmoving, because motion implies change in Space and change in Time, and He, being beyond Time and Space, is immutable. He possesses eternally in Himself all that is, has been or ever can be, and He therefore does not increase or diminish. He is beyond causality and relativity and therefore there is no change of relations in His being.

"SWIFTER THAN MIND"

The world is a cyclic movement (*saṁsāra*) of the Divine Consciousness in Space and Time. Its law and, in a sense, its object is progression; it exists by movement and would be dissolved by cessation of movement. But the basis of this movement is not material; it is the energy of active consciousness which, by its motion and multiplication in different principles (different in appearance, the same in essence), creates oppositions of unity and multiplicity, divisions of Time and Space, relations and groupings of circumstance and Causality. All these things are real in consciousness, but only symbolic of the Being, somewhat as the imaginations of a creative Mind are true representations

*4 One unmoving that is swifter than Mind; That the Gods reach not, for It progresses ever in front. That, standing, passes beyond others as they run. In That the Master of Life establishes the Waters.

5 That moves and That moves not; That is far and the same is near; That is within all this and That also is outside all this.

of itself, yet not quite real in comparison with itself, or real with a different kind of reality.

But mental consciousness is not the Power that creates the universe. That is something infinitely more puissant, swift and unfettered than the mind. It is the pure omnipotent self-awareness of the Absolute unbound by any law of the relativity. The laws of the relativity, upheld by the gods, are Its temporary creations. Their apparent eternity is only the duration, immeasurable to us, of the world which they govern. They are laws regularising motion and change, not laws binding the Lord of the movement. The gods, therefore, are described as continually running in their course. But the Lord is free and unaffected by His own movement.

"THAT MOVES, THAT MOVES NOT"

The motion of the world works under the government of a perpetual stability. Change represents the constant shifting of apparent relations in an eternal Immutability.

It is these truths that are expressed in the formulae of the one Unmoving that is swifter than Mind, That which moves and moves not, the one Stable which outstrips in the speed of its effective consciousness the others who run.

TRANSITIONAL THOUGHT
THE MANY[1]

If the One is pre-eminently real, "the others", the Many are not unreal. The world is not a figment of the Mind.

Unity is the eternal truth of things, diversity a play of the unity. The sense of unity has therefore been termed Knowledge, Vidya, the sense of diversity Ignorance, Avidya. But diversity is not false except when it is divorced from the sense of its true and eternal unity.

---

[1] The series of ideas under this heading seem to me to be the indispensable metaphysical basis of the Upanishad. The Isha Upanishad does not teach a pure and exclusive Monism; it declares the One without denying the Many and its method is to see the One in the Many. It asserts the simultaneous validity of Vidya and Avidya and upholds as the object of action and knowledge an immortality consistent with Life and Birth in this world. It regards every object as itself, the universe and every soul as itself, the divine Purusha. The ensemble of these ideas is consistent only with a synthetic or comprehensive as opposed to an illusionist or exclusive Monism.

Brahman is one, not numerically, but in essence. Numerical oneness would either exclude multiplicity or would be a pluralistic and divisible oneness with the Many as its parts. That is not the unity of Brahman, which can neither be diminished, nor increased, nor divided.

The Many in the universe are sometimes called parts of the universal Brahman as the waves are parts of the sea. But, in truth, these waves are each of them that sea, their diversities being those of frontal or superficial appearances caused by the sea's motion. As each object in the universe is really the whole universe in a different frontal appearance, so each individual soul is all Brahman regarding Itself and world from a centre of cosmic consciousness.

For That is identical, not single. It is identical always and everywhere in Time and Space, as well as identical beyond Time and Space. Numerical oneness and multiplicity are equally valid terms of its essential unity.

These two terms, as we see them, are like all others, representations in Chit, in the free and all-creative self-awareness of the Absolute regarding itself variously, infinitely, innumerably and formulating what it regards. Chit is a power not only of knowledge, but of expressive will, not only of receptive vision, but of formative representation; the two are indeed one power. For Chit is an action of Being, not of the Void. What it sees, that becomes. It sees itself beyond Space and Time; that becomes in the conditions of Space and Time.

Creation is not a making of something out of nothing or of one thing out of another, but a self-projection of Brahman into the conditions of Space and Time. Creation is not a making, but a becoming in terms and forms of conscious existence.

In the becoming each individual is Brahman variously represented and entering into various relations with Itself in the play of the divine consciousness; in being, each individual is all Brahman.

Brahman as the Absolute or the Universal has the power of standing back from Itself in the relativity. It conceives, by a subordinate movement of consciousness, the individual as other than the universal, the relative as different from the Absolute. With-

out this separative movement, the individual would always tend
to lose itself in the universal, the relative to disappear into the
Absolute. Thus, It supports a corresponding reaction in the individual who regards himself as "other" than the transcendent
and universal Brahman and "other" than the rest of the Many.
He puts identity behind him and enforces the play of Being
in the separate Ego.

The individual may regard himself as eternally different from
the One, or as eternally one with It, yet different, or he may go
back entirely in his consciousness to the pure Identity.[1] But he
can never regard himself as independent of some kind of Unity,
for such a view would correspond to no conceivable truth in the
universe or beyond it.

These three attitudes correspond to three truths of the
Brahman which are simultaneously valid and none of them
entirely true without the others as its complements. Their co-
existence, difficult of conception to the logical intellect, can be
experienced by identity in consciousness with Brahman.

Even in asserting Oneness, we must remember that Brahman
is beyond our mental distinctions and is a fact not of Thought
that discriminates, but of Being which is absolute, infinite and
escapes discrimination. Our consciousness is representative and
symbolic; it cannot conceive the thing-in-itself, the Absolute,
except by negation, in a sort of void, by emptying it of all that it
seems in the universe to contain. But the Absolute is not a void
or negation. It is all that is here in Time and beyond Time.

Even oneness is a representation and exists in relation to
multiplicity. Vidya and Avidya are equally eternal powers of the
supreme Chit. Neither Vidya nor Avidya by itself is the absolute
knowledge. (*Verses 9-11*)

Still, of all relations oneness is the secret base, not multiplicity. Oneness constitutes and upholds the multiplicity, multiplicity does not constitute and uphold the oneness.

Therefore we have to conceive of oneness as our self and the
essential nature of Being, multiplicity as a representation of Self
and a becoming. We have to conceive of the Brahman as One

---

[1] The positions, in inverse order, of the three principal philosophical schools of Vedanta,
Monism, Qualified Monism and Dualism.

Self of all and then return upon the Many as becomings of the One Being (*bhūtāni...ātmānam*). But both the Self and the becomings are Brahman; we cannot regard the one as Brahman and the others as unreal and not Brahman. Both are real, the one with a constituent and comprehensive, the others with a derivative or dependent reality.

THE RUNNING OF THE GODS

Brahman representing Itself in the universe as the Stable, by Its immutable existence (Sat), is Purusha, God, Spirit; representing Itself as the Motional, by Its power of active Consciousness (Chit), is Nature, Force or World-Principle (Prakriti, Shakti, Maya).[1] The play of these two principles is the Life of the universe.

The Gods are Brahman representing Itself in cosmic Personalities expressive of the one Godhead who, in their impersonal action, appear as the various play of the principles of Nature.

The "others" are *sarvāṇi bhūtāni* of a later verse, all becomings, Brahman representing itself in the separative consciousness of the Many.

Everything in the universe, even the Gods, seems to itself to be moving in the general movement towards a goal outside itself or other than its immediate idea of itself. Brahman is the goal; for It is both the beginning and the end, the cause and the result of all movement.

But the idea of a final goal in the movement of Nature itself is illusory. For Brahman is Absolute and Infinite. The Gods, labouring to reach him, find, at every goal that they realise, Brahman still moving forward in front to a farther realisation. Nothing in the appearances of the universe can be entirely That to the relative consciousness; all is only a symbolic representa-

---

[1] Prakriti, executive Nature as opposed to Purusha, which is the Soul governing, taking cognisance of and enjoying the works of Prakriti. Shakti, the self-existent, self-cognitive, self-effective Power of the Lord (Ishwara, Deva or Purusha), which expresses itself in the workings of Prakriti. Maya, signifying originally in the Veda comprehensive and creative knowledge, Wisdom that is from of old; afterwards taken in its second and derivative sense, cunning, magic, Illusion. In this second significance it can really be appropriate only to the workings of the lower Nature, *aparā prakṛti*, which has put behind it the Divine Wisdom and is absorbed in the experiences of the separative Ego. It is in the more ancient sense that the word Maya is used in the Upanishads, where, indeed, it occurs but rarely.

tion of the Unknowable.

All things are already realised in Brahman. The running of the Others in the course of Nature is only a working out (Prakriti), by Causality, in Time and Space, of something that Brahman already possesses.

Even in Its universal being Brahman exceeds the Movement. Exceeding Time, It contains in Itself past, present and future simultaneously and has not to run to the end of conceivable Time. Exceeding Space, It contains all formations in Itself coincidently and has not to run to the end of conceivable Space. Exceeding Causality, It contains freely in Itself all eventualities as well as all potentialities without being bound by the apparent chain of causality by which they are linked in the universe. Everything is already realised by It as the Lord before it can be accomplished by the separated Personalities in the movement.

THE PRINCIPLE OF LIFE

MATARISHWAN AND THE WATERS

What then is Its intention in the movement?

The movement is a rhythm, a harmony which That, as the Universal Life, works out by figures of Itself in the terms of conscious Being. It is a formula symbolically expressive of the Unknowable, — so arranged that every level of consciousness really represents something beyond itself, depth of depth, continent of continent. It is a play[1] of the divine Consciousness existing for its own satisfaction and adding nothing to That, which is already complete. It is a fact of conscious being, justified by its own existence, with no purpose ulterior to itself. The idea of purpose, of a goal is born of the progressive self-unfolding by the world of its own true nature to the individual Souls inhabiting its forms; for the Being is gradually self-revealed within its own becomings, real Unity emerges out of the Multiplicity and changes entirely the values of the latter to our consciousness.

This self-unfolding is governed by conditions determined by the complexity of consciousness in its cosmic action.

For consciousness is not simple or homogeneous, it is sep-

---

[1] This is the Vaishnava image of the Lila applied usually to the play of the Personal Deity in the world, but equally applicable to the active impersonal Brahman.

tuple. That is to say, it constitutes itself into seven forms or grades of conscious activity descending from pure Being to physical being. Their interplay creates the worlds, determines all activities, constitutes all becomings.

Brahman is always the continent of this play or this working. Brahman self-extended in Space and Time is the universe.

In this extension Brahman represents Itself as formative Nature, the universal Mother of things, who appears to us, first, as Matter, called *prthivī*, the Earth-Principle.

Brahman in Matter or physical being represents Itself as the universal Life-Power, Matarishwan, which moves there as a dynamic energy, *prāṇa*, and presides effectively over all arrangement and formation.

Universal Life establishes, involved in Matter, the septuple consciousness; and the action of *prāṇa*, the dynamic energy, on the Matrix of things evolves out of it its different forms and serves as a basis for all their evolutions.

TRANSITIONAL THOUGHT
THE WATERS

There are, then, seven constituents of Chit active in the universe.

We are habitually aware of three elements in our being, Mind, Life and Body. These constitute for us a divided and mutable existence which is in a condition of unstable harmony and works by a strife of positive and negative forces between the two poles of Birth and Death. For all life is a constant birth or becoming (*sambhava, sambhūti* of *Verses 12-14*). All birth entails a constant death or dissolution of that which becomes, in order that it may change into a new becoming. Therefore this state of existence is called *mrtyu*, Death, and described as a stage which has to be passed through and transcended. (*Verses 11,14*)

For this is not the whole of our being and, therefore, not our pure being. We have, behind, a superconscious existence which has also three constituents, *sat, cit-tapas* and *ānanda*.

Sat is essence of our being, pure infinite and undivided, as opposed to this divisible being which founds itself on the constant changeableness of physical substance. Sat is the divine counterpart of physical substance.

Chit-Tapas is pure energy of Consciousness, free in its rest or its action, sovereign in its will, as opposed to the hampered dynamic energies of Prana which, feeding upon physical substances, are dependent on and limited by their sustenance.[1] Tapas is the divine counterpart of this lower nervous or vital energy.

Ananda is Beatitude, the bliss of pure conscious existence and energy, as opposed to the life of the sensations and emotions which are at the mercy of the outward touches of Life and Matter and their positive and negative reactions, joy and grief, pleasure and pain. Ananda is the divine counterpart of the lower emotional and sensational being.

This higher existence, proper to the divine Sachchidananda, is unified, self-existent, not confused by the figures of Birth and Death. It is called, therefore, *amrtam*, Immortality, and offered to us as the goal to be aimed at and the felicity to be enjoyed when we have transcended the state of death. (*Verses 11, 14, 17, 18*)

The higher divine is linked to the lower mortal existence by the causal Idea[2] or supramental Knowledge-Will, *vijñāna*. It is the causal Idea which, by supporting and secretly guiding the confused activities of the Mind, Life and Body, ensures and compels the right arrangement of the universe. It is called in the Veda the Truth because it represents by direct vision the truth of things both inclusive and independent of their appearances; the Right or Law, because, containing in itself the effective power of Chit, it works out all things according to their nature with a perfect knowledge and prevision; the Vast, because it is of the nature of an infinite cosmic Intelligence comprehensive of all particular activities.

Vijnana, as the Truth, leads the divided consciousness back to the One. It also sees the truth of things in the multiplicity.

---

[1] Therefore physical substance is called in the Upanishads *annam*, Food. In its origin, however, the word meant simply being or substance.

[2] Not the abstract mental idea, but the supramental Real-Idea, the Consciousness, Force and Delight of the Being precipitated into a comprehensive and discriminative awareness of all the truths and powers of its own existence, carrying in its self-knowledge the will of self-manifestation, the power of all its potentialities and the power of all its forms. It is power that acts and effectuates, as well as knowledge master of its own action.

Vijnana is the divine counterpart of the lower divided intelligence.

These seven powers of Chit are spoken of by the Vedic Rishis as the Waters, they are imaged as currents flowing into or rising out of the general sea of Consciousness in the human being.[1]

They are all co-existent in the universe eternally and inseparably, but capable of being involved and remanifested in each other. They are actually involved in physical Nature and must necessarily evolve out of it. They can be withdrawn into pure infinite Being and can again be manifested out of it.

The infolding and unfolding of the One in the Many and the Many in the One is therefore the law of the eternally recurrent cosmic Cycles.

THE VISION OF THE BRAHMAN

The Upanishad teaches us how to perceive Brahman in the universe and in our self-existence.

We have to perceive Brahman comprehensively as both the Stable and the Moving. We must see It in eternal and immutable Spirit and in all the changing manifestations of universe and relativity.

We have to perceive all things in Space and Time, the far and the near, the immemorial Past, the immediate Present, the infinite Future with all their contents and happenings as the One Brahman.

We have to perceive Brahman as that which exceeds, contains and supports all individual things as well as all universe, transcendentally of Time and Space and Causality. We have to perceive It also as that which lives in and possesses the universe and all it contains.

This is the transcendental, universal and individual Brahman, Lord, Continent and Indwelling Spirit, which is the object of all knowledge. Its realisation is the condition of perfection and the way of Immortality.

---

[1] *Hṛdya samudra*, Ocean of the Heart. Rv. IV. 58. 5.

2. SELF-REALISATION

Verses 6 - 7*

SELF-REALISATION

Brahman is, subjectively, Atman, the Self or immutable existence of all that is in the universe. Everything that changes in us, mind, life, body, character, temperament, action, is not our real and unchanging self, but becomings of the Self in the movement, *jagati*.

In Nature, therefore, all things that exist, animate or inanimate, are becomings of the one Self of all. All these different creatures are one indivisible existence. This is the truth each being has to realise.

When this unity has been realised by the individual in every part of his being, he becomes perfect, pure, liberated from ego and the dualities, possessed of the entire divine felicity.

ATMAN

Atman, our true self, is Brahman; it is pure indivisible Being, self-luminous, self-concentrated in consciousness, self-concentrated in force, self-delighted. Its existence is light and bliss. It is timeless, spaceless and free.

THE THREEFOLD PURUSHA[1]

Atman represents itself to the consciousness of the creature in three states, dependent on the relations between *puruṣa* and *prakṛti*, the Soul and Nature. These three states are *akṣara*, unmoving or immutable; *kṣara*, moving or mutable; and *para* or *uttama*, Supreme or Highest.

---

*6 But he who sees everywhere the Self in all existences and all existences in the Self, shrinks not thereafter from aught.

7 He in whom it is the Self-Being that has become all existences that are Becomings, for he has the perfect knowledge, how shall he be deluded, whence shall he have grief who sees everywhere oneness?

[1] Gita XV. 16, 17. See also XIII *passim*.

Kshara Purusha is the Self reflecting the changes and movements of Nature, participating in them, immersed in the consciousness of the movement and seeming in it to be born and die, increase and diminish, progress and change. Atman, as the Kshara, enjoys change and division and duality; controls secretly its own changes but seems to be controlled by them; enjoys the oppositions of pleasure and pain, good and bad, but appears to be their victim; possesses and upholds the action of Nature, by which it seems to be created. For, always and inalienably, the Self is Ishwara, the Lord.

Akshara Purusha is the Self, standing back from the changes and movements of Nature, calm, pure, impartial, indifferent, watching them and not participating, above them as on a summit, not immersed in these Waters. This calm Self is the sky that never moves and changes looking down upon the waters that are never at rest. The Akshara is the hidden freedom of the Kshara.

Para Purusha or Purushottama is the Self containing and enjoying both the stillness and the movement, but conditioned and limited by neither of them. It is the Lord, Brahman, the All, the Indefinable and Unknowable.

It is this supreme Self that has to be realised in both the unmoving and the mutable.

PURUSHA IN PRAKRITI[1]

Atman, the Self, represents itself differently in the sevenfold movement of Nature according to the dominant principle of the consciousness in the individual being.

In the physical consciousness Atman becomes the material being, *annamaya puruṣa*.

In the vital or nervous consciousness Atman becomes the vital or dynamic being, *prāṇamaya puruṣa*.

In the mental consciousness Atman becomes the mental being, *manomaya puruṣa*.

In the supra-intellectual consciousness, dominated by the Truth or causal Idea (called in Veda *satyam ṛtam bṛhat*, the True, the Right, the Vast), Atman becomes the ideal being or

[1] *Taittiriya Upanishad* II. 1-6.

great Soul, *vijñānamaya puruṣa* or *mahat ātman*.[1]

In the consciousness proper to the universal Beatitude, Atman becomes the all-blissful being or all-enjoying and all-productive Soul, *ānandamaya puruṣa.*

In the consciousness proper to the infinite divine self-awareness which is also the infinite all-effective Will (*cit-tapas*), Atman is the all-conscious Soul that is source and lord of the universe, *caitanya puruṣa.*

In the consciousness proper to the state of pure divine existence, Atman is *sat puruṣa*, the pure divine Self.

Man, being one in his true Self with the Lord who inhabits all forms, can live in any of these states of the Self in the world and partake of its experiences. He can be anything he wills from the material to the all-blissful being. Through the Anandamaya he can enter into the Chaitanya and Sat Purusha.

SACHCHIDANANDA

Sachchidananda is the manifestation of the higher Purusha; its nature of infinite being, consciousness, power and bliss is the higher Nature, *parā prakṛti*. Mind, life and body are the lower nature, *aparā prakṛti.*

The state of Sachchidananda is the higher half of universal existence, *parārdha*, the nature of which is Immortality, *amṛtam*. The state of mortal existence in Matter is the lower half, *aparārdha*, the nature of which is death, *mṛtyu.*

Mind and life in the body are in the state of Death because by Ignorance they fail to realise Sachchidananda. Realising perfectly Sachchidananda, they can convert themselves, Mind into the nature of the Truth, *vijñāna*, Life into the nature of *caitanya*, Body into the nature of *sat*, that is, into the pure essence.

When this cannot be done perfectly in the body, the soul realises its true state in other forms of existence or worlds, the "sunlit" worlds and states of felicity, and returns upon material existence to complete its evolution in the body.

A progressively perfect realisation in the body is the aim of human evolution.

---

[1] The *mahat ātman* or Vast Self is frequently referred to in the Upanishads. It is also called *bhūmā*, the Large.

It is also possible for the soul to withdraw for an indefinable period into the pure state of Sachchidananda.

The realisation of the Self as Sachchidananda is the aim of human existence.

THE CONDITION OF SELF-REALISATION[1]

Sachchidananda is always the pure state of Atman; it may either remain self-contained as if apart from the universe or overlook, embrace and possess it as the Lord.

In fact, it does both simultaneously. (*Verse 8*)

The Lord pervades the universe as the Virat Purusha, the Cosmic Soul (*paribhūḥ* of the eighth verse, the One who becomes everywhere); He enters into each object in the movement, to the Knowledge as Brahman supporting individual consciousness and individual form, to the Ignorance as an individualised and limited being. He manifests as the Jivatman or individual self in the living creature.

From the standpoint of our lower state in the kingdom of death and limitation Atman is Sachchidananda, supra-mental, but reflected in the mind. If the mind is pure, bright and still, there is the right reflection; if it is unpurified, troubled and obscured, the reflection is distorted and subjected to the crooked action of the Ignorance.

According to the state of the reflecting mind we may have either purity of self-knowledge or an obscuration and distortion of knowledge in the dualities of truth and error; a pure activity of unegoistic Will or an obscuration and deflection of Will in the dualities of right and wrong action, sin and virtue; a pure state and unmixed play of beatitude or an obscuration and perversion of it in the dualities of right and wrong enjoyment, pleasure and pain, joy and grief.

It is the mental ego-sense that creates this distortion by division and limitation of the Self. The limitation is brought about through the Kshara Purusha identifying itself with the changeable

---

[1] I have collected under this and the preceding headings the principal ideas of the Upanishads with regard to the Self, although not expressly mentioned or alluded to in our text, because they are indispensable to an understanding of the complete philosophy of these Scriptures and to the relations of the thought which is developed in the Isha.

formations of Nature in the separate body, the individual life and the egoistic mind, to the exclusion of the sense of unity with all existence and with all existences.

This exclusion is a fixed habit of the understanding due to our past evolution in the movement, not an ineffugable law of human consciousness. Its diminution and final disappearance are the condition of self-realisation.

The beginning of wisdom, perfection and beatitude is the vision of the One.

THE STAGES OF SELF-REALISATION

THE VISION OF THE ALL

The first movement of self-realisation is the sense of unity with other existences in the universe. Its early or crude form is the attempt to understand or sympathise with others, the tendency of a widening love or compassion or fellow-feeling for others, the impulsion of work for the sake of others.

The oneness so realised is a pluralistic unity, the drawing together of similar units resulting in a collectivity or solidarity rather than in real oneness. The Many remain to the consciousness as the real existences; the One is only their result.

Real knowledge begins with the perception of essential oneness, — one Matter, one Life, one Mind, one Soul playing in many forms.

When this Soul of things is seen to be Sachchidananda, then knowledge is perfected. For we see Matter to be only a play of Life, Life a play of Mind energising itself in substance, Mind a play of Truth or causal Idea representing truth of being variously in all possible mental forms, Truth a play of Sachchidananda, Sachchidananda the self-manifestation of a supreme Unknowable, Para-Brahman or Para-Purusha.

We perceive the soul in all bodies to be this one Self or Sachchidananda multiplying itself in individual consciousness. We see also all minds, lives, bodies to be active formations of the same existence in the extended being of the Self.

This is the vision of all existences in the Self and of the Self in all existences which is the foundation of perfect internal liberty and perfect joy and peace.

For by this vision, in proportion as it increases in intensity and completeness, there disappears from the individual mentality all *jugupsā*, that is to say, all repulsion, shrinking, dislike, fear, hatred and other perversions of feeling which arise from division and personal opposition to other beings or to the objectivities that surround us. Perfect equality[1] of soul is established.

THE VISION OF THE SELF IN ITS BECOMINGS

Vision is not sufficient; one must become what inwardly one sees. The whole inner life must be changed so as to represent perfectly in all parts of the being what is understood by the intellect and seen by the inner perception.

In the individual soul extending itself to the All by the vision of unity (*ekatvam anupaśyataḥ*, seeing everywhere oneness) arranging its thoughts, emotions and sensations according to the perfect knowledge of the right relation of things which comes by the realisation of the Truth (*vijānataḥ*, having the perfect knowledge), there must be repeated the divine act of consciousness by which the one Being, eternally self-existent, manifests in itself the multiplicity of the world (*sarvāṇi bhūtāni ātmaiva abhūt*, the Self-Being became all Becomings).

That is to say, the human or egoistic view is that of a world of innumerable separate creatures each self-existent and different from the others, each trying to get its utmost possible profit out of the others and the world, but the divine view, the way in which God sees the world, is Himself, as the sole Being, living in innumerable existences that are Himself, supporting all, helping all impartially, working out to a divine fulfilment and under terms fixed from the beginning, from years sempiternal, a great progressive harmony of Becoming whose last term is Sachchidananda or Immortality. This is the viewpoint of the Self as Lord inhabiting the whole movement. The individual soul has to change the human or egoistic for the divine, supreme and universal view and live in that realisation.

---

[1] The state described in the Gita as *samatva*. *Jugupsā* is the feeling of repulsion caused by the sense of a want of harmony between one's own limited self-formation and the contacts of the external with a consequent recoil of grief, fear, hatred, discomfort, suffering. It is the opposite of attraction which is the source of desire and attachment. Repulsion and attraction removed, we have *samatva*.

It is necessary, therefore, to have the knowledge of the transcendent Self, the sole unity, in the equation *so'ham*, I am He, and in that knowledge to extend one's conscious existence so as to embrace the whole Multiplicity.

This is the double or synthetic ideal of the Isha Upanishad; to embrace simultaneously Vidya and Avidya, the One and the Many; to exist in the world, but change the terms of the Death into the terms of the Immortality; to have the freedom and peace of the Non-Birth simultaneously with the activity of the Birth. (*Verses 9-14*)

All parts of the lower being must consent to this realisation; to perceive with the intellect is not enough. The heart must consent in a universal love and delight, the sense-mind in a sensation of God and self everywhere, the life in the comprehension of all aims and energies in the world as part of its own being.

THE ACTIVE BEATITUDE

This realisation is the perfect and complete Beatitude, embracing action, but delivered from sorrow and self-delusion.

There is no possibility of self-delusion (*moha*); for the soul, having attained to the perception of the Unknowable behind all existence, is no longer attached to the Becoming and no longer attributes an absolute value to any particularity in the universe, as if that were an object in itself and desirable in itself. All is enjoyable and has a value as the manifestation of the Self and for the sake of the Self which is manifested in it, but none for its own.[1] Desire and illusion are removed; illusion is replaced by knowledge, desire by the active beatitude of universal possession.

There is no possibility of sorrow; for all is seen as Sachchidananda and therefore in the terms of the infinite conscious existence, the infinite will, the infinite felicity. Even pain and grief are seen to be perverse terms of Ananda, and that Ananda which they veil here and for which they prepare the lower existence (for all suffering in the evolution is a preparation of strength and bliss) is already seized, known and enjoyed by the soul thus liberated and perfected. For it possesses the eternal Reality of which they are the appearances.

[1] *Brihadaranyaka Upanishad.*

Thus it is possible, by the realisation of the unity of God and the world (*iś* and *jagat*) in the complete knowledge of the Brahman, to renounce desire and illusion through the ascent to the pure Self and the Non-Becoming and yet to enjoy by means of all things in the manifestation God in the universe through a free and illuminated self-identification with Sachchidananda in all existences.

CONCLUSION

We have, therefore, in the second movement the explanation of the first verse of the Upanishad. The first line, asserting that all souls are the one Lord inhabiting every object in the universe and that every object is universe in universe, movement in the general movement, has been explained in the terms of complete oneness by the Brahman, transcendental and universal even in the individual, One in the Many, Many in the One, Stable and Motional, exceeding and reconciling all opposites. The second line, fixing as the rule of divine life universal renunciation of desire as the condition of universal enjoyment in the spirit, has been explained by the state of self-realisation, the realisation of the free and transcendent Self as one's own true being, of that Self as Sachchidananda and of the universe seen as the Becoming of Sachchidananda and possessed in the terms of the right Knowledge and no longer in the terms of the Ignorance which is the cause of all attraction and repulsion, self-delusion and sorrow.

I. THE LORD

Verse 8*

"HE"

In its third movement the Upanishad takes up the justification of works already stated in general terms in its second verse and founds it more precisely upon the conception of Brahman or the Self as the Lord, — *iś, iśvara, para puruṣa, saḥ* (He) — who is the cause of personality and governs by His law of works the rhythm of the Movement and the process of the worlds that He conceives and realises throughout eternal Time in His own self-existence.

It is an error to conceive that the Upanishads teach the true existence only of an impersonal and actionless Brahman, an impersonal God without power or qualities. They declare rather an Unknowable that manifests itself to us in a double aspect of Personality and Impersonality. When they wish to speak of this Unknowable in the most comprehensive and general way, they use the neuter and call it *tat*, That; but this neuter does not exclude the aspect of universal and transcendent Personality acting and governing the world (cf. *Kena Upanishad* III). Still, when they intend to make prominent the latter idea they more often prefer to use the masculine *saḥ*, He, or else they employ the term Deva, God or the Divine, or Purusha, the conscious Soul, of whom Prakriti or Maya is the executive Puissance, the Shakti.

The Isha Upanishad, having declared the Brahman as the sole reality manifesting itself in many aspects and forms, having presented this Brahman subjectively as the Self, the one Being of whom all existences are Becomings, and as that which we have to realise in ourselves and in all things and beyond all things, now

*8 It is He that has gone abroad — That which is bright, bodiless, without scar of imperfection, without sinews, pure, unpierced by evil. The Seer, the Thinker, the One who becomes everywhere, the Self-existent has ordered objects perfectly according to their nature from years sempiternal.

proceeds to assert the same Brahman more objectively as the Lord, the Purusha who both contains and inhabits the universe.

It is He that went abroad. This Brahman, this Self is identical with the Lord, the Ish, with whose name the Upanishad opens, the Inhabitant of all forms: and, as we shall find, identical with the universal Purusha of the 16th verse, — "The Purusha there and there, He am I." It is He who has become all things and beings, — a conscious Being, the sole Existent and Self-existent, who is Master and Enjoyer of all He becomes. And the Upanishad proceeds to formulate the nature and manner, the general law of that becoming of God which we call the world. For on this conception depends the Vedic idea of the two poles of death and immortality, the reason for the existence of Avidya, the Ignorance, and the justification of works in the world.

TRANSITIONAL THOUGHT
THE DIVINE PERSONALITY

The Vedantic idea of God, "He", Deva or Ishwara, must not be confused with the ordinary notions attached to the conception of a Personal God. Personality is generally conceived as identical with individuality and the vulgar idea of a Personal God is a magnified individual like man in His nature but yet different, greater, more vast and all-overpowering. Vedanta admits the human manifestation of Brahman in man and to man, but does not admit that this is the real nature of the Ishwara.

God is Sachchidananda. He manifests Himself as infinite existence of which the essentiality is consciousness, of which again the essentiality is bliss, is self-delight. Delight cognising variety of itself, seeking its own variety, as it were, becomes the universe. But these are abstract terms; abstract ideas in themselves cannot produce concrete realities. They are impersonal states; impersonal states cannot in themselves produce personal activities.

This becomes still clearer if we consider the manifestation of Sachchidananda. In that manifestation Delight translates itself into Love; Consciousness translates itself into double terms, conceptive Knowledge, executive Force; Existence translates itself into Being, that is to say, into Person and Substance. But

Love is incomplete without a Lover and an object of Love, Knowledge without a Knower and an object of Knowledge, Force without a Worker and a Work, Substance without a Person cognising and constituting it.

This is because the original terms also are not really impersonal abstractions. In delight of Brahman there is an Enjoyer of delight, in consciousness of Brahman a Conscient, in existence of Brahman an Existent; but the object of Brahman's delight and consciousness and the term and stuff of Its existence are Itself. In the divine Being Knowledge, the Knower and the Known and, therefore, necessarily also Delight, the Enjoyer and the Enjoyed are one.

This Self-Awareness and Self-Delight of Brahman has two modes of its Force of consciousness, its Prakriti or Maya, — intensive in self-absorption, diffusive in self-extension. The intensive mode is proper to the pure and silent Brahman; the diffusive to the active Brahman. It is the diffusion of the Self-existent in the term and stuff of His own existence that we call the world, the becoming or the perpetual movement (*bhuvanam, jagat*). It is Brahman that becomes; what He becomes is also the Brahman. The object of Love is the self of the Lover; the work is the self-figuration of the Worker; Universe is body and action of the Lord.

When, therefore, we consider the abstract and impersonal aspect of the infinite existence, we say, "That"; when we consider the Existent self-aware and self-blissful, we say, "He". Neither conception is entirely complete. Brahman itself is the Unknowable beyond all conceptions of Personality and Impersonality. We may call it "That" to show that we exile from our affirmation all term and definition. We may equally call it "He", provided we speak with the same intention of rigorous exclusion. *Tat* and *sah* are always the same, One that escapes definition.

In the universe there is a constant relation of Oneness and Multiplicity. This expresses itself as the universal Personality and the many Persons, and both between the One and the Many and among the Many themselves there is the possibility of an infinite variety of relations. These relations are determined by the play of the divine existence, the Lord, entering into His manifested habitations. They exist at first as conscious relations between individual souls; they are then taken up by them and used as a means of entering into conscious relation with the One. It is this entering into various relations with the One which is the object and function of Religion. All religions are justified by this essential necessity; all express one Truth in various ways and move by various paths to one goal.

The Divine Personality reveals Himself in various forms and names to the individual soul. These forms and names are in a sense created in the human consciousness; in another they are eternal symbols revealed by the Divine who thus concretises Himself in mind-form to the multiple consciousness and aids it in its return to its own Unity.[1]

HE THAT WENT ABROAD

It is He that has extended Himself in the relative consciousness whose totality of finite and changeable circumstances dependent on an equal, immutable and eternal Infinity is what we call the Universe. *Sa paryagāt.*

In this extension we have, therefore, two aspects, one of pure infinite relationless immutability, another of a totality of objects in Time and Space working out their relations through causality. Both are different and mutually complementary expressions of the same unknowable "He".

To express the infinite Immutability the Upanishad uses a series of neuter adjectives, "Bright, bodiless, without scar, without sinews, pure, unpierced by evil." To express the same Absolute as cause, continent and governing Inhabitant of the totality of objects and of each object in the totality (*jagatyām jagat*) it uses four masculine epithets, "The Seer, the Thinker, the One who becomes everywhere, the Self-existent" or "the Self-Becoming".

The Immutable is the still and secret foundation of the play and the movement, extended equally, impartially in all things, *samam brahma*,[2] lending its support to all without choice or

---

[1] It would be an error to suppose that these conceptions are in their essence later developments of philosophical Hinduism. The conception of the many forms and names of the One is as old as the Rig-veda.

[2] "The equal Brahman." — Gita.

active participation. Secure and free in His eternal immutability the Lord projects Himself into the play and the movement, becoming there in His self-existence all that the Seer in Him visualises and the Thinker in Him conceives. *Kavir maniṣī paribhūḥ svayambhūḥ.*

THE PURE IMMUTABLE

The pure immutability of the Lord is "bright". It is luminosity of pure concentrated Self-awareness, not broken by refractions, not breaking out into colour and form. It is the pure self-knowledge of the Purusha, the conscious Soul, with his Power, his executive Force contained and inactive.

It is "bodiless", — without form, indivisible and without appearance of division. It is one equal Purusha in all things, not divided by the divisions of Space and Time, — a pure self-conscious Absolute.

It is without scar, that is, without defect, break or imperfection. It is untouched and unaffected by the mutabilities. It supports their clash of relations, their play of more and less, of increase and diminution, of irruption and interpenetration. For Itself is without action, *acalaḥ sanātanaḥ*,[1] "motionless, sempiternal."

It is without sinews. The reason for Its being without scar is that It does not put out Power, does not dispense Force in multiple channels, does not lose it here, increase it there, replenish its loss or seek by love or by violence its complementary or its food. It is without nerves of force; It does not pour itself out in the energies of the Pranic dynamism, of Life, of Matarishwan.

It is pure, unpierced by evil. What we call sin or evil, is merely excess and defect, wrong placement, inharmonious action and reaction. By its equality, by its inaction even while it supports all action, the conscious Soul retains its eternal freedom and eternal purity. For it is unmodified; It watches as the Sakshi, the witness, the modifications effected by Prakriti, but does not partake of them, does not get clogged with them, receives not their impression. *Na lipyate.*

[1] Gita II. 24.

THE SOUL INALIENABLY FREE

What is the relation of the active Brahman and of the human soul to this pure Inactive? They too are That. Action does not change the nature of the Self, but only the nature of the diverse forms. The Self is always pure, blissful, perfect, whether inactive or participating in action.

The Self is all things and exceeds them. It exceeds always that in which the mind is engrossed, that which it takes in a particular time and space as a figure of itself. The boundless whole is always perfect. The totality of things is a complete harmony without wound or flaw. The viewpoint of the part taken for a whole, in other words the Ignorance, is the broken reflection which creates the consciousness of limitation, incompleteness and discord. We shall see that this Ignorance has a use in the play of the Brahman; but in itself it appears at first to be only a parent of evil.

Ignorance is a veil that separates the mind, body and life from their source and reality, Sachchidananda. Thus obscured the mind feels itself pierced by the evil that Ignorance creates. But the Active Brahman is always Sachchidananda using for its self-becoming the forms of mind, body and life. All their experiences are therefore seen by It in the terms of Sachchidananda. It is not pierced by the evil. For It also is the One and sees everywhere Oneness. It is not mastered by the Ignorance that It uses as a minor term of its conception.

The human soul is one with the Lord; it also is in its completeness Sachchidananda using Ignorance as the minor term of its being. But it has projected its conceptions into this minor term and established there in limited mind its centre of vision, its viewpoint. It assumes to itself the incompleteness and the resultant sense of want, discord, desire, suffering. The Real Man behind is not affected by all this confusion; but the apparent or exterior Man is affected. To recover its freedom it must recover its completeness; it must identify itself with the divine Inhabitant within, its true and complete self. It can then, like the Lord, conduct the action of Prakriti without undergoing the false impression of identification with the results of its action. It is this idea on which the Upanishad bases the assertion, "Action cleaveth not to a man."

To this end it must recover the silent Brahman within. The Lord possesses always His double term and conducts the action of the universe, extended in it, but not attached to or limited by His works. The human soul, entangled in mind, is obscured in vision by the rushing stream of Prakriti's works and fancies itself to be a part of that stream and swept in its currents and in its eddies. It has to go back in its self-existence to the silent Purusha even while participating in its self-becoming in the movement of Prakriti. It becomes then, not only like the silent Purusha, the witness and upholder, but also the Lord and the free enjoyer of Prakriti and her works. An absolute calm and passivity, purity and equality within, a sovereign and inexhaustible activity without is the nature of Brahman as we see it manifested in the universe.

There is therefore no farther objection to works. On the contrary, works are justified by the participation or self-identification of the soul with the Lord in His double aspect of passivity and activity. Tranquillity for the Soul, activity for the energy, is the balance of the divine rhythm in man.

THE LAW OF THINGS

The totality of objects (*arthān*) is the becoming of the Lord in the extension of His own being. Its principle is double. There is consciousness; there is Being. Consciousness dwells in energy (*tapas*) upon its self-being to produce Idea of itself (*vijñāna*) and form and action inevitably corresponding to the Idea. This is the original Indian conception of creation, self-production or projection into form (*sṛṣṭi, prasava*). Being uses its self-awareness to evolve infinite forms of itself governed by the expansion of the innate Idea in the form. This is the original Indian conception of evolution, prominent in certain philosophies such as the Sankhya (*pariṇāma, vikāra, vivarta*). It is the same phenomenon diversely stated.

In the idea of some thinkers the world is a purely subjective evolution (*vivarta*), not real as objective facts; in the idea of others it is an objective fact, a real modification (*pariṇāma*), but one which makes no difference to the essence of Being. Both notions claim to derive from the Upanishads as their authority, and their opposition comes in fact by the separation of what in the ancient Vedanta was viewed as one, — as we see in this passage.

Brahman is His own subject and His own object, whether in His pure self-existence or in His varied self-becoming. He is the object of His own self-awareness; He is the Knower of His own self-being. The two aspects are inseparable, even though they seem to disappear into each other and emerge again from each other. All appearance of pure subjectivity holds itself as an object implicit in its very subjectivity; all appearance of pure objectivity holds itself as subject implicit in its very objectivity.

All objective existence is the Self-existent, the Self-becoming, *svayambhū*, becoming by the force of the Idea within it. The Idea is, self-contained, the Fact that it becomes. For *svayambhū* sees or comprehends Himself in the essence of the Fact as *kavi*, thinks Himself out in the evolution of its possibilities as *manīṣī*, becomes form of Himself in the movement in Space and Time as *paribhū*. These three are one operation appearing as successive in the relative, temporal and spatial Consciousness.

It follows that every object holds in itself the law of its own being eternally, *śāśvatībhyaḥ samābhyaḥ*, from years sempiternal, in perpetual Time. All relations in the totality of objects are thus determined by their Inhabitant, the Self-existent, the Self-becoming, and stand contained in the nature of things by the omnipresence of the One, the Lord, by His self-vision which is their inherent subjective Truth, by His self-becoming which, against a background of boundless possibilities, is the Law of their inevitable evolution in the objective Fact.

Therefore all things are arranged by Him perfectly, *yāthā-tathyataḥ*, as they should be in their nature. There is an imperative harmony in the All, which governs the apparent discords of individualisation. That discord would be real and operate in eternal chaos, if there were only a mass of individual forms and forces, if each form and force did not contain in itself and were not in its reality the self-existent All, the Lord.

THE PROCESS OF THINGS

The Lord appears to us in the relative notion of the process of things first as Kavi, the Wise, the Seer. The Kavi sees the Truth in itself, the truth in its becoming, in its essence, possibilities, actuality. He contains all that in the Idea, the Vijnana, called the Truth and Law, *satyam ṛtam*. He contains it comprehensively, not piecemeal; the Truth and Law of things is the *bṛhat*, the Large. Viewed by itself, the realm of Vijnana would seem a realm of predetermination, of concentration, of compelling seed-state. But it is a determination not in previous Time, but in perpetual Time; a Fate compelled by the Soul, not compelling it, compelling rather the action and result, present in the expansion of the movement as well as in the concentration of the Idea. Therefore the truth of the Soul is freedom and mastery, not subjection and bondage. Purusha commands Prakriti, Prakriti does not compel Purusha. *Na karma lipyate nare.*

The Manishi takes his stand in the possibilities. He has behind him the freedom of the Infinite and brings it in as a background for the determination of the finite. Therefore every action in the world seems to emerge from a balancing and clashing of various possibilities. None of these, however, are effective in the determination except by their secret consonance with the Law of that which has to become. The Kavi is in the Manishi and upholds him in his working. But viewed by itself the realm of the Manishi would seem to be a state of plasticity, of free-will, of the interaction of forces, but of a free-will in thought which is met by a fate in things.

For the action of the Manishi is meant to eventuate in the becoming of the Paribhu. The Paribhu, called also Virat, extends Himself in the realm of eventualities. He fulfils what is contained in the Truth, what works out in the possibilities reflected by the mind, what appears to us as the fact objectively realised. The realm of Virat would seem, if taken separately, to be that of a Law and Predetermination which compels all things that evolve in that realm, — the iron chain of Karma, the rule of mechanical necessity, the despotism of an inexplicable Law.

But the becoming of Virat is always the becoming of the self-existent Lord, — *paribhūḥ svayambhūḥ*. Therefore to realise the truth of that becoming we have to go back and re-embrace all that stands behind; — we have to return to the full truth of the free and infinite Sachchidananda.

This is the truth of things as seen from above and from the Unity. It is the divine standpoint; but we have to take account of the human standpoint which starts from below, proceeds from the Ignorance, and perceives these principles successively, not comprehensively, as separate states of consciousness. Humanity is that which returns in experience to Sachchidananda, and it must begin from below, in Avidya, with the mind embodied in matter, the Thinker imprisoned and emerging from the objective Fact. This imprisoned Thinker is Man, the "Manu".

He has to start from death and division and arrive at unity and immortality. He has to realise the universal in the individual and the Absolute in the relative. He is Brahman growing self-conscious in the objective multiplicity. He is the ego in the cosmos vindicating himself as the All and the Transcendent.

THIRD MOVEMENT

2. KNOWLEDGE AND IGNORANCE

Verses 9 - 11*

VIDYA AND AVIDYA

All manifestation proceeds by the two terms, Vidya and Avidya, the consciousness of Unity and the consciousness of Multiplicity. They are the two aspects of the Maya, the formative self-conception of the Eternal.

Unity is the eternal and fundamental fact, without which all multiplicity would be unreal and an impossible illusion. The consciousness of Unity is therefore called Vidya, the Knowledge.

Multiplicity is the play or varied self-expansion of the One, shifting in its terms, divisible in its view of itself, by force of which the One occupies many centres of consciousness, inhabits many formations of energy in the universal Movement. Multiplicity is implicit or explicit in unity. Without it the Unity would be either a void of non-existence or a powerless, sterile limitation to the state of indiscriminate self-absorption or of blank repose.

But the consciousness of multiplicity separated from the true knowledge in the many of their own essential oneness, — the viewpoint of the separate ego identifying itself with the divided form and the limited action, — is a state of error and delusion. In man this is the form taken by the consciousness of multiplicity. Therefore it is given the name of Avidya, the Ignorance.

Brahman, the Lord, is one and all-blissful, but free from limitation by His unity; all-powerful, He is able to conceive Himself from multiple centres in multiple forms from which and upon

*9 Into a blind darkness they enter who follow after the Ignorance, they as if into a greater darkness who devote themselves to the Knowledge alone.

10 Other, verily, it is said, is that which comes by the Knowledge, other that which comes by the Ignorance; this is the lore we have received from the wise who revealed That to our understanding.

11 He who knows That as both in one, the Knowledge and the Ignorance, by the Ignorance crosses beyond death and by the Knowledge enjoys Immortality.

which flow multiple currents of energy, seen by us as actions or play of forces. When He is thus multiple, He is not bound by His multiplicity, but amid all variations dwells eternally in His own oneness. He is Lord of Vidya and Avidya. They are the two sides of His self-conception (Maya), the twin powers of His Energy (Chit-Shakti).

Brahman, exceeding as well as dwelling in the play of His Maya, is *iś*, lord of it and free. Man, dwelling in the play, is *aniś*, not lord, not free, subject to Avidya. But this subjection is itself a play of the Ignorance, unreal in essential fact (*para-mārtha*), real only in practical relation (*vyavahāra*), in the working out of the actions of the divine Energy, the Chit-Shakti. To get back to the essential fact of his freedom he must recover the sense of Oneness, the consciousness of Brahman, of the Lord, realise his oneness in Brahman and with the Lord. Recovering his freedom, realising his oneness with all existences as becomings of the One Being who is always himself (*so'ham asmi*, He am I), he is able to carry out divine actions in the world, no longer sub-ject to the Ignorance, because free in the Knowledge.

The perfection of man, therefore, is the full manifestation of the Divine in the individual through the supreme accord be-tween Vidya and Avidya. Multiplicity must become conscious of its oneness, Oneness embrace its multiplicity.

THE EXTREME PATHS

The purpose of the Lord in the world cannot be fulfilled by following Vidya alone or Avidya alone.

Those who are devoted entirely to the principle of multi-plicity and division and take their orientation away from oneness enter into a blind darkness of Ignorance. For this tendency is one of increasing contraction and limitation, disaggregation of the gains of knowledge and greater and greater subjection to the mechanical necessities of Prakriti and finally to her separative and self-destructive forces. To turn away from the progression towards Oneness is to turn away from existence and from light.

Those who are devoted entirely to the principle of indiscri-minate Unity and seek to put away from them the integrality of the Brahman, also put away from them knowledge and completeness and enter as if into a greater darkness. They enter into some special state and accept it for the whole, mistaking exclusion in consciousness for transcendence in consciousness. They ignore by choice of knowledge, as the others are ignorant by compulsion of error. Knowing all to transcend all is the right path of Vidya.

Although a higher state than the other, this supreme Night is termed a greater darkness, because the lower is one of chaos from which reconstitution is always possible, the higher is a conception of Void or Asat, an attachment to non-existence of Self from which it is more difficult to return to fulfilment of Self.

THE GAINS IN EITHER PATH

Pursued with a less entire attachment the paths of Vidya and Avidya have each their legitimate gains for the human soul, but neither of these are the full and perfect thing undertaken by the individual in the manifestation.

By Vidya one may attain to the state of the silent Brahman or the Akshara Purusha regarding the universe without actively participating in it or to His self-absorbed state of Chit in Sat from which the universe proceeds and towards which it returns. Both these states are conditions of serenity, plenitude, freedom from the confusions and sufferings of the world.

But the highest goal of man is neither fulfilment in the movement as a separate individual nor in the Silence separated from the movement, but in the Uttama Purusha, the Lord, He who went abroad and upholds in Himself both the Kshara and the Akshara as modes of His being. The self of man, the Jivatman, is here in order to realise in the individual and for the universe that one highest Self of all. The ego created by Avidya is a necessary mechanism for affirming individuality in the universal as a starting-point for this supreme achievement.

By Avidya one may attain to a sort of fullness of power, joy, world-knowledge, largeness of being, which is that of the Titans or of the Gods, of Indra, of Prajapati. This is gained in the path of self-enlargement by an ample acceptance of the multiplicity in all its possibilities and a constant enrichment of the individual by all the materials that the universe can pour into him. But this also is not the goal of man; for though it brings transcendence of the ordinary human limits, it does not bring the divine transcendence of the universe in the Lord of the universe. One transcends confusion of Ignorance, but not limitation of Knowledge, — transcends death of the body, but not limitation of being, — transcends subjection to sorrow, but not subjection to joy, — transcends the lower Prakriti, but not the higher. To gain the real freedom and the perfect Immortality one would have to descend again to all that had been rejected and make the right use of death, sorrow and ignorance.

The real knowledge is that which perceives Brahman in His integrality and does not follow eagerly after one consciousness rather than another, is no more attached to Vidya than to Avidya. This was the knowledge of the ancient sages who were *dhira,* steadfast in the gaze of their thought, not drawn away from the completeness of knowledge by one light or by another and whose perception of Brahman was consequently entire and comprehensive and their teaching founded on that perception equally entire and comprehensive (*vicacakṣire*). It is the knowledge handed down from these Ancients that is being set forth in the Upanishad.

THE COMPLETE PATH

Brahman embraces in His manifestation both Vidya and Avidya and if they are both present in the manifestation, it is because they are both necessary to its existence and its accomplishment. Avidya subsists because Vidya supports and embraces it; Vidya depends upon Avidya for the preparation and the advance of the soul towards the great Unity. Neither could exist without the other; for if either were abolished, they would both pass away into something which would be neither the one nor the other, something inconceivable and ineffable beyond all manifestation.

In the worst Ignorance there is some point of the knowledge which constitutes that form of Ignorance and some support of Unity which prevents it in its most extreme division, limitation, obscurity from ceasing to exist by dissolving into nothingness. The destiny of the Ignorance is not that it should be dissolved out of existence, but that its elements should be enlightened, united, that which they strive to express delivered, fulfilled and in the fulfilment transmuted and transfigured.

In the uttermost unity of which knowledge is capable the contents of the Multiplicity are inherent and implicit and can any moment be released into activity. The office of Vidya is not to destroy Avidya as a thing that ought never to have been manifested but to draw it continually towards itself, supporting it the while and helping it to deliver itself progressively from that character of Ignorance, of the oblivion of its essential Oneness, which gives it its name.

Avidya fulfilled by turning more and more to Vidya enables the individual and the universal to become what the Lord is in Himself, conscious of His manifestation, conscious of His non-manifestation, free in birth, free in non-birth.

Man represents the point at which the multiplicity in the universe becomes consciously capable of this turning and fulfilment. His own natural fulfilment comes by following the complete path of Avidya surrendering itself to Vidya, the Multiplicity to the Unity, the Ego to the One in all and beyond all, and of Vidya accepting Avidya into itself, the Unity fulfilling the Multiplicity, the One manifesting Himself unveiled in the individual and in the universe.

MORTALITY AND IMMORTALITY

MORTALITY

By Avidya fulfilled man passes beyond death, by Vidya accepting Avidya into itself he enjoys immortality.

By death is meant the state of mortality which is a subjection to the process of constant birth and dying as a limited ego bound to the dualities of joy and sorrow, good and evil, truth and error, love and hatred, pleasure and suffering.

This state comes by limitation and self-division from the One who is all and in all and beyond all and by attachment of the idea of self to a single formation in Time and Space of body, life and mind, by which the Self excludes from its view all that it verily is with the exception of a mass of experiences flowing out from and in upon a particular centre and limited by the capacities of a

particular mental, vital and bodily frame. This mass of experiences it organises around the ego-centre in the mind and linking
them together in Time by a double action of memory, passive in
state, active in work, says continually, "This is I."

The result is that the soul attributes to itself a certain portion
only of the play of Prakriti or Chit-Shakti and consequently a
certain limited capacity of force of consciousness which has to
bear all the impact of what the soul does not regard as itself but
as a rush of alien forces; against them it defends its separate
formation of individuality from dissolution into Nature or mastery by Nature. It seeks to assert in the individual form and by
its means its innate character of Ish or Lord and so to possess
and enjoy its world.

But by the very definition of the ego its capacity is limited.
It accepts as itself a form made of the movement of Nature which
cannot endure in the general flux of things. It has to form it by
the process of the movement and this is birth, it dissolves it by
the process of the movement and this is death.

It can master by the understanding only so much of its experiences as assimilate with its own viewpoint and in a way which
must always be imperfect and subject to error because it is not the
view of all or the viewpoint of the All. Its knowledge is partly
error and all the rest it ignores.

It can only accept and harmonise itself with a certain number
of its experiences, precisely because these are the only ones it can
understand sufficiently to assimilate. This is its joy; the rest is
sorrow or indifference.

It is only capable of harmonising with the force in its body,
nerves and mind a certain number of impacts of alien forces. In
these it takes pleasure. The rest it receives with insensibility or
pain.

Death therefore is the constant denial by the All of the ego's
false self-limitation in the individual frame of mind, life and body.

Error is the constant denial by the All of the ego's false sufficiency in a limited knowledge.

Suffering of mind and body is the constant denial by the All
of the ego's attempt to confine the universal Ananda to a false
and self-regarding formation of limited and exclusive enjoyments.

It is only by accepting the oneness of the All that the individual can escape from this constant and necessary denial and attain beyond. Then All-being, All-force, All-consciousness, All-truth, All-delight take possession of the individual soul. It changes mortality for immortality.

MORTALITY AND AVIDYA

But the way of attaining to immortality is not by the self-dissolution of the individual formation into the flux of Prakriti, neither is it by prematurely dissolving it into the All-soul which Prakriti expresses. Man moves towards something which fulfils the universe by transcending it. He has to prepare his individual soul for the transcendence and for the fulfilment.

If Avidya is the cause of mortality, it is also the path out of mortality. The limitation has been created precisely in order that the individual may affirm himself against the flux of Prakriti in order eventually to transcend, possess and transform it.

The first necessity is therefore for man continually to enlarge himself in being, knowledge, joy, power in the limits of the ego so that he may arrive at the conception of something which progressively manifests itself in him in these terms and becomes more and more powerful to deal with the oppositions of Prakriti and to change, individually, more and more the terms of ignorance, suffering and weakness into the terms of knowledge, joy and power and even death into a means of wider life.

This self-enlargement has then to awaken to the perception of something exceeding itself, exceeding the personal manifestation. Man has so to enlarge his conception of self as to see all in himself and himself in all (*Verse 6*). He has to see that this "I" which contains all and is contained in all, is the One, is universal and not his personal ego. To That he has to subject his ego, That he has to reproduce in his nature and become, That is what he has to possess and enjoy with an equal soul in all its forms and movements.

He has to see that this universal One is something entirely transcendent, the sole Being, and that the universe and all its forms, actions, egos are only becomings of that Being (*Verse 7*). World is a becoming which seeks always to express in motion of

Time and Space, by progression in mind, life and body what is beyond all becoming, beyond Time and Space, beyond mind, life and body.

Thus Avidya becomes one with Vidya. By Avidya man passes beyond that death, suffering, ignorance, weakness which were the first terms he had to deal with, the first assertions of the One in the birth affirming Himself amid the limitations and divisions of the Multiplicity. By Vidya he enjoys even in the birth the Immortality.

IMMORTALITY

Immortality does not mean survival of the self or the ego after dissolution of the body. The Self always survives the dissolution of the body, because it always pre-existed before the birth of the body. The self is unborn and undying. The survival of the ego is only the first condition by which the individual soul is able to continue and link together its experiences in Avidya so as to pursue with an increasing self-possession and mastery that process of self-enlargement which culminates in Vidya.

By immortality is meant the consciousness which is beyond birth and death, beyond the chain of cause and effect, beyond all bondage and limitation, free, blissful, self-existent in conscious-being, the consciousness of the Lord, of the supreme Purusha, of Sachchidananda.

IMMORTALITY AND BIRTH

On this realisation man can base his free activity in the universe.

But having so far attained, what further utility has the soul for birth or for works? None for itself, everything for God and the universe.

Immortality beyond the universe is not the object of manifestation in the universe, for that the Self always possessed. Man exists in order that through him the Self may enjoy Immortality in the birth as well as in the non-becoming.

Nor is individual salvation the end; for that would only be the sublime of the ego, not its self-realisation through the Lord in all.

Having realised his own immortality, the individual has yet to fulfil God's work in the universe. He has to help the life, the mind and the body in all beings to express progressively Immortality and not mortality.

This he may do by the becoming in the material body which we ordinarily call birth, or from some status in another world or even, it is possible, from beyond world. But birth in the body is the most close, divine and effective form of help which the liberated can give to those who are themselves still bound to the progression of birth in the lowest world of the Ignorance.

3. BIRTH AND NON-BIRTH

Verses 12 - 14*

THE BIRTH AND THE NON-BIRTH

The Self outside Nature does not become; it is immutable as well as eternal. The Self in Nature becomes, it changes its states and forms. This entry into various states and forms in the succession of Time is Birth in Nature.

Because of these two positions of the Self, in Nature and out of Nature, moving in the movement and seated above the movement, active in the development and eating the fruits of the tree of Life or inactive and simply regarding, there are two possible states of conscious existence directly opposed to each other of which the human soul is capable, the state of Birth, the state of Non-Birth.

Man starts from the troubled state of Birth, he arrives at that tranquil poise of conscious existence liberated from the movement which is the Non-Birth. The knot of the Birth is the ego-sense; the dissolution of the ego-sense brings us to the Non-Birth. Therefore the Non-Birth is also called the Dissolution (*vināśa*).

Birth and Non-Birth are not essentially physical conditions, but soul-states. A man may break the knot of the ego-sense and yet remain in the physical body; but if he concentrates himself solely in the state of dissolution of ego, then he is not born again in the body. He is liberated from birth as soon as the present impulse of Nature which continues the action of the mind and body has been exhausted. On the other hand if he attaches him-

---

*12 Into a blind darkness they enter who follow after the Non-Birth, they as if into a greater darkness who devote themselves to the Birth alone.

13 Other, verily, it is said, is that which comes by the Birth, other that which comes by the Non-Birth; this is the lore we have received from the wise who revealed That to our understanding.

14 He who knows That as both in one, the Birth and the dissolution of Birth, by the dissolution crosses beyond death and by the Birth enjoys Immortality.

self to the Birth, the ego-principle in him seeks continually to clothe itself in fresh mental and physical forms.

THE EVIL OF THE EXTREMES

Neither attachment to Non-Birth nor attachment to Birth is the perfect way. For all attachment is an act of ignorance and a violence committed upon the Truth. Its end also is ignorance, a state of blind darkness.

Exclusive attachment to Non-Birth leads to a dissolution into indiscriminate Nature or into the Nihil, into the Void, and both of these are states of blind darkness. For the Nihil is an attempt not to transcend the state of existence in birth, but to annul it, not to pass from a limited into an illimitable existence, but from existence into its opposite. The opposite of existence can only be the Night of negative consciousness, a state of ignorance and not of release.

On the other hand, attachment to Birth in the body means a constant self-limitation and an interminable round of egoistic births in the lower forms of egoism without issue or release. This is, from a certain point of view, a worse darkness than the other; for it is ignorant even of the impulse of release. It is not an error in the grasping after truth, but a perpetual contentment with the state of blindness. It cannot lead even eventually to any greater good, because it does not dream of any higher condition.

THE GOOD OF THE EXTREMES

On the other hand each of these tendencies, pursued with a certain relativeness to the other, has its own fruit and its own good. Non-Birth pursued as the goal of Birth and a higher, fuller and truer existence may lead to withdrawal into the silent Brahman or into the pure liberty of the Non-Being. Birth, pursued as a means of progress and self-enlargement, leads to a greater and fuller life which may, in its turn, become a vestibule to the final achievement.

THE PERFECT WAY

But neither of these results is perfect in itself nor the true goal of humanity. Each of them brings its intended portion into the perfect good of the human soul only when it is completed by the other.

Brahman is both Vidya and Avidya, both Birth and Non-Birth. The realisation of the Self as the unborn and the poise of the soul beyond the dualities of birth and death in the infinite and transcendent existence are the conditions of a free and divine life in the Becoming. The one is necessary to the other. It is by participation in the pure unity of the Immobile (Akshara) Brahman that the soul is released from its absorption in the stream of the movement. So released it identifies itself with the Lord to whom becoming and non-becoming are only modes of His existence and is able to enjoy immortality in the manifestation without being caught in the wheel of Nature's delusions. The necessity of birth ceases, its personal object having been fulfilled; the freedom of becoming remains. For the Divine enjoys equally and simultaneously the freedom of His eternity and the freedom of His becoming.

It may even be said that to have had the conscious experience of a dissolution of the very idea of Being into the supreme Non-Being is necessary for the fullest and freest possession of Being itself. This would be from the synthetic standpoint the justification of the great effort of Buddhism to exceed the conception of all positive being even in its widest or purest essentiality.

Thus by dissolution of ego and of the attachment to birth the soul crosses beyond death; it is liberated from all limitation in the dualities. Having attained this liberation it accepts becoming as a process of Nature subject to the soul and not binding upon it and by this free and divine becoming enjoys Immortality.

THE JUSTIFICATION OF LIFE

Thus, the third movement of the Upanishad is a justification of life and works, which were enjoined upon the seeker of the Truth in its second verse. Works are the essence of Life. Life is a manifestation of the Brahman; in Brahman the Life Principle arranges a harmony of the seven principles of conscious being by which that manifestation works out its involution and evolution. In Brahman Matarishwan disposes the waters, the sevenfold movement of the divine Existence.

That divine Existence is the Lord who has gone abroad in the movement and unrolled the universe in His three modes as All-Seer of the Truth of things, Thinker-out of their possibilities, Realiser of their actualities. He has determined all things sovereignly in their own nature, development and goal from years sempiternal.

That determination works out through His double power of Vidya and Avidya, consciousness of essential unity and consciousness of phenomenal multiplicity.

The Multiplicity carried to its extreme limit returns upon itself in the conscious individual who is the Lord inhabiting the forms of the movement and enjoying first the play of the Ignorance. Afterwards by development in the Ignorance the soul returns to the capacity of Knowledge and enjoys by the Knowledge Immortality.

This Immortality is gained by the dissolution of the limited ego and its chain of births into the consciousness of the unborn and undying, the Eternal, the Lord, the ever-free. But it is enjoyed by a free and divine becoming in the universe and not outside the universe; for there it is always possessed, but here in the material body it is to be worked out and enjoyed by the divine Inhabitant under circumstances that are in appearance the most opposite to its terms, in the life of the individual and in the multiple life of the universe.

Life has to be transcended in order that it may be freely accepted; the works of the universe have to be over-passed in order that they may be divinely fulfilled.

The soul even in apparent bondage is really free and only plays at being bound; but it has to go back to the consciousness of freedom and possess and enjoy universally not this or that but the Divine and the All.

1. THE WORLDS — SURYA

Verses 15 - 16*

THE WORLDS AFTER DEATH

In the third verse the Upanishad has spoken of sunless worlds enveloped in blind gloom. In its third movement it also speaks twice of the soul entering into a blind gloom, but here it is a state of consciousness that seems to be indicated and not a world. Nevertheless, the two statements differ little in effect; for in the Vedantic conception a world is only a condition of conscious being organised in the terms of the seven constituent principles of manifested existence. According to the state of consciousness which we reach here in the body, will be our state of consciousness and the surroundings organised by it when the mental being passes out of the body. For the individual soul out of the body must either disappear into the general constituents of its existence, merge itself into Brahman or persist in an organisation of consciousness other than the terrestrial and in relations with the universe other than those which are appropriate to life in the body. This state of consciousness and the relations belonging to it are the other worlds, the worlds after death.

THE THREE STATES

The Upanishad admits three states of the soul in relation to the manifested universe, — terrestrial life by birth in the body, the survival of the individual soul after death in other states and the immortal existence which being beyond birth and death, beyond manifestation can yet enter into forms as the Inhabitant and embrace Nature as its lord. The two former conditions appertain to the Becoming; Immortality stands in the Self, in the

---

*15 The face of Truth is covered with a brilliant golden lid; that do thou remove, O Fosterer, for the law of the Truth, for sight.

16 O Fosterer, O sole Seer, O Ordainer, O illumining Sun, O power of the Father of creatures, marshal thy rays, draw together thy light; the Lustre which is thy most blessed form of all, that in Thee I behold. The Purusha there and there, He am I.

Non-Birth, and enjoys the Becoming.

The Upanishad, although it does not speak expressly of rebirth in an earthly body, yet implies that belief in its thought and language, — especially in the 17th verse. On the basis of this belief in rebirth man may aim at three distinct objects beyond death, — a better or more fortunate life or lives upon earth, eternal enjoyment of bliss in an ultra-terrestrial world of light and joy or a transcendence exclusive of all universal existence, merged in the Supreme as in one's true self, but having no relation with the actual or possible contents of its infinite consciousness.

REBIRTH

The attainment of a better life or lives upon earth is not the consummation offered to the soul by the thought of the Upanishad. But it is an important intermediate object so long as the soul is in a state of growth and self-enlargement and has not attained to liberation. The obligation of birth and death is a sign that the mental being has not yet unified itself with its true supramental self and spirit, but is dwelling "in Avidya and enclosed within it".[1] To attain that union the life of man upon earth is its appointed means. After liberation the soul is free, but may still participate in the entire movement and return to birth no longer for its own sake but for the sake of others and according to the will in it of its divine Self, the Lord of its movement.

HEAVEN AND HELL

The enjoyment of beatitude in a heaven beyond is also not the supreme consummation. But Vedantic thought did not envisage rebirth as an immediate entry after death into a new body; the mental being in man is not so rigidly bound to the vital and physical, — on the contrary, the latter are ordinarily dissolved together after death, and there must therefore be, before the soul is attracted back towards terrestrial existence, an interval in which it assimilates its terrestrial experiences in order to be able to constitute a new vital and physical being upon

---

[1] *Avidyāyām antare vartamānāḥ.* — *Katha Upanishad* I. 2.5; *Mundaka* I. 2. 8.

earth. During this interval it must dwell in states or worlds beyond and these may be favourable or unfavourable to its future development. They are favourable in proportion as the light of the Supreme Truth of which Surya is a symbol enters into them, but states of intermediate ignorance or darkness are harmful to the soul in its progress. Those enter into them, as has been affirmed in the third verse, who do hurt to themselves by shutting themselves to the light or distorting the natural course of their development. The Vedantic heavens are states of light and the soul's expansion; darkness, self-obscuration and self-distortion are the nature of the Hells which it has to shun.

In relation to the soul's individual development, therefore, the life in worlds beyond, like the life upon earth, is a means and not an object in itself. After liberation the soul may possess these worlds as it possesses the material birth, accepting in them a means towards the divine manifestation in which they form a condition of its fullness, each being one of the parts in a series of organised states of conscious being which is linked with and supports all the rest.

TRANSCENDENCE

Transcendence is the goal of the development, but it does not exclude the possession of that which is transcended. The soul need not and should not push transcendence so far as to aim at its own extinction. Nirvana is extinction of the ego-limitations, but not of all possibility of manifestation, since it can be possessed even in the body.

The desire of the exclusive liberation is the last desire that the soul in its expanding knowledge has to abandon; the delusion that it is bound by birth is the last delusion that it has to destroy.

SURYA AND AGNI

On the basis of this conception of the worlds and the relation of these different soul-states to each other the Upanishad proceeds to indicate the two lines of knowledge and action which lead to the supreme vision and the divine felicity. This is done under the form of an invocation to Surya and Agni, the

Vedic godheads, representative one of the supreme Truth and its illuminations, the other of the divine Will raising, purifying and perfecting human action.

THE ORDER OF THE WORLDS

To understand entirely the place and function of Surya we must enter a little more profoundly into the Vedic conception of the seven worlds and the principles of consciousness they represent.

All conscious being is one and indivisible in itself, but in manifestation it becomes a complex rhythm, a scale of harmonies, a hierarchy of states or movements. For what we call a state is only the organisation of a complex movement. This hierarchy is composed by a descending or involutive and an ascending or evolutive movement of which Spirit and Matter are the highest and lowest terms.

Spirit is Sat or pure existence, pure in self-awareness (Chit), pure in self-delight (Ananda). Therefore Spirit can be regarded as a triune basis of all conscious being. There are three terms, but they are really one. For all pure existence is in its essence pure self-conscience and all pure self-conscience is in its essence pure self-delight. At the same time our consciousness is capable of separating these three by the Idea and the Word and even of creating for itself in its divided or limited movements the sense of their apparent opposites.

An integral intuition into the nature of conscious being shows us that it is indeed one in essence, but also that it is capable of an infinite potential complexity and multiplicity in self-experience. The working of this potential complexity and multiplicity in the One is what we call from our point of view manifestation or creation or world or becoming — (*bhuvana, bhāva*). Without it no world-existence is possible.

The agent of this becoming is always the self-conscience of the Being. The power by which the self-conscience brings out of itself its potential complexities is termed Tapas, Force or Energy, and, being self-conscious, is obviously of the nature of Will. But not Will as we understand it, something exterior to its object, other than its works, labouring on material outside itself, but Will inherent in the Being, inherent in the becoming, one with the movement of existence, — self-conscious Will that becomes what it sees and knows in itself, Will that is expressed as Force of its own work and formulates itself in the result of its work. By this Will, Tapas or Chit-Shakti, the worlds are created.

THE HIGHER WORLDS

All organisation of self-conscient being which takes as its basis the unity of pure existence belongs to the world of the highest creation, *parārdha*, — the worlds of the Spirit.

We can conceive three principal formations.

When *tapas* or energy of self-conscience dwells upon *sat* or pure existence as its basis, the result is *satyaloka* or world of true existence. The soul in *satyaloka* is one with all its manifestations by oneness of essence and therefore one in self-conscience and in energy of self-conscience and one also in bliss.

When *tapas* dwells upon active power of *cit* as its basis, the result is *tapoloka* or world of energy of self-conscience. The soul in *tapoloka* is one with all manifestations in this Energy and therefore enjoys oneness also in the totality of their bliss and possesses equally their unity of essence.

When *tapas* dwells upon active Delight of being as its basis, the result is *janaloka*, world of creative Delight. The soul in *janaloka* is one in delight of being with all manifestation and through that bliss one also in conscious energy and in essence of being.

All these are states of consciousness in which unity and multiplicity have not yet been separated from each other. All is in all, each in all and all in each, inherently, by the very nature of conscious being and without effort of conception or travail of perception. There is no night, no obscurity. Neither is there, properly speaking, any dominant action of illuminating Surya. For the whole of consciousness there is self-luminous and needs no light other than itself. The distinct existence of Surya is lost in the oneness of the Lord or Purusha; that luminous oneness is Surya's most blessed form of all.

THE LOWER CREATION

In the lower creation also there are three principles, Matter,

Life, and Mind. Sat or pure existence appears there as extended substance or Matter; Will or Force appears as Life which is in its nature creative or manifesting Force and that Force is in its nature a self-conscient will involved and obscure in the forms of its creation. It is liberated from the involution and obscurity by delight of being struggling to become conscious of itself in desire and sensation; the result is the emergence of Mind. So at least it appears to us in the ascending or evolutive movement.

Wherever there is Matter, Life and Mind are present involved or evolving. So also, Life and Mind have some kind of material form as the condition of their activities. These three appear not as triune, owing to their domination by the dividing principle of Avidya, but as triple.

In the organisation of consciousness to which we belong, Tapas dwells upon Matter as its basis. Our consciousness is determined by the divisibility of extended substance in its apparent forms. This is Bhurloka, the material world, the world of formal becoming.

But we may conceive of a world in which dynamic Life-force with sensation emergent in it is the basis and determines without the gross obstacle of Matter the forms that it shall take. This organisation of consciousness has for its field Bhuvarloka, the world of free vital becoming in form.

We may conceive also of an organised state of consciousness in which Mind liberates itself from subjection to material sensation and becoming dominant determines its own forms instead of being itself determined by the forms in which it finds itself as a result of life-evolution. This formation is Swarloka or world of free, pure and luminous mentality.

In these lower worlds consciousness is normally broken up and divided. The light of Surya, the Truth, is imprisoned in the night of the subconscient or appears only reflected in limited centres or with its rays received by those centres and utilised according to their individual nature.

THE INTERMEDIATE WORLD

Between these two creations, linking them together, is the world or organisation of consciousness of which the infinite Truth of things is the foundation. There dominant individualisation no longer usurps the all-pervading soul and the foundation of consciousness is its own vast totality arranging in itself individualised movements which never lose the consciousness of their integrality and total oneness with all others. Multiplicity no longer prevails and divides, but even in the complexity of its movements always refers back to essential unity and its own integral totality. This world is therefore called Maharloka or world of large consciousness.

The principle of Maharloka is Vijnana, the Idea. But this Vijnana is intuitional or rather gnostic Idea,[1] not intellectual conception. The difference is that intellectual conception not only tends towards form, but determines itself in the form of the idea and once determined distinguishes itself sharply from other conceptions. But pure intuitional or gnostic Idea sees itself in the Being as well as in the Becoming. It is one with the existence which throws out the form as a symbol of itself and it therefore carries with it always the knowledge of the Truth behind the form. It is in its nature self-conscience of the being and power of the One, aware always of its totality, starting therefore from the totality of all existence and perceiving directly its contents. Its nature is *dṛṣṭi*, seeing, not conceiving. It is the vision at once of the essence and the image. It is this intuition or gnosis which is the Vedic Truth, the self-vision and all-vision of Surya.

THE LAW OF THE TRUTH

The face of this Truth is covered as with a brilliant shield, as with a golden lid; covered, that is to say, from the view of our human consciousness. For we are mental beings and our highest ordinary mental sight is composed of the concepts and percepts of the mind, which are indeed a means of knowledge, rays of the Truth, but not in their nature truth of existence, only truth of form. By them we arrange our knowledge of the appearances of things and try to infer the truth behind. The true knowledge is

---

[1] Intuition (revelation, inspiration, intuitive perception, intuitive discrimination) is Vijnana working in mind under the conditions and in the forms of mind. Gnosis or true supermind is a power above mind working in its own law, out of the direct identity of the supreme Self, his absolute self-conscious Truth knowing herself by her own power of absolute Light without any need of seeking, even the most luminous seeking.

truth of existence, *satyam*, not mere truth of form or appearance.

We can only arrive at the true Truth, if Surya works in us to remove this brilliant formation of concepts and percepts and replaces them by the self-vision and all-vision.

For this it is necessary that the law and action of the Truth should be manifested in us. We must learn to see things as they are, see ourselves as we are. Our present action is one in which self-knowledge and will are divided. We start with a fundamental falsehood, that we have a separate existence from others and we try to know the relations of separate beings in their separateness and act on the knowledge so formed for an individual utility. The law of the Truth would work in us if we saw the totality of our existence containing all others its forms created by the action of the totality, its powers working in and by the action of the totality. Our internal and external action would then well naturally and directly out of our self-existence, out of the very truth of things and not in obedience to an intermediate principle which is in its nature a falsifying reflection.

THE FULFILMENT OF SURYA IN MAN

Nevertheless even in our ordinary action there is the beginning or at least the seed of the Truth which must liberate us. Behind every act and perception there is an intuition, a truth which, if it is continually falsified in the form, yet preserves itself in the essence and works to lead us by increasing light and largeness to truth in the manifestation. Behind all this travail of differentiation and division there is an insistent unifying tendency which is also continually falsified in the separate result, but yet leads persistently towards our eventual integrality in knowledge, in being and in will.

Surya is Pushan, fosterer or increaser. His work must be to effect this enlargement of the divided self-perception and action of will into the integral will and knowledge. He is sole seer and replacing other forms of knowledge by his unifying vision enables us to arrive finally at oneness. That intuitive vision of the totality, of one in All and All in one, becomes the ordainer of the right law of action in us, the law of the Truth. For Surya is Yama, the Ordainer or Controller who assures the law, the

Dharma. Thus we arrive at the fullness of action of the Illu-
miner in us, accomplish the entirety of the Truth-Consciousness.
We are then able to see that all that is contained in the being of
Surya, in the Vijnana which builds up the worlds is becoming
of existence in the one existence and one Lord of all becoming,
the Purusha, Sachchidananda. All becoming is born in the
Being who himself exceeds all becomings and is their Lord,
Prajapati.

By the revelation of the vision of Surya the true knowledge
is formed. In this formation the Upanishad indicates two successive actions. First, there is an arrangement or marshalling
of the rays of Surya, that is to say, the truths concealed behind
our concepts and percepts are brought out by separate intuitions
of the image and the essence of the image and arranged in their
true relations to each other. So we arrive at totalities of intuitive
knowledge and can finally go beyond to unity. This is the drawing together of the light of Surya. This double movement is neces-
sitated by the constitution of our minds which cannot, like the
original Truth-Consciousness, start at once from the totality and
perceive its contents from within. The mind can hardly conceive unity except as an abstraction, a sum or a void. Therefore
it has to be gradually led from its own manner to that which
exceeds it. It has to carry out its own characteristic action of
arrangement, but with the help and by the operation of the higher
faculty, no longer arbitrarily, but following the very action of the
Truth of existence itself. Afterwards, by thus gradually correc-
ting the manner of its own characteristic action it can succeed in
reversing that characteristic action itself and learn to proceed
from the whole to the contents instead of proceeding from
"parts"[1] mistaken for entities to an apparent whole which is still
a "part" and still mistaken for an entity.

THE ONE EXISTENT

Thus by the action of Surya we arrive at that light of the
supreme super-conscient in which even the intuitive knowledge
of the truth of things based upon the total vision passes into the
self-luminous self-vision of the one existent, one in all infinite

---

[1] There are really no parts, existence being indivisible.

complexities of a self-experience which never loses its unity or its self-luminousness. This is Surya's godliest form of all. For it is the supreme Light, the supreme Will, the supreme Delight of existence.

This is the Lord, the Purusha, the self-conscient Being. When we have this vision, there is the integral self-knowledge, the perfect seeing, expressed in the great cry of the Upanishad, *so'ham*. The Purusha there and there, He am I. The Lord manifests Himself in the movements and inhabits many forms, but it is One who inhabits all. This self-conscient being, this real "I" whom the mental being individualised in the form is aware of as his true self — it is He. It is the All; and it is that which transcends the All.

2. ACTION AND THE DIVINE WILL

Verses 17 - 18*

THE SIDE OF ACTION

Through Surya then, through the growth of the illumination in the mind which enables it eventually to pass beyond itself, we have the first principle of progress from mortality to immortality. It is by the Sun as a door or gate[1] that the individual, the limited consciousness attains to the full consciousness and life in the one, supreme and all-embracing Soul.

Both consciousness and life are included in the formula of Immortality; Knowledge is incomplete without action. Chit fulfils itself by Tapas, Consciousness by energy. And as Surya represents the divine Light, so Agni to the ancient Rishis represented divine Force, Power or Will-in-Consciousness. The prayer to Agni completes the prayer to Surya.

THE INDIVIDUAL WILL

As in knowledge, so in action, unity is the true foundation. The individual, accepting division as his law, isolating himself in his own egoistic limits, is necessarily mortal, obscure and ignorant in his workings. He follows in his aims and in his methods a knowledge that is personal, governed by desire, habits of thought, obscure subconscious impulses or, at best, a broken partial and shifting light. He lives by rays and not in the full blaze of the Sun. His knowledge is narrow in its objectivity, narrow in its subjectivity, in neither one with the integral know-

---

*17 The Breath of things is an immortal life, but of this body ashes are the end — OM! O Will, remember, that which was done remember! O Will, remember, that which was done remember.

18 O god Agni, knowing all things that are manifested, lead us by the good path to the felicity; remove from us the devious attraction of sin. To thee completest speech of submission we address.

[1] *Sūryadvāreṇa — Mundaka Upanishad* I. 2. 11.

ledge and the total working and total will in the universe. His action, therefore, is crooked, many-branching, hesitating and fluctuating in its impulsion and direction; it beats about among falsehoods to find the Truth, tosses or scraps fragments together to piece out the whole, stumbles among errors and sins to find the right. Being neither one-visioned nor whole-visioned, having neither the totality of the universal Will nor the concentrated oneness of the transcendent, the individual will cannot walk straight on the right or good path towards the Truth and the Immortality. Governed by desire, exposed to the shock of the forces around it with which its egoism and ignorance forbid it to put itself in harmony, it is subject to the twin children of the Ignorance, suffering and falsehood. Not having the divine Truth and Right, it cannot have the divine Felicity.

AGNI, THE DIVINE WILL

But as there is in and behind all the falsehoods of our material mind and reason a Light that prepares by this twilight the full dawn of the Truth in man, so there is in and behind all our errors, sins and stumblings a secret Will, tending towards Love and Harmony, which knows where it is going and prepares and combines our crooked branchings towards the straight path which will be the final result of their toil and seeking. The emergence of this Will and that Light is the condition of immortality.

This Will is Agni. Agni is in the Rig-veda, from which the closing verse of the Upanishad is taken, the flame of the Divine Will or Force of Consciousness working in the worlds. He is described as the immortal in mortals, the leader of the journey, the divine Horse that bears us on the road, the "son of crookedness" who himself knows and is the straightness and the Truth. Concealed and hard to seize in the workings of this world because they are all falsified by desire and egoism, he uses them to transcend them and emerges as the universal in Man or universal Power, Agni Vaishwanara, who contains in himself all the gods and all the worlds, upholds all the universal workings and finally fulfils the godhead, the immortality. He is the worker of the divine Work. It is these symbols which govern the sense of the two final verses of the Upanishad.

THE IMMORTAL LIFE-PRINCIPLE

Life is the condition from which the Will and the Light emerge. It is said in the Veda that Vayu or Matarishwan, the Life-principle, is he who brings down Agni from Surya in the high and far-off supreme world. Life calls down the divine Will from the Truth-Consciousness into the realm of mind and body to prepare here, in Life, its own manifestation. Agni, enjoying and devouring the things of Life, generates the Maruts, nervous forces of Life that become forces of thought; they, upheld by Agni, prepare the action of Indra, the luminous Mind, who is for our life-powers their Rishi or finder of the Truth and Right. Indra slays Vritra, the Coverer, dispels the darkness, causes Surya to rise upon our being and go abroad over its whole field with the rays of the Truth. Surya is the Creator or manifester, Savitri, who manifests in this mortal world the world or state of immortality, dispels the evil dream of egoism, sin and suffering and transforms Life into the immortality, the good, the beatitude. The Vedic gods are a parable of human life emerging, mounting, lifting itself towards the Godhead.

Life, body, action, will, these are our first materials. Matter supplies us with the body; but it is only a temporary knot of the movement, a dwelling-place of the Purusha in which he presides over the activities generated out of the Life-principle. Once it is thrown aside by the Life-principle it is dissolved; ashes are its end. Therefore the body is not ourselves, but only an outer tool and instrument. For Matter is the principle of obscurity and division, of birth and death, of formation and dissolution. It is the assertion of death. Immortal man must not identify himself with the body.

The Life-principle in us survives. It is the immortal Breath[1] or, as the phrase really means, the subtle force of existence which is superior to the principle of birth and death. At first sight it may appear that birth and death are attributes of the Life, but it is not really so: birth and death are processes of Matter, of the body. The Life-principle is not formed and dissolved in the formulation and dissolution of the body; if that were so, there could be no continuity of the individual existence and all would go back

---

[1] *Anilam amṛtam.*

at death into the formless. Life forms body, it is not formed by
it. It is the thread upon which the continuity of our successive
bodily lives is arranged, precisely because it is itself immortal.
It associates itself with the perishable body and carries forward
the mental being, the Purusha in the mind, upon his journey.

WILL AND MEMORY

This journey consists in a series of activities continued from
life to life in this world with intervals of life in other states. The
Life-principle maintains them; it supplies their material in the
formative energy which takes shape in them. But their presiding
god is not the Life-principle; it is the Will. Will is *kratu*, the
effective power behind the act. It is of the nature of consciousness; it is energy of consciousness, and although present in all
forms, conscious, subconscious or superconscious, vital, physical
or mental, yet comes into its kingdom only when it emerges in
Mind. It uses the mental faculty of memory to link together and
direct consciously the activities towards the goal of the individual.

In man the use of consciousness by the mental will is imperfect, because memory is limited. Our action is both dispersed and
circumscribed because mentally we live from hour to hour in the
current of Time, holding only to that which attracts or seems immediately useful to our egoistic mind. We live in what we are
doing, we do not control what has been done, but are rather
controlled by our past works which we have forgotten. This is
because we dwell in the action and its fruits instead of living in
the soul and viewing the stream of action from behind it. The
Lord, the true Will, stands back from the actions and therefore
is their lord and not bound by them.

The Upanishad solemnly invokes the Will to remember the
thing that has been done, so as to contain and be conscious of the
becoming, so as to become a power of knowledge and self-
possession and not only a power of impulsion and self-formula-
tion. It will thus more and more approximate itself to the true
Will and preside over the co-ordination of the successive lives
with a conscious control. Instead of being carried from life to
life in a crooked path, as by winds, it will be able to proceed
more and more straight in an ordered series, linking life to life

with an increasing force of knowledge and direction until it becomes the fully conscious Will moving with illumination on the straight path towards the immortal felicity. The mental will, *kratu*, becomes what it at present only represents, the divine Will, Agni.

WILL AND KNOWLEDGE

The essentiality of the divine Will is that in it Consciousness and Energy, Knowledge and Force are one. It knows all manifestations, all things that take birth in the worlds. It is Jatavedas, that which has right knowledge of all births. It knows them in the law of their being, in their relation to other births, in their aim and method, in their process and goal, in their unity with all and their difference from all. It is this divine Will that conducts the universe; it is one with all the things that it combines and its being, its knowledge, its action are inseparable from each other. What it is, it knows; what it knows, that it does and becomes.

But as soon as egoistic consciousness emerges and interferes, there is a disturbance, a division, a false action. Will becomes an impulsion ignorant of its secret motive and aim, knowledge becomes a dubious and partial ray not in possession of the will, the act and the result, but only striving to possess and inform them. This is because we are not in possession of our self,[1] our true being, but only of the ego. What we are, we know not; what we know, we cannot effect. For knowledge is real and action in harmony with true knowledge only when they proceed naturally out of the conscious, illumined and self-possessing soul, in which being, knowledge and action are one movement.

SURRENDER TO THE DIVINE WILL

This is the change that happens when, the mental will approximating more and more to the divine, Agni burns out in us. It is that increasing knowledge and force which carries us finally into the straight or good path out of the crookedness. It is the divine Will, one with the divine knowledge, which leads us towards felicity, towards the state of Immortality. All that belongs to the deviations of the ego, all that obscures and drives or

---

[1] *ātmavān*.

draws us into this or that false path with its false lures and stumblings are put away from us by it. These things fall away from the
divinised Will and cease to find lodging in our consciousness.

Therefore the sign of right action is the increasing and finally
the complete submission of the individual to the divine Will
which the illumination of Surya reveals in him. Although manifested in his consciousness, this Will is not individual. It is the
will of the Purusha who is in all things and transcends them. It
is the will of the Lord.

Knowledge of the Lord as the One in the fully self-conscious
being, submission to the Lord as the universal and transcendent
in the fully self-conscious action, are the two keys of the divine
gates, the gates of Immortality.

And the nature of the two united is an illuminated Devotion
which accepts, aspires to and fulfils God in the human existence.

CONCLUSION

Thus the fourth movement indicates psychologically the
double process of that attainment of Immortality which is the
subject of the third movement, the state of bliss and truth within
and the worlds of Light after death culminating in the identity
of the self-luminous One. At the same time it particularises
under the cover of Vedic symbols the process of that self-knowledge and identification with the Self and all its becomings which
is the subject of the second movement and of that liberated action
in the assertion of which the first culminates. It is thus a fitting
close and consummation to the Upanishad.

Conclusion and Summary

THE Isha Upanishad is one of the more ancient of the Vedantic writings in style, substance and versification, subsequent certainly to the Chhandogya, Brihadaranyaka and perhaps to the Taittiriya and Aitareya, but certainly the most antique of the extant metrical Upanishads. Upanishadic thought falls naturally into two great periods; in one, the earlier, it still kept close to its Vedic roots, reflected the old psychological system of the Vedic Rishis and preserved what may be called their spiritual pragmatism; in the other and later, in which the form and thought became more modern and independent of early symbols and origins, some of the principal elements of Vedic thought and psychology begin to be omitted or to lose their previous connotation and the foundations of the later ascetic and anti-pragmatic Vedanta begin to appear. The Isha belongs to the earlier or Vedic group. It is already face to face with the problem of reconciling human life and activity with the Monistic standpoint and its large solution of the difficulty is one of the most interesting passages of Vedantic literature. It is the sole Upanishad which offered almost insuperable difficulties to the extreme illusionism and anti-pragmatism of Shankaracharya and it was even, for this reason, excised from the list of authoritative Upanishads by one of his greatest followers.

THE PRINCIPLE OF THE UPANISHAD

The principle it follows throughout is the uncompromising reconciliation of uncompromising extremes. Later thought took one series of terms, — the World, Enjoyment, Action, the Many, Birth, the Ignorance, — and gave them a more and more secondary position, exalting the opposite series, God, Renunciation, Quietism, the One, Cessation of Birth, the Knowledge until this trend of thought culminated in Illusionism and the idea of existence in the world as a snare and a meaningless burden imposed inexplicably on the soul by itself, which must be cast aside as

soon as possible. It ended in a violent cutting of the knot of the
great enigma. This Upanishad tries instead to get hold of the
extreme ends of the knots, disengage and place them alongside
of each other in a release that will be at the same time a right
placing and relation. It will not qualify or subordinate unduly
any of the extremes, although it recognises a dependence of one
on the other. Renunciation is to go to the extreme, but also
enjoyment is to be equally integral; Action has to be complete
and ungrudging, but also freedom of the soul from its works
must be absolute; Unity utter and absolute is the goal, but this
absoluteness has to be brought to its highest term by including in
it the whole infinite multiplicity of things.

So great is this scruple in the Upanishad that having so expressed itself in the formula "By the Ignorance having crossed
over death by the knowledge one enjoys Immortality" that Life
in the world might be interpreted as only a preliminary to an
existence beyond, it at once rights the balance by reversing the
order in the parallel formula "By dissolution having crossed
over death by birth one enjoys Immortality", and thus makes life
itself the field of the immortal existence which is the goal and
aspiration of all life. In this conclusion it agrees with the early
Vedic thought which believed all the worlds and existence and
non-existence and death and life and immortality to be here in
the embodied human being, there evolvent, there realisable and
to be possessed and enjoyed, not dependent either for acquisition
or enjoyment on the renunciation of life and bodily existence.
This thought has never entirely passed out of Indian philosophy,
but has become secondary and a side admission not strong
enough to qualify seriously the increasing assertion of the extinction of mundane existence as the condition of our freedom
and our sole wise and worthy aim.

THE OPPOSITES

The pairs of opposites successively taken up by the Upanishad and resolved are, in the order of their succession:

1. The Conscious Lord and phenomenal Nature.
2. Renunciation and Enjoyment.
3. Action in Nature and Freedom in the Soul.

4. The One stable Brahman and the multiple Movement.
5. Being and Becoming.
6. The Active Lord and the indifferent Akshara Brahman.
7. Vidya and Avidya.
8. Birth and Non-Birth.
9. Works and Knowledge.

These discords are thus successively resolved:

GOD AND NATURE

1. Phenomenal Nature is a movement of the conscious Lord. The object of the movement is to create forms of His consciousness in motion in which He as the one soul in many bodies can take up his habitation and enjoy the multiplicity and the movement with all their relations.[1]

ENJOYMENT AND RENUNCIATION

2. Real integral enjoyment of all this movement and multiplicity in its truth and in its infinity depends upon an absolute renunciation; but the renunciation intended is an absolute renunciation of the principle of desire founded on the principle of egoism and not a renunciation of world-existence.[2] This solution depends on the idea that desire is only an egoistic and vital deformation of the divine Ananda or delight of being from which the world is born; by extirpation of ego and desire Ananda again becomes the conscious principle of existence. This substitution is the essence of the change from life in death to life in immortality. The enjoyment of the infinite delight of existence free from ego, founded on oneness of all in the Lord, is what is meant by the enjoyment of Immortality.

ACTION AND FREEDOM

3. Actions are not inconsistent with the soul's freedom. Man is not bound by works, but only seems to be bound. He has

---

[1] This is also the view of the Gita and generally accepted.

[2] This, again, is the central standpoint of the Gita, which, however, admits also the renunciation of world-existence. The general trend of Vedantic thought would accept the renunciation of desire and egoism as the essential but would hold that renunciation of egoism means the renunciation of all world-existence, for it sees desire and not Ananda as the cause of world-existence.

to recover the consciousness of his inalienable freedom by recovering the consciousness of unity in the Lord, unity in himself, unity with all existence.[1] This done, life and works can and should be accepted in their fullness; for the manifestation of the Lord in life and works is the law of our being and the object of our world-existence.

THE QUIESCENCE AND THE MOVEMENT

4. What then of the Quiescence of the Supreme Being and how is persistence in the Movement compatible with that Quiescence which is generally recognised as an essential condition of the supreme Bliss?

The Quiescence and the Movement are equally one Brahman and the distinction drawn between them is only a phenomenon of our consciousness. So it is with the idea of space and time, the far and the near, the subjective and the objective, internal and external, myself and others, one and many. Brahman, the real existence, is all these things to our consciousness, but in itself ineffably superior to all such practical distinctions. The Movement is a phenomenon of the Quiescence, the Quiescence itself may be conceived as a Movement too rapid for the gods, that is to say, for our various functions of consciousness to follow in its real nature. But it is no formal, material, spatial, temporal movement, only a movement in consciousness. Knowledge sees it all as one, Ignorance divides and creates oppositions where there is no opposition but simply relations of one consciousness in itself. The ego in the body says, "I am within, all else is outside; and in what is outside, this is near to me in Time and Space, that is far." All this is true in present relation; but in essence it is all one indivisible movement of Brahman which is not material movement but a way of seeing things in the one consciousness.

BEING AND BECOMING

5. Everything depends on what we see, how we look at existence in our soul's view of things. Being and Becoming, One and Many are both true and are both the same thing: Being

---

[1] This truth would, again, be generally admitted, but not the conclusion that is drawn from it.

is one, Becomings are many; but this simply means that all Becomings are one Being who places Himself variously in the phenomenal movement of His consciousness. We have to see the One Being, but we have not to cease to see the many Becomings, for they exist and are included in Brahman's view of Himself. Only, we must see with knowledge and not with ignorance. We have to realise our true self as the one unchangeable, indivisible Brahman. We have to see all becomings as developments of the movement in our true self and this self as one inhabiting all bodies and not our body only. We have to be consciously, in our relations with this world, what we really are, — this one self becoming everything that we observe. All the movement, all energies, all forms, all happenings we must see as those of our one and real self in many existences, as the play of the Will and Knowledge and Delight of the Lord in His world-existence.

We shall then be delivered from egoism and desire and the sense of separate existence and therefore from all grief and delusion and shrinking; for all grief is born of the shrinking of the ego from the contacts of existence, its sense of fear, weakness, want, dislike, etc.; and this is born from the delusion of separate existence, the sense of being my separate ego exposed to all these contacts of so much that is not myself. Get rid of this, see oneness everywhere, be the One manifesting Himself in all creatures; ego will disappear; desire born of the sense of not being this, not having that, will disappear; the free inalienable delight of the One in His own existence will take the place of desire and its satisfactions and dissatisfactions.[1] Immortality will be yours, death born of division will be overcome.

THE ACTIVE AND INACTIVE BRAHMAN

6. The Inactive and the Active Brahman are simply two aspects of the one Self, the one Brahman, who is the Lord. It is He who has gone abroad in the movement. He maintains Himself free from all modifications in His inactive existence. The inaction is the basis of the action and exists in the action; it is His

---

[1] In the ordinary view all this would be admitted, but the practical possibility of maintaining this state of consciousness and birth in the world together would be doubted.

freedom from all He does and becomes and in all He does and
becomes. These are the positive and negative poles of one indivisible consciousness. We embrace both in one quiescence and
one movement, inseparable from each other, dependent on
each other. The quiescence exists relatively to the movement,
the movement to the quiescence. He is beyond both. This is a
different point of view from that of the identity of the Movement
and Quiescence which are one in reality; it expresses rather their
relation in our consciousness once they are admitted as a practical necessity of that consciousness. It is obvious that we also
by becoming one with the Lord would share in this biune conscious existence.[1]

VIDYA AND AVIDYA

7. The knowledge of the One and the knowledge of the
Many are a result of the movement of the one consciousness,
which sees all things as One in their truth-Idea but differentiates
them in their mentality and formal becoming. If the mind (*maniṣī*) absorbs itself in God as the formal becoming (*paribhū*) and
separates itself from God in the true Idea (*kavi*), then it loses
Vidya, the knowledge of the One, and has only the knowledge of
the Many which becomes no longer knowledge at all but ignorance, Avidya. This is the cause of the separate ego-sense.

Avidya is accepted by the Lord in the Mind (*maniṣī*) in order
to develop individual relations to their utmost in all the possibilities of division and its consequences and then through these
individual relations to come back individually to the knowledge
of the One in all. That knowledge has remained all along un-
abrogated in the consciousness of the true seer or Kavi. This seer
in ourselves stands back from the mental thinker; the latter,
thus separated, has to conquer death and division by a developing experience as the individual Inhabitant and finally to recover
by the reunited knowledge of the One and the Many the state
of Immortality. This is our proper course and not either to devote ourselves exclusively to the life of Avidya or to reject it entirely for motionless absorption in the One.

---

[1] In the ordinary view the Jiva cannot exist in both at the same time; his dissolution is
into the Quiescence and not into unity with the Lord in the action and inaction.

BIRTH AND NON-BIRTH

8. The reason for this double movement of the Thinker is
that we are intended to realise immortality in the Birth. The self
is uniform and undying and in itself always possesses immortality. It does not need to descend into Avidya and Birth to get
that immortality of Non-Birth; for it possesses it always. It
descends in order to realise and possess it as the individual Brahman in the play of world-existence. It accepts Birth and Death,
assumes the ego and then dissolving the ego by the recovery of
unity realises itself as the Lord, the One, and Birth as only a becoming of the Lord in mental and formal being; this becoming
is now governed by the true sight of the Seer and, once this is
done, becoming is no longer inconsistent with Being, birth becomes a means and not an obstacle to the enjoyment of immortality by the lord of this formal habitation.[1] This is our proper
course and not to remain for ever in the chain of birth and death,
nor to flee from birth into a pure non-becoming. The bondage
does not consist in the physical act of becoming, but in the persistence of the ignorant sense of the separate ego. The Mind
creates the chain and not the body.

WORKS AND KNOWLEDGE

9. The opposition between works and knowledge exists as
long as works and knowledge are only of the egoistic mental
character. Mental knowledge is not true knowledge; true knowledge is that which is based on the true sight, the sight of the Seer,
of Surya, of the Kavi. Mental thought is not knowledge, it is
a golden lid placed over the face of the Truth, the Sight, the divine
Ideation, the Truth-Consciousness. When that is removed,
sight replaces mental thought, the all-embracing truth-ideation,
mahas, *veda*, *dṛṣṭi*, replaces the fragmentary mental activity.
True Buddhi (*vijñāna*) emerges from the dissipated action of the
Buddhi which is all that is possible on the basis of the sense-
mind, the Manas. Vijnana leads us to pure knowledge (*jñāna*),

---

[1] This is the stumbling-block to the ordinary philosophies which are impregnated with
the idea of the illusoriness of the world, even when they do not go the whole way with the
Mayavada. Birth, they would say, is a play of ignorance, it cannot subsist along with entire
knowledge.

pure consciousness (*cit*). There we realise our entire identity with the Lord in all at the very roots of our being.

But in Chit, Will and Seeing are one. Therefore in Vijnana or truth-ideation also which comes luminously out of Chit, Will and Sight are combined and no longer as in the mind separated from each other. Therefore when we have the sight and live in the Truth-Consciousness, our will becomes the spontaneous law of the truth in us and, knowing all its acts and their sense and objective, leads straight to the human goal, which was always the enjoyment of the Ananda, the Lord's delight in self-being, the state of Immortality. In our acts also we become one with all beings and our life grows into a representation of oneness, truth and divine joy and no longer proceeds on the crooked path of egoism full of division, error and stumbling. In a word, we attain to the object of our existence which is to manifest in itself whether on earth in a terrestrial body and against the resistance of Matter or in the worlds beyond or enter beyond all world the glory of the divine Life and the divine Being.

KENA UPANISHAD

Kena Upanishad

FIRST PART

केनेषितं पतति प्रेषितं मनः । केन प्राणः प्रथमः प्रैति युक्तः ।
केनेषितां वाचमिमां वदन्ति । चक्षुः श्रोत्रं क उ देवो युनक्ति ॥१॥

1. By whom missioned falls the mind shot to its mark? By
   whom yoked moves the first life-breath forward on its
   paths? By whom impelled is this word that men speak?
   What god set eye and ear to their workings?

श्रोत्रस्य श्रोत्रं मनसो मनो यत् । वाचो ह वाचं स उ प्राणस्य प्राणः ।
चक्षुषश्चक्षुरतिमुच्य धीराः । प्रेत्यास्माल्लोकादमृता भवन्ति ॥२॥

2. That which is hearing of our hearing, mind of our mind,
   speech of our speech, that too is life of our life-breath and
   sight of our sight. The wise are released beyond and they
   pass from this world and become immortal.

न तत्र चक्षुर्गच्छति न वाग्गच्छति नो मनो
न विद्मो न विजानीमो यथैतदनुशिष्यात् ।
अन्यदेव तद्विदितादथो अविदितादधि ।
इति शुश्रुम पूर्वेषां ये नस्तद्व्याचचक्षिरे ॥३॥

3. There sight travels not, nor speech, nor the mind. We know
   It not nor can distinguish how one should teach of It:
   for It is other than the known; It is there above the
   unknown. It is so we have heard from men of old who
   declared That to our understanding.

यद्वाचानभ्युदितं येन वागभ्युद्यते ।
तदेव ब्रह्म त्वं विद्धि नेदं यदिदमुपासते ॥४॥

4. That which is unexpressed by the word, that by which the

word is expressed, know That to be the Brahman and not
this which men follow after here.

यन्मनसा न मनुते येनाहुर्मनो मतम् ।
तदेव ब्रह्म त्वं विद्धि नेदं यदिदमुपासते ॥५॥

5. That which thinks not by the mind,[1] that by which the mind
   is thought, know That to be the Brahman and not this which
   men follow after here.

यच्चक्षुषा न पश्यति येन चक्षूंषि पश्यति ।
तदेव ब्रह्म त्वं विद्धि नेदं यदिदमुपासते ॥६॥

6. That which sees not with the eye,[2] that by which one sees
   the eye's seeings, know That to be the Brahman and not
   this which men follow after here.

यच्छ्रोत्रेण न शृणोति येन श्रोत्रमिदं श्रुतम् ।
तदेव ब्रह्म त्वं विद्धि नेदं यदिदमुपासते ॥७॥

7. That which hears not with the ear,[3] that by which the ear's
   hearing is heard, know That to be the Brahman and not
   this which men follow after here.

यत्प्राणेन न प्राणिति येन प्राणः प्रणीयते ।
तदेव ब्रह्म त्वं विद्धि नेदं यदिदमुपासते ॥८॥

8. That which breathes not with the breath,[4] that by which the
   life-breath is led forward in its paths, know That to be
   the Brahman and not this which men follow after here.

---

[1] Or, "that which one thinks not with the mind,".
[2] Or, "that which one sees not with the eye,".
[3] Or, "that which one hears not with the ear,".
[4] Or, "that which one breathes not (i.e. smells not) with the breath,".

SECOND PART

यदि मन्यसे सुवेदेति दभ्रमेवापि नूनं त्वं वेत्थ ब्रह्मणो रूपम् ।
यदस्य त्वं यदस्य देवेष्वथ नु मीमांस्यमेव ते मन्ये विदितम् ॥१॥

1. If thou thinkest that thou knowest It well, little indeed dost thou know the form of the Brahman. That of It which is thou, that of It which is in the gods, this thou hast to think out. I think It known.

नाहं मन्ये सुवेदेति नो न वेदेति वेद च ।
यो नस्तद्वेद तद्वेद नो न वेदेति वेद च ॥२॥

2. I think not that I know It well and yet I know that It is not unknown to me. He of us who knows It, knows That; he knows that It is not unknown to him.

यस्यामतं तस्य मतं मतं यस्य न वेद सः ।
अविज्ञातं विजानतां विज्ञातमविजानताम् ॥३॥

3. He by whom It is not thought out, has the thought of It; he by whom It is thought out, knows It not. It is unknown to the discernment of those who discern of It, by those who seek not to discern of It, It is discerned.

प्रतिबोधविदितं मतममृतत्वं हि विन्दते ।
आत्मना विन्दते वीर्यं विद्यया विन्दतेऽमृतम् ॥४॥

4. When It is known by perception that reflects It, then one has the thought of It, for one finds immortality; by the self one finds the force to attain and by the knowledge one finds immortality.

इह चेदवेदीदथ सत्यमस्ति । न चेदिहावेदीन्महती विनष्टिः ।
भूतेषु भूतेषु विचित्य धीराः । प्रेत्यास्माल्लोकादमृता भवन्ति ॥५॥

5. If here one comes to that knowledge, then one truly is; if here one comes not to the knowledge, then great is the per-

dition. The wise distinguish That in all kinds of becomings and they pass forward from this world and become immortal.

THIRD PART

ब्रह्म ह देवेभ्यो विजिग्ये तस्य ह ब्रह्मणो विजये देवा अमही-
यन्त । त ऐक्षन्तास्माकमेवायं विजयोऽस्माकमेवायं महिमेति ॥१॥

1. The Eternal conquered for the gods and in the victory of the Eternal the gods grew to greatness. This was what they saw, "Ours the victory, ours the greatness."

तद्धैषां विजज्ञौ तेभ्यो ह प्रादुर्बभूव तन्न व्यजानत किमिदं यक्ष-
मिति ॥२॥

2. The Eternal knew their thought and appeared before them; and they knew not what was this mighty Daemon.

तेऽग्निमब्रुवन् जातवेद एतद्विजानीहि किमेतद्यक्षमिति तथेति ॥३॥

3. They said to Agni, "O thou that knowest all things born, learn of this thing, what may be this mighty Daemon," and he said, "So be it."

तदभ्यद्रवत्तमभ्यवदत्कोऽसीत्यग्निर्वा अहमस्मीत्यब्रवीज्जातवेदा वा
अहमस्मीति ॥४॥

4. He rushed towards the Eternal and It said to him, "Who art thou?" "I am Agni," he said, "I am he that knows all things born."

तस्मिंस्त्वयि किं वीर्यमित्यपीदꣳ सर्वं दहेयं यदिदं पृथिव्यामिति ॥५॥

5. "Since such thou art, what is the force in thee?" "Even all this I could burn, all that is upon the earth."

तस्मै तृणं निदधावेतद्दहेति तदुपप्रेयाय सर्वजवेन तन्न शशाक दग्धुं
स तत एव निववृते नैतदशकं विज्ञातुं यदेतद्यक्षमिति ॥६॥

6. The Eternal set before him a blade of grass; "This burn," and he made towards it with all his speed, but he could not burn it. There he ceased, and turned back; "I could not know of It, what might be this mighty Daemon."

अथ वायुमब्रुवन् वायवेतद्विजानीहि किमेतद्यक्षमिति तथेति ॥७॥

7. Then they said to Vayu, "O Vayu, this discern, what is this mighty Daemon." He said, "So be it."

तदभ्यद्रवत्तमभ्यववत् कोऽसीति वायुर्वा अहमस्मीत्यब्रवीन्मातरिश्वा
वा अहमस्मीति ॥८॥

8. He rushed upon That; It said to him, "Who art thou?" "I am Vayu," he said, "and I am he that expands in the Mother of things."

तस्मिँस्त्वयि किं वीर्यमित्यपीदं सर्वमाददीय यदिदं पृथिव्यामिति ॥९॥

9. "Since such thou art, what is the force in thee?" "Even all this I can take for myself, all this that is upon the earth."

तस्मै तृणं निदधावेतदादत्स्वेति तदुपप्रेयाय सर्वजवेन तन्न शशाकादातुं
स तत एव निववृते नैतदशकं विज्ञातुं यदेतद्यक्षमिति ॥१०॥

10. That set before him a blade of grass, "This take." He went towards it with all his speed and he could not take it. Even there he ceased, even thence he returned; "I could not discern of That, what is this mighty Daemon."

अथेन्द्रमब्रुवन्मघवन्नेतद्विजानीहि किमेतद्यक्षमिति तथेति तदभ्यद्रवत्
तस्मात्तिरोदधे ॥११॥

11. Then they said to Indra, "Master of plenitudes, get thou the knowledge, what is this mighty Daemon." He said, "So be

it." He rushed upon That. That vanished from before him.

स तस्मिन्नेवाकाशे स्त्रियमाजगाम बहुशोभमानामुमां हैमवतीं तां होवाच किमेतद्यक्षमिति ॥१२॥

12. He in the same ether came upon the Woman, even upon Her who shines out in many forms, Uma daughter of the snowy summits. To her he said, "What was this mighty Daemon?"

FOURTH PART

सा ब्रह्मेति होवाच ब्रह्मणो वा एतद्विजये महीयध्वमिति ततो हैव विदाञ्चकार ब्रह्मेति ॥१॥

1. She said to him, "It is the Eternal. Of the Eternal is this victory in which ye shall grow to greatness." Then alone he came to know that this was the Brahman.

तस्माद्वा एते देवा अतितरामिवान्यान्देवान्यदग्निर्वायुरिन्द्रस्ते ह्येन- न्नेदिष्ठं पस्पर्शुंस्ते ह्येनत्प्रथमो विदाञ्चकार ब्रह्मेति ॥२॥

2. Therefore are these gods as it were beyond all the other gods, even Agni and Vayu and Indra, because they came nearest to the touch of That....[1]

तस्माद् वा इन्द्रोऽतितरामिवान्यान्देवान्स ह्येनन्नेदिष्ठं पस्पर्श स ह्येनत्प्रथमो विदाञ्चकार ब्रह्मेति ॥३॥

3. Therefore is Indra as it were beyond all the other gods because he came nearest to the touch of That, because

---

[1] By some mistake of early memorisers or later copyists the rest of the verse has become hopelessly corrupted. It runs, "They he first came to know that it was the Brahman", which is neither fact nor sense nor grammar. The close of the third verse has crept into and replaced the original close of the second.

he first knew that it was the Brahman.

तस्यैष आदेशो यदेतद्विद्युतो व्यद्युतदा इतीन्यमीमिषदा इत्यधि-
दैवतम् ॥४॥

4. Now this is the indication of That, — as is this flash of the
lightning upon us or as is this falling of the eyelid, so in that
which is of the gods.

अथाध्यात्मं यदेतद् गच्छतीव च मनोऽनेन चैतदुपस्मरत्यभीक्ष्णं
सङ्कल्पः ॥५॥

5. Then in that which is of the Self, — as the motion of this
mind seems to attain to That and by it afterwards the will
in the thought continually remembers It.

तद्ध तद्वनं नाम तद्वनमित्युपासितव्यं स य एतदेवं वेदाभि हैनं सर्वाणि
भूतानि संवाञ्छन्ति ॥६॥

6. The name of That is "That Delight"; as That Delight one
should follow after It. He who so knows That, towards
him verily all existences yearn.

उपनिषवं भो ब्रूहीत्युक्ता त उपनिषद् ब्राह्मीं वाव त उपनिषद-
मब्रूमेति ॥७॥

7. Thou hast said "Speak to me Upanishad";[1] spoken to thee
is Upanishad. Of the Eternal verily is the Upanishad that
we have spoken.

तस्यै तपो दमः कर्मेति प्रतिष्ठा वेदाः सर्वाङ्गानि सत्यमायतनम् ॥८॥

8. Of this knowledge austerity and self-conquest and works
are the foundation, the Vedas are all its limbs, truth is its
dwelling place.

---

[1] Upanishad means inner knowledge, that which enters into the final Truth and
settles in it.

यो वा एतामेवं वेदापहत्य पाप्मानमनन्ते स्वर्गे लोके ज्येये प्रति-
तिष्ठति प्रतितिष्ठति ॥९॥

9. He who knows this knowledge, smites evil away from him
    and in that vaster world and infinite heaven finds his founda-
    tion, yea, he finds his foundation.

COMMENTARY

1 - The Subject of the Upanishad

THE twelve great Upanishads are written round one body of ancient knowledge; but they approach it from different sides. Into the great kingdom of the Brahmavidya each enters by its own gates, follows its own path or detour, aims at its own point of arrival. The Isha Upanishad and the Kena are both concerned with the same grand problem, the winning of the state of Immortality, the relations of the divine, all-ruling, all-possessing Brahman to the world and to the human consciousness, the means of passing out of our present state of divided self, ignorance and suffering into the unity, the truth, the divine beatitude. As the Isha closes with the aspiration towards the supreme felicity, so the Kena closes with the definition of Brahman as the Delight and the injunction to worship and seek after That as the Delight. Nevertheless there is a variation in the starting-point, even in the standpoint, a certain sensible divergence in the attitude.

For the precise subject of the two Upanishads is not identical. The Isha is concerned with the whole problem of the world and life and works and human destiny in their relation to the supreme truth of the Brahman. It embraces in its brief eighteen verses most of the fundamental problems of Life and scans them swiftly with the idea of the supreme Self and its becomings, the supreme Lord and His workings as the key that shall unlock all gates. The oneness of all existences is its dominating note.

The Kena Upanishad approaches a more restricted problem, starts with a more precise and narrow inquiry. It concerns itself only with the relation of mind-consciousness to Brahman-consciousness and does not stray outside the strict boundaries of its subject. The material world and the physical life are taken for granted, they are hardly mentioned. But the material world and the physical life exist for us only by virtue of our internal self and our internal life. According as our mental instruments represent to us the external world, according as our vital force in obedience to the mind deals with its impacts and objects, so

will be our outward life and existence. The world is for us, not
fundamentally but practically at any rate, what our mind and
senses declare it to be; life is what our mentality or at least our
half-mentalised vital being determines that it shall become. The
question is asked by the Upanishad, what then are these mental
instruments? what is this mental life which uses the external?
Are they the last witnesses, the supreme and final power? Are
mind and life and body all or is this human existence only a veil
of something greater, mightier, more remote and profound than
itself?

The Upanishad replies that there is such a greater existence
behind, which is to the mind and its instruments, to the life-
force and its workings what they are to the material world. Matter
does not know Mind, Mind knows Matter; it is only when the
creature embodied in Matter develops mind, becomes the mental
being that he can know his mental self and know by that self
Matter also in its reality to Mind. So also Mind does not know
That which is behind it, That knows Mind; and it is only when
the being involved in Mind can deliver out of its appearances
his true Self that he can become That, know it as himself and by it
know also Mind in its reality to that which is more real than
Mind. How to rise beyond the mind and its instruments, enter
into himself, attain to the Brahman becomes then the supreme
aim for the mental being, the all-important problem of his existence.

For given that there is a more real existence than the mental
existence, a greater life than the physical life, it follows that the
lower life with its forms and enjoyments which are all that men
here ordinarily worship and pursue, can no longer be an object
of desire for the awakened spirit. He must aspire beyond; he
must free himself from this world of death and mere phenomena
to become himself in his true state of immortality beyond them.
Then alone he really exists when here in this mortal life itself he
can free himself from the mortal consciousness and know and be
the Immortal and Eternal. Otherwise he feels that he has lost
himself, has fallen from his true salvation.

But this Brahman-consciousness is not represented by the
Upanishad as something quite alien to the mental and physical

world, aloof from it and in no way active upon it or concerned with its activities. On the contrary, it is the Lord and ruler of all the world; the energies of the gods in the mortal consciousness are its energies; when they conquer and grow great, it is because Brahman has fought and won. This world therefore is an inferior action, a superficial representation of something infinitely greater, more perfect, more real than itself.

What is that something? It is the All-Bliss which is infinite being and immortal force. It is that pure and utter bliss and not the desires and enjoyments of this world which men ought to worship and to seek. How to seek it is the one question that matters; to follow after it with all one's being is the only truth and the only wisdom.

2- The Question. *What Godhead?*

MIND is the principal agent of the lower or phenomenal consciousness; vital force or the life-breath, speech and the five senses of knowledge are the instruments of the mind. Prana, the life-force in the nervous system, is indeed the one main instrument of our mental consciousness; for it is that by which the mind receives the contacts of the physical world through the organs of knowledge, sight, hearing, smell, touch and taste, and reacts upon its object by speech and the other four organs of action; all these senses are dependent upon the nervous life-force for their functioning. The Upanishad therefore begins by a query as to the final source or control of the activities of the Mind, Life-Force, Speech, Senses.

The question is, *kena*, by whom or what? In the ancient conception of the universe our material existence is formed from the five elemental states of Matter, the ethereal, aerial, fiery, liquid and solid; everything that has to do with our material existence is called the elemental, *adhibhūta*. In this material there move non-material powers manifesting through the Mind-Force and Life-Force that work upon Matter, and these are called Gods or Devas; everything that has to do with the working of the non-material in us is called *adhidaiva*, that which pertains to the Gods. But above the non-material powers, containing them, greater than they is the Self or Spirit, *ātman*, and everything that has to do with this highest existence in us is called the spiritual, *adhyātma*. For the purpose of the Upanishads the *adhidaiva* is the subtle in us; it is that which is represented by Mind and Life as opposed to gross Matter; for in Mind and Life we have the characteristic action of the Gods.

The Upanishad is not concerned with the elemental, the *adhibhūta*; it is concerned with the relation between the subtle existence and the spiritual, the *adhidaiva* and *adhyātma*. But the Mind, the Life, the speech, the senses are governed by cosmic powers, by Gods, by Indra, Vayu, Agni. Are these subtle cosmic powers the beginning of existence, the true movers of mind and life, or is there some superior unifying force, one in itself behind them all?

By whom or what is the mind missioned and sent on its errand so that it falls on its object like an arrow shot by a skilful archer at its predetermined mark, like a messenger, an envoy sent by his master to a fixed place for a fixed object? What is it within us or without us that sends forth the mind on its errand? What guides it to its object?

Then there is the life-force, the Prana, that works in our vital being and nervous system. The Upanishad speaks of it as the first or supreme Breath; elsewhere in the sacred writings it is spoken of as the chief Breath or the Breath of the mouth, *mukhya, āsanya*; it is that which carries in it the Word, the creative expression. In the body of man there are said to be five workings of the life-force called the five Pranas. One specially termed Prana moves in the upper part of the body and is pre-eminently the breath of life, because it brings the universal life-force into the physical system and gives it there to be distributed. A second in the lower part of the trunk, termed Apana, is the breath of death; for it gives away the vital force out of the body. A third, the Samana, regulates the interchange of these two forces at their meeting-place, equalises them and is the most important agent in maintaining the equilibrium of the vital forces and their functions. A fourth, the Vyana, pervasive, distributes the vital energies throughout the body. A fifth, the Udana, moves upward from the body to the crown of the head and is a regular channel of communication between the physical life and the greater life of the spirit. None of these are the first or supreme Breath, although the Prana most nearly represents it; the Breath to which so much importance is given in the Upanishads, is the pure life-force itself, — first, because all the others are secondary to it, born from it and only exist as its special functions. It is imaged in the Veda as the Horse; its various energies are the forces that draw the chariots of the Gods. The Vedic image is recalled by the choice of the terms employed in the Upanishad, *yukta*, yoked, *praiti*, goes forward, as a horse driven by the charioteer advances in its path.

Who then has yoked this life-force to the many workings of existence or by what power superior to itself does it move forward in its paths? For it is not primal, self-existent or its own agent. We are conscious of a power behind which guides, drives, controls, uses it.

The force of the vital breath enables us to bring up and speed outward from the body this speech that we use to express, to throw out into a world of action and new-creation the willings and thought-formations of the mind. It is propelled by Vayu, the life-breath; it is formed by Agni, the secret will-force and fiery shaping energy in the mind and body. But these are the agents. Who or what is the secret Power that is behind them, the master of the word that men speak, its real former and the origin of that which expresses itself?

The ear hears the sound, the eye sees the form; but hearing and vision are particular operations of the life-force in us used by the mind in order to put itself into communication with the world in which the mental being dwells and to interpret it in the forms of sense. The life-force shapes them, the mind uses them, but something other than the life-force and the mind enables them to shape and to use their objects and their instruments. What God sets eye and ear to their workings? Not Surya, the God of light, not Ether and his regions; for these are only conditions of vision and hearing.

The Gods combine, each bringing his contribution, the operations of the physical world that we observe as of the mental world that is our means of observation; but the whole universal action is one, not a sum of fortuitous atoms; it is one, arranged in its parts, combined in its multiple functionings by virtue of a single conscient existence which can never be constructed or put together (*akṛta*) but is for ever anterior to all these workings. The Gods work only by this Power anterior to themselves, live only by its life, think only by its thought, act only for its purposes. We look into ourselves and all things and become aware of it there, an "I", an "Is", a Self, which is other, firmer, vaster than any separate or individual being.

But since it is not anything that the mind can make its object or the senses throw into form for the mind, what then is it — or who? What absolute Spirit? What one, supreme and eternal Godhead? *Ko devaḥ.*

3- The Supramental Godhead

THE eternal question has been put which turns man's eyes away from the visible and the outward to that which is utterly within, away from the little known that he has become to the vast unknown he is behind these surfaces and must yet grow into and be, because that is his Reality and out of all masquerade of phenomenon and becoming the Real Being must eventually deliver itself. The human soul once seized by this compelling direction can no longer be satisfied with looking forth at mortalities and seemings through those doors of the mind and sense which the Self-existent has made to open outward upon a world of forms; it is driven to gaze inward into a new world of realities.

Here in the world that man knows, he possesses something which, however imperfect and insecure, he yet values. For he aims at and to some extent he procures enlarged being, increasing knowledge, more and more joy and satisfaction and these things are so precious to him that for what he can get of them he is ready to pay the price of continual suffering from the shock of their opposites. If then he has to abandon what he here pursues and clasps, there must be a far more powerful attraction drawing him to the Beyond, a secret offer of something so great as to be a full reward for all possible renunciation that can be demanded of him here. This is offered, — not an enlarged becoming, but infinite being; not always relative piecings of knowledge mistaken in their hour for the whole of knowledge, but the possession of our essential consciousness and the flood of its luminous realities; not partial satisfactions, but *the* delight. In a word, Immortality.

The language of the Upanishad makes it strikingly clear that it is no metaphysical abstraction, no void Silence, no indeterminate Absolute which is offered to the soul that aspires, but rather the absolute of all that is possessed by it here in the relative world of its sojourning. All here in the mental is a growing light, consciousness and life; all there in the supramental is an

infinite life, light and consciousness. That which is here sha-
dowed, is there found; the incomplete here is there the fulfilled.
The Beyond is not an annullation, but a transfiguration of all
that we are here in our world of forms; it is sovran Mind of this
mind, secret Life of this life, the absolute Sense which supports
and justifies our limited senses.

We renounce ourselves in order to find ourselves; for in the
mental life there is only a seeking, but never an ultimate finding
till mind is overpassed. Therefore there is behind all our mentality a perfection of ourselves which appears to us as an antinomy
and contrast to what we are. For here we are a constant becoming; there we possess our eternal being. Here we conceive
of ourselves as a changeful consciousness developed and always
developing by a hampered effort in the drive of Time; there
we are an immutable consciousness of which Time is not the
master but the instrument as well as the field of all that it creates
and watches. Here we live in an organisation of mortal consciousness which takes the form of a transient world; there we
are liberated into the harmonies of an infinite self-seeing which
knows all world in the light of the eternal and immortal. The
Beyond is our reality; that is our plenitude; that is the absolute
satisfaction of our self-existence. It is immortality and it is "That
Delight".

Here in our imprisoned mentality the ego strives to be master
and possessor of its inner field and its outer environment, yet
cannot hold anything to enjoy it, because it is not possible really
to possess what is not-self to us. But there in the freedom of the
eternal our self-existence possesses without strife by the sufficient fact that all things are itself. Here is the apparent man,
there the real man, the Purusha: here are gods, there is the
Divine: here is the attempt to exist, Life flowering out of an all-
devouring death, there Existence itself and a dateless immortality.

The answer that is thus given is involved in the very form of
the original question. The Truth behind Mind, Life, Sense must
be that which controls by exceeding it; it is the Lord, the all-
possessing Deva. This was the conclusion at which the Isha
Upanishad arrived by the synthesis of all existences; the Kena
arrives at it by the antithesis of one governing self-existence

to all this that exists variously by another power of being than its own. Each follows its own method for the resolution of all things into the one Reality, but the conclusion is identical. It is the All-possessing and All-enjoying, who is reached by the renunciation of separate being, separate possession and separate delight.

But the Isha addresses itself to the awakened seeker; it begins therefore with the all-inhabiting Lord, proceeds to the all-becoming Self and returns to the Lord as the Self of the cosmic movement, because it has to justify works to the seeker of the Uncreated and to institute a divine life founded on the joy of immortality and on the unified consciousness of the individual made one with the universal. The Kena addresses itself to the soul still attracted by the external life, not yet wholly awakened nor wholly a seeker; it begins therefore with the Brahman as the Self beyond Mind and proceeds to the Brahman as the hidden Lord of all our mental and vital activities, because it has to point this soul upward beyond its apparent and outward existence. But the two opening chapters of the Kena only state less widely from this other viewpoint the Isha's doctrine of the Self and its becomings; the last two repeat in other terms of thought the Isha's doctrine of the Lord and His movement.

4- The Eternal Beyond the Mind

THE Upanishad first affirms the existence of this profounder, vaster, more puissant consciousness behind our mental being. That, it affirms, is Brahman. Mind, Life, Sense, Speech are not the utter Brahman; they are only inferior modes and external instruments. Brahman-consciousness is our real self and our true existence.

Mind and body are not our real self; they are mutable formations or images which we go on constructing in the drive of Time as a result of the mass of our past energies. For although those energies seem to us to lie dead in the past because their history is behind us, yet are they still existent in their mass and always active in the present and the future.

Neither is the ego-function our real self. Ego is only a faculty put forward by the discriminative mind to centralise round itself the experiences of the sense-mind and to serve as a sort of lynch-pin in the wheel which keeps together the movement. It is no more than an instrument, although it is true that so long as we are limited by our normal mentality, we are compelled by the nature of that mentality and the purpose of the instrument to mistake our ego-function for our very self.

Neither is it the memory that constitutes our real self. Memory is another instrument, a selective instrument for the practical management of our conscious activities. The ego-function uses it as a rest and support so as to preserve the sense of continuity without which our mental and vital activities could not be organised for a spacious enjoyment by the individual. But even our mental self comprises and is influenced in its being by a host of things which are not present to our memory, are subconscious and hardly grasped at all by our surface existence. Memory is essential to the continuity of the ego-sense, but it is not the constituent of the ego-sense, still less of the being.

Neither is moral personality our real self. It is only a changing formation, a pliable mould framed and used by our subjective life in order to give some appearance of fixity to the constantly mutable becoming which our mental limitations successfully tempt us to call ourselves.

Neither is the totality of that mutable conscious becoming, although enriched by all that subconsciously underlies it, our real self. What we become is a fluent mass of life, a stream of experience pouring through time, a flux of Nature upon the crest of which our mentality rides. What we are is the eternal essence of that life, the immutable consciousness that bears the experience, the immortal substance of Nature and mentality.

For behind all and dominating all that we become and experience, there is something that originates, uses, determines, enjoys, yet is not changed by its origination, not affected by its instruments, not determined by its determinations, not worked upon by its enjoyings. What that is, we cannot know unless we go behind the veil of our mental being which knows only what is affected, what is determined, what is worked upon, what is changed. The mind can only be aware of that as something which we indefinably are, not as something which it definably knows. For the moment our mentality tries to fix this something, it loses itself in the flux and the movement, grasps at parts, functions, fictions, appearances which it uses as planks of safety in the welter or tries to cut out a form from the infinite and say, "This is I." In the words of the Veda, "when the mind approaches That and studies it, That vanishes."

But behind the Mind is this other or Brahman-consciousness, Mind of our mind, Sense of our senses, Speech of our speech, Life of our life. Arriving at that, we arrive at Self; we can draw back from mind the image into Brahman the Reality.

But what differentiates that real from this apparent self? Or — since we can say no more than we have said already in the way of definition, since we can only indicate that "That" is not what "this" is, but is the mentally inexpressible absolute of all that is here, — what is the relation of this phenomenon to that reality? For it is the question of the relation that the Upanishad makes its starting-point; its opening question assumes that there is a relation and that the reality originates and governs the phenomenon.

Obviously, Brahman is not a thing subject to our mind,

senses, speech or life-force; it is no object seen, heard, expressed, sensed, formed by thought, nor any state of body or mind that we become in the changing movement of the life. But the thought of the Upanishad attempts to awaken deeper echoes from our gulfs than this obvious denial of the mental and sensuous objectivity of the Brahman. It affirms that not only is it not an object of mind or a formation of life, but it is not even dependent on our mind, life and senses for the exercise of its lordship and activity. It is that which does not think by the mind, does not live by the life, does not sense by the senses, does not find expression in the speech, but rather makes these things themselves the object of its superior, all-comprehending, all-knowing consciousness.

Brahman thinks out the mind by that which is beyond mind; it sees the sight and hears the hearing by that absolute vision and audition which are not phenomenal and instrumental but direct and inherent; it forms our expressive speech out of its creative word; it speeds out this life we cling to from that eternal movement of its energy which is not parcelled out into forms but has always the freedom of its own inexhaustible infinity.

Thus the Upanishad begins its reply to its own question. It first describes Brahman as Mind of the mind, Sight of the sight, Hearing of the hearing, Speech of the speech, Life of the life. It then takes up each of these expressions and throws them successively into a more expanded form so as to suggest a more definite and ample idea of their meaning, so far as that can be done by words. To the expression "Mind of the mind" corresponds the expanded phrase "That which thinks not with the mind, that by which the mind is thought" and so on with each of the original descriptive expressions to the closing definition of the Life behind this life as "That which breathes not with the life-breath, that by which the life-power is brought forward into its movement".

And each of these exegetic lines is emphasised by the reiterated admonition, "That Brahman seek to know and not this which men follow after here." Neither Mind, Life, Sense and Speech nor their objects and expressions are the Reality which we have to know and pursue. True knowledge is of That which forms these instruments for us but is itself independent of their utilities. True possession and enjoyment is of that which, while it creates these objects of our pursuit, itself makes nothing the object of its pursuit and passion, but is eternally satisfied with all things in the joy of its immortal being.

5- The Supreme Word

THE Upanishad, reversing the usual order of our logical thought which would put Mind and Sense first or Life first and Speech last as a subordinate function, begins its negative description of Brahman with an explanation of the very striking phrase, Speech of our speech. And we can see that it means a Speech beyond ours, an absolute expression of which human language is only a shadow and as if an artificial counterfeit. What idea underlies this phrase of the Upanishad and this precedence given to the faculty of speech?

Continually, in studying the Upanishads, we have to divest ourselves of modern notions and to realise as closely as possible the associations that lay behind the early Vedantic use of words. We must recollect that in the Vedic system the Word was the creatrix; by the Word Brahma creates the forms of the universe. Moreover, human speech at its highest merely attempts to recover by revelation and inspiration an absolute expression of Truth which already exists in the Infinite above our mental comprehension. Equally, then, must that Word be above our power of mental construction.

All creation is expression by the Word; but the form which is expressed is only a symbol or representation of the thing which is. We see this in human speech which only presents to the mind a mental form of the object; but the object it seeks to express is itself only a form or presentation of another Reality. That Reality is Brahman. Brahman expresses by the Word a form or presentation of himself in the objects of sense and consciousness which constitute the universe, just as the human word expresses a mental image of those objects. That Word is creative in a deeper and more original sense than human speech and with a power of which the utmost creativeness of human speech can be only a far-off and feeble analogy.

The word used here for utterance means literally a raising up to confront the mind. Brahman, says the Upanishad, is that which cannot be so raised up before the mind by speech.

Human speech, as we see, raises up only the presentation of a presentation, the mental figure of an object which is itself only a figure of the sole Reality, Brahman. It has indeed a power of new creation, but even that power only extends to the creation of new mental images, that is to say, of adaptive formations based upon previous mental images. Such a limited power gives no idea of the original creative puissance which the old thinkers attributed to the divine Word.

If, however, we go a little deeper below the surface, we shall arrive at a power in human speech which does give us a remote image of the original creative Word. We know that vibration of sound has the power to create — and to destroy — forms; this is a commonplace of modern Science. Let us suppose that behind all forms there has been a creative vibration of sound.

Next, let us examine the relation of human speech to sound in general. We see at once that speech is only a particular application of the principle of sound, a vibration made by pressure of the breath in its passage through the throat and mouth. At first, beyond doubt, it must have been formed naturally and spontaneously to express the sensations and emotions created by an object or occurrence and only afterwards seized upon by the mind to express first the idea of the object and then ideas about the object. The value of speech would therefore seem to be only representative and not creative.

But, in fact, speech is creative. It creates forms of emotion, mental images and impulses of action. The ancient Vedic theory and practice extended this creative action of speech by the use of the Mantra. The theory of the Mantra is that it is a word of power born out of the secret depths of our being where it has been brooded upon by a deeper consciousness than the mental, framed in the heart and not originally constructed by the intellect, held in the mind, again concentrated on by the waking mental consciousness and then thrown out silently or vocally — the silent word is perhaps held to be more potent than the spoken — precisely for the work of creation. The Mantra can not only create new subjective states in ourselves, alter our psychical being, reveal knowledge and faculties we did not before possess, can not only produce similar results in other minds than that of the user, but can produce vibrations in the mental and vital atmosphere which result in effects, in actions and even in the production of material forms on the physical plane.

As a matter of fact, even ordinarily, even daily and hourly we do produce by the word within us thought-vibrations, thought-forms which result in corresponding vital and physical vibrations, act upon ourselves, act upon others, and end in the indirect creation of actions and of forms in the physical world. Man is constantly acting upon man both by the silent and the spoken word and he so acts and creates, though less directly and powerfully, even in the rest of Nature. But because we are stupidly engrossed with the external forms and phenomena of the world and do not trouble to examine its subtle and non-physical processes, we remain ignorant of all this field of science behind.

The Vedic use of the Mantra is only a conscious utilisation of this secret power of the word. And if we take the theory that underlies it together with our previous hypothesis of a creative vibration of sound behind every formation, we shall begin to understand the idea of the original creative Word. Let us suppose a conscious use of the vibrations of sound which will produce corresponding forms or changes of form. But Matter is only, in the ancient view, the lowest of the planes of existence. Let us realise then that a vibration of sound on the material plane presupposes a corresponding vibration on the vital without which it could not have come into play; that again presupposes a corresponding originative vibration on the mental; the mental presupposes a corresponding originative vibration on the supramental at the very root of things. But a mental vibration implies thought and perception and a supramental vibration implies a supreme vision and discernment. All vibration of sound on that higher plane is, then, instinct with and expressive of this supreme discernment of a truth in things and is at the same time creative, instinct with a supreme power which casts into forms the truth discerned and eventually, descending from plane to plane, reproduces it in the physical form or object created in Matter by etheric sound. Thus we see that the theory of creation by the Word which is the absolute expression of the Truth, and the theory of the material creation by sound-vibration in the ether correspond and are two logical poles of the same idea. They both belong to the same ancient Vedic system.

This, then, is the supreme Word, Speech of our speech. It is vibration of pure Existence, instinct with the perceptive and originative power of infinite and omnipotent consciousness, shaped by the Mind behind mind into the inevitable word of the Truth of things; out of whatever substance on whatever plane, the form or physical expression emerges by its creative agency. The Supermind using the Word is the creative Logos.

The Word has its seed-sounds — suggesting the eternal syllable of the Veda, A U M, and the seed-sounds of the Tantriks — which carry in them the principles of things; it has its forms which stand behind the revelatory and inspired speech that comes to man's supreme faculties, and these compel the forms of things in the universe; it has its rhythms, — for it is no disordered vibration, but moves out into great cosmic measures, — and according to the rhythm is the law, arrangement, harmony, processes of the world it builds. Life itself is a rhythm of God.

But what is it that is expressed or raised up before the mental consciousness by the Word in the phenomenal world? Not Brahman, but truths, forms and phenomena of Brahman. Brahman is not, cannot be expressed by the Word; he does not use the word here to express his very self, but is known only to his own self-awareness. And even the truths of himself that stand behind the forms of cosmic things are in their true reality always self-expressed to his eternal vision in a higher than the mental vibration, a rhythm and voice of themselves that is their own very soul of movement. Speech, a lesser thing, creates, expresses, but is itself only a creation and expression. Brahman is not expressed by speech, but speech is itself expressed by Brahman. And that which expresses speech in us, brings it up out of our consciousness with its strivings to raise up the truth of things to our mind, is Brahman himself as the Word, a Thing that is in the supreme superconscience. That Word, Speech of our speech, is in its essence of Power the Eternal himself and in its supreme movements a part of his very form and everlasting spiritual body, *brahmaṇo rūpam.*

Therefore it is not the happenings and phenomena of the world that we have to accept finally as our object of pursuit, but That which brings out from itself the Word by which they were thrown into form for our observation by the consciousness and for our pursuit by the will. In other words, the supreme Existence that has originated all.

Human speech is only a secondary expression and at its highest a shadow of the divine Word, of the seed-sounds, the satisfying rhythms, the revealing forms of sound that are the omniscient and omnipotent speech of the eternal Thinker, Harmonist, Creator. The highest inspired speech to which the human mind can attain, the word most unanalysably expressive of supreme truth, the most puissant syllable or *mantra* can only be its far-off representation.

6- The Necessity of Supermind

As THE Upanishad asserts a speech behind this speech, which is the expressive aspect of the Brahman-consciousness, so it asserts a Mind behind this mind which is its cognitive aspect. And as we asked ourselves what could be the rational basis for the theory of the divine Word superior to our speech, so we have now to ask ourselves what can be the rational basis for this theory of a cognitive faculty or principle superior to Mind. We may say indeed that if we grant a divine Word creative of all things, we must also grant a divine Mind cognitive of the Word and of all that it expresses. But this is not a sufficient foundation; for the theory of the divine Word presents itself only as a rational possibility. A cognition higher than Mind presents itself on the other hand as a necessity which arises from the very nature of Mind itself, a necessity from which we cannot logically escape.

In the ancient system which admitted the soul's survival of the body, Mind was the man, in a very profound and radical sense of the phrase. It is not only that the human being is the one reasoning animal upon earth, the thinking race; he is essentially the mental being in a terrestrial body, the *manu*. Quite apart from the existence of a soul or self one in all creatures, the body is not even the phenomenal self of man; the physical life also is not himself; both may be dissolved, man will persist. But if the mental being also is dissolved, man as man ceases to be; for this is his centre and the nodus of his organism.

On the contrary, according to the theory of a material evolution upheld by modern Science, man is only Matter that has developed mind by an increasing sensibility to the shocks of its environment; and Matter being the basis of existence, there is nothing, except the physical elements, that can survive the dissolution of the body. But this formula is at most the obverse and inferior side of a much larger truth. Matter could not develop Mind if in or behind the force that constitutes physical forms there were not already a principle of Mind striving towards self-manifestation. The will to enlighten and consciously govern the life and the form must have been already existent in that which appears to us inconscient; it must have been there before mind was evolved. For, if there were no such necessity of Mind in Matter, if the stuff of mentality were not there already and the will to mentalise, Mind could not possibly have come into being out of inconscient substance.

But in the mere chemical elements which go to constitute material forms or in electricity or in any other purely physical factor, whatever unconscious will or sensation they may be possessed by or possess, we can discover nothing which could explain the emergence of conscious sensation, which could constitute a will towards the evolution of thought or which could impose the necessity of such an evolution on inconscient physical substance. It is not then in the form of Matter itself, but in the Force which is at work in Matter, that we must seek the origin of Mind. That Force must either be itself conscious or contain the grain of mental consciousness inherent in its being and therefore the potentiality and indeed the necessity of its emergence. This imprisoned consciousness, though originally absorbed in the creation first of forms and then of physical relations and reactions between physical forms, must still have held in itself from the beginning, however long kept back and suppressed, a will to the ultimate enlightenment of these relations by the creation of corresponding conscious or mental values. Mind is then a concealed necessity which the subconscient holds in itself from the commencement of things; it is the thing that must emerge once the attractions and repulsions of Matter begin to be established; it is the suppressed secret and cause of the reactions of life in the metal, plant and animal.

If on the other hand we say that Mind in some such secret and suppressed form is not already existent in Matter, we must then suppose that it exists outside Matter and embraces it or enters into it. We must suppose a mental plane of existence which presses upon the physical and tends to possess it. In that case the mental being would be in its origin an entity which is formed outside the material world; but it prepares in that world bodies which become progressively more and more able to house and express Mind. We may image it forming, entering into and possessing the body, breaking into it, as it were, — as the Purusha in the Aitareya Upanishad is said to form the body and then to enter in by breaking open a door in Matter. Man would in this view be a mental being incarnate in the living body who at its dissolution leaves it with full possession of his mentality.

The two theories are far from being incompatible with each other; they can be viewed as complements forming a single truth. For the involution of Mind, its latency in the material Force of the physical universe and in all its movements does not preclude the existence of a mental world beyond and above the reign of the physical principle. In fact, the emergence of such a latent Mind might well depend upon and would certainly profit by the aid and pressure of forces from a supra-physical kingdom, a mental plane of existence.

There are always two possible views of the universe. The one supposes, with modern Science, Matter to be the beginning of things and studies everything as an evolution from Matter; or, if not Matter, then, with the Sankhya philosophy, an indeterminate inconscient active Force or Prakriti of which even mind and reason are mechanical operations, — the conscious soul, if any exists, being a quite different and, although conscient, yet inactive entity. The other supposes the conscious soul, the Purusha, to be the material as well as the cause of the universe and Prakriti to be only its Shakti or the Force of its conscious being which operates upon itself as the material of forms.[1] The latter is the view of the Upanishads. Certainly, if we study the material world only, excluding all evidence of other planes as a dream or a hallucination, if we equally exclude all evidence of operations in mind which exceed the material limitation and study only its ordinary equation with Matter, we must necessarily accept the theory of Matter as the origin and as the indispensable basis and continent. Otherwise, we shall be irresistibly led towards the early Vedantic conclusions.

However this may be, even from the standpoint of the sole material world Man in the substance of his manhood is a mind

---

[1] For example, the Aitareya Upanishad which shows us the Atman or Self using the Purusha as that in which all the operations of Nature are formed.

occupying and using the life of the body — a mind that is greater than the Matter in which it has emerged. He is the highest present expression of the will in the material universe; the Force that has built up the worlds, so far as we are able to judge of its intention from its actual operations as we see them in their present formula upon earth, arrives in him at the thing it was seeking to express. It has brought out the hidden principle of Mind that now operates consciously and intelligently on the life and the body. Man is the satisfaction of the necessity which Nature bore secretly in her from the very commencement of her works; he is the highest possible Name or Numen on this planet; he is the realised terrestrial godhead.

But all this is true only if we assume that for Nature's terrestrial activities Mind is the ultimate formula. In reality and when we study more deeply the phenomena of consciousness, the facts of mentality, the secret tendency, aspiration and necessity of man's own nature, we see that he cannot be the highest term. He is the highest realised here and now; he is not the highest realisable. As there is something below him, so there is something, if even only a possibility, above. As physical Nature concealed a secret beyond herself which in him she has released into creation, so he too conceals a secret beyond himself which he in turn must deliver to the light. That is his destiny.

This must necessarily be so because Mind too is not the first principle of things and therefore cannot be their last possibility. As Matter contained Life in itself, contained it as its own secret necessity and had to be delivered of that birth, and as Life contained Mind in itself, contained it as its own secret necessity and had to be delivered of the birth it held, so Mind too contains in itself that which is beyond itself, contains it as its own secret necessity and presses to be delivered, it also, of this supreme birth.

What is the rational necessity which forbids us to suppose Mind to be Nature's last birth and compels us to posit something beyond it of which itself is the indication? A consideration of the nature and working of mentality supplies us with the answer. For mentality is composed of three principal elements, thought, will and sensation. Sensation may be described as an attempt of divided consciousness to seize upon its object and enjoy it, thought as its attempt to seize upon the truth of the object and possess it, will as its attempt to seize upon the potentiality of the object and use it. At least these three things are such an attempt in their essentiality, in their instinct, in their subconscious purpose. But obviously the attempt is imperfect in its conditions and its success; its very terms indicate a barrier, a gulf, an incapacity. As Life is limited and hampered by the conditions of its synthesis with Matter, so Mind is limited and hampered by the conditions of its synthesis with Life in Matter. Neither Matter nor Life has found anything proper to their own formula which could help to conquer or sufficiently expand its limitations; they have been compelled each to call in a new principle, Matter to call into itself Life, Life to call into itself Mind. Mind also is not able to find anything proper to its own formula which can conquer or sufficiently expand the limitations imposed upon its workings; Mind also has to call in a new principle beyond itself, freer than itself and more powerful.

In other words, Mind does not exhaust the possibilities of consciousness and therefore cannot be its last and highest expression. Mind tries to arrive at Truth and succeeds only in touching it imperfectly with a veil between; there must be in the nature of things a faculty or principle which sees the Truth unveiled, an eternal faculty of knowledge which corresponds to the eternal fact of the Truth. There is, says the Veda, such a principle; it is the Truth-Consciousness which sees the Truth directly and is in possession of it spontaneously. Mind labours to effect the will in it and succeeds only in accomplishing partially, with difficulty and insecurely the potentiality at which it works; there must be a faculty or principle of conscious effective force which corresponds to the unconscious automatic principle of self-fulfilment in Nature, and this principle must be sought for in the form of consciousness that exceeds Mind. Mind, finally, aspires to seize and enjoy the essential delight-giving quality, the *rasa* of things, but it succeeds only in attaining to it indirectly, holding it in an imperfect grasp and enjoying it externally and fragmentarily; there must be a principle which can attain directly, hold rightly, enjoy intimately and securely.

There is, says the Veda, an eternal Bliss-consciousness which corresponds to the eternal *rasa* or essential delight-giving quality of all experience and is not limited by the insecure approximations of the sense in Mind.

If, then, such a deeper principle of consciousness exists, it must be that and not mind which is the original and fundamental intention concealed in Nature and which eventually and somewhere must emerge. But is there any reason for supposing that it must emerge here and in Mind, as Mind has emerged in Life and Life in Matter? We answer in the affirmative because Mind has in itself, however obscurely, that tendency, that aspiration and, at bottom, that necessity. There is one law from the lowest to the highest. Matter, when we examine it closely, proves to be instinct with the stuff of Life — the vibrations, actions and reactions, attractions and repulsions, contractions and expansions, the tendencies of combination, formation and growth, the seekings and responses which are the very substance of life; but the visible principle of life can only emerge when the necessary material conditions have been prepared which will permit it to organise itself in Matter. So also Life is instinct with the stuff of Mind, abounds with an unconscious[1] sensation, will, intelligence, but the visible principle of Mind can only emerge when the necessary vital conditions have been prepared which will permit it to organise itself in living Matter. Mind too is instinct with the stuff of supermind — sympathies, unities, intuitions, emergences of pre-existent knowledge, instincts, imperative lights and movements, inherent self-effectivities of will which disguise themselves in a mental form; but the visible principle of supermind can only emerge when the necessary mental conditions are prepared which will permit it to organise itself in man, the mental living creature.

This necessary preparation is proceeding in human development as the corresponding preparations were developed in the lower stages of the evolution, — with the same gradations, retardations, inequalities; but still it is more enlightened, increasingly self-conscious, nearer to a conscious sureness. And the very fact that this progress is attended by less absorption in the detail,

---

[1] I use the language of the materialist Haeckel in spite of its paradoxical form.

less timidity of error, a less conservative attachment to the step gained suggests as much as it contradicts the hope and almost the assurance that when the new principle emerges it will not be by the creation of a new and quite different type which, separated after its creation, will leave the rest of mankind in the same position to it as are the animals to man, but, if not by the elevation of humanity as a whole to a higher level, yet by an opening of the greater possibility to all of the race who have the will to rise. For Man, first among Nature's children, has shown the capacity to change himself by his own effort and the conscious aspiration to transcend.

These considerations justify to the reason the idea of a Mind beyond our mind, but only as a final evolution out of Matter. The Upanishad, however, enthrones it as the already existing creator and ruler of Mind; it is a secret principle already conscient and not merely contained inconsciently in the very stuff of things. But this is the natural conclusion — even apart from spiritual experience — from the nature of the supramental principle. For it is at its highest an eternal knowledge, will, bliss and conscious being and it is more reasonable to conclude that it is eternally conscious, though we are not conscious of it, and the source of the universe, than that it is eternally inconscient and only becomes conscient in Time as a result of the universe. Our inconscience of it is no proof that it is inconscient of us: and yet our own incapacity is the only real basis left for the denial of an eternal Mind beyond mind superior to its creations and originative of the cosmos.

All other foundations for the rejection of this ancient wisdom have disappeared or are disappearing before the increasing light of modern knowledge.

7- Mind and Supermind

WE ARRIVE then at this affirmation of an all-cognitive principle superior to Mind and exceeding it in nature, scope and capacity. For the Upanishad affirms a Mind beyond mind as the result of intuition and spiritual experience and its existence is equally a necessary conclusion from the facts of the cosmic evolution. What then is this Mind beyond mind? how does it function? or by what means shall we arrive at the knowledge of it or possess it?

The Upanishad asserts about this supreme cognitive principle, first, that it is beyond the reach of mind and the senses; secondly, that it does not itself think with the mind; thirdly, that it is that by which mind itself is thought or mentalised; fourthly, that it is the very nature or description of the Brahman-consciousness.

When we say, however, that "Mind of mind" is the nature or description of the Brahman-consciousness, we must not forget that the absolute Brahman in itself is held to be unknowable and therefore beyond description. It is unknowable, not because it is a void and capable of no description except that of nothingness, nor because, although positive in existence, it has no content or quality, but because it is beyond all things that our present instruments of knowledge can conceive and because the methods of ideation and expression proper to our mentality do not apply to it. It is the absolute of all things that we know and of each thing that we know and yet nothing nor any sum of things can exhaust or characterise its essential being. For its manner of being is other than that which we call existence; its unity resists all analysis, its multiple infinities exceed every synthesis. Therefore it is not in its absolute essentiality that it can be described as Mind of the mind, but in its fundamental nature in regard to our mental existence. Brahman-consciousness is the eternal outlook of the Absolute upon the relative.

But even of this outlook we may say that it is beyond the reach of mind and speech and senses. Yet mind, speech and senses seem to be our only available means for acquiring and expressing knowledge. Must we not say then that this Brahman-consciousness also is unknowable and that we can never hope to know it or possess it while in this body? Yet the Upanishad commands us to *know* this Brahman and by knowledge to possess it — for the knowledge intended by the words *viddhi, avedīt*, is a knowledge that discovers and takes possession, — and it declares later on that it is here, in this body and on this earth that we must thus possess Brahman in knowledge, otherwise great is the perdition. A good deal of confusion has been brought into the interpretation of this Upanishad by a too trenchant dealing with the subtlety of its distinctions between the knowability and the unknowability of the Brahman. We must therefore try to observe exactly what the Upanishad says and especially to seize the whole of its drift by synthetic intuition rather than cut up its meaning so as to make it subject to our logical mentality.

The Upanishad sets out by saying that this Ruler of the mind, senses, speech and life is Mind of our mind, Life of our life, Sense of our senses, Speech of our speech; and it then proceeds to explain what it intends by these challenging phrases. But it introduces between the description and the explanation a warning that neither the description nor the explanation must be pushed beyond their proper limits or understood as more than guideposts pointing us towards our goal. For neither Mind, Speech nor Sense can travel to the Brahman; therefore Brahman must be beyond all these things in its very nature, otherwise it would be attainable by them in their function. The Upanishad, although it is about to teach of the Brahman, yet affirms, "we know It not, we cannot distinguish how one should teach of it." The two Sanskrit words that are here used, *vidmaḥ* and *vijānīmaḥ*, seem to indicate the one a general grasp and possession in knowledge, the other a total and exact comprehension in whole and detail, by synthesis and analysis. The reason of this entire inability is next given, "because Brahman is other than the known and It is there over the unknown", possessing it and, as it were, presiding over it. The known is all that we grasp and possess by our present mentality; it is all that is not the supreme Brahman but only form and phenomenon of it to our sense and mental cognition. The un-

known is that which is beyond the known and though unknown
is not unknowable if we can enlarge our faculties or attain to
others that we do not yet possess.

Yet the Upanishad next proceeds to maintain and explain
its first description and to enjoin on us the knowledge of the
Brahman which it so describes. This contradiction is not at
once reconciled; it is only in the second chapter that the difficulty
is solved and only in the fourth that the means of knowledge are
indicated. The contradiction arises from the nature of our knowledge itself which is a relation between the consciousness that
seeks and the consciousness that is sought; where that relation
disappears, knowledge is replaced by sheer identity. In what we
call existence, the highest knowledge can be no more than the
highest relation between that which seeks and that which is
sought, and it consists in a modified identity through which
we may pass beyond knowledge to the absolute identity. This
metaphysical distinction is of importance because it prevents us
from mistaking any relation in knowledge for the absolute and
from becoming so bound by our experience as to lose or miss the
fundamental awareness of the absolute which is beyond all possible description and behind all formulated experience. But it
does not render the highest relation in our knowledge, the modified identity in experience worthless or otiose. On the contrary,
it is that we must aim at as the consummation of our existence
in the world. For if we possess it without being limited by it, —
and if we are limited by it we have not true possession of it, —
then in and through it we shall, even while in this body,
remain in touch with the Absolute.

The means for the attainment of this highest knowledge is
the constant preparation of the mind by the admission into it of
a working higher than itself until the mind is capable of giving
itself up to the supramental action which exceeds it and which
will finally replace it. In fact, Mind also has to follow the law of
natural progression which has governed our evolution in this
world from Matter into Life and Life into Mind. For just as
Life-consciousness is beyond the imprisoned material being and
unattainable by it through its own instruments, just as mind-
consciousness is beyond the first inconscient movements of life,

so too this supramental consciousness is beyond the divided and dividing nature of Mind and unattainable by it through its own instruments. But as Matter is constantly prepared for the manifestation of Life until Life is able to move in it, possess it, manage in it its own action and reaction, and as Life is constantly prepared for the manifestation of Mind until Mind is able to use it, enlighten its actions and reactions by higher and higher mental values, so must it be with Mind and that which is beyond Mind.

And all this progression is possible because these things are only different formations of one being and one consciousness. Life only reveals in Matter that which is involved in Matter, that which is the secret meaning and essence of Matter. It reveals, as it were, to material existence its own soul, its own end. So too Mind reveals in Life all that Life means, all that it obscurely is in essence but cannot realise because it is absorbed in its own practical motion and its own characteristic form. So also Supermind must intervene to reveal Mind to itself, to liberate it from its absorption in its own practical motion and characteristic form and enable the mental being to realise that which is the hidden secret of all its formal practice and action. Thus shall man come to the knowledge of that which rules within him and missions his mind to its mark, sends forth his speech, impels the life-force in its paths and sets his senses to their workings.

This supreme cognitive Principle does not think by the mind. Mind is to it an inferior and secondary action, not its own proper mode. For Mind, based on limitation and division, can act only from a given centre in the lower and obscured existence; but Supermind is founded on unity and it comprehends and pervades; its action is in the universal and is in conscious communion with a transcendent source eternal and beyond the formations of the universe. Supermind regards the individual in the universal and does not begin with him or make of him a separate being. It starts from the Transcendent and sees the universal and individual as they are in relation to it, as its terms, as its formulas; it does not start from the individual and universal to arrive at the Transcendent. Mind acquires knowledge and mastery; it reaches it by a constant mentalising and willing: Supermind possesses knowledge and mastery; possessing, it throws itself out freely in various willing and knowing. Mind gropes by divided sensation; it arrives at a sort of oneness through sympathy: Supermind possesses by a free and all-embracing sense; it lives in the unity of which various love and sympathy are only a secondary play of manifestation. Supermind starts from the whole and sees in it its parts and properties, it does not build up the knowledge of the whole by an increasing knowledge of the parts and properties; and even the whole is to it only a unity of sum, only a partial and inferior term of the higher unity of infinite essence.

We see, then, that these two cognitive Principles start from two opposite poles and act in opposite directions by opposite methods. Yet it is by the higher cognitive that the lower is formed and governed. Mind is thought by that which is beyond Mind; the mentalising consciousness shapes and directs its movement according to the knowledge and impulse it receives from this higher Supermind and even the stuff of which it is formed belongs to that Principle. Mentality exists because that which is beyond Mind has conceived an inverse action of itself working in a thinner, poorer, darker, less powerful substance of conscious being and founded upon its self-concentration on different points in its own being and in different forms of its own being. Supermind fixes these points, sees how consciousness must act from them on other forms of itself and in obedience to the pressure of those other forms, once a particular rhythm or law of universal action is given; it governs the whole action of mentality according to what it thus fixes and sees. Even our ignorance is only the distorted action of a truth projected from the Supermind and could not exist except as such a distortion; and so likewise all our dualities of knowledge, sensation, emotion, force proceed from that higher vision, obey it and are a secondary and, as one might say, perverse action of the concealed Supermind itself which governs always this lower action in harmony with its first conception of a located consciousness, divided indeed and therefore not in possession of its world or itself, but feeling out towards that possession and towards the unity which, because of the Supermind in us, it instinctively, if obscurely, knows to be its true nature and right.

But, for this very reason, the feeling out, the attempt at acquisition can only succeed in proportion as the mental being abandons his characteristic mentality and its limitations in order to rise beyond to that Mind of the mind which is his origin and his secret governing principle. His mentality must admit Supramentality as Life has admitted Mind. So long as he worships, follows after, adheres to all this that he now accepts as the object of his pursuit, to the mind and its aims, to its broken methods, its constructions of will and opinion and emotion dependent on egoism, division and ignorance, he cannot rise beyond this death to that immortality which the Upanishad promises to the seeker. That Brahman we have to know and seek after and not this which men here adore and pursue.

THE Upanishad is not satisfied with the definition of the Brahman-consciousness as Mind of the mind. Just as it has described it as Speech of the speech, so also it describes it as Eye of the eye, Ear of the ear. Not only is it an absolute cognition behind the play of expression, but also an absolute Sense behind the action of the senses. Every part of our being finds its fulfilment in that which is beyond its present forms of functioning and not in those forms themselves.

This conception of the all-governing supreme consciousness does not fall in with our ordinary theories about sense and mind and the Brahman. We know of sense only as an action of the organs through which embodied mind communicates with external Matter, and these sense-organs have been separately developed in the course of evolution; the senses therefore are not fundamental things, but only subordinate conveniences and temporary physical functionings of the embodied mind. Brahman, on the other hand, we conceive of by the elimination of all that is not fundamental, by the elimination even of the Mind itself. It is a sort of positive zero, an X or unknowable which corresponds to no possible equation of physical or psychological quantities. In essence this may or may not be true; but we have now to think not of the Unknowable but of its highest manifestation in consciousness; and this we have described as the outlook of the Absolute on the relative and as that which is the cause and governing power of all that we and the universe are. There in that governing cause there must be something essential and supreme of which all our fundamental functionings here are a rendering in the terms of embodied consciousness.

Sense, however, is not or does not appear to be fundamental; it is only an instrumentation of Mind using the nervous system. It is not even a pure mental functioning, but depends so much upon the currents of the Life-force, upon its electric energy vibrating up and down the nerves, that in the Upanishads the senses are called Pranas, powers or functionings of the Life-force. It is true that Mind turns these nervous impressions when communicated to it into mental values, but the sense-action itself seems to be rather nervous than mental. In any case there would, at first sight, appear to be no warrant in reason for attributing a Sense of the sense to that which is not embodied, to a supramental consciousness which has no need of any such instrumentation.

But this is not the last word about sense; this is only its outward appearance behind which we must penetrate. What, not in its functioning, but in its essence, is the thing we call sense? In its functioning, if we analyse that thoroughly, we see that it is the contact of the mind with an eidolon of Matter, — whether that eidolon be of a vibration of sound, a light-image of form, a volley of earth-particles giving the sense of odour, an impression of *rasa* or sap that gives the sense of taste, or that direct sense of disturbance of our nervous being which we call touch. No doubt, the contact of Matter with Matter is the original cause of these sensations; but it is only the eidolon of Matter, as for instance the image of the form cast upon the eye, with which the mind is directly concerned. For the mind operates upon Matter not directly, but through the Life-force; that is its instrument of communication and the Life-force, being in us a nervous energy and not anything material, can seize on Matter only through nervous impressions of form, through contactual images, as it were, which create corresponding values in the energy-consciousness called in the Upanishads the Prana. Mind takes these up and replies to them with corresponding mental values, mental impressions of form, so that the thing sensed comes to us after a triple process of translation, first the material eidolon, secondly the nervous or energy-image, third the image reproduced in stuff of mind.

This elaborate process is concealed from us by the lightning-like rapidity with which it is managed, — rapidity in our impressions of Time; for in another notation of Time by a creature differently constituted each part of the operation might be distinctly sensible. But the triple translation is always there, because there are really three sheaths of consciousness in us, the material, *annakoṣa*, in which the physical contact and image are received and formed, the vital and nervous, *prāṇakoṣa*, in which there is a nervous contact and formation, the mental, *manaḥkoṣa*, in which there is mental contact and imaging. We dwell centred in the mental sheath and therefore the experience of the material world has to come through the other two sheaths before it can reach us.

The foundation of sense, therefore, is contact, and the essential contact is the mental without which there would not be sense at all. The plant, for instance, feels nervously, feels in terms of life-energy, precisely as the human nervous system does, and it has precisely the same reactions; but it is only if the plant has rudimentary mind that we can suppose it to be, as we understand the word, sensible of these nervous or vital impressions and reactions. For then it would feel not only nervously, but in terms of mind. Sense, then, may be described as in its essence mental contact with an object and the mental reproduction of its image.

All these things we observe and reason of in terms of this embodiment of mind in Matter; for these sheaths or *koṣas* are formations in a more and more subtle substance reposing on gross Matter as their base. Let us imagine that there is a mental world in which Mind and not Matter is the base. There sense would be quite a different thing in its operation. It would feel mentally an image in Mind and throw it out into form in more and more gross substance; and whatever physical formations there might already be in that world would respond rapidly to the Mind and obey its modifying suggestions. Mind would be masterful, creative, originative, not as with us either obedient to Matter and merely reproductive or else in struggle with it and only with difficulty able to modify a material predetermined and dully reluctant to its touch. It would be, subject to whatever supramental power might be above it, master of a ductile and easily responsive material. But still Sense would be there, because contact in mental consciousness and formation of images would still be part of the law of being.

Mind, in fact, or active consciousness generally has four necessary functions which are indispensable to it wherever and however it may act and of which the Upanishads speak in the four terms, *vijñāna*, *prajñāna*, *saṁjñāna* and *ājñāna*. Vijnana is the original comprehensive consciousness which holds an image of things at once in its essence, its totality and its parts and pro-

perties; it is the original, spontaneous, true and complete view
of it which belongs properly to the supermind and of which mind
has only a shadow in the highest operations of the comprehensive
intellect. Prajnana is the consciousness which holds an image
of things before it as an object with which it has to enter into
relations and to possess by apprehension and a combined ana-
lytic and synthetic cognition. Sanjnana is the contact of consciousness with an image of things by which there is a sensible
possession of it in its substance; if Prajnana can be described as
the outgoing of apprehensive consciousness to possess its object
in conscious energy, to know it, Sanjnana can be described as
the inbringing movement of apprehensive consciousness which
draws the object placed before it back to itself so as to possess
it in conscious substance, to feel it. Ajnana is the operation by
which consciousness dwells on an image of things so as to hold,
govern and possess it in power. These four, therefore, are the
basis of all conscious action.

As our human psychology is constituted, we begin with Sanjnana, the sense of an object in its image; the apprehension of it
in knowledge follows. Afterwards we try to arrive at the comprehension of it in knowledge and the possession of it in power.
There are secret operations in us, in our subconscient and superconscient selves, which precede this action, but of these we are
not aware in our surface being and therefore for us they do
not exist. If we knew of them, our whole conscious functioning
would be changed. As it is what happens is a rapid process by
which we sense an image and have of it an apprehensive percept
and concept, and a slower process of the intellect by which we
try to comprehend and possess it. The former process is the
natural action of the mind which has entirely developed in us;
the latter is an acquired action, an action of the intellect and the
intelligent will which represent in Mind an attempt of the mental
being to do what can only be done with perfect spontaneity and
mastery by something higher than Mind. The intellect and intelligent will form a bridge by which the mental being is trying to establish a conscious connection with the supramental and to prepare
the embodied soul for the descent into it of a supramental action.
Therefore the first process is comparatively easy, spontaneous,

rapid, perfect; the second slow, laboured, imperfect. In proportion as the intellectual action becomes associated with and dominated by a rudimentary supramental action, — and it is this which constitutes the phenomenon of genius, — the second process also becomes more and more easy, spontaneous, rapid and perfect.

If we suppose a supreme consciousness, master of the world, which really conducts behind the veil all the operations the mental gods attribute to themselves, it will be obvious that that consciousness will be the entire Knower and Lord. The basis of its action or government of the world will be the perfect, original and all-possessing Vijnana and Ajnana. It will comprehend all things in its energy of conscious knowledge, control all things in its energy of conscious power. These energies will be the spontaneous inherent action of its conscious being creative and possessive of the forms of the universe. What part then will be left for the apprehensive consciousness and the sense? They will be not independent functions, but subordinate operations involved in the action of the comprehensive consciousness itself. In fact, all four there will be one rapid movement. If we had all these four acting in us with the unified rapidity with which the Prajnana and Sanjnana act, we should then have in our notation of Time some inadequate image of the unity of the supreme action of the supreme energy.

If we consider, we shall see that this must be so. The supreme consciousness must not only comprehend and possess in its conscious being the images of things which it creates as its self-expression, but it must place them before it — always in its own being, not externally — and have a certain relation with them by the two terms of apprehensive consciousness. Otherwise the universe would not take the form that it has for us; for we only reflect in the terms of our organisation the movements of the supreme Energy. But by the very fact that the images of things are there held in front of an apprehending consciousness within the comprehending conscious being and not externalised as our individual mind externalises them, the supreme Mind and supreme Sense will be something quite different from our mentality and our forms of sensation. They will be terms of an entire knowledge and self-possession and not terms of an ignorance and limitation which strives to know and possess.

In its essential and general term our sense must reflect and be the creation of this supreme Sense. But the Upanishad speaks of a Sight behind our sight and a Hearing behind our hearing, not in general terms of a Sense behind our sense. Certainly eye and ear are only taken as typical of the senses, and are chosen because they are the highest and subtlest of them all. But still the differentiation of sense which forms part of our mentality is evidently held to correspond with a differentiation of some kind in the supreme Sense. How is this possible? It is what we have next to unravel by examining the nature and source of the functioning of the separate senses in ourselves, — their source in our mentality and not merely their functioning in the actual terms of our life-energy and our body. What is it in Mind that is fundamental to sight and hearing? Why do we see and hear and not simply sense with the mind?

Mind was called by Indian psychologists
the eleventh and ranks as the supreme sense. In the ancient
arrangement of the senses, five of knowledge and five of action,
it was the sixth of the organs of knowledge and at the same
time the sixth of the organs of action. It is a commonplace of
psychology that the effective functioning of the senses of knowledge is inoperative without the assistance of the mind; the eye
may see, the ear may hear, all the senses may act, but if the mind
pays no attention, the man has not heard, seen, felt, touched or
tasted. Similarly, according to psychology, the organs of action
act only by the force of the mind operating as will or, physio-
logically, by the reactive nervous force from the brain which
must be according to materialistic notions the true self and
essence of all will. In any case, the senses or all senses, if there
are other than the ten, — according to a text in the Upanishad
there should be at least fourteen, seven and seven, — all senses
appear to be only organisations, functionings, instrumentations
of the mind-consciousness, devices which it has formed in the
course of its evolution in living Matter.

Modern psychology has extended our knowledge and has
admitted us to a truth which the ancients already knew but expressed in other language. We know now or we rediscover the
truth that the conscious operation of mind is only a surface
action. There is a much vaster and more potent subconscious
mind which loses nothing of what the senses bring to it; it keeps
all its wealth in an inexhaustible store of memory, *akṣitam
śravaḥ*. The surface mind may pay no attention, still the subconscious mind attends, receives, treasures up with an infallible
accuracy. The illiterate servant-girl hears daily her master
reciting Hebrew in his study; the surface mind pays no attention
to the unintelligible gibberish, but the subconscious mind hears,
remembers and, when in an abnormal condition it comes up to
the surface, reproduces those learned recitations with a porten-
tous accuracy which the most correct and retentive scholar might

envy. The man or mind has not heard because he did not attend; the greater man or mind within has heard because he always attends, or rather sub-tends, with an infinite capacity. So too a man put under an anaesthetic and operated upon has felt nothing; but release his subconscious mind by hypnosis and he will relate accurately every detail of the operation and its appropriate sufferings; for the stupor of the physical sense-organ could not prevent the larger mind within from observing and feeling.

Similarly we know that a large part of our physical action is instinctive and directed not by the surface but by the subconscious mind. And we know now that it is a mind that acts and not merely an ignorant nervous reaction from the brute physical brain. The subconscious mind in the catering insect knows the anatomy of the victim it intends to immobilise and make food for its young and it directs the sting accordingly, as unerringly as the most skilful surgeon, provided the mere limited surface mind with its groping and faltering nervous action does not get in the way and falsify the inner knowledge or the inner will-force.

These examples point us to truths which western psychology, hampered by past ignorance posing as scientific orthodoxy, still ignores or refuses to acknowledge. The Upanishads declare that the Mind in us is infinite; it knows not only what has been seen but what has not been seen, not only what has been heard but what has not been heard, not only what has been discriminated by the thought but what has not been discriminated by the thought. Let us say, then, in the tongue of our modern knowledge that the surface man in us is limited by his physical experiences; he knows only what his nervous life in the body brings to his embodied mind; and even of those bringings he knows, he can retain and utilise only so much as his surface mind-sense attends to and consciously remembers; but there is a larger subliminal consciousness within him which is not thus limited. That consciousness senses what has not been sensed by the surface mind and its organs and knows what the surface mind has not learned by its acquisitive thought. That in the insect knows the anatomy of its victim; that in the man outwardly insensible not only feels and remembers the action of the surgeon's knife, but knows the appropriate reactions of suffering which were in the physical body inhibited by the anaesthetic and therefore non-existent; that in the illiterate servant-girl heard and retained accurately the words of an unknown language and could, as Yogic experience knows, by a higher action of itself understand those superficially unintelligible sounds.

To return to the Vedantic words we have been using, there is a vaster action of the Sanjnana which is not limited by the action of the physical sense-organs; it was this which sensed perfectly and made its own through the ear the words of the unknown language, through the touch the movements of the unfelt surgeon's knife, through the sense-mind or sixth sense the exact location of the centres of locomotion in the victim insect. There is also associated with it a corresponding vaster action of Prajnana, Ajnana and Vijnana not limited by the smaller apprehensive and comprehensive faculties of the external mind. It is this vaster Prajnana which perceived the proper relation of the words to each other, of the movement of the knife to the unfelt suffering of the nerves and of the successive relation in space of the articulations in the insect's body. Such perception was inherent in the right reproduction of the words, the right narration of the sufferings, the right successive action of the sting. The Ajnana or Knowledge-Will originating all these actions was also vaster, not limited by the faltering force that governs the operations directed by the surface mind. And although in these examples the action of the vaster Vijnana is not so apparent, yet it was evidently there working through them and ensuring their co-ordination.

But at present it is with the Sanjnana that we are concerned. Here we should note, first of all, that there is an action of the sense-mind which is superior to the particular action of the senses and is aware of things even without imaging them in forms of sight, sound, contact, but which also as a sort of subordinate operation, subordinate but necessary to completeness of presentation, does image in these forms. This is evident in psychical phenomena. Those who have carried the study and experimentation of them to a certain extent, have found that we can sense things known only to the minds of others, things that exist only at a great distance, things that belong to another plane than the terrestrial but have here their effects; we can both sense them in their images and also feel, as it were, all that they are without any definite image proper to the five senses.

This shows, in the first place, that sight and the other senses are not mere results of the development of our physical organs in the terrestrial evolution. Mind, subconscious in all Matter and evolving in Matter, has developed these physical organs in order to apply its inherent capacities of sight, hearing etc., on the physical plane by physical means for a physical life; but they are inherent capacities and not dependent on the circumstance of terrestrial evolution and they can be employed without the use of the physical eye, ear, skin, palate. Supposing that there are psychical senses which act through a psychical body, and we thus explain these psychical phenomena, still that action also is only an organisation of the inherent functioning of the essential sense, the Sanjnana, which in itself can operate without bodily organs. This essential sense is the original capacity of consciousness to feel in itself all that consciousness has formed and to feel it in all the essential properties and operations of that which has form, whether represented materially by vibration of sound or images of light or any other physical symbol.

The trend of knowledge leads more and more to the conclusion that not only are the properties of form, even the most obvious such as colour, light etc., merely operations of Force, but form itself is only an operation of Force. This Force again proves to be self-power of conscious-being[1] in a state of energy and activity. Practically, therefore, all form is only an operation of consciousness impressing itself with presentations of its own workings. We see colour because that is the presentation which consciousness makes to itself of one of its own operations; but colour is only an operation of Force working in the form of Light, and Light again is only a movement, that is to say an operation of Force. The question is what is essential to this operation of Force taking on itself the presentation of form? For it is this that must determine the working of Sanjnana or Sense on whatever plane it may operate.

Everything begins with vibration or movement, the original

---

[1] *devātmaśaktiṁ svaguṇair nigūḍhām*, self-power of the divine Existent hidden by its own modes. Shwetashwatara Upanishad.

kṣobha or disturbance. If there is no movement of the conscious being, it can only know its own pure static existence. Without vibration[1] or movement of being in consciousness there can be no act of knowledge and therefore no sense; without vibration or movement of being in force there can be no object of sense. Movement of conscious being as knowledge becoming sensible of itself as movement of force, in other words the knowledge separating itself from its own working to watch that and take it into itself again by feeling, — this is the basis of universal Sanjnana. This is true both of our internal and external operations. I become anger by a vibration of conscious force acting as nervous emotion and I feel the anger that I have become by another movement of conscious force acting as light of knowledge. I am conscious of my body because I have myself become the body; that same force of conscious being which has made this form of itself, this presentation of its workings knows it in that form, in that presentation. I can know nothing except what I myself am; if I know others, it is because they also are myself, because my self has assumed these apparently alien presentations as well as that which is nearest to my own mental centre. All sensation, all action of sense is thus the same in essence whether external or internal, physical or psychical.

But this vibration of conscious being is presented to itself by various forms of sense which answer to the successive operations of movement in its assumption of form. For first we have intensity of vibration creating regular rhythm which is the basis or constituent of all creative formation; secondly, contact or intermiscence of the movements of conscious being which constitute the rhythm; thirdly, definition of the grouping of movements which are in contact, their shape; fourthly, the constant welling up of the essential force to support in its continuity the movement that has been thus defined; fifthly, the actual enforcement and compression of the force in its own movement which maintains the form that has been assumed. In Matter these five constituent operations are said by the Sankhyas to represent themselves as five elemental conditions of substance, the etheric, atmo-

---

[1] The term is used not because it is entirely adequate or accurate, no physical term can be, but because it is most suggestive of the original outgoing of consciousness to seek itself.

spheric, igneous, liquid and solid; and the rhythm of vibration
is seen by them as *śabda*, sound, the basis of hearing, the intermiscence as contact, the basis of touch, the definition as shape,
the basis of sight, the upflow of force as *rasa*, sap, the basis of
taste, and the discharge of the atomic compression as *gandha*,
odour, the basis of smell. It is true that this is only predicated of
pure or subtle Matter; the physical matter of our world being
a mixed operation of force, these five elemental states are not
found there separately except in a very modified form. But all
these are only the physical workings or symbols. Essentially
all formation, to the most subtle and most beyond our senses
such as form of mind, form of character, form of soul, amount
when scrutinised to this fivefold operation of conscious-force
in movement.

All these operations, then, the Sanjnana or essential sense
must be able to seize, to make its own by that union in knowledge of knower and object which is peculiar to itself. Its sense of
the rhythm or intensity of the vibrations which contain in themselves all the meaning of the form, will be the basis of the essential hearing of which our apprehension of physical sound or the
spoken word is only the most outward result; so also its sense
of the contact or intermiscence of conscious force with conscious force must be the basis of the essential touch; its sense of
the definition or form of force must be the basis of the essential
sight; its sense of the upflow of essential being in the form, that
which is the secret of its self-delight, must be the basis of the
essential taste; its sense of the compression of force and the self-
discharge of its essence of being must be the basis of the essential inhalation grossly represented in physical substance by the
sense of smell. On whatever plane, to whatever kind of formation these essentialities of sense will apply themselves and on
each they will seek an appropriate organisation, an appropriate
functioning.

This various sense will, it is obvious, be in the highest
consciousness a complex unity, just as we have seen that there the
various operation of knowledge is also a complex unity. Even if
we examine the physical senses, say, the sense of hearing, if we
observe how the underlying mind receives their action, we shall

see that in their essence all the senses are in each other. That mind is not only aware of the vibration which we call sound; it is aware also of the contact and interchange between the force in the sound and the nervous force in us with which that inter-mixes; it is aware of the definition or form of the sound and of the complex contacts or relations which make up the form; it is aware of the essence or outwelling conscious force which constitutes and maintains the sound and prolongs its vibrations in our nervous being; it is aware of our own nervous inhalation of the vibratory discharge proceeding from the compression of force which makes, so to speak, the solidity of the sound. All these sensations enter into the sensitive reception and joy of mu-sic which is the highest physical form of this operation of force, — they constitute our physical sensitiveness to it and the joy of our nervous being in it; diminish one of them and the joy and the sensitiveness are to that extent dulled. Much more must there be this complex unity in a higher than the physical con-sciousness and most of all must there be unity in the highest. But the essential sense must be capable also of seizing the secret essence of all conscious being in action, in itself and not only through the results of the operation; its appreciation of these results can be nothing more than itself an outcome of this deeper sense which it has of the essence of the Thing behind its appearances.

If we consider these things thus subtly in the light of our own deeper psychology and pursue them beyond the physical appear-ances by which they are covered, we shall get to some intellectual conception of the sense behind our senses or rather the Sense of our senses, the Sight of our sight and the Hearing of our hearing. The Brahman-consciousness of which the Upanishad speaks is not the Absolute withdrawn into itself, but that Absolute in its outlook on the relative; it is the Lord, the Master-Soul, the governing Transcendent and All, He who constitutes and con-trols the action of the gods on the different planes of our being. Since it constitutes them, all our workings can be no more than psychical and physical results and representations of some-thing essential proper to its supreme creative outlook, our sense a shadow of the divine Sense, our sight of the divine Sight, our hearing of the divine Hearing. Nor is that divine Sight and Hearing limited to things physical, but extend themselves to all forms and operations of conscious being.

The supreme Consciousness does not depend on what we call sight and hearing for its own essential seeing and audition. It operates by a supreme Sense, creative and comprehensive, of which our physical and psychical sight and hearing are external results and partial operations. Neither is it ignorant of these, nor excludes them; for since it constitutes and controls, it must be aware of them but from a supreme plane, *param dhāma*, which includes all in its view; for its original action is that highest movement of Vishnu which, the Veda tells us, the seers behold like an eye extended in heaven. It is that by which the soul sees its seeings and hears its hearings; but all sense only assumes its true value and attains to its absolute, its immortal reality when we cease to pursue the satisfactions of the mere external and physical senses and go beyond even the psychical being to this spiritual or essential which is the source and fountain, the knower, constituent and true valuer of all the rest.

This spiritual sense of things, secret and superconscient in us, alone gives their being, worth and reality to the psychical and physical sense; in themselves they have none. When we attain to it, these inferior operations are as it were taken up into it and the whole world and everything in it changes to us and takes on a different and a non-material value. That Master-consciousness in us senses our sensations of objects, sees our seeings, hears our hearings no longer for the benefit of the senses and their desires, but with the embrace of the self-existent Bliss which has no cause, beginning or end, eternal in its own immortality.

10- The Superlife—Life of Our Life

BUT the Brahman-consciousness is not only Mind of our mind, Speech of our speech, Sense of our sense; it is also Life of our life. In other words, it is a supreme and universal energy of existence of which our own material life and its sustaining energy are only an inferior result, a physical symbol, an external and limited functioning. That which governs our existence and its functionings, does not live and act by them, but is their superior cause and the supra-vital principle out of which they are formed and by which they are controlled.

The English word life does duty for many very different shades of meaning; but the word Prana familiar in the Upanishad and in the language of Yoga is restricted to the life-force whether viewed in itself or in its functionings. The popular significance of Prana was indeed the breath drawn into and thrown out from the lungs and so, in its most material and common sense, the life or the life-breath; but this is not the philosophic significance of the word as it is used in the Upanishads. The Prana of the Upanishads is the life-energy itself which was supposed to occupy and act in the body with a fivefold movement, each with its characteristic name and each quite as necessary to the functioning of the life of the body as the act of respiration. Respiration in fact is only one action of the chief movement of the life-energy, the first of the five, — the action which is most normally necessary and vital to the maintenance and distribution of the energy in the physical frame, but which can yet be suspended without the life being necessarily destroyed.

The existence of a vital force or life-energy has been doubted by western Science, because that Science concerns itself only with the most external operations of Nature and has as yet no true knowledge of anything except the physical and outward. This Prana, this life-force is not physical in itself; it is not material energy, but rather a different principle supporting Matter and involved in it. It supports and occupies all forms and without it no physical form could have come into being or could remain in

being. It acts in all material forces such as electricity and is
nearest to self-manifestation in those that are nearest to pure
force; material forces could not exist or act without it, for from
it they derive their energy and movement and they are its
vehicles. But all material aspects are only field and form of the
Prana which is in itself a pure energy, their cause and not their
result. It cannot therefore be detected by any physical analysis;
physical analysis can only resolve for us the combinations of
those material happenings which are its results and the external
signs and symbols of its presence and operation.

How then do we become aware of its existence? By that
purification of our mind and body and that subtilisation of our
means of sensation and knowledge which become possible
through Yoga. We become capable of analysis other than the
resolution of forms into their gross physical elements and are
able to distinguish the operations of the pure mental principle
from those of the material and both of these from the vital or
dynamic which forms a link between them and supports them
both. We are then able to distinguish the movements of the Pranic currents not only in the physical body which is all that we are
normally aware of, but in that subtle frame of our being which
Yoga detects underlying and sustaining the physical. This is
ordinarily done by the process of Pranayama, the government
and control of the respiration. By Pranayama the Hathayogin is
able to control, suspend and transcend the ordinary fixed operation of the Pranic energy which is all that Nature needs for the
normal functioning of the body and of the physical life and mind,
and he becomes aware of the channels in which that energy distributes itself in all its workings and is therefore able to do things
with his body which seem miraculous to the ignorant, just as the
physical scientist by his knowledge of the workings of material
forces is able to do things with them which would seem to us
magic if their law and process were not divulged. For all the
workings of life in the physical form are governed by the Prana
and not only those which are normal and constant and those
which, being always potential, can be easily brought forward and
set in action, but those which are of a more remote potentiality
and seem to our average experience difficult or impossible.

But the Pranic energy supports not only the operations of
our physical life, but also those of the mind in the living body.
Therefore by the control of the Pranic energy it is not only possible to control our physical and vital functionings and to transcend their ordinary operation, but to control also the workings of
the mind and to transcend its ordinary operations. The human
mind in fact depends always on the Pranic force which links it
with the body through which it manifests itself, and it is able to
deploy its own force only in proportion as it can make that energy
available for its own uses and subservient to its own purposes.
In proportion, therefore, as the Yogin gets back to the control of
the Prana, and by the direction of its batteries opens up those
nervous centres (*cakras*) in which it is now sluggish or only
partially operative, he is able to manifest powers of mind, sense
and consciousness which transcend our ordinary experience.
The so-called occult powers of Yoga are such faculties which thus
open up of themselves as the Yogin advances in the control of
the Pranic force and, purifying the channels of its movement,
establishes an increasing communication between the consciousness of his subtle subliminal being and the consciousness of his
gross physical and superficial existence.

Thus the Prana is vital or nervous force which bears the
operations of mind and body, is yoked by them as it were like a
horse to a chariot and driven by the mind along the paths on
which it wishes to travel to the goal of its desire. Therefore it is
described in this Upanishad as yoked and moving forward and
again as being led forward, the images recalling the Vedic symbol
of the Horse by which the Pranic force is constantly designated
in the Rig-veda. It is in fact that which does all the action of the
world in obedience to conscious or subconscious mind and in the
conditions of material force and material form. While the mind
is that movement of Nature in us which represents in the mould
of our material and phenomenal existence and within the triple
term of the Ignorance the knowledge aspect of the Brahman, the
consciousness of the knower, and body is that which similarly
represents the being of the existent in the mask of phenomenally
divisible substance, so Prana or life-energy represents in the flux
of phenomenal things the force, the active dynamis of the Lord

who controls and enjoys the manifestation of His own being.[1] It is a universal energy present in every atom and particle of the universe, and active in every stirring and current of the constant flux and interchange which constitutes the world.

But just as mind is only an inferior movement of the supreme Conscious-Being and above mind there is a divine and infinite principle of consciousness, will and knowledge which controls the ignorant action of mind, and it is by this superior principle and not by mind that Brahman cognises His own being whether in itself or in its manifestation, so also it must be with this Life-force. The characteristics of the Life-force as it manifests itself in us are desire, hunger, an enjoyment which devours the object enjoyed and a sensational movement and activity of response which gropes after possession and seeks to pervade, embrace, take into itself the object of its desire.[2] It is not in this breath of desire and mortal enjoyment that the true life can consist or the highest, divine energy act, any more than the supreme know-ledge can think in the terms of ignorant, groping, limited and divided mind. As the movements of mind are merely represen-tations in the terms of the duality and the ignorance, reflections of a supreme consciousness and knowledge, so the movements of this life-force can only be similar representations of a supreme energy expressing a higher and truer existence possessed of that consciousness and knowledge and therefore free from de-sire, hunger, transient enjoyment and hampered activity. What is desire here must there be self-existent Will or Love; what is hunger here must there be desireless satisfaction; what is here enjoyment must there be self-existent delight; what is here a groping action and response, must be there self-possessing and all-possessing energy, — such must be the Life of our life by which this inferior action is sustained and led to its goal. Brah-man does not breathe with the breath, does not live by this Life-force and its dual terms of birth and death.

What then is this Life of our life? It is the supreme Energy[3]

---

[1] The three are the reverse aspects of Chit, Sat and Chit-Tapas.

[2] All these significances are intended by the Vedic Rishis in their use of the word *aśva*, Horse, for the *prāṇa*, the root being capable of all of them as we see from the words *āśā*, hope; *aśanā*, hunger; *aś*, to eat; *aś*, to enjoy; *āśu*, swift; *aś*, to move, attain, pervade, etc.

[3] Tapas or Chit-Shakti.

which is nothing but the infinite force in action of the supreme conscious Being in His own illumined self. The Self-existent is luminously aware of Himself and full of His own delight; and that self-awareness is a timeless self-possession which in action reveals itself as a force of infinite consciousness omnipotent as well as omniscient; for it exists between two poles, one of eternal stillness and pure identity, the other of eternal energy and identity of All with itself, the stillness eternally supporting the energy. That is the true existence, the Life from which our life proceeds; that is the immortality, while what we cling to as life is "hunger that is death". Therefore the object of the wise must be to pass in their illumined consciousness beyond the false and phenomenal terms of life and death to this immortality.

Yet is this Life-force, however inferior its workings, instinct with the being, will, light of that which it represents, of that which transcends it; by That it is "led forward" on its paths to a goal which its own existence implies by the very imperfection of its movements and renderings. This death called life is not only a dark figure of that light, but it is the passage by which we pass through transmutation of our being from the death-sleep of Matter into the spirit's infinite immortality.

11- The Great Transition

THE thought of the Upanishad as expressed in its first chapter in the brief and pregnant sentences of the Upanishadic style, amounts then to this result that the life of the mind, senses, vital activities in which we dwell is not the whole or the chief part of our existence, not the highest, not self-existent, not master of itself. It is an outer fringe, a lower result, an inferior working of something beyond; a superconscient Existence has developed, supports and governs this partial and fragmentary, this incomplete and unsatisfying consciousness and activity of the mind, life and senses. To rise out of this external and surface consciousness towards and into that superconscient is our progress, our goal, our destiny of completeness and satisfaction.

The Upanishad does not assert the unreality, but only the incompleteness and inferiority of our present existence. All that we follow after here is an imperfect representation, a broken and divided functioning of what is eternally in an absolute perfection on that higher plane of existence. This mind of ours unpossessed of its object, groping, purblind, besieged by error and incapacity, its action founded on an external vision of things, is only the shadow thrown by a superconscient Knowledge which possesses, creates and securely uses the truth of things because nothing is external to it, nothing is other than itself, nothing is divided or at war within its all-comprehensive self-awareness. That is the Mind of our mind. Our speech, limited, mechanical, imperfectly interpretative of the outsides of things, restricted by the narrow circle of the mind, based on the appearances of sense is only the far-off and feeble response, the ignorant vibration returned to a creative and revelatory Word which has built up all the forms which our mind and speech seek to comprehend and express. Our sense, a movement in stuff of consciousness vibratory to outward impacts, attempting imperfectly to grasp them by laboured and separately converging reactions, is only the faulty image of a supreme Sense which at once, fully, harmoniously unites itself with and enjoys all that the supreme Mind and

Speech create in the self-joyous activity of the divine and infinite existence. Our life, a breath of force and movement and possession attached to a form of mind and body and restricted by the form, limited in its force, hampered in its movement, besieged in its possession and therefore a thing of discords at war with itself and its environment, hungering and unsatisfied, moving inconstantly from object to object and unable to embrace and retain their multiplicity, devouring its objects of enjoyment and therefore transient in its enjoyments, is only a broken movement of the one, undivided, infinite Life which is all-possessing and ever satisfied because in all it enjoys its eternal self unimprisoned by the divisions of Space, unoccupied by the moments of Time, undeluded by the successions of Cause and Circumstance.

This superconscient Existence, one, conscious of itself, conscious both of its eternal peace and its omniscient and omnipotent force, is also conscious of our cosmic existence which it holds in itself, inspires secretly and omnipotently governs. It is the Lord of the Isha Upanishad who inhabits all the creations of His Force, all form of movement in the ever mobile principle of cosmos. It is our self and that of which and by which we are constituted in all our being and activities, the Brahman. The mortal life is a dual representation of That with two conflicting elements in it, negative and positive. Its negative elements of death, suffering, incapacity, strife, division, limitation are a dark figure which conceal and serve the development of that which its positive elements cannot yet achieve, — immortality hiding itself from life in the figure of death, delight hiding itself from pleasure in the figure of suffering, infinite force hiding itself from finite effort in the figure of incapacity, fusion of love hiding itself from desire in the figure of strife, unity hiding itself from acquisition in the figure of division, infinity hiding itself from growth in the figure of limitation. The positive elements suggest what the Brahman is, but never are what the Brahman is, although their victory, the victory of the gods, is always the victory of the Brahman over its own self-negations, always the self-affirmation of His vastness against the denials of the dark and limiting figure of things. Still, it is not this vastness merely, but the absolute infinity which is Brahman itself. And therefore within this dual figure of things

we cannot attain to our self, our Highest; we have to transcend
in order to attain. Our pursuit of the positive elements of this
existence, our worship of the gods of the mind, life, sense is only
a preparatory to the real travail of the soul, and we must leave
this lower Brahman and know that Higher if we are to fulfil ourselves. We pursue, for instance, our mental growth, we become
mental beings full of an accomplished thought-power and
thought-acquisition, *dhīrāḥ*, in order that we may by thought of
mind go beyond mind itself to the Eternal. For always the life
of mind and senses is the jurisdiction of death and limitation;
beyond is the immortality.

The wise, therefore, the souls seated and accomplished in
luminous thought-power put away from them the dualities of
our mind, life and senses and go forward from this world; they
go beyond to the unity and the immortality. The word used for
going forward is that which expresses the passage of death; it is
also that which the Upanishad uses for the forward movement of
the Life-force yoked to the car of embodied mind and sense on
the paths of life. And in this coincidence we can find a double
and most pregnant suggestion.

It is not by abandoning life on earth in order to pursue immortality on other more favourable planes of existence that the
great achievement becomes possible. It is here, *ihaiva*, in this
mortal life and body that immortality must be won, here in this
lower Brahman and by this embodied soul that the Higher must
be known and possessed. "If here one find it not, great is the perdition." This Life-force in us is led forward by the attraction of the
supreme Life on its path of constant acquisition through types of
the Brahman until it reaches a point where it has to go entirely
forward, to go across out of the mortal life, the mortal vision of
things to some Beyond. So long as death is not entirely conquered, this going beyond is represented in the terms of death
and by a passing into other worlds where death is not present,
where a type of immortality is tasted corresponding to that which
we have found here in our soul-experience; but the attraction
of death and limitation is not overpassed because they still conceal something of immortality and infinity which we have not
yet achieved; therefore there is a necessity of return, an insistent

utility of farther life in the mortal body which we do not overcome until we have passed beyond all types to the very being of
the Infinite, One and Immortal.

The worlds of which the Upanishad speaks are essentially
soul-conditions and not geographical divisions of the cosmos.
This material universe is itself only existence as we see it when
the soul dwells on the plane of material movement and experience
in which the spirit involves itself in form, and therefore all the
framework of things in which it moves by the life and which it
embraces by the consciousness is determined by the principle of
infinite division and aggregation proper to Matter, to substance of
form. This becomes then its world or vision of things. And to whatever soul-condition it climbs, its vision of things will change from
the material vision and correspond to that other condition, and
in that other framework it will move in its living and embrace it in
its consciousness. These are the worlds of the ancient tradition.

But the soul that has entirely realised immortality passes
beyond all worlds and is free from frameworks. It enters into the
being of the Lord; like this supreme superconscient Self and
Brahman, it is not subdued to life and death. It is no longer subject to the necessity of entering into the cycle of rebirth, of tra-
velling continually between the imprisoning dualities of death
and birth, affirmation and negation; for it has transcended name
and form. This victory, this supreme immortality it must achieve
here as an embodied soul in the mortal framework of things.
Afterwards, like the Brahman, it transcends and yet embraces the
cosmic existence without being subject to it. Personal freedom,
personal fulfilment is then achieved by the liberation of the soul
from imprisonment in the form of this changing personality and
by its ascent to the One that is the All. If afterwards there is any
assumption of the figure of mortality, it is an assumption and not
a subjection, a help brought to the world and not a help to be derived from it, a descent of the ensouled superconscient existence
not from any personal necessity, but from the universal need in
the cosmic labour for those yet unfree and unfulfilled to be helped
and strengthened by the force that has already described the
path up to the goal in its experience and achieved under the same
conditions the Work and the Sacrifice.

BEFORE we can proceed to the problem how, being what we are and the Brahman being what it is, we can effect the transition from the status of mind, life and senses proper to man over to the status proper to the supreme Consciousness which is master of mind, life and senses, another and prior question arises. The Upanishad does not state it explicitly, but implies and answers it with the strongest emphasis on the solution and the subtlest variety in its repetition of the apparent paradox that is presented.

The Master-Consciousness of the Brahman is that for which we have to abandon this lesser status of the mere creature subject to the movement of Nature in the cosmos; but after all this Master-Consciousness, however high and great a thing it may be, has a relation to the universe and the cosmic movement; it cannot be the utter Absolute, Brahman superior to all relativities. This Conscious-Being who originates, supports and governs our mind, life, senses is the Lord; but where there is no universe of relativities, there can be no Lord, for there is no movement to transcend and govern. Is not then this Lord, as one might say in a later language, not so much the creator of Maya as himself a creation of Maya? Do not both Lord and cosmos disappear when we go beyond all cosmos? And is it not beyond all cosmos that the only true reality exists? Is it not this only true reality and not the Mind of our mind, the Sense of our sense, the Life of our life, the Word behind our speech, which we have to know and possess? As we must go behind all effects to the Cause, must we not equally go beyond the Cause to that in which neither cause nor effects exist? Is not even the immortality spoken of in the Veda and Upanishads a petty thing to be overpassed and abandoned? and should we not reach towards the utter Ineffable where mortality and immortality cease to have any meaning?

The Upanishad does not put to itself the question in this form and language which only became possible when Nihilistic Buddhism and Vedantic Illusionism had passed over the face of our thought and modified philosophical speech and concepts. But it knows of the ineffable Absolute which is the utter reality and absoluteness of the Lord even as the Lord is the absolute of all that is in the cosmos. Of That it proceeds to speak in the only way in which it can be spoken of by the human mind.

Its answer to the problem is that That is precisely the Unknowable[1] of which no relations can be affirmed[2] and about which therefore our intellect must for ever be silent. The injunction to know the utterly Unknowable would be without any sense or practical meaning. Not that That is a Nihil, a pure Negative, but it cannot either be described by any of the positives of which our mind, speech or perception is capable, nor even can it be indicated by any of them. It is only a little that we know; it is only in the terms of the little that we can put the mental forms of our knowledge. Even when we go beyond to the real form of the Brahman which is not this universe, we can only indicate, we cannot really describe. If then we think we have known it perfectly, we betray our ignorance; we show that we know very little indeed, not even the little that we can put into the forms of our knowledge. For the universe seen as our mind sees it is the little, the divided, the parcelling out of existence and consciousness in which we know and express things by fragments, and we can never really cage in our intellectual and verbal fictions that infinite totality. Yet it is through the principles manifested in the universe that we have to arrive at That, through the life, through the mind and through that highest mental knowledge which grasps at the fundamental Ideas that are like doors concealing behind them the Brahman and yet seeming to reveal Him.

Much less, then, if we can only thus know the Master-Consciousness which is the form of the Brahman, can we pretend to know its utter ineffable reality which is beyond all knowledge. But if this were all, there would be no hope for the soul and a resigned Agnosticism would be the last word of wisdom. The truth is that though thus beyond our mentality and our highest ideative knowledge, the Supreme does give Himself both to this knowledge and to our mentality in the way proper to each and by following that way we can arrive at Him, but only

[1] *ajñeyam atarkyam.*   [2] *avyavahāryam.*

on condition that we do not take our mentalising by the mind and our knowing by the higher thought for the full knowledge and rest in that with a satisfied possession.

The way is to use our mind rightly for such knowledge as is open to its highest, purified capacity. We have to know the form of the Brahman, the Master-Consciousness of the Lord through and yet beyond the universe in which we live. But first we must put aside what is mere form and phenomenon in the universe; for that has nothing to do with the form of the Brahman, the body of the Self, since it is not His form, but only His most external mask. Our first step therefore must be to get behind the forms of Matter, the forms of Life, the forms of Mind and go back to that which is essential, most real, nearest to actual entity. And when we have gone on thus eliminating, thus analysing all forms into the fundamental entities of the cosmos, we shall find that these fundamental entities are really only two, ourselves and the gods.

The gods of the Upanishad have been supposed to be a figure for the senses, but although they act in the senses, they are yet much more than that. They represent the divine power in its great and fundamental cosmic functionings whether in man or in mind and life and matter in general; they are not the functionings themselves but something of the Divine which is essential to their operation and its immediate possessor and cause. They are, as we see from other Upanishads, positive self-representations of the Brahman leading to good, joy, light, love, immortality as against all that is a dark negation of these things. And it is necessarily in the mind, life, senses and speech of man that the battle here reaches its height and approaches to its full meaning. The gods seek to lead these to good and light; the Titans, sons of darkness, seek to pierce them with ignorance and evil.[1] Behind the gods is the Master-Consciousness of which they are the positive cosmic self-representations.

The other entity which represents the Brahman in the cosmos is the self of the living and thinking creature, man. This self also is not an external mask; it is not form of the mind or form of the life or form of the body. It is something that supports these and

---

[1] *Chhandogya* and *Brihadaranyaka Upanishads.*

makes them possible, something that can say positively like the
gods, "I am" and not only "I seem". We have then to scrutinise
these two entities and see what they are in relation to each other
and to the Brahman; or, as the Upanishad puts it, "That of it
which is thou, that of it which is in the gods, *this* is what thy mind
has to resolve." Well, but what then of the Brahman is myself?
and what of the Brahman is in the Gods? The answer is evident.
I am a representation in the cosmos, but for all purposes of the
cosmos a real representation of the Self; and the gods are a representation in the cosmos — a real representation since without
them the cosmos could not continue — of the Lord. The one
supreme Self is the essentiality of all these individual existences;
the one supreme Lord is the Godhead in the gods.

The Self and the Lord are one Brahman, whom we can realise through our self and realise through that which is essential
in the cosmic movement. Just as our self constitutes our mind,
body, life, senses, so that Self constitutes all mind, body, life,
senses; it is the origin and essentiality of things. Just as the gods
govern, supported by our self, the cosmos of our individual being,
the action of our mind, senses and life, so the Lord governs as
Mind of the mind, Sense of the sense, Life of the life, supporting
His active divinity by His silent essential self-being, all cosmos
and all form of being. As we have gone behind the forms of the
cosmos to that which is essential in their being and movement
and found our self and the gods, so we have to go behind our self
and the gods and find the one supreme Self and the one supreme
Godhead. Then we can say, "I think that I know."

But at once we have to qualify our assertion. I think not
that I know perfectly, for that is impossible in the terms of our
instruments of knowledge. I do not think for a moment that I
know the Unknowable, that that can be put into the forms
through which I must arrive at the Self and Lord; but at the same
time I am no longer in ignorance, I know the Brahman in the
only way in which I can know Him, in His self-revelation to me
in terms not beyond the grasp of my psychology, manifest as the
Self and the Lord. The mystery of existence is revealed in a way
that utterly satisfies my being because it enables me first to comprehend it through these figures as far as it can be comprehended

by me and, secondly, to enter into, to live in, to be one in law and being with and even to merge myself in the Brahman.

If we fancy that we have grasped the Brahman by the mind and in that delusion fix down our knowledge of Him to the terms our mentality has found, then our knowledge is no knowledge; it is the little knowledge that turns to falsehood. So too those who try to fix Him into our notion of the fundamental ideas in which we discern Him by the thought that rises above ordinary mental perception, have no real discernment of the Brahman, since they take certain idea-symbols for the Reality. On the other hand, if we recognise that our mental perceptions are simply so many clues by which we can rise beyond mental perception and if we use these fundamental idea-symbols and the arrangement of them which our uttermost thought makes in order to go beyond the symbol to that reality, then we have rightly used mind and the higher discernment for their supreme purpose. Mind and the higher discernment are satisfied of the Brahman even in being exceeded by Him.

The mind can only reflect in a sort of supreme understanding and experience the form, the image of the supreme as He shows Himself to our mentality. Through this reflection we find, we know; the purpose of knowledge is accomplished, for we find immortality, we enter into the law, the being, the beatitude of the Brahman-consciousness. By self-realisation of Brahman as our self we find the force, the divine energy which lifts us beyond the limitation, weakness, darkness, sorrow, all-pervading death of our mortal existence; by the knowledge of the one Brahman in all beings and in all the various movement of the cosmos we attain beyond these things to the infinity, the omnipotent being, the omniscient light, the pure beatitude of that divine existence.

This great achievement must be done here in this mortal world, in this limited body; for if we do it, we arrive at our true existence and are no longer bound down to our phenomenal becoming. But if here we find it not, great is the loss and perdition; for we remain continually immersed in the phenomenal life of the mind and body and do not rise above it into the true supramental existence. Nor, if we miss it here, will death give it to us by our passage to another and less difficult world. Only those who use their awakened self and enlightened powers to distinguish and discover that One and Immortal in all existences, the all-originating self, the all-inhabiting Lord, can make the real passage which transcends life and death, can pass out of this mortal status, can press beyond and rise upward into a world-transcending immortality.

This, then, and no other is the means to be seized on and the goal to be reached. "There is no other path for the great journey." The Self and the Lord are that indeterminable, unknowable, ineffable Parabrahman and when we seek rather that which is indeterminable and unknowable to us, it is still the Self and the Lord always that we find, though by an attempt which is not the straight and possible road intended for the embodied soul seeking here to accomplish its true existence.[1] They are the self-manifested Reality which so places itself before man as the object of his highest aspiration and the fulfilment of all his activities.

[1] *Gita.*

13- The Parable of the Gods

FROM its assertion of the relative knowableness of the unknowable Brahman and the justification of the soul's aspiration towards that which is beyond its present capacity and status the Upanishad turns to the question of the means by which that high-reaching aspiration can put itself into relation with the object of its search. How is the veil to be penetrated and the subject consciousness of man to enter into the master-consciousness of the Lord? What bridge is there over this gulf? Knowledge has already been pointed out as the supreme means open to us, a knowledge which begins by a sort of reflection of the true existence in the awakened mental understanding. But Mind is one of the gods; the Light behind it is indeed the greatest of the gods, Indra. Then, an awakening of all the gods through their greatest to the essence of that which they are, the one Godhead which they represent. By the mentality opening itself to the Mind of our mind, the sense and speech also will open themselves to the Sense of our sense and to the Word behind our speech and the life to the Life of our life. The Upanishad proceeds to develop this consequence of its central suggestion by a striking parable or apologue.

The gods, the powers that affirm the Good, the Light, the Joy and Beauty, the Strength and Mastery have found themselves victorious in their eternal battle with the powers that deny. It is Brahman that has stood behind the gods and conquered for them; the Master of all who guides all has thrown His deciding will into the balance, put down His darkened children and exalted the children of Light. In this victory of the Master of all the gods are conscious of a mighty development of themselves, a splendid efflorescence of their greatness in man, their joy, their light, their glory, their power and pleasure. But their vision is as yet sealed to their own deeper truth; they know of themselves, they know not the Eternal; they know the godheads, they do not know God. Therefore they see the victory as their own, the greatness as their own. This opulent efflorescence of the gods and uplifting of their greatness and light is the advance of man to his ordinary ideal of a perfectly enlightened mentality, a strong and sane vitality, a well-ordered body and senses, a harmonious, rich, active and happy life, the Hellenic ideal which the modern world holds to be our ultimate potentiality. When such an efflorescence takes place whether in the individual or the kind, the gods in man grow luminous, strong, happy; they feel they have conquered the world and they proceed to divide it among themselves and enjoy it.

But such is not the full intention of Brahman in the universe or in the creature. The greatness of the gods is His own victory and greatness, but it is only given in order that man may grow nearer to the point at which his faculties will be strong enough to go beyond themselves and realise the Transcendent. Therefore Brahman manifests Himself before the exultant gods in their well-ordered world and puts to them by His silence the heart-shaking, the world-shaking question, "If ye are all, then what am I? for see, I am and I am here." Though He manifests, He does not reveal Himself, but is seen and felt by them as a vague and tremendous presence, the Yaksha, the Daemon, the Spirit, the unknown Power, the Terrible beyond good and evil for whom good and evil are instruments towards His final self-expression. Then there is alarm and confusion in the divine assembly; they feel a demand and a menace, on the side of the evil the possibility of monstrous and appalling powers yet unknown and un-mastered which may wreck the fair world they have built, up-heave and shatter to pieces the brilliant harmony of the intellect, the aesthetic mind, the moral nature, the vital desires, the body and senses which they have with such labour established, on the side of the good the demand of things unknown which are beyond all these and therefore are equally a menace, since the little which is realised cannot stand against the much that is un-realised, cannot shut out the vast, the infinite that presses against the fragile walls we have erected to define and shelter our limited being and pleasure. Brahman presents itself to them as the Unknown; the gods knew not what was this Daemon.

Therefore Agni first arises at their bidding to discover its nature, limits, identity. The gods of the Upanishad differ in one all-important respect from the gods of the Rig-veda; for the latter are not only powers of the One, but conscious of their source and true identity; they know the Brahman, they dwell in the supreme Godhead, their origin, home and proper plane is the superconscient Truth. It is true they manifest themselves in man in the form of human faculties and assume the appearance of human limitations, manifest themselves in the lower cosmos and assume the mould of its cosmic operations; but this is only their lesser and lower movement and beyond it they are for ever the One, the Transcendent and Wonderful, the Master of Force and Delight and Knowledge and Being. But in the Upanishads the Brahman idea has grown and cast down the gods from this high pre-eminence so that they appear only in their lesser human and cosmic workings. Much of their other Vedic aspects they keep. Here the three gods Indra, Vayu, Agni represent the cosmic Divine on each of its three planes, Indra on the mental, Vayu on the vital, Agni on the material. In that order, therefore, beginning from the material they approach the Brahman.

Agni is the heat and flame of the conscious force in Matter which has built up the universe; it is he who has made life and mind possible and developed them in the material universe where he is the greatest deity. Especially he is the primary impeller of speech of which Vayu is the medium and Indra the lord. This heat of conscious force in Matter is Agni Jatavedas, the knower of all births: of all things born, of every cosmic phenomenon he knows the law, the process, the limit, the relation. If then it is some mighty Birth of the cosmos that stands before them, some new indeterminate developed in the cosmic struggle and process, who shall know him, determine his limits, strength, potentialities if not Agni Jatavedas?

Full of confidence he rushes towards the object of his search and is met by the challenge, "Who art thou? What is the force in thee?" His name is Agni Jatavedas, the Power that is at the basis of all birth and process in the material universe and embraces and knows their workings and the force in him is this that all that is thus born, he as the flame of Time and Death can devour. All things are his food which he assimilates and turns into material of new birth and formation. But this all-devourer

cannot devour with all his force a fragile blade of grass so long
as it has behind it the power of the Eternal. Agni is compelled to
return, not having discovered. One thing only is settled that this
Daemon is no Birth of the material cosmos, no transient thing
that is subject to the flame and breath of Time; it is too great
for Agni.

Another god rises to the call. It is Vayu Matarishwan, the
great Life-Principle, he who moves, breathes, expands infinitely
in the mother element. All things in the universe are the movement of this mighty Life; it is he who has brought Agni and
placed him secretly in all existence; for him the worlds have
been upbuilded that Life may move in them, that it may act, that
it may riot and enjoy. If this Daemon be no birth of Matter, but
some stupendous Life-force active whether in the depths or on
the heights of being, who shall know it, who shall seize it in his
universal expansion if not Vayu Matarishwan?

There is the same confident advance upon the object, the
same formidable challenge, "Who art thou? What is the force
in thee?" This is Vayu Matarishwan and the power in him is this
that he, the Life, can take all things in his stride and growth and
seize on them for his mastery and enjoyment. But even the
veriest frailest trifle he cannot seize and master so long as it is
protected against him by the shield of the Omnipotent. Vayu too
returns, not having discovered. One thing only is settled that this
is no form or force of cosmic Life which operates within the
limits of the all-grasping vital impulse; it is too great for Vayu.

Indra next arises, the Puissant, the Opulent. Indra is the
power of the Mind; the senses which the Life uses for enjoyment,
are operations of Indra which he conducts for knowledge and all
things that Agni has upbuilt and supports and destroys in the
universe are Indra's field and the subject of his functioning. If
then this unknown Existence is something that the senses can
grasp or, if it is something that the mind can envisage, Indra shall
know it and make it part of his opulent possessions. But it is
nothing that the senses can grasp or the mind envisage, for as
soon as Indra approaches it, it vanishes. The mind can only
envisage what is limited by Time and Space and this Brahman
is that which, as the Rig-veda has said, is neither today nor

tomorrow and though it moves and can be approached in the conscious being of all conscious existences, yet when the mind tries to approach it and study it in itself, it vanishes from the view of the mind. The Omnipresent cannot be seized by the senses, the Omniscient cannot be known by the mentality.

But Indra does not turn back from the quest like Agni and Vayu; he pursues his way through the highest ether of the pure mentality and there he approaches the Woman, the many-shining, Uma Haimavati; from her he learns that this Daemon is the Brahman by whom alone the gods of mind and life and body conquer and affirm themselves, and in whom alone they are great. Uma is the supreme Nature from whom the whole cosmic action takes its birth; she is the pure summit and highest power of the One who here shines out in many forms. From this supreme Nature which is also the supreme Consciousness the gods must learn their own truth; they must proceed by reflecting it in themselves instead of limiting themselves to their own lower movement. For she has the knowledge and consciousness of the One, while the lower nature of mind, life and body can only envisage the many. Although therefore Indra, Vayu and Agni are the greatest of the gods, the first coming to know the existence of the Brahman, the others approaching and feeling the touch of it, yet it is only by entering into contact with the supreme consciousness and reflecting its nature and by the elimination of the vital, mental, physical egoism so that their whole function shall be to reflect the One and Supreme that Brahman can be known by the gods in us and possessed. The conscious force that supports our embodied life must become simply and purely a reflector of that supreme Consciousness and Power of which its highest ordinary action is only a twilight figure; the Life must become a passively potent reflection and pure image of that supreme Life which is greater than all our utmost actual and potential vitality; the Mind must resign itself to be no more than a faithful mirror of the image of the superconscient Existence. By this conscious surrender of mind, life and senses to the Master of our senses, life and mind who alone really governs their action, by this turning of the cosmic existence into a passive reflection of the eternal being and a faithful reproducer of the nature of the Eternal we may hope to know and through knowledge to rise into that which is superconscient to us; we shall enter into the Silence that is master of an eternal, infinite, free and all-blissful activity.

14 - The Transfiguration of the Self and the Gods

THE means of the knowledge of Brahman are, we have seen, to get back behind the forms of the universe to that which is essential in the cosmos, — and that which is essential is twofold, the gods in Nature and the self in the individual, — and then to get behind these to the Beyond which they represent. The practical relation of the gods to Brahman in this process of divine knowledge has been already determined. The cosmic functionings through which the gods act, mind, life, speech, senses, body, must become aware of something beyond them which governs them, by which they are and move, by whose force they evolve, enlarge themselves and arrive at power and joy and capacity; to that they must turn from their ordinary operations; leaving these, leaving the false idea of independent action and self-ordering which is an egoism of mind and life and sense they must become consciously passive to the power, light and joy of something which is beyond themselves. What happens then is that this divine Unnameable reflects Himself openly in the gods. His light takes possession of the thinking mind, His power and joy of the life, His light and rapture of the emotional mind and the senses. Something of the supreme image of Brahman falls upon the world-nature and changes it into divine nature.

All this is not done by a sudden miracle. It comes by flashes, revelations, sudden touches and glimpses; there is as if a leap of the lightning of revelation flaming out from those heavens for a moment and then returning into its secret source; as if the lifting of the eyelid of an inner vision and its falling again because the eye cannot look long and steadily on the utter light. The repetition of these touches and visitings from the Beyond fixes the gods in their upward gaze and expectation, constant repetition fixes them in a constant passivity; not moving out any longer to grasp at the forms of the universe mind, life and senses will more and more be fixed in the memory, in the understanding, in the joy of the touch and vision of that transcendent glory which they have now resolved to make their sole object; to that only they will learn to respond and not to the touches of outward things. The silence which has fallen on them and which is now their foundation and status will become their knowledge of the eternal silence which is Brahman; the response of their functioning to a supernal light, power, joy will become their knowledge of the eternal activity which is Brahman. Other status, other response and activity they will not know. The mind will know nothing but the Brahman, think of nothing but the Brahman, the Life will move to, embrace, enjoy nothing but the Brahman, the eye will see, the ear hear, the other senses sense nothing but the Brahman.

But is then a complete oblivion of the external the goal? Must the mind and senses recede inward and fall into an unending trance and the life be for ever stilled? This is possible, if the soul so wills, but it is not inevitable and indispensable. The Mind is cosmic, one in all the universe; so too are the Life, and the Sense, so too is Matter of the body; and when they exist in and for the Brahman only, they will not only know this but will sense, feel and live in that universal unity. Therefore to whatever thing they turn which to the individual sense and mind and life seems now external to them, there also it is not the mere form of things which they will know, think of, sense, embrace and enjoy, but always and only the Brahman. Moreover, the external will cease to exist for them, because nothing will be external but all things internal to us, even the whole world and all that is in it. For the limit of ego, the wall of individuality will break; the individual Mind will cease to know itself as individual, it will be conscious only of universal Mind one everywhere in which individuals are only knots of the one mentality; so the individual life will lose its sense of separateness and live only in and as the one life in which all individuals are simply whirls of the indivisible flood of Pranic activity; the very body and senses will be no longer conscious of a separated existence, but the real body which the man will feel himself to be physically will be the whole Earth and the whole universe and the whole indivisible form of things wheresoever existent, and the senses also will be converted to this principle of sensation so that even in what we call the external, the eye will see Brahman only in every sight, the ear will hear Brahman only in every sound, the inner and outer body will feel Brahman only in every touch and the touch itself as if internal in the greater body. The soul whose gods are thus converted to this supreme law and religion, will realise in the cosmos itself and in all its multiplicity the truth of the One besides whom there is no other or second. Moreover, becoming one with the formless and infinite, it will exceed the universe itself and see all the worlds not as external, not even as commensurate with itself, but as if within it.

And in fact, in the higher realisation it will not be Mind, Life, Sense of which even the mind, life and sense themselves will be originally aware, but rather that which constitutes them. By this process of constant visiting and divine touch and influence the Mind of the mind, that is to say, the superconscient Knowledge will take possession of the mental understanding and begin to turn all its vision and thinking into luminous stuff and vibration of light of the Supermind. So too the sense will be changed by the visitings of the Sense behind the sense and the whole sense-view of the universe itself will be altered so that the vital, mental and supramental will become visible to the senses with the physical only as their last, outermost and smallest result. So too the Life will become a superlife, a conscious movement of the infinite Conscious-Force; it will be impersonal, unlimited by any particular acts and enjoyment, unbound to their results, untroubled by the dualities or the touch of sin and suffering, grandiose, boundless, immortal. The material world itself will become for these gods a figure of the infinite, luminous and blissful Superconscient.

This will be the transfiguration of the gods, but what of the self? For we have seen that there are two fundamental entities, the gods and the self, and the self in us is greater than the cosmic Powers, its Godward destination more vital to our perfection and self-fulfilment than any transfiguration of these lesser deities. Therefore not only must the gods find their one Godhead and resolve themselves into it; that is to say, not only must the cosmic principles working in us resolve themselves into the working of the One, the Principle of all principles, so that they shall become only a unified existence and single action of That in spite of all play of differentiation, but also and with a more fundamental necessity the self in us which supports the action of the gods must find and enter into the one Self of all individual existences, the indivisible Spirit to whom all souls are no more than dark or luminous centres of its consciousness.

This the self of man, since it is the essentiality of a mental being, will do through the mind. In the gods the transfiguration is effected by the Superconscient itself visiting their substance and opening their vision with its flashes until it has transformed them; but the mind is capable of another action which is only apparently movement of mind, but really the movement of the self towards its own reality. The mind seems to go to That, to attain to it; it is lifted out of itself into something beyond and, although it falls back, still by the mind the will of knowledge in the mental thought continually and at last continuously remembers that into which it has entered. On this the Self through the mind seizes and repeatedly dwells and so doing it is finally caught up into it and at last able to dwell securely in that transcendence. It transcends the mind, it transcends its own mental individualisation of the being, that which it now knows as itself; it ascends and takes foundation in the Self of all and in the status of self-joyous infinity which is the supreme manifestation of the Self. This is the transcendent immortality, this is the spiritual existence which the Upanishads declare to be the goal of man and by which we pass out of the mortal state into the heaven of the Spirit.

What then happens to the gods and the cosmos and all that the Lord develops in His being? Does it not all disappear? Is not the transfiguration of the gods even a mere secondary state through which we pass towards that culmination and which drops away from us as soon as we reach it? And with the disappearance of the gods and the cosmos does not the Lord too, the Master-Consciousness, disappear so that nothing is left but the one pure indeterminate Existence self-blissful in an eternal inaction and non-creation? Such was the conclusion of the later Vedanta in its extreme monistic form and such was the sense which it tried to read into all the Upanishads; but it must be recognised that in the language whether of the Isha or the Kena Upanishad there is absolutely nothing, not even a shade or a nuance pointing to it. If we want to find it there, we have to put it in by force; for the actual language used favours instead the conclusion of other Vedantic systems, which considered the goal to be the eternal joy of the soul in a Brahmaloka or world of the Brahman in which it is one with the infinite existence and yet in a sense still a soul able to enjoy differentiation in the oneness.

In the next verse we have the culmination of the teaching of the Upanishad, the result of the great transcendence which it has been setting forth and afterwards the description of the immortality to which the souls of knowledge attain when they pass beyond the mortal status. It declares that Brahman is in its nature "That Delight", *tad vanam*. "Vana" is the Vedic word for delight or delightful, and *"tad vanam"* means therefore the transcendent Delight, the all-blissful Ananda of which the Taittiriya Upanishad speaks as the highest Brahman from which all existences are born, by which all existences live and increase and into which all existences arrive in their passing out of death and birth. It is as this transcendent Delight that the Brahman must be worshipped and sought. It is this beatitude therefore which is meant by the immortality of the Upanishads. And what will be the result of knowing and possessing Brahman as the supreme Ananda? It is that towards the knower and possessor of the Brahman is directed the desire of all creatures. In other words, he becomes a centre of the divine Delight shedding it on all the world and attracting all to it as to a fountain of joy and love and self-fulfilment in the universe.

This is the culmination of the teaching of the Upanishad; there was a demand for the secret teaching that enters into the ultimate truth, for the "Upanishad", and in response this doctrine has been given. It has been uttered, the Upanishad of the Brahman, the hidden ultimate truth of the supreme Existence; its beginning was the search for the Lord, Master of mind, life, speech and senses in whom is the absolute of mind, the absolute of life, the absolute of speech and senses and its close is the finding of Him as the transcendent Beatitude and the elevation of the soul that finds and possesses it into a living centre of that Delight towards which all creatures in the universe shall turn as to a fountain of its ecstasies.

*
**

The Upanishad closes with two verses which seem to review and characterise the whole work in the manner of the ancient writings when they have drawn to their close. This Upanishad or gospel of the inmost Truth of things has for its foundation, it is said, the practice of self-mastery, action and the subdual of the sense-life to the power of the Spirit. In other words, life and works are to be used as a means of arriving out of the state of subjection proper to the soul in the ignorance into a state of mastery which brings it nearer to the absolute self-mastery and all-mastery of the supreme Soul seated in the knowledge. The Vedas, that is to say, the utterances of the inspired seers and the truths they hold, are described as all the limbs of the Upanishad; in other words, all the convergent lines and aspects, all the necessary elements of this great practice, this profound psychological self-training and spiritual aspiration are set forth in these great Scriptures, channels of supreme knowledge and indicators of a supreme discipline. Truth is its home; and this Truth is not merely intellectual verity, — for that is not the sense of the word in the Vedic writings, — but man's ultimate human state of true being, true consciousness, right knowledge, right works, right joy of existence, all indeed that is contrary to the falsehood of egoism and ignorance. It is by these means, by using works and self-discipline for mastery of oneself and for the generation of spiritual energy, by fathoming in all its parts the knowledge and repeating the high example of the great Vedic seers and by living in the Truth that one becomes capable of the great ascent which the Upanishad opens to us.

The goal of the ascent is the world of the true and vast existence of which the Veda speaks as the Truth that is the final goal and home of man. It is described here as the greater infinite heavenly world, (Swargaloka, Swarloka of the Veda), which is not the lesser Swarga of the Puranas or the lesser Brahma-loka of the Mundaka Upanishad, its world of the sun's rays to which the soul arrives by works of virtue and piety, but falls from them by the exhaustion of their merit; it is the higher Swarga or Brahman-world of the Katha which is beyond the dual symbols of birth and death, the higher Brahman-worlds of the Mundaka which the soul enters by knowledge and renunciation. It is therefore a state not belonging to the Ignorance, but to Knowledge. It is, in fact, the infinite existence and beatitude of the soul in the being of the all-blissful existence; it is too the higher status, the light of the Mind beyond the mind, the joy and eternal mastery of the Life beyond the life, the riches of the Sense beyond the senses. And the soul finds in it not only its own largeness but finds too and possesses the infinity of the One and it has firm foundation in that immortal state because there a supreme Silence and eternal Peace are the secure foundation of eternal Knowledge and absolute Joy.

15- A Last Word

WE HAVE now completed our review of this Upanishad; we have considered minutely the bearings of its successive utterances and striven to make as precise as we can to the intelligence the sense of the puissant phrases in which it gives us its leading clues to that which can never be entirely expressed by human speech. We have some idea of what it means by that Brahman, by the Mind of mind, the Life of life, the Sense of sense, the Speech of speech, by the opposition of ourselves and the gods, by the Unknowable who is yet not utterly unknowable to us, by the transcendence of the mortal state and the conquest of immortality.

Fundamentally its teaching reposes on the assertion of three states of existence, the human and mortal, the Brahman-consciousness which is the absolute of our relativities, and the utter Absolute which is unknowable. The first is in a sense a false status of misrepresentation because it is a continual term of apparent opposites and balancings where the truth of things is a secret unity; we have here a bright or positive figure and a dark or negative figure and both are figures, neither the Truth; still in that we now live and through that we have to move to the Beyond. The second is the Lord of all this dual action who is beyond it; He is the truth of Brahman and not in any way a falsehood or misrepresentation, but the truth of it as attained by us in our eternal supramental being; in Him are the absolutes of all that here we experience in partial figures. The Unknowable is beyond our grasp because though it is the same Reality, yet it exceeds even our highest term of eternal being and is beyond Existence and Non-existence; it is therefore to the Brahman, the Lord who has a relation to what we are that we must direct our search if we would attain beyond what temporarily seems to what eternally is.

The attainment of the Brahman is our escape from the mortal status into Immortality, by which we understand not the survival of death, but the finding of our true self of eternal being and bliss beyond the dual symbols of birth and death. By immortality we mean the absolute life of the soul as opposed to the transient and mutable life in the body which it assumes by birth and death and rebirth and superior also to its life as the mere mental being who dwells in the world subjected helplessly to this law of death and birth or seems at least by his ignorance to be subjected to this and to other laws of the lower Nature. To know and possess its true nature, free, absolute, master of itself and its embodiments is the soul's means of transcendence, and to know and possess this is to know and possess the Brahman. It is also to rise out of mortal world into immortal world, out of world of bondage into world of largeness, out of finite world into infinite world. It is to ascend out of earthly joy and sorrow into a transcendent Beatitude.

This must be done by the abandonment of our attachment to the figure of things in the mortal world. We must put from us its death and dualities if we would compass the unity and immortality. Therefore it follows that we must cease to make the goods of this world or even its right, light and beauty our object of pursuit; we must go beyond these to a supreme Good, a transcendent Truth, Light and Beauty in which the opposite figures of what we call evil disappear. But still, being in this world, it is only through something in this world itself that we can transcend it; it is through its figures that we must find the absolute. Therefore, we scrutinise them and perceive that there are first these forms of mind, life, speech and sense, all of them figures and imperfect suggestions, and then behind them the cosmic principles through which the One acts. It is to these cosmic principles that we must proceed and turn them from their ordinary aim and movement in the world to find their own supreme aim and absolute movement in their own one Godhead, the Lord, the Brahman; they must be drawn to leave the workings of ordinary mind and find the superconscient Mind, to leave the workings of ordinary speech and sense and find the supramental Sense and original Word, to leave the apparent workings of mundane Life and find the transcendent Life.

Besides the gods, there is our self, the spirit within who supports all this action of the gods. Our spirit too must turn from its absorption in its figure of itself as it sees it involved in the movement of individual life, mind, body and subject to it and must direct its gaze upward to its own supreme Self who is beyond all this movement and master of it all. Therefore the mind must indeed become passive to the divine Mind, the sense to the divine Sense, the life to the divine Life and by receptivity to constant touches and visitings of the highest be transfigured into a reflection of these transcendences; but also the individual self must through the mind's aspiration upwards, through up-liftings of itself beyond, through constant memory of the supreme Reality in which during these divine moments it has lived, ascend finally into that Bliss and Power and Light.

But this will not necessarily mean the immersion into an all-oblivious Being eternally absorbed in His own inactive self-existence. For the mind, sense, life going beyond their individual formations find that they are only one centre of the sole Mind, Life, Form of things and therefore they find Brahman in that also and not only in an individual transcendence; they bring down the vision of the superconscient into that also and not only into their own individual workings. The mind of the individual escapes from its limits and becomes the one universal mind, his life the one universal life, his bodily sense the sense of the whole universe and even more as his own indivisible Brahman-body. He perceives the universe in himself and he perceives also his self in all existences and knows it to be the one, the omnipresent, the single-multiple all-inhabiting Lord and Reality. Without this realisation he has not fulfilled the conditions of immortality. Therefore it is said that what the sages seek is to distinguish and see the Brahman in all existences; by that discovery, realisation and possession of Him everywhere and in all they attain to their immortal existence.

Still although the victory of the gods, that is to say, the progressive perfection of the mind, life, body in the positive terms of good, right, joy, knowledge, power is recognised as a victory of the Brahman and the necessity of using life and human works in the world as a means of preparation and self-mastery is admitted, yet a final passing away into the infinite heavenly world or status of the Brahman-consciousness is held out as the goal.

And this would seem to imply a rejection of the life of the cosmos. Well then may we ask, we the modern humanity more and more conscious of the inner warning of that which created us, be it Nature or God, that there is a work for the race, a divine purpose in its creation which exceeds the salvation of the individual soul, because the universal is as real or even more real than the individual, we who feel more and more, in the language of the Koran, that the Lord did not create heaven and earth in a jest, that Brahman did not begin dreaming this world-dream in a moment of aberration and delirium, — well may we ask whether this gospel of individual salvation is all the message even of this purer, earlier, more catholic Vedanta. If so, then Vedanta at its best is a gospel for the saint, the ascetic, the monk, the solitary, but it has not a message which the widening consciousness of the world can joyfully accept as the word for which it was waiting. For there is evidently something vital that has escaped it, a profound word of the riddle of existence from which it has turned its eyes or which it was unable or thought it not worth while to solve.

Now certainly there is an emphasis in the Upanishads increasing steadily as time goes on into an over-emphasis, on the salvation of the individual, on his rejection of the lower cosmic life. This note increases in them as they become later in date, it swells afterwards into the rejection of all cosmic life whatever and that becomes finally in later Hinduism almost the one dominant and all-challenging cry. It does not exist in the earlier Vedic revelation where individual salvation is regarded as a means towards a great cosmic victory, the eventual conquest of heaven and earth by the superconscient Truth and Bliss and those who have achieved the victory in the past are the conscious helpers of their yet battling posterity. If this earlier note is missing in the Upanishads, then, — for great as are these Scriptures, luminous, profound, sublime in their unsurpassed truth, beauty and power, yet it is only the ignorant soul that will make itself the slave of a book, — then in using them as an aid to knowledge we must insistently call back that earlier missing note, we must seek elsewhere a solution for the word of the riddle that has been ignored. The Upanishad alone of extant scriptures gives us without veil or stinting, with plenitude and a noble catholicity the truth of the

Brahman; its aid to humanity is therefore indispensable. Only, where anything essential is missing, we must go beyond the Upanishads to seek it, — as for instance when we add to its emphasis on divine knowledge the indispensable ardent emphasis of the later teachings upon divine love and the high emphasis of the Veda upon divine works.

The Vedic gospel of a supreme victory in heaven and on earth for the divine in man, the Christian gospel of a kingdom of God and divine city upon earth, the Puranic idea of progressing Avataras ending in the kingdom of the perfect and the restoration of the Golden Age, not only contain behind their forms a profound truth, but they are necessary to the religious sense in mankind. Without it the teaching of the vanity of human life and of a passionate fleeing and renunciation can only be powerful in passing epochs or else on the few strong souls in each age that are really capable of these things. The rest of humanity will either reject the creed which makes that its foundation or ignore it in practice while professing it in precept or else must sink under the weight of its own impotence and the sense of the illusion of life or of the curse of God upon the world as mediaeval Christendom sank into ignorance and obscurantism or later India into stagnant torpor and the pettiness of a life of aimless egoism. The promise for the individual is well, but the promise for the race is also needed. Our father Heaven must remain bright with the hope of deliverance, but also our mother Earth must not feel herself for ever accursed.

It was necessary at one time to insist even exclusively on the idea of individual salvation so that the sense of a Beyond might be driven into man's mentality, as it was necessary at one time to insist on a heaven of joys for the virtuous and pious so that man might be drawn by that shining bait towards the practice of religion and the suppression of his unbridled animality. But as the lures of earth have to be conquered, so also have the lures of heaven. The lure of a pleasant Paradise of the rewards of virtue has been rejected by man; the Upanishads belittled it ages ago in India and it is now no longer dominant in the mind of the people; the similar lure in popular Christianity and popular Islam has no meaning for the conscience of modern humanity.

The lure of a release from birth and death and withdrawal from the cosmic labour must also be rejected, as it was rejected by Mahayanist Buddhism which held compassion and helpfulness to be greater than Nirvana. As the virtues we practise must be done without demand of earthly or heavenly reward, so the salvation we seek must be purely internal and impersonal; it must be the release from egoism, the union with the Divine, the realisation of our universality as well as our transcendence, and no salvation should be valued which takes us away from the love of God in his manifestation and the help we can give to the world. If need be, it must be taught for a time, "Better this hell with our other suffering selves than a solitary salvation."

Fortunately, there is no need to go to such lengths and deny one side of the truth in order to establish another. The Upanishad itself suggests the door of escape from any over-emphasis in its own statement of the truth. For the man who knows and possesses the supreme Brahman as the transcendent Beatitude becomes a centre of that delight to which all his fellows shall come, a well from which they can draw the divine waters. Here is the clue that we need. The connection with the universe is preserved for the one reason which supremely justifies that connection; it must subsist not from the desire of personal earthly joy, as with those who are still bound, but for help to all creatures. Two then are the objects of the high-reaching soul, to attain the Supreme and to be for ever for the good of all the world, — even as Brahman Himself; whether here or elsewhere, does not essentially matter. Still where the struggle is thickest, there should be the hero of the spirit, that is surely the highest choice of the son of Immortality; the earth calls most, because it has most need of him, to the soul that has become one with the universe.

And the nature of the highest good that can be done is also indicated, — though other lower forms of help are not therefore excluded. To assist in the lesser victories of the gods which must prepare the supreme victory of the Brahman may well be and must be in some way or other a part of our task; but the greatest helpfulness of all is this, to be a human centre of the Light, the Glory, the Bliss, the Strength, the Knowledge of the Divine

Existence, one through whom it shall communicate itself lavishly to other men and attract by its magnet of delight their souls to that which is the Highest.

MANDUKYA UPANISHAD

Mundaka Upanishad

CHAPTER ONE : SECTION I

ब्रह्मा देवानां प्रथमः सम्बभूव विश्वस्य कर्त्ता भुवनस्य गोप्ता ।
स ब्रह्मविद्यां सर्वविद्याप्रतिष्ठामथर्वाय ज्येष्ठपुत्राय प्राह ॥१॥

1. Brahma first of the Gods was born, the creator of all, the world's protector; he to Atharvan, his eldest son, declared the God-knowledge in which all sciences have their foundation.

अथर्वणे यां प्रवदेत ब्रह्माथर्वा तां पुरोवाचाङ्गिरे ब्रह्मविद्याम् ।
स भारद्वाजाय सत्यवहाय प्राह भारद्वाजोऽङ्गिरसे परावराम् ॥२॥

2. The God-knowledge by Brahma declared to Atharvan, Atharvan of old declared to Angir; he to Satyavaha the Bharadwaja told it, the Bharadwaja to Angiras, both the higher and the lower knowledge.

शौनको ह वै महाशालोऽङ्गिरसं विधिवदुपसन्नः पप्रच्छ ।
कस्मिन् नु भगवो विज्ञाते सर्वमिदं विज्ञातं भवतीति ॥३॥

3. Shaunaka, the great house-lord, came to Angiras in the due way of the disciple and asked of him, "Lord, by knowing what does all this that is become known?"

तस्मै स होवाच — द्वे विद्ये वेदितव्ये इति ह स्म यद् ब्रह्मविदो
वदन्ति परा चैवापरा च ॥४॥

4. To him thus spoke Angiras: Twofold is the knowledge that must be known of which the knowers of the Brahman tell, the higher and the lower knowledge.

तत्रापरा ऋग्वेदो यजुर्वेदः सामवेदोऽथर्ववेदः शिक्षा कल्पो व्याकरणं
निरुक्तं छन्दो ज्योतिषमिति । अथ परा यया तदक्षरमधिगम्यते ॥५॥

5. Of which the lower, the Rig-veda and the Yajur-veda,
    and the Sama-veda and the Atharva-veda, chanting, ritual,
    grammar, etymological interpretation, and prosody and
    astronomy. And then the higher by which is known the
    Immutable.

यत् तदद्रेश्यमग्राह्यमगोत्रमवर्णमचक्षुःश्रोत्रं तदपाणिपादम् ।
नित्यं विभुं सर्वगतं सुसूक्ष्मं तदव्ययं यद् भूतयोनिं परिपश्यन्ति धीराः ॥६॥

6. That the invisible, that the unseizable, without connections,
    without hue, without eye or ear, that which is without
    hands or feet, eternal, pervading, which is in all things and
    impalpable, that which is Imperishable, that which is the
    womb of creatures sages behold everywhere.

यथोर्णनाभिः सृजते गृह्णते च यथा पृथिव्यामोषधयः सम्भवन्ति ।
यथा सतः पुरुषात् केशलोमानि तथाक्षरात् सम्भवतीह विश्वम् ॥७॥

7. As the spider puts out and gathers in, as herbs spring up
    upon the earth, as hair of head and body grow from a living
    man, so here all is born from the Immutable.

तपसा चीयते ब्रह्म ततोऽन्नमभिजायते ।
अन्नात् प्राणो मनः सत्यं लोकाः कर्मसु चामृतम् ॥८॥

8. Brahman grows by his energy at work, and then from Him
    is Matter born, and out of Matter life, and mind and truth
    and the worlds, and in works immortality.

यः सर्वज्ञः सर्वविद् यस्य ज्ञानमयं तपः ।
तस्मादेतद् ब्रह्म नाम रूपमन्नं च जायते ॥९॥

9. He who is the Omniscient, the all-wise, He whose energy
    is all made of knowledge, from Him is born this that is
    Brahman here, this Name and Form and Matter.

तदेतत् सत्यं मन्त्रेषु कर्माणि कवयो
यान्यपश्यंस्तानि त्रेतायां बहुधा सन्ततानि ।
तान्याचरथ नियतं सत्यकामा
एष वः पन्थाः सुकृतस्य लोके ॥१॥

1. This is That, the Truth of things: works which the sages beheld in the Mantras[1] were in the Treta[2] manifoldly extended. Works do ye perform religiously with one passion for the Truth; this is your road to the heaven of good deeds.

यदा लेलायते ह्यर्चिः समिद्धे हव्यवाहने ।
तदाज्यभागावन्तरेणाहुतीः प्रतिपादयेच्छ्रद्धयाहुतम् ॥२॥

2. When the fire of the sacrifice is kindled and the flame sways and quivers, then between the double pourings of butter cast therein with faith thy offerings.

यस्याग्निहोत्रमदर्शमपौर्णमास-
मचातुर्मास्यमनाग्रयणमतिथिवर्जितं च ।
अहुतमवैश्वदेवमविधिना हुत-
मासप्तमांस्तस्य लोकान् हिनस्ति ॥३॥

3. For he whose altar-fires are empty of the new-moon offering and the full-moon offering and the offering of the rains and the offering of the first fruits, or unfed, or fed without right ritual, or without guests or without the dues to the Vishwa-Devas, destroys his hope of all the seven worlds.

काली कराली च मनोजवा च सुलोहिता या च सुधूम्रवर्णा ।
स्फुलिङ्गिनी विश्वरुची च देवी लेलायमाना इति सप्त जिह्वाः ॥४॥

4. Kali, the black, Karali, the terrible, Manojava, thought-swift, Sulohita, blood-red, Sudhumravarna, smoke-hued, Sphulingini, scattering sparks, Vishwaruchi, the all-beauti-

---

[1] The inspired verses of the Veda. [2] The second of the four ages.

ful, these are the seven swaying tongues of the fire.

एतेषु यश्चरते भ्राजमानेषु यथाकालं चाहुतयो ह्याददायन् ।
तं नयन्त्येताः सूर्यस्य रश्मयो यत्र देवानां पतिरेकोऽधिवासः ॥५॥

5. He who in these when they are blazing bright performs the rites, in their due season, him his fires of sacrifice take and they lead him, these rays of the sun, there where the Over-lord of the Gods is the Inhabitant on high.

एह्येहीति तमाहुतयः सुवर्चसः सूर्यस्य रश्मिभिर्यजमानं वहन्ति ।
प्रियां वाचमभिवदन्त्योऽर्चयन्त्य एष वः पुण्यः सुकृतो ब्रह्मलोकः ॥६॥

6. "Come with us", "Come with us", they cry to him, these luminous fires of sacrifice and they bear him by the rays of the sun speaking to him pleasant words of sweetness, doing him homage, "This is your holy world of Brahman and the heaven of your righteousness."

प्लवा ह्येते अदृढा यज्ञरूपा अष्टादशोक्तमवरं येषु कर्म ।
एतच्छ्रेयो येऽभिनन्दन्ति मूढा जरामृत्युं ते पुनरेवापि यन्ति ॥७॥

7. But frail are the ships of sacrifice, frail these forms of sacrifice, all the eighteen of them, in which are declared the lower works; fools are they who hail them as the highest good and they come yet again to this world of age and death.

अविद्यायामन्तरे वर्तमानाः स्वयं धीराः पण्डितं मन्यमानाः ।
जङ्घन्यमानाः परियन्ति मूढा अन्धेनैव नीयमाना यथान्धाः ॥८॥

8. They who dwell shut within the ignorance and they hold themselves for learned men thinking, "We, even we are the wise and the sages" — fools are they and they wander around beaten and stumbling like blind men led by the blind.

अविद्यायां बहुधा वर्तमाना वयं कृतार्था इत्यभिमन्यन्ति बालाः ।
यत् कर्मिणो न प्रवेदयन्ति रागात् तेनातुराः क्षीणलोकाश्च्यवन्ते ॥९॥

9. They dwell in many bonds of the ignorance, children thinking, "We have achieved our aim of Paradise"; for when the
men of works are held by their affections, and arrive not at
the Knowledge, then they are overtaken by anguish, then
their Paradise wastes by enjoying and they fall from their
heavens.

इष्टापूर्तं मन्यमाना वरिष्ठं नान्यच्छ्रेयो वेदयन्ते प्रमूढाः ।
नाकस्य पृष्ठे ते सुकृतेऽनुभूत्वेमं लोकं हीनतरं वा विशन्ति ॥१०॥

10. Minds bewildered who hold the oblation offered and the
well dug for the greatest righteousness and know not any
other highest good, on the back of heaven they enjoy the
world won by their righteousness and enter again this or
even a lower world.

तपःश्रद्धे ये ह्युपवसन्त्यरण्ये शान्ता विद्वांसो भैक्ष्यचर्यां चरन्तः ।
सूर्यद्वारेण ते विरजाः प्रयान्ति यत्रामृतः स पुरुषो ह्यव्ययात्मा ॥११॥

11. But they who in the forest follow after faith and self-
discipline, calm and full of knowledge, living upon alms, cast
from them the dust of their passions, and through the gate
of the Sun they pass on there where is the Immortal, the
Spirit, the Self undecaying and imperishable.

परीक्ष्य लोकान् कर्मचितान् ब्राह्मणो निर्वेदमायान्नास्त्यकृतः कृतेन ।
तद्विज्ञानार्थं स गुरुमेवाभिगच्छेत् समित्पाणिः श्रोत्रियं ब्रह्मनिष्ठम् ॥१२॥

12. The seeker of the Brahman, having put to the test the worlds
piled up by works, arrives at world-distaste, for not by
work done is reached He who is Uncreated.[1] For the knowledge of That, let him approach, fuel in hand, a Guru, one
who is learned in the Veda and is devoted to contemplation
of the Brahman.

---

[1] Or, "He, the uncreated, lives not by that which is made." Literally, "not by the made
(or, by that which is done) the Unmade (He who is uncreated)."

तस्मै स विद्वानुपसन्नाय सम्यक् प्रशान्तचित्ताय शमान्विताय ।
येनाक्षरं पुरुषं वेद सत्यं प्रोवाच तां तत्त्वतो ब्रह्मविद्याम् ॥१३॥

13. To him because he has taken entire refuge with him, with a heart tranquillised and a spirit at peace, that man of know-ledge declares in its principles the science of the Brahman by which one comes to know the Immutable Spirit, the True and Real.

तदेतत् सत्यं यथा सुदीप्तात् पावकाद्
विस्फुलिङ्गाः सहस्रशः प्रभवन्ते सरूपाः ।
तथाक्षराद् विविधाः सोम्य भावाः
प्रजायन्ते तत्र चैवापि यन्ति ॥१॥

1. This is That, the Truth of things: as from one high-kindled
   fire thousands of different sparks are born and all have the
   same form of fire, so, O fair son, from the immutable
   manifold becomings are born and even into that they depart.

दिव्यो ह्यमूर्तः पुरुषः स बाह्याभ्यन्तरो ह्यजः ।
अप्राणो ह्यमनाः शुभ्रो ह्यक्षरात् परतः परः ॥२॥

2. He, the divine, the formless Spirit, even He is the outward
   and the inward and He the Unborn; He is beyond life, beyond mind, luminous, Supreme beyond the immutable.

एतस्माज्जायते प्राणो मनः सर्वेन्द्रियाणि च ।
खं वायुर्ज्योतिरापः पृथिवी विश्वस्य धारिणी ॥३॥

3. Life and mind and the senses are born from Him and the
   sky, and the wind, and light, and the waters and earth up-
   holding all that is.

अग्निर्मूर्धा चक्षुषी चन्द्रसूर्यौ दिशः श्रोत्रे वाग् विवृताश्च वेदाः ।
वायुः प्राणो हृदयं विश्वमस्य पद्भ्यां पृथिवी ह्येष सर्वभूतान्तरात्मा ॥४॥

4. Fire is the head of Him and His eyes are the Sun and Moon,
   the quarters His organs of hearing and the revealed Vedas
   are His voice, air is His breath, the universe is His heart,
   Earth lies at His feet. He is the inner Self in all beings.

तस्मादग्निः समिधो यस्य सूर्यः सोमात् पर्जन्य ओषधयः पृथिव्याम् ।
पुमान् रेतः सिञ्चति योषितायां बह्वीः प्रजाः पुरुषात् सम्प्रसूताः ॥५॥

5. From Him is fire, of which the Sun is the fuel, then rain
    from the Soma, herbs upon the earth, and the male casts
    his seed into woman: thus are these many peoples born
    from the Spirit.

तस्मादृचः साम यजूंषि दीक्षा यज्ञाश्च सर्वे क्रतवो दक्षिणाश्च ।
संवत्सरश्च यजमानश्च लोकाः सोमो यत्र पवते यत्र सूर्यः ॥६॥

6. From Him are the hymns of the Rig-veda, the Sama and
    the Yajur, initiation, and all sacrifices and works of sacrifice,
    and dues given, the year and the giver of the sacrifice and
    the worlds, on which the moon shines and the sun.

तस्माच्च देवा बहुधा सम्प्रसूताः साध्या मनुष्याः पशवो वयांसि ।
प्राणापानौ व्रीहियवौ तपश्च श्रद्धा सत्यं ब्रह्मचर्यं विधिश्च ॥७॥

7. And from Him have issued many gods, and demi-gods
    and men and beasts and birds, the main breath and down-
    ward breath, and rice and barley, and askesis and faith and
    Truth, and chastity and rule of right practice.

सप्त प्राणाः प्रभवन्ति तस्मात् सप्तार्चिषः समिधः सप्त होमाः ।
सप्त इमे लोका येषु चरन्ति प्राणा गुहाशया निहिताः सप्त सप्त ॥८॥

8. The seven breaths are born from Him and the seven lights
    and kinds of fuel and the seven oblations and these seven
    worlds in which move the life-breaths set within with the
    secret heart for their dwelling-place, seven and seven.

अतः समुद्रा गिरयश्च सर्वेऽस्मात् स्यन्दन्ते सिन्धवः सर्वरूपाः ।
अतश्च सर्वा ओषधयो रसश्च येनैष भूतैस्तिष्ठते ह्यन्तरात्मा ॥९॥

9. From Him are the oceans and all these mountains and from
    Him flow rivers of all forms, and from Him are all plants,
    and sensible delight which makes the soul to abide with the
    material elements.

पुरुष एवेदं विश्वं कर्म तपो ब्रह्म परामृतम् ।
एतद् यो वेद निहितं गुहायां
सोऽविद्याग्रन्थि विकिरतीह सोम्य ॥१०॥

10. The Spirit is all this universe; He is works and askesis and
the Brahman, supreme and immortal. O fair son, he who
knows this hidden in the secret heart, scatters even here in
this world the knot of the Ignorance.

आविः सन्निहितं गुहाचरं नाम
महत् पदमत्रैतत् समर्पितम् ।
एजत् प्राणन्निमिषच्च यदेतज्जानथ सदस-
द्वरेण्यं परं विज्ञानाद् यद् वरिष्ठं प्रजानाम् ॥१॥

1. Manifested, it is here set close within, moving in the secret heart, this is the mighty foundation and into it is consigned all that moves and breathes and sees. This that is that great foundation here, know, as the Is and Is-not, the supremely desirable, greatest and the Most High, beyond the knowledge of creatures.

यदर्चिमद् यदणुभ्योऽणु च
यस्मिंल्लोका निहिता लोकिनश्च ।
तदेतदक्षरं ब्रह्म स प्राणस्तदु वाङ्मनः
तदेतत् सत्यं तदमृतं तद् वेद्ध्यं सोम्य विद्धि ॥२॥

2. That which is the Luminous, that which is smaller than the atoms, that in which are set the worlds and their peoples, That is This, — it is Brahman immutable: life is That, it is speech and mind. That is This, the True and Real, it is That which is immortal: it is into That that thou must pierce, O fair son, into That penetrate.

धनु गृ्हीत्वौपनिषदं महास्त्रं शरं ह्युपासानिशितं सन्धयीत ।
आयम्य तद्भावगतेन चेतसा लक्ष्यं तदेवाक्षरं सोम्य विद्धि ॥३॥

3. Take up the bow of the Upanishad, that mighty weapon, set to it an arrow sharpened by adoration, draw the bow with a heart wholly devoted to the contemplation of That, and O fair son, penetrate into That as thy target, even into the Immutable.

प्रणवो धनुः शरो ह्यात्मा ब्रह्म तल्लक्ष्यमुच्यते ।
अप्रमत्तेन वेद्ध्यं शरवत् तन्मयो भवेत् ॥४॥

4. OM is the bow and the soul is the arrow, and That, even the Brahman, is spoken of as the target. That must be pierced with an unfaltering aim; one must be absorbed into That as an arrow is lost in its target.

यस्मिन् द्यौः पृथिवी चान्तरिक्षमोतं मनः सह प्राणैश्च सर्वैः ।
तमेवैकं जानथ आत्मानमन्या वाचो विमुञ्चथामृतस्यैष सेतुः ॥५॥

5. He in whom are inwoven heaven and earth and the mid-region, and mind with all the life-currents, Him know to be the one Self; other words put away from you: this is the bridge to immortality.

अरा इव रथनाभौ संहता यत्र नाडघः
स एषोऽन्तश्चरते बहुधा जायमानः ।
ओमित्येवं ध्यायथ आत्मानं
स्वस्ति वः पाराय तमसः परस्तात् ॥६॥

6. Where the nerves are brought close together like the spokes in the nave of a chariot-wheel, this is He that moves within, — there is He manifoldly born. Meditate on the Self as OM and happy be your passage to the other shore beyond the darkness.

यः सर्वज्ञः सर्वविद् यस्यैष महिमा भुवि ।
दिव्ये ब्रह्मपुरे ह्येष व्योम्न्यात्मा प्रतिष्ठितः ॥७॥

7. The Omniscient, the All-wise, whose is this might and majesty upon the earth, is this Self enthroned in the Divine city of the Brahman, in his ethereal heaven.

मनोमयः प्राणशरीरनेता
प्रतिष्ठितोऽन्ने हृदयं सन्निधाय ।
तद् विज्ञानेन परिपश्यन्ति धीरा
आनन्दरूपममृतं यद् विभाति ॥८॥

8. A mental being, leader of the life and the body, has set a heart in matter, in matter he has taken his firm foundation.

By its knowing the wise see everywhere around them That
which shines in its effulgence, a shape of Bliss and Immortal.

भिद्यते हृदयग्रन्थिश्छिद्यन्ते सर्वसंशयाः ।
क्षीयन्ते चास्य कर्माणि तस्मिन् दृष्टे पराबरे ॥९॥

9. The knot of the heart-strings is rent, cut away are all doubts,
and a man's works are spent and perish, when is seen That
which is at once the being below and the Supreme.

हिरण्मये परे कोशे विरजं ब्रह्म निष्कलम् ।
तच्छुभ्रं ज्योतिषां ज्योतिस्तद् यदात्मविदो विदुः ॥१०॥

10. In a supreme golden sheath the Brahman lies, stainless, without parts. A Splendour is That, It is the Light of Lights, It is
That which the self-knowers know.

न तत्र सूर्यो भाति न चन्द्रतारकं
नेमा विद्युतो भान्ति कुतोऽयमग्निः ।
तमेव भान्तमनुभाति सर्वं
तस्य भासा सर्वमिदं विभाति ॥११॥

11. There the sun shines not and the moon has no splendour and
the stars are blind; there these lightnings flash not, how then
shall burn this earthly fire? All that shines is but the shadow
of His shining; all this universe is effulgent with His light.

ब्रह्मैवेदममृतं पुरस्ताद् ब्रह्म पश्चाद् ब्रह्म दक्षिणतश्चोत्तरेण ।
अधश्चोर्ध्वं च प्रसृतं ब्रह्मैवेदं विश्वमिदं वरिष्ठम् ॥१२॥

12. All this is Brahman immortal, naught else; Brahman is in
front of us, Brahman behind us, and to the south of us and to
the north of us[1] and below us and above us; it stretches
everywhere. All this is Brahman alone, all this magnificent
universe.

---

[1] Or, "to the right and the left of us".

द्वा सुपर्णा सयुजा सखाया समानं वृक्षं परिषस्वजाते ।
तयोरन्यः पिप्पलं स्वाद्वत्त्यनश्नन्नन्यो अभिचाकशीति ॥१॥

1. Two birds, beautiful of wing, close companions, cling to one
   common tree: of the two one eats the sweet fruit of the tree,
   the other eats not but watches his fellow.

समाने वृक्षे पुरुषो निमग्नोऽनीशया शोचति मुह्यमानः ।
जुष्टं यदा पश्यत्यन्यमीशमस्य महिमानमिति वीतशोकः ॥२॥

2. The soul is the bird that sits immersed on the one common
   tree; but because he is not lord he is bewildered and has
   sorrow. But when he sees that other who is the Lord and
   beloved, he knows that all is His greatness and his sorrow
   passes away from him.

यदा पश्यः पश्यते रुक्मवर्णं कर्तारमीशं पुरुषं ब्रह्मयोनिम् ।
तदा विद्वान् पुण्यपापे विधूय निरञ्जनः परमं साम्यमुपैति ॥३॥

3. When, a seer, he sees the Golden-hued, the maker, the Lord,
   the Spirit who is the source of Brahman,[1] then he becomes
   the knower and shakes from his wings sin and virtue; pure of
   all stain he reaches the supreme identity.[2]

प्राणो ह्येष यः सर्वभूतैर्विभाति
विजानन् विद्वान् भवते नातिवादी ।
आत्मक्रीड आत्मरतिः
क्रियावानेष ब्रह्मविदां वरिष्ठः ॥४॥

4. This is the life in things that shines manifested by all these
   beings; a man of knowledge coming wholly to know this,
   draws back from creeds and too much disputings. In the

---

[1] Or, "whose source is Brahman"; Shankara admits the other meaning as an alternative,
but explains it as "the source of the lower Brahman".

[2] Or, "pure of all staining tinge he reaches to a supreme equality".

Self his delight, at play in the Self, doing works, — the best is he among the knowers of the Eternal.

सत्येन लभ्यस्तपसा ह्येष आत्मा
सम्यग्ज्ञानेन ब्रह्मचर्येण नित्यम् ।
अन्तःशरीरे ज्योतिर्मयो हि शुभ्रो
यं पश्यन्ति यतयः क्षीणदोषाः ॥५॥

5. The Self can always be won by truth, by self-discipline, by integral knowledge, by a life of purity, — this Self that is in the inner body, radiant, made all of light whom, by the perishing of their blemishes, the doers of askesis behold.

सत्यमेव जयते नानृतं सत्येन पन्था विततो देवयानः ।
येनाक्रमन्त्यृषयो ह्याप्तकामा यत्र तत् सत्यस्य परमं निधानम् ॥६॥

6. It is Truth that conquers and not falsehood; by Truth was stretched out the path of the journey of the gods, by which the sages winning their desire ascend there where Truth has its Supreme abode.

बृहच्च तद् दिव्यमचिन्त्यरूपं सूक्ष्माच्च तत् सूक्ष्मतरं विभाति ।
दूरात् सुदूरे तदिहान्तिके च पश्यत्स्विहैव निहितं गुहायाम् ॥७॥

7. Vast is That, divine, its form unthinkable; it shines out subtler than the subtle:[1] very far and farther than farness, it is here close to us, for those who have vision it is even here in this world; it is here, hidden in the secret heart.

न चक्षुषा गृह्यते नापि वाचा नान्यैर्देवैस्तपसा कर्मणा वा ।
ज्ञानप्रसादेन विशुद्धसत्त्वस्ततस्तु तं पश्यते निष्कलं ध्यायमानः ॥८॥

8. Eye cannot seize, speech cannot grasp Him, nor these other godheads; not by austerity can he be held nor by works: only when the inner being is purified by a glad serenity of

---

[1] Or, "minuter than the minute:".

knowledge, then indeed, meditating, one beholds the Spirit indivisible.

एषोऽणुरात्मा चेतसा वेदितव्यो
यस्मिन् प्राणः पञ्चधा संविवेश ।
प्राणैश्चित्तं सर्वमोतं प्रजानां
यस्मिन् विशुद्धे विभवत्येष आत्मा ॥९॥

9. This self is subtle and has to be known by a thought-mind into which the life-force has made its fivefold entry: all the conscious heart of creatures is shot through and inwoven with the currents of the life-force and only when it is purified can this Self manifest its power.[1]

यं यं लोकं मनसा संविभाति
विशुद्धसत्त्वः कामयते यांश्च कामान् ।
तं तं लोकं जयते तांश्च कामां-
स्तस्मादात्मज्ञं ह्यर्चयेद् भूतिकामः ॥१०॥

10. Whatever world the man whose inner being is purified sheds the light of his mind upon, and whatsoever desires he cherishes, that world he takes by conquest, and those desires. Then, let whosoever seeks for success and well-being approach with homage a self-knower.

---

[1] The verb *vibhavati* seems here to have a complex sense and to mean, "to manifest its full power and pervading presence".

स वेदैतत् परमं ब्रह्म धाम यत्र विश्वं निहितं भाति शुभ्रम् ।
उपासते पुरुषं ये ह्यकामास्ते शुक्रमेतदतिवर्तन्ति धीराः ॥१॥

1. He knows this supreme Brahman as the highest abiding place in which shines out, inset, the radiant world. The wise who are without desire and worship the Spirit pass beyond this sperm.[1]

कामान् यः कामयते मन्यमानः स कामभिर्जायते तत्र तत्र ।
पर्याप्तकामस्य कृतात्मनस्तु इहैव सर्वे प्रविलीयन्ति कामाः ॥२॥

2. He who cherishes desires and his mind dwells with his longings, is by his desires born again wherever they lead him, but the man who has won all his desire[2] and has found his soul, for him even here in this world vanish away all desires.

नायमात्मा प्रवचनेन लभ्यो न मेधया न बहुना श्रुतेन ।
यमेवैष वृणुते तेन लभ्यस्तस्यैष आत्मा विवृणुते तनुं स्वाम् ॥३॥

3. This Self is not won by exegesis, nor by brain-power, nor by much learning of Scripture. Only by him whom It chooses can it be won; to him this Self unveils its own body.

नायमात्मा बलहीनेन लभ्यो न च प्रमादात् तपसो वाप्यलिङ्गात् ।
एतैरुपायैर्यतते यस्तु विद्वांस्तस्यैष आत्मा विशते ब्रह्मधाम ॥४॥

4. This Self cannot be won by any who is without strength, nor with error in the seeking, nor by an askesis without the true mark: but when a man of knowledge strives by these means his Self enters into Brahman, his abiding place.

---

[1] Shankara takes it so in the sense of *semen virile*, which is the cause of birth into the cosmos. But it is possible that it means rather "pass beyond this brilliant universe"; the radiant world which has just been spoken of, to the greater Light which is its abiding place and source, the supreme Brahman.

[2] Or, "finished with desires".

संप्राप्यैनमृषयो ज्ञानतृप्ताः कृतात्मानो वीतरागाः प्रशान्ताः ।
ते सर्वगं सर्वतः प्राप्य धीरा युक्तात्मानः सर्वमेवाविशन्ति ॥५॥

5. Attaining to him, seers glad with fullness of knowledge,
perfected in the self, all passions cast from them, tranquillised, — these, the wise, come to the all-pervading from
every side, and, uniting themselves with him enter utterly
the All.

वेदान्तविज्ञानसुनिश्चितार्थाः संन्यासयोगाद् यतयः शुद्धसत्त्वाः ।
ते ब्रह्मलोकेषु परान्तकाले परामृताः परिमुच्यन्ति सर्वे ॥६॥

6. Doers of askesis who have made sure of the aim[1] of the
whole-knowledge of Vedanta, the inner being purified by the
Yoga of renunciation, all in the hour of their last end passing beyond death are released into the worlds of the
Brahman.

गताः कलाः पञ्चदश प्रतिष्ठा देवाश्च सर्वे प्रतिदेवतासु ।
कर्माणि विज्ञानमयश्च आत्मा परेऽव्यये सर्वे एकीभवन्ति ॥७॥

7. The fifteen parts return into their foundations, and all the
gods pass into their proper godheads, works and the Self of
Knowledge, — all become one in the Supreme and Imperishable.

यथा नद्यः स्यन्दमानाः समुद्रेऽस्तं गच्छन्ति नामरूपे विहाय ।
तथा विद्वान् नामरूपाद् विमुक्तः परात्परं पुरुषमुपैति दिव्यम् ॥८॥

8. As rivers in their flowing reach their home[2] in the ocean and
cast off their names and forms, even so one who knows is
delivered from name and form and reaches the Supreme
beyond the Most High, even the Divine Person.

स यो ह वै तत् परमं ब्रह्म वेद
ब्रह्मैव भवति नास्याब्रह्मवित् कुले भवति ।

---

[1] Or, "meaning". [2] Or, "come to their end".

तरति शोकं तरति पाप्मानं
गुहाग्रन्थिभ्यो विमुक्तोऽमृतो भवति ॥९॥

9. He, verily, who knows that Supreme Brahman becomes himself Brahman; in his lineage none is born who knows not the Brahman. He crosses beyond sorrow, he crosses beyond sin, he is delivered from the knotted cord of the secret heart and becomes immortal.

तदेतदृचाऽभ्युक्तम् ॥
क्रियावन्तः श्रोत्रिया ब्रह्मनिष्ठाः
स्वयं जुह्वत एकर्षि श्रद्धयन्तः ।
तेषामेवैतां ब्रह्मविद्यां वदेत
शिरोव्रतं विधिवद् यैस्तु चीर्णम् ॥१०॥

10. This is That declared by the Rig-veda. Doers of works, versed in the Veda, men absorbed in the Brahman, who putting their faith in the sole-seer offer themselves to him sacrifice, — to them one should speak this Brahman-Knowledge, men by whom the Vow of the Head has been done according to the rite.

तदेतत् सत्यमृषिरङ्गिराः पुरोवाच नैतदचीर्णव्रतोऽधीते ।
नमः परमऋषिभ्यो नमः परमऋषिभ्यः ॥११॥

11. This is That, the Truth of things which the seer Angiras spoke of old. This none learns who has not performed the Vow of the Head. Salutation to the seers supreme! Salutation to the seers supreme!

KATHA UPANISHAD

Katha Upanishad

FIRST CYCLE : FIRST CHAPTER

ॐ उशन् ह वै वाजश्रवसः सर्ववेदसं ददौ ।
तस्य ह नचिकेता नाम पुत्र आस ॥१॥

1. Vajashravasa, desiring, gave all he had. Now Vajashravasa had a son named Nachiketas.

तश्ह कुमारश् सन्तं दक्षिणासु नीयमानासु श्रद्धाऽऽविवेश ।
सोऽमन्यत ॥२॥

2. As the gifts were led past, faith took possession of him who was yet a boy unwed and he pondered:

पीतोदका जग्धतृणा दुग्धदोहा निरिन्द्रियाः ।
अनन्दा नाम ते लोकास्तान्स गच्छति ता ददत् ॥३॥

3. "Cattle that have drunk their water, eaten their grass, yielded their milk, worn out their organs, of undelight are the worlds which he reaches who gives such as these."

स होवाच पितरं तत कस्मै मां दास्यसीति ।
द्वितीयं तृतीयं तं होवाच मृत्यवे त्वा ददामीति ॥४॥

4. He said to his father, "Me, O my father, to whom wilt thou give?" A second time and a third he said it, and he replied, "To Death I give thee."

बहूनामेमि प्रथमो बहूनामेमि मध्यमः ।
किं स्विद्यमस्य कर्तव्यं यन्मयाद्य करिष्यति ॥५॥

5. "Among many I walk the first, among many I walk the midmost; something Death means to do which today by me he will accomplish.

अनुपश्य यथा पूर्वे प्रतिपश्य तथाऽपरे ।
सस्यमिव मर्त्यः पच्यते सस्यमिवाजायते पुनः ॥६॥

6. "Look back and see, even as were the men of old, — look round! — even so are they that have come after. Mortal man withers like the fruits of the field and like the fruits of the field he is born again."

वैश्वानरः प्रविशत्यतिथिर्ब्राह्मणो गृहान् ।
तस्यैतां शान्ति कुर्वन्ति हर वैवस्वतोदकम् ॥७॥

His attendants say to Yama:

7. "Fire is the Brahmin who enters as a guest the houses of men; him thus they appease. Bring, O son of Vivasvan,[1] the water of the guest-rite.

आशाप्रतीक्षे संगतं सूनृतां चेष्टापूर्ते पुत्रपशूंश्च सर्वान् ।
एतद् वृङ्क्ते पुरुषस्याल्पमेधसो यस्यानश्नन्नवसति ब्राह्मणो गृहे ॥८॥

8. "That man of little understanding in whose house a Brahmin dwells fasting, all his hope and his expectation and all he has gained and the good and truth that he has spoken and the wells he has dug and the sacrifices he has offered and all his sons and his cattle are torn from him by that guest unhonoured."

तिस्रो रात्रीर्यदवात्सीर्गृहे मेऽनश्नन्ब्रह्मन्नतिथिर्नमस्यः ।
नमस्तेऽस्तु ब्रह्मन्स्वस्ति मेऽस्तु तस्मात्प्रति श्रीन्वरान्वृणीष्व ॥९॥

Yama speaks:

9. "Because for three nights thou hast dwelt in my house, O Brahmin, a guest worthy of reverence, — salutation to thee, O Brahmin, on me let there be the weal, — therefore three boons do thou choose, for each night a boon."

---

[1] Yama, lord of death, is also the master of the Law in the world, and he is therefore the child of the Sun, luminous Master of Truth from which the Law is born.

शान्तसंकल्पः सुमना यथा स्याद्वीतमन्युर्गौतमो माभि मृत्यो ।
त्वत्प्रसृष्टं माभिवदेत्प्रतीत एतत्त्रयाणां प्रथमं वरं वृणे ॥१०॥

Nachiketas speaks:

"Tranquillised in his thought and serene of mind be the
Gautama, my father, let his passion over me pass away
from him; assured in heart let him greet me from thy grasp
delivered; this boon I choose, the first of three."

यथा पुरस्ताद् भविता प्रतीत औद्दालकिरारुणिर्मंत्रप्रसृष्टः ।
सुखं रात्रीः शयिता वीतमन्युस्त्वां ददृशिवान्मृत्युमुखात्प्रमुक्तम् ॥११॥

Yama speaks:

11. "Even as before assured in heart and by me released shall he
be, Auddalaki Aruni, thy father; sweetly shall he sleep
through the nights and his passion shall pass away from him,
having seen thee from death's jaws delivered."

स्वर्गे लोके न भयं किंचनास्ति न तत्र त्वं न जरया बिभेति ।
उभे तीर्त्वाऽशनायापिपासे शोकातिगो मोदते स्वर्गलोके ॥१२॥

Nachiketas speaks:

12. "In heaven fear is not at all, in heaven, O Death, thou art
not, nor old age and its terrors; crossing over hunger and
thirst as over two rivers, leaving sorrow behind the soul in
heaven rejoices.

स त्वाग्निं स्वर्ग्यमध्येषि मृत्यो प्रब्रूहि त्वं श्रद्दधानाय मह्यम् ।
स्वर्गलोका अमृतत्वं भजन्त एतद् द्वितीयेन वृणे वरेण ॥१३॥

13. "Therefore that heavenly Flame[1] which thou, O Death,
studiest, expound unto me, for I believe. They who win
their world of heaven, have immortality for their portion.
This for the second boon I have chosen."

---

[1] The celestial force concealed subsciently in man's mortality by the kindling of which
and its right ordering man transcends his earthly nature; not the physical flame of the external
sacrifice to which these profound phrases are inapplicable.

प्र ते ब्रवीमि तदु मे निबोध स्वर्ग्यमग्निं नचिकेतः प्रजानन् ।
अनन्तलोकाप्तिमथो प्रतिष्ठां विद्धि त्वमेतं निहितं गुहायाम् ॥१४॥

Yama speaks:

14. "Hearken to me and understand, O Nachiketas; I declare to thee that heavenly Flame, for I know it. Know this to be the possession of infinite existence and the foundation and the thing hidden in the secret cave of our being."

लोकादिमग्निं तमुवाच तस्मै या इष्टका यावतीर्वा यथा वा ।
स चापि तत्प्रत्यवदद्यथोक्तमथास्य मृत्युः पुनरेवाह तुष्टः ॥१५॥

15. Of the Flame that is the world's beginning[1] he told him and what are the bricks to him and how many and the way of their setting; and Nachiketas too repeated it even as it was told; then Death was pleased and said to him yet farther;

तमब्रवीत्प्रीयमाणो महात्मा वरं तवेहाद्य ददामि भूयः ।
तवैव नाम्ना भवितायमग्निः सृङ्कां चेमामनेकरूपां गृहाण ॥१६॥

16. Yea, the Great Soul was gratified and said to him, "Yet a farther boon today I give thee; for even by thy name shall this Fire be called; this necklace also take unto thee, a necklace[2] of many figures.

त्रिणाचिकेतस्त्रिभिरेत्य सन्धिं त्रिकर्मकृत्तरति जन्ममृत्यू ।
ब्रह्मजज्ञं देवमीड्यं विदित्वा निचाय्येमाँ शान्तिमत्यन्तमेति ॥१७॥

17. "Whoso lights the three fires[3] of Nachiketas and comes to union with the Three[4] and does the triple works,[5] beyond

---

[1] The Divine Force concealed in the subconscient is that which has originated and built up the worlds. At the other end in the superconscient it reveals itself as the Divine Being, Lord and Knower who has manifested Himself out of the Brahman.

[2] The necklace of many figures is Prakriti, creative Nature which comes under the control of the soul that has attained to the divine existence.

[3] Probably, the Divine Force utilised to raise to divinity the triple being of man.

[4] Possibly, the three Purushas, soul-states or Personalities of the Divine Being, indicated by the three letters A U M. The highest Brahman is beyond the three letters of the mystic syllable.

[5] The sacrifice of the lower existence to the divine, consummated on the three planes of

birth and death he crosses; for he finds the God of our adoration, the Knower[1] who is born from the Brahman, whom having beheld he attains to surpassing peace.

त्रिणाचिकेतस्त्रयमेतद्विदित्वा य एवं विद्वाँश्चिनुते नाचिकेतम् ।
स मृत्युपाशान्पुरतः प्रणोद्य शोकातिगो मोदते स्वर्गलोके ॥१८॥

18. "When a man has the three flames of Nachiketas and knows this that is Triple, when so knowing he beholds the Flame of Nachiketas, then he thrusts from in front of him the meshes of the snare of death; leaving sorrow behind him he in heaven rejoices.

एष तेऽग्निनॅचिकेतः स्वर्ग्यो यमवृणीथा द्वितीयेन वरेण ।
एतमग्निं तवॅव प्रवक्ष्यन्ति जनासस्तृतीयं वरं नचिकेतो वृणीष्व ॥१९॥

19. "This is the heavenly Flame, O Nachiketas, which thou hast chosen for the second boon; of this Flame the peoples shall speak that it is thine indeed. A third boon choose, O Nachiketas."

येयं प्रेते विचिकित्सा मनुष्येऽस्तीत्येके नायमस्तीति चॅके ।
एतद्विद्यामनुशिष्टस्त्वयाऽहं वराणामेष वरस्तृतीयः ॥२०॥

Nachiketas speaks:

20. "This debate that there is over the man who has passed and some say 'This he is not' and some that he is, that, taught by thee, I would know; this is the third boon of the boons of my choosing."

देवॅरत्रापि विचिकित्सितं पुरा न हि सुविज्ञेयमणुरेष धर्मः ।
अन्यं वरं नचिकेतो वृणीष्व मा मोपरोत्सीरति मा सृजैनम् ॥२१॥

Yama speaks:

21. "Even by the gods was this debated of old; for it is not

---
man's physical, vital and mental consciousness.

[1] The Purusha or Divine Being, Knower of the Field, who dwells within all and for whose pleasure Prakriti fulfils the cosmic play.

easy of knowledge, since very subtle is the law of it. Another boon choose, O Nachiketas; importune me not, nor urge me; this, this abandon."

देवैरत्रापि विचिकित्सितं किल त्वं च मृत्यो यन्न सुज्ञेयमात्थ ।
वक्ता चास्य त्वादृगन्यो न लभ्यो नान्यो वरस्तुल्य एतस्य कश्चित् ॥२२॥

Nachiketas speaks:

22. "Even by the gods was this debated, it is sure, and thou thyself hast said that it is not easy of knowledge; never shall I find another like thee[1] to tell of it, nor is there any other boon that is its equal."

शतायुषः पुत्रपौत्रान्वृणीष्व बहून्पशून्हस्तिहिरण्यमश्वान् ।
भूमेर्महदायतनं वृणीष्व स्वयं च जीव शरदो यावदिच्छसि ॥२३॥

Yama speaks:

23. "Choose sons and grandsons who shall live each a hundred years, choose much cattle and elephants and gold and horses; choose a mighty reach of earth and thyself live for as many years as thou listest.

एतत्तुल्यं यदि मन्यसे वरं वृणीष्व वित्तं चिरजीविकां च ।
महाभूमौ नचिकेतस्त्वमेधि कामानां त्वा कामभाजं करोमि ॥२४॥

24. "This boon if thou deemest equal to that of thy asking, choose wealth and long living; possess thou, O Nachiketas, a mighty country; I give thee thy desire of all desirable things for thy portion.

ये ये कामा दुर्लभा मर्त्यलोके सर्वान्कामाँश्छन्दतः प्रार्थयस्व ।
इमा रामाः सरथाः सतूर्या नहीदृशा लम्भनीया मनुष्यैः ।
आभिर्मत्प्रत्ताभिः परिचारयस्व नचिकेतो मरणं मानुप्राक्षीः ॥२५॥

25. "Yea, all desires that are hard to win in the world of mortals, all demand at thy pleasure; lo, these delectable women with

---

[1] Yama is the knower and keeper of the cosmic Law through which the soul has to rise by death and life to the freedom of Immortality.

their chariots and their bugles, whose like are not to be won by men, these I will give thee, live with them for thy hand-maidens. But of death question not, O Nachiketas."

श्वोभावा मर्त्यस्य यदन्तकैतत्सर्वेन्द्रियाणां जरयन्ति तेजः।
अपि सर्वं जीवितमल्पमेव तवैव वाहास्तव नृत्यगीते ॥२६॥

Nachiketas speaks:

26. "Until the morrow mortal man has these things, O Ender, and they wear away all this keenness and glory of his senses; nay, all life is even for a little. Thine are these chariots and thine the dancing of these women and their singing.

न वित्तेन तर्पणीयो मनुष्यो लप्स्यामहे वित्तमद्राक्ष्म चेत्त्वा।
जीविष्यामो यावदीशिष्यसि त्वं वरस्तु मे वरणीयः स एव ॥२७॥

27. "Man is not to be satisfied by riches, and riches we shall have if we have beheld thee and shall live as long as thou shalt be lord of us.[1] This boon and no other is for my choosing.

अजीर्यताममृतानामुपेत्य जीर्यन्मर्त्यः क्वधःस्थः प्रजानन्।
अभिध्यायन्वर्णरतिप्रमोदानतिदीर्घे जीविते को रमेत ॥२८॥

28. "Who that is a mortal man and grows old and dwells down upon the unhappy earth, when he has come into the presence of the ageless Immortals and knows, yea, who when he looks very close at beauty and enjoyment and pleasure, can take delight in overlong living?

यस्मिन्निदं विचिकित्सन्ति मृत्यो यत्साम्पराये महति ब्रूहि नस्तत्।
योऽयं वरो गूढमनुप्रविष्टो नान्यं तस्मान्नचिकेता वृणीते ॥२९॥

29. "This of which they thus debate, O Death, declare to me, even that which is in the great passage; than this boon which enters in into the secret that is hidden from us, no other chooses Nachiketas."

---

[1] Life being a figure of death and Death of life, the only true existence is the infinite, divine and immortal.

अन्यच्छ्रेयोऽन्यदुतैव प्रेयस्ते उभे नानार्थे पुरुषं सिनीतः ।
तयोः श्रेय आददानस्य साधु भवति हीयतेऽर्थाद्य उ प्रेयो वृणीते ॥१॥

Yama speaks:

1. "One thing is the good and quite another thing is the pleasant, and both seize upon a man with different meanings.
Of these whoso takes the good, it is well with him; he falls
from the aim of life who chooses the pleasant.

श्रेयश्च प्रेयश्च मनुष्यमेतस्तौ सम्परीत्य विविनक्ति धीरः ।
श्रेयो हि धीरोऽभि प्रेयसो वृणीते प्रेयो मन्दो योगक्षेमाद्वृणीते ॥२॥

2. "The good and the pleasant come to a man and the thought-
ful mind turns all around them and distinguishes. The wise
chooses out the good from the pleasant, but the dull soul
chooses the pleasant rather than the getting of his good and
its having.

स त्वं प्रियान्प्रियरूपांश्च कामानभिध्यायन्नचिकेतोऽत्यस्राक्षीः ।
नैतां सृङ्कां वित्तमयीमवाप्तो यस्यां मज्जन्ति बहवो मनुष्याः ॥३॥

3. "And thou, O Nachiketas, hast looked close at the objects
of desire, at pleasant things and beautiful, and thou hast
cast them from thee: thou hast not entered into the net of
riches in which many men sink to perdition.

दूरमेते विपरीते विषूची अविद्या या च विद्येति ज्ञाता ।
विद्याभीप्सिनं नचिकेतसं मन्ये न त्वा कामा बहवोऽलोलुपन्त ॥४॥

4. "For far apart are these, opposite, divergent, the one that is
known as the Ignorance and the other the Knowledge. But
Nachiketas I deem truly desirous of the knowledge whom
so many desirable things could not make to lust after them.

अविद्यायामन्तरे वर्तमानाः स्वयं धीराः पण्डितंमन्यमानाः ।
दन्द्रम्यमाणाः परियन्ति मूढा अन्धेनैव नीयमाना यथान्धाः ॥५॥

5. "They who dwell in the ignorance, within it, wise in their own wit and deeming themselves very learned, men bewildered are they who wander about round and round circling[1] like blind men led by the blind.

न साम्परायः प्रतिभाति बालं प्रमाद्यन्तं वित्तमोहेन मूढम् ।
अयं लोको नास्ति पर इति मानी पुनः पुनर्वशमापद्यते मे ॥६॥

6. "The childish wit bewildered and drunken with the illusion of riches cannot open its eyes to see the passage to heaven: for he that thinks this world is and there is no other, comes again and again into Death's thraldom.

श्रवणायापि बहुभिर्यो न लभ्यः शृण्वन्तोऽपि बहवो यं न विद्युः ।
आश्चर्यो वक्ता कुशलोऽस्य लब्धाश्चर्यो ज्ञाता कुशलानुशिष्टः ॥७॥

7. "He that is not easy even to be heard of by many, and even of those that have heard, they are many who have not known Him, — a miracle is the man that can speak of Him wisely or is skilful to win Him, and when one is found, a miracle is the listener who can know God even when taught of Him by the knower.

न नरेणावरेण प्रोक्त एष सुविज्ञेयो बहुधा चिन्त्यमानः ।
अनन्यप्रोक्ते गतिरत्र नास्त्यणीयान् ह्यतर्क्यमणुप्रमाणात् ॥८॥

8. "An inferior man cannot tell you of Him; for thus told thou canst not truly know Him, since He is thought of in many aspects. Yet unless told of Him by another thou canst not find thy way there to Him; for He is subtler than subtlety and that which logic cannot reach.

नैषा तर्केण मतिरापनेया प्रोक्तान्येनैव सुज्ञानाय प्रेष्ठ ।
यां त्वमापः सत्यधृतिर्बतासि त्वादृङ् नो भूयान्नचिकेतः प्रष्टा ॥९॥

9. "This wisdom is not to be had by reasoning, O beloved

---

[1] *Doubtful reading.*

Nachiketas; only when told thee by another it brings real knowledge, — the wisdom which thou hast gotten. Truly thou art steadfast in the Truth! Even such a questioner as thou art may I meet with always."

जानाम्यहं शेवधिरित्यनित्यं न ह्यधुवैः प्राप्यते हि धुवं तत् ।
ततो मया नाचिकेतश्चितोऽग्निरनित्यैर्द्रव्यैः प्राप्तवानस्मि नित्यम् ॥१०॥

Nachiketas speaks:

10. "I know of treasure that it is not for ever; for not by things unstable shall one attain That One which is stable; therefore I heaped the fire of Nachiketas, and by the sacrifice of transitory things I won the Eternal."

कामस्याप्तिं जगतः प्रतिष्ठां क्रतोरानन्त्यमभयस्य पारम् ।
स्तोमं महदुरुगायं प्रतिष्ठां दृष्ट्वा धृत्या धीरो नचिकेतोऽत्यस्राक्षीः ॥११॥

Yama speaks:

11. "When thou hast seen in thy grasp, O Nachiketas, the possession of desire and the firm foundation of this world and an infinity of power and the other shore of security and great praise and wide-moving firm foundation,[1] wise and strong in steadfastness thou didst cast these things from thee.

तं दुर्दर्शं गूढमनुप्रविष्टं गुहाहितं गह्वरेष्ठं पुराणम् ।
अध्यात्मयोगाधिगमेन देवं मत्वा धीरो हर्षशोकौ जहाति ॥१२॥

12. "Realising God by attainment to Him through spiritual Yoga, even the Ancient of Days who has entered deep into that which is hidden and is hard to see, for he is established in our secret being and lodged in the cavern heart of things, the wise and steadfast man casts far from him joy and sorrow.

एतच्छ्रुत्वा सम्परिगृह्य मर्त्यः प्रवृह्य धर्म्यमणुमेतमाप्य ।
स मोदते मोदनीयं हि लब्ध्वा विवृतं सद्म नचिकेतसं मन्ये ॥१३॥

---

[1] Or, "and great fame chanted through widest regions,".

13. "When mortal man has heard, when he has grasped, when he has forcefully separated the Righteous One from his body and won that subtle Being, then he has delight, for he has got that which one can indeed delight in. Verily I deem of Nachiketas as a house wide open."

अन्यत्र धर्मादन्यत्राधर्मादन्यत्रास्मात्कृताकृतात् ।
अन्यत्र भूताच्च भव्याच्च यत्तत्पश्यसि तद्ब्रव ॥१४॥

Nachiketas speaks:

14. "Tell me of That which thou seest otherwhere than in virtue and otherwhere than in unrighteousness, otherwhere than in the created and the uncreated, otherwhere than in that which has been and that which shall be."

सर्वे वेदा यत्पदमामनन्ति तपांसि सर्वाणि च यद्वदन्ति ।
यदिच्छन्तो ब्रह्मचर्यं चरन्ति तत्ते पदं संग्रहेण ब्रवीम्योमित्येतत् ॥१५॥

Yama speaks:

15. "The seat and goal that all the Vedas glorify and which all austerities declare, for the desire of which men practise holy living, of That will I tell thee in brief compass. OM is that goal, O Nachiketas.

एतद्ध्येवाक्षरं ब्रह्म एतद्ध्येवाक्षरं परम् ।
एतद्ध्येवाक्षरं ज्ञात्वा यो यदिच्छति तस्य तत् ॥१६॥

16. "For this Syllable is Brahman, this Syllable is the Most High: this Syllable if one know, whatsoever one shall desire, it is his.

एतदालम्बनं श्रेष्ठमेतदालम्बनं परम् ।
एतदालम्बनं ज्ञात्वा ब्रह्मलोके महीयते ॥१७॥

17. "This support is the best, this support is the highest, knowing this support one grows great in the world of the Brahman.

न जायते म्रियते वा विपश्चिन्नायं कुतश्चिन्न बभूव कश्चित् ।
अजो नित्यः शाश्वतोऽयं पुराणो न हन्यते हन्यमाने शरीरे ॥१८॥

18. "The Wise One is not born, neither does He die: He came not
from anywhere, neither is He anyone: He is unborn, He is
everlasting, He is ancient and sempiternal: He is not slain in
the slaying of the body.

हन्ता चेन्मन्यते हन्तुं हतश्चेन्मन्यते हतम् ।
उभौ तौ न विजानीतो नायं हन्ति न हन्यते ॥१९॥

19. "If the slayer think that he slays, if the slain think that he is
slain, both of these have not the knowledge. This slays not,
neither is He slain.

अणोरणीयान्महतो महीयानात्मास्य जन्तोर्निहितो गुहायाम् ।
तमक्रतुः पश्यति वीतशोको धातुप्रसादान्महिमानमात्मनः ॥२०॥

20. "Finer than the fine, huger than the huge the Self hides in the
secret heart of the creature: when a man strips himself of will
and is weaned from sorrow, then he beholds Him; purified
from the mental elements he sees the greatness of the Self-
being.

आसीनो दूरं व्रजति शयानो याति सर्वतः ।
कस्तं मदामदं देवं मदन्यो ज्ञातुमर्हति ॥२१॥

21. "Seated He journeys far off, lying down He goes everywhere.
Who other than I is fit to know God, even Him who is rapture and the transcendence of rapture?

अशरीरं शरीरेष्वनवस्थेष्ववस्थितम् ।
महान्तं विभुमात्मानं मत्वा धीरो न शोचति ॥२२॥

22. "Realising the Bodiless in bodies, the Established in things
unsettled, the Great and Omnipresent Self, the wise and
steadfast soul grieves no longer.

नायमात्मा प्रवचनेन लभ्यो न मेधया न बहुना श्रुतेन ।
यमेवैष वृणुते तेन लभ्यस्तस्यैष आत्मा विवृणुते तनूं स्वाम् ॥२३॥

23. "The Self is not to be won by eloquent teaching, nor by brain
power, nor by much learning: but only he whom this Being
chooses can win Him; for to him this Self bares His body.

नाविरतो दुश्चरिताप्राशान्तो नासमाहितः ।
नाशान्तमानसो वापि प्रज्ञानेनैनमाप्नुयात् ॥२४॥

24. "None who has not ceased from doing evil, or who is not
calm, or not concentrated in his being, or whose mind has
not been tranquillised, can by wisdom attain to Him.

यस्य ब्रह्म च क्षत्रं च उभे भवत ओदनः ।
मृत्युर्यस्योपसेचनं क इत्था वेद यत्र सः ॥२५॥

25. "He to whom the sages are as meat and heroes as food for
his eating and Death is an ingredient of His banquet, how
thus shall one know of Him where He abides?"

ऋतं पिबन्तौ सुकृतस्य लोके गुहां प्रविष्टौ परमे परार्धे ।
छायातपौ ब्रह्मविदो वदन्ति पञ्चाग्नयो ये च त्रिणाचिकेताः ॥१॥

Yama speaks:

1. "There are two that drink deep of the truth in the world of
   work well-accomplished: they are lodged in the secret plane
   of being and in the highest kingdom of the most High is their
   dwelling: as of light and shade the knowers of the Brahman
   speak of them, and those of the five fires and those who
   kindle thrice the fire of Nachiketas.

यः सेतुरीजानानामक्षरं ब्रह्म यत्परम् ।
अभयं तितीर्षतां पारं नाचिकेतश्शकेमहि ॥२॥

2. "May we have strength to kindle Agni Nachiketas, for he
   is the bridge of those who do sacrifice and he is Brahman
   supreme and imperishable, and the far shore of security to
   those who would cross this ocean.

आत्मानं रथिनं विद्धि शरीरं रथमेव तु ।
बुद्धिं तु सारथिं विद्धि मनः प्रग्रहमेव च ॥३॥

3. "Know the body for a chariot and the soul for the master of
   the chariot: know Reason for the charioteer and the mind
   for the reins only.

इन्द्रियाणि हयानाहुर्विषयांस्तेषु गोचरान् ।
आत्मेन्द्रियमनोयुक्तं भोक्तेत्याहुर्मनीषिणः ॥४॥

4. "The senses they speak of as the steeds and the objects of
   sense as the paths in which they move; and One yoked with
   Self and the mind and the senses, is the enjoyer, say the
   thinkers.

यस्त्वविज्ञानवान्भवत्ययुक्तेन मनसा सदा ।
तस्येन्द्रियाण्यवश्यानि दुष्टाश्वा इव सारथेः ॥५॥

5. "Now he that is without knowledge with his mind ever un-
applied, his senses are to him as wild horses and will not
obey their driver of the chariot.

यस्तु विज्ञानवान्भवति युक्तेन मनसा सदा ।
तस्येन्द्रियाणि वश्यानि सदश्वा इव सारथेः ॥६॥

6. "But he that has knowledge with his mind ever applied, his
senses are to him as noble steeds and they obey the driver.

यस्त्वविज्ञानवान्भवत्यमनस्कः सदाऽशुचिः ।
न स तत्पदमाप्नोति संसारं चाधिगच्छति ॥७॥

7. "Yea, he that is without knowledge and is unmindful and is
ever unclean, reaches not that goal, but wanders in the cycle
of phenomena.

यस्तु विज्ञानवान्भवति समनस्कः सदा शुचिः ।
स तु तत्पदमाप्नोति यस्माद् भूयो न जायते ॥८॥

8. "But he that has knowledge and is mindful and pure always,
reaches that goal whence he is not born again.

विज्ञानसारथिर्यस्तु मनःप्रग्रहवान्नरः ।
सोऽध्वनः पारमाप्नोति तद्विष्णोः परमं पदम् ॥९॥

9. "That man who uses the mind for reins and the knowledge
for the driver, reaches the end of his road, that highest seat
of Vishnu.

इन्द्रियेभ्यः परा ह्यर्था अर्थेभ्यश्च परं मनः ।
मनसस्तु परा बुद्धिर्बुद्धेरात्मा महान्परः ॥१०॥

10. "Than the senses the objects of sense are higher: and higher
than the objects of sense is the Mind: and higher than the

Mind is the faculty of knowledge: and than that the Great-Self is higher.

महतः परमव्यक्तमव्यक्तात्पुरुषः परः ।
पुरुषान्न परं किञ्चित्सा काष्ठा सा परा गतिः ॥११॥

11. "And higher than the Great-Self is the Unmanifest and higher than the Unmanifest is the Purusha: than the Purusha there is none higher: He is the culmination, He is the highest goal of the journey.

एष सर्वेषु भूतेषु गूढोत्मा न प्रकाशते ।
दृश्यते त्वग्र्यया बुद्ध्या सूक्ष्मया सूक्ष्मदर्शिभिः ॥१२॥

12. "He is the secret Self in all existences and does not manifest Himself to the vision: yet is He seen by the seers of the subtle by a subtle and perfect understanding.

यच्छेद्वाङ्मनसी प्राज्ञस्तद्यच्छेज्ज्ञान आत्मनि ।
ज्ञानमात्मनि महति नियच्छेत्तद्यच्छेच्छान्त आत्मनि ॥१३॥

13. "Let the wise man restrain speech in his mind and mind in Self, and knowledge in the Great-Self, and that again let him restrain in the Self that is at peace.

उत्तिष्ठत जाग्रत प्राप्य वरान्निबोधत ।
क्षुरस्य धारा निशिता दुरत्यया दुर्गं पथस्तत्कवयो वदन्ति ॥१४॥

14. "Arise, awake, find out the great ones and learn of them: for sharp as a razor's edge, hard to traverse, difficult of going is that path, say the sages.

अशब्दमस्पर्शमरूपमव्ययं तथाऽरसं नित्यमगन्धवच्च यत् ।
अनाद्यनन्तं महतः परं ध्रुवं निचाय्य तन्मृत्युमुखात्प्रमुच्यते ॥१५॥

15. "That in which sound is not, nor touch, nor shape, nor diminution, nor taste, nor smell, that which is eternal, and It is without end or beginning, higher than the Great-Self, the

Stable, that having seen, from the mouth of death there is deliverance."

नाचिकेतमुपाख्यानं मृत्युप्रोक्तं सनातनम् ।
उक्त्वा श्रुत्वा च मेधावी ब्रह्मलोके महीयते ॥१६॥

16.   The man of intelligence having spoken or heard the eternal story of Nachiketas wherein Death was the speaker, grows great in the world of the Brahman.

य इमं परमं गुह्यां श्रावयेद् ब्रह्मसंसदि ।
प्रयतः श्राद्धकाले वा तदानन्त्याय कल्पते
तदानन्त्याय कल्पत इति ॥१७॥

17.   He who being pure recites this supreme secret at the time of the Shraddha in the assembly of the Brahmins, that turns for him to infinite existence.

परात्र्चि खानि व्यतृणत्स्वयम्भूस्तस्मात्पराङ् पश्यति नान्तरात्मन् ।
कश्चिद्धीरः प्रत्यगात्मानमैक्षदावृत्तचक्षुरमृतत्वमिच्छन् ॥१॥

Yama speaks:

1. "The Self-born has set the doors of the body to face out-
   wards, therefore the soul of a man gazes outward and not
   at the Self within : hardly a wise man here and there, desiring
   immortality, turns his eyes inward and sees the Self within
   him.

पराचः कामाननुयन्ति बालास्ते मृत्योर्यन्ति विततस्य पाशम् ।
अथ धीरा अमृतत्वं विदित्वा ध्रुवमध्रुवेष्विह न प्रार्थयन्ते ॥२॥

2. "The rest childishly follow after desire and pleasure and walk
   into the snare of Death that gapes wide for them. But calm
   souls having learned of immortality seek not for perma-
   nence in the things of this world that pass and are not.

येन रूपं रसं गन्धं शब्दान्स्पर्शांश्च मैथुनान् ।
एतेनैव विजानाति किमत्र परिशिष्यते । एतद्वै तत् ॥३॥

3. "By the Self one knows form and taste and smell, by the
   Self one knows sound and touch and the joy of man with
   woman : what is there left in this world of which the Self
   not knows?
   This is That thou seekest.

स्वप्नान्तं जागरितान्तं चोभौ येनानुपश्यति ।
महान्तं विभुमात्मानं मत्वा धीरो न शोचति ॥४॥

4. "The calm soul having comprehended the great Lord, the
   omnipresent Self by whom one beholds both to the end of
   dream and to the end of waking, ceases from grieving.

य इमं मध्ववं वेद आत्मानं जीवमन्तिकात् ।
ईशानं भूतभव्यस्य न ततो विजुगुप्सते । एतद्वै तत् ॥५॥

5. "He that has known from very close this Eater of sweetness, the Jiva, the self within that is lord of what was and what shall be, shrinks not thereafter from aught nor abhors any.
This is That thou seekest.

य: पूर्वं तपसो जातमद्भ्य: पूर्वमजायत ।
गुहां प्रविश्य तिष्ठन्तं यो भूतेभिर्व्यपश्यत ।   एतद्वै तत् ॥६॥

6. "He is the seer that sees Him who came into being before austerity and was before the waters: deep in the heart of the creature he sees Him, for there He stands by the mingling of the elements.
This is That thou seekest.

या प्राणेन सम्भवत्यदितिर्देवतामयी ।
गुहां प्रविश्य तिष्ठन्तीं या भूतेभिर्व्यजायत ।   एतद्वै तत् ॥७॥

7. "This is Aditi, the mother of the Gods, who was born through the Prana and by the mingling of the elements had her being: deep in the heart of things she has entered, there she is seated.
This is That thou seekest.

अरण्योर्निहितो जातवेदा गर्भ इव सुभृतो गर्भिणीभि: ।
दिवे दिव ईड्यो जागृवद्भिर्हविष्मद्भिर्मनुष्येभिरग्नि: ।   एतद्वै तत् ॥८॥

8. "As a woman carries with care the unborn child in her womb, so is the Master of Knowledge lodged in the tinders: and day by day should men worship Him, who live the waking life and stand before Him with sacrifices; for He is that Agni.
This is That thou seekest.

यतश्चोदेति सूर्योऽस्तं यत्र च गच्छति ।
तं देवा: सर्वेऽर्पितास्तदु नात्येति कश्चन ।   एतद्वै तत् ॥९॥

9.   "He from whom the sun arises and to whom the sun returns,
      and in Him are all the Gods established; none passes
      beyond Him.
      This is That thou seekest.

यदेवेह तदमुत्र यदमुत्र तदन्विह।
मृत्योः स मृत्युमाप्नोति य इह नानेव पश्यति ॥१०॥

10.   "What is in this world, is also in the other: and what is
      in the other, that again is in this: who thinks he sees diffe-
      rence here, from death to death he goes.

मनसैवेदमाप्तव्यं नेह नानास्ति किञ्चन।
मृत्योः स मृत्युं गच्छति य इह नानेव पश्यति ॥११॥

11.   "Through the mind must we understand that there is
      nothing in this world that really varies: who thinks he sees
      difference here, from death to death he goes.

अङ्गुष्ठमात्रः पुरुषो मध्य आत्मनि तिष्ठति।
ईशानो भूतभव्यस्य न ततो विजुगुप्सते। एतद्वै तत् ॥१२॥

12.   "The Purusha who is seated in the midst of our self is no
      larger than the finger of a man; He is the Lord of what was
      and what shall be. Him having seen one shrinks not from
      aught, nor abhors any.
      This is That thou seekest.

अङ्गुष्ठमात्रः पुरुषो ज्योतिरिवाधूमकः।
ईशानो भूतभव्यस्य स एवाद्य स उ श्वः। एतद्वै तत् ॥१३॥

13.   "The Purusha that is within us is no larger than the finger
      of a man; He is like a blazing fire that is without smoke,
      He is lord of His past and His future. He alone is today
      and He alone shall be tomorrow.
      This is That thou seekest.

यथोदकं दुर्गे वृष्टं पर्वतेषु विधावति ।
एवं धर्मान्पृथक् पश्यंस्तानेवानुविधावति ॥१४॥

14. "As water that rains in the rough and difficult places, runs
to many sides on the mountain-tops, so he that sees separate
law and action of the One Spirit, follows in the track of what
he sees.

यथोदकं शुद्धे शुद्धमासिक्तं तादृगेव भवति ।
एवं मुनेर्विजानत आत्मा भवति गौतम ॥१५॥

15. "But as pure water that is poured into pure water, even as
it was such it remains, so is it with the soul of the thinker
who knows God, O seed of Gautama."

पुरमेकादशद्वारमजस्याबऋचेतसः ।
अनुष्ठाय न शोचति विमुक्तश्च विमुच्यते ।   एतद्धै तत् ॥१॥

Yama speaks:

1. "The unborn who is not devious-minded has a city with
    eleven gates: when he takes up his abode in it, he grieves
    not, but when he is set free from it, that is his deliverance.
    This is That thou seekest.

हꣳसः शुचिषद्वसुरन्तरिक्षसद्धोता वेदिषदतिथिर्दुरोणसत् ।
नृषद्वरसदृतसद्व्योमसदब्जा गोजा ऋतजा अद्रिजा ऋतं बृहत् ॥२॥

2. "Lo, the Swan whose dwelling is in the purity, He is the
    Vasu in the inter-regions, the Sacrificer at the altar, the Guest
    in the vessel of the drinking: He is in man and in the Great
    Ones and His home is in the law, and His dwelling is in the
    firmament: He is all that is born of water and all that is born
    of earth and all that is born on the mountains. He is the
    Truth and He is the Mighty One.

ऊर्ध्वं प्राणमुन्नयत्यपानं प्रत्यगस्यति ।
मध्ये वामनमासीनं विश्वे देवा उपासते ॥३॥

3. "This is He that draws the main breath upward and casts
    the lower breath downward. The Dwarf that sits in the
    centre, to Him all the Gods do homage.

अस्य विस्रंसमानस्य शरीरस्थस्य देहिनः ।
देहाद्विमुच्यमानस्य किमत्र परिशिष्यते ।   एतद्धै तत् ॥४॥

4. "When this encased Spirit that is in the body, falls away
    from it, when He is freed from its casing, what is there
    then that remains?
    This is That thou seekest.

न प्राणेन नापानेन मर्त्यो जीवति कश्चन ।
इतरेण तु जीवन्ति यस्मिन्नेतावुपाश्रितौ ॥५॥

5. "Man that is mortal lives not by the breath, no, nor by the lower breath; but by something else we live in which both these have their being.

हन्त त इदं प्रवक्ष्यामि गुह्यं ब्रह्म सनातनम् ।
यथा च मरणं प्राप्य आत्मा भवति गौतम ॥६॥

6. "Surely, O Gautama, I will tell thee of this secret and eternal Brahman and likewise what becomes of the soul when one dies.

योनिमन्ये प्रपद्यन्ते शरीरत्वाय देहिनः ।
स्थाणुमन्येऽनुसंयन्ति यथाकर्म यथाश्रुतम् ॥७॥

7. "For some enter a womb to the embodying of the Spirit and others follow after the Immovable: according to their deeds is their goal and after the measure of their revealed knowledge.

य एष सुप्तेषु जागर्ति कामं कामं पुरुषो निर्मिमाणः ।
तदेव शुक्रं तद् ब्रह्म तदेवामृतमुच्यते ।
तस्मिँल्लोकाः श्रिताः सर्वे तदु नात्येति कश्चन । एतद्वै तत् ॥८॥

8. "This that wakes in the sleepers creating desire upon desire, this Purusha, Him they call the Bright One, Him Brahman, Him Immortality, and in Him are all the worlds established: none goes beyond Him.
This is That thou seekest.

अग्निर्यथैको भुवनं प्रविष्टो रूपं रूपं प्रतिरूपो बभूव ।
एकस्तथा सर्वभूतान्तरात्मा रूपं रूपं प्रतिरूपो बहिश्च ॥९॥

9. "Even as one Fire has entered into the world, but it shapes itself to the forms it meets, so there is one Spirit within all creatures, but it shapes itself to form and form: it is likewise outside these.

वायुर्यथैको भुवनं प्रविष्टो रूपं रूपं प्रतिरूपो बभूव ।
एकस्तथा सर्वभूतान्तरात्मा रूपं रूपं प्रतिरूपो बहिश्च ॥१०॥

10. "Even as one Air has entered into the world, but it shapes
itself to the forms it meets, so there is one Spirit within all
creatures, but it shapes itself to form and form: it is likewise outside these.

सूर्यो यथा सर्वलोकस्य चक्षुर्न लिप्यते चाक्षुषैर्बाह्यदोषैः ।
एकस्तथा सर्वभूतान्तरात्मा न लिप्यते लोकदुःखेन बाह्यः ॥११॥

11. "Even as the Sun is the eye of all this world, yet is not soiled
by the outward blemishes of the visual, so there is one
Spirit within all creatures, but the sorrow of this world soils
it not: for it is beyond grief and his danger.

एको वशी सर्वभूतान्तरात्मा एकं रूपं बहुधा यः करोति ।
तमात्मस्थं येऽनुपश्यन्ति धीरास्तेषां सुखं शाश्वतं नेतरेषाम् ॥१२॥

12. "One calm and controlling Spirit within all creatures that
makes one form into many fashions: the calm and strong
who see Him in their self as in a mirror, theirs is eternal felicity and 'tis not for others.

नित्योऽनित्यानां चेतनश्चेतनानामेको बहूनां यो विदधाति कामान् ।
तमात्मस्थं येऽनुपश्यन्ति धीरास्तेषां शान्तिः शाश्वती नेतरेषाम् ॥१३॥

13. "The One Eternal in the transient, the One consciousness
in many conscious beings, who being One orders the desires
of many: the calm and strong who behold Him in their self
as in a mirror, theirs is eternal peace and 'tis not for others.

तदेतदिति मन्यन्तेऽनिर्देश्यं परमं सुखम् ।
कथं नु तद्विजानीयां किमु भाति विभाति वा ॥१४॥

14. " 'This is He' is all they can realise of Him, a highest felicity
which none can point to nor any define it. How shall I know
of Him whether He shines or reflects one light and another?

न तत्र सूर्यो भाति न चन्द्रतारकं नेमा विद्युतो भान्ति कुतोऽयमग्निः।
तमेव भान्तमनुभाति सर्वं तस्य भासा सर्वमिदं विभाति ॥१५॥

15. "There the sun cannot shine and the moon has no lustre: all the stars are blind: there our lightnings flash not, neither any earthly fire. For all that is bright is but the shadow of His brightness and by His shining all this shines."

ऊर्ध्वमूलोऽवाक्शाख एषोऽश्वत्थः सनातनः ।
तदेव शुक्रं तद् ब्रह्म तदेवामृतमुच्यते ।
तस्मिँल्लोकाः श्रिताः सर्वे तदु नात्येति कश्चन ।   एतद्वै तत् ॥१॥

Yama speaks:

1. "This is an eternal Ashwattha-tree whose root is above, but
    its branches are downward. It is He that is called the Bright
    One and Brahman, and Immortality, and in Him are all
    the worlds established, none goes beyond Him.
    This is That thou seekest.

यदिदं किञ्च जगत्सर्वं प्राण एजति निःसृतम् ।
महद् भयं वज्रमुद्यतं य एतद्विदुरमृतास्ते भवन्ति ॥२॥

2. "All this universe of motion moves in the Prana and from
    the Prana also it proceeded: a mighty terror is He, yea, a
    thunderbolt uplifted. Who know Him, are the immortals.

भयादस्याग्निस्तपति भयात्तपति सूर्यः ।
भयादिन्द्रश्च वायुश्च मृत्युर्धावति पञ्चमः ॥३॥

3. "For fear of Him the Fire burns: for fear of Him the Sun
    gives heat: for fear of Him Indra and Vayu and Death
    hasten in their courses.

इह चेदशकद्बोद्धुं प्राक् शरीरस्य विस्रसः ।
ततः सर्गेषु लोकेषु शरीरत्वाय कल्पते ॥४॥

4. "If in this world of men and before thy body fall from thee,
    thou wert able to apprehend it, then thou availest for
    embodiment in the worlds that He creates.

यथाऽऽदर्शे तथात्मनि यथा स्वप्ने तथा पितृलोके ।
यथाप्सु परीव ददृशे तथा गन्धर्वलोके छायातपयोरिव ब्रह्मलोके ॥५॥

5. "In the self one sees God as in a mirror, but as in a dream in the world of the Fathers: and as in water one sees the surface of an object, so one sees Him in the world of the Gandharvas. But He is seen as light and shade in the heaven of the Spirit.

इन्द्रियाणां पृथग्भावमुदयास्तमयौ च यत् ।
पृथगुत्पद्यमानानां मत्वा धीरो न शोचति ॥६॥

6. "The calm soul having comprehended the separateness of the senses and the rising of them and their setting and their separate emergence, puts from him pain and sorrow.

इन्द्रियेभ्यः परं मनो मनसः सत्त्वमुत्तमम् ।
सत्त्वादधि महानात्मा महतोऽव्यक्तमुत्तमम् ॥७॥

7. "The mind is higher than the senses, and higher than the mind is the genius, and above the genius is the Mighty Spirit, and higher than the Mighty One is the Unmanifested.

अव्यक्तात्तु परः पुरुषो व्यापकोऽलिङ्ग एव च ।
यं ज्ञात्वा मुच्यते जन्तुरमृतत्वं च गच्छति ॥८॥

8. "But highest above the Unmanifested is the Purusha who pervades all and alone has no sign nor feature. Mortal man knowing Him is released into immortality.

न संदृशे तिष्ठति रूपमस्य न चक्षुषा पश्यति कश्चनैनम् ।
हृदा मनीषा मनसाभिक्लृप्तो य एतद्विदुरमृतास्ते भवन्ति ॥९॥

9. "God has not set His body within the ken of seeing, neither does any man with the eye behold Him, but to the heart and the mind and the super-mind He is manifest. Who know Him are the immortals.

यदा पञ्चावतिष्ठन्ते ज्ञानानि मनसा सह ।
बुद्धिश्च न विचेष्टति तामाहुः परमां गतिम् ॥१०॥

10. "When the five senses cease and are at rest and the mind rests with them and the higher mind ceases from its workings, that is the highest state, say thinkers.

तां योगमिति मन्यन्ते स्थिरामिन्द्रियधारणाम् ।
अप्रमत्तस्तदा भवति योगो हि प्रभवाप्ययौ ॥११॥

11. "The state unperturbed when the senses are imprisoned in the mind, of this they say 'It is Yoga.' Then man becomes very vigilant, for Yoga is the birth of things and their ending.[1]

नैव वाचा न मनसा प्राप्तुं शक्यो न चक्षुषा ।
अस्तीति ब्रुवतोऽन्यत्र कथं तदुपलभ्यते ॥१२॥

12. "Not with the mind has man the power to get God, no, nor through speech, nor by the eye. Unless one says 'He is', how can one become sensible of Him?

अस्तीत्येवोपलब्धव्यस्तत्त्वभावेन चोभयोः ।
अस्तीत्येवोपलब्धस्य तत्त्वभावः प्रसीदति ॥१३॥

13. "One must apprehend God in the concept 'He is' and also in His essential: but when he has grasped Him as the 'Is', then the essential of God dawns upon a man.

यदा सर्वे प्रमुच्यन्ते कामा येऽस्य हृदि श्रिताः ।
अथ मर्त्योऽमृतो भवत्यत्र ब्रह्म समश्नुते ॥१४॥

14. "When every desire that finds lodging in the heart of man, has been loosened from its moorings, then this mortal puts on immortality: even here he tastes God, in this human body.

यदा सर्वे प्रभिद्यन्ते हृदयस्येह ग्रन्थयः ।
अथ मर्त्योऽमृतो भवत्येतावद्ध्यनुशासनम् ॥१५॥

---

[1] Shankara interprets, "as Yoga has a beginning (birth) so has it an ending". But this is not what the Sruti says.

15.   "Yea, when all the strings of the heart are rent asunder, even here, in this human birth, then the mortal becomes immortal. This is the whole teaching of the Scriptures.

शतं चैका च हृदयस्य नाडघस्तासां मूर्धानमभिनिःसृतैका ।
तयोर्ध्वमायन्नमृतत्वमेति विश्वङ्ङन्या उत्क्रमणे भवन्ति ॥१६॥

16.   "A hundred and one are the nerves of the heart, and of all these only one issues out through the head of a man: by this his soul mounts up to its immortal home, but the rest lead him to all sorts and conditions of births in his passing.

अङ्गुष्ठमात्रः पुरुषोऽन्तरात्मा सदा जनानां हृदये सन्निविष्टः ।
तं स्वाच्छरीरात्प्रवृहेन्मुञ्जादिवेषीकां धैर्येण ।
तं विद्याच्छुक्रममृतं तं विद्याच्छुक्रममृतमिति ॥१७॥

17.   "The Purusha, the Spirit within, who is no larger than the finger of a man is seated for ever in the heart of creatures: one must separate Him with patience from one's own body as one separates from a blade of grass its main fibre. Thou shalt know Him for the Bright Immortal, yea, for the Bright Immortal."

मृत्युप्रोक्तां नचिकेतोऽथ लब्ध्वा विद्यामेतां योगविधिं च कृत्स्नम् ।
ब्रह्मप्राप्तो विरजोऽभूद्विमृत्युरन्योऽप्येवं यो विदध्यात्ममेव ॥१८॥

18.   Thus did Nachiketas with Death for his teacher win the God-knowledge: he learned likewise the whole ordinance of Yoga: thereafter he obtained God and became void of stain and void of death. So shall another be who comes likewise to the Science of the Spirit.

READINGS IN THE TAITTIRIYA UPANISHAD

The Knowledge of Brahman

> The knower of Brahman reacheth that which is supreme.
> This is that verse which was spoken; "Truth, Knowledge,
>   Infinity the Brahman,
> He who knoweth that hidden in the secrecy in the supreme
>   ether,
> Enjoyeth all desires along with the wise-thinking Brahman."

This is the burden of the opening sentences of the Taittiriya Upanishad's second section; they begin its elucidation of the highest truth. Or in the Sanskrit,

ब्रह्मविद् आप्नोति परम् —
तद् एषाभ्युक्ता — सत्यं ज्ञानम् अनन्तं ब्रह्म —
यो वेद निहितं गुहायां — परमे व्योमन् —
सोऽश्नुते सर्वान् कामान् — सह ब्रह्मणा विपश्चितेति ।

But what is Brahman?
Whatever reality is in existence, by which all the rest subsists, that is Brahman. An Eternal behind all instabilities, a Truth of things which is implied, if it is hidden in all appearances, a Constant which supports all mutations, but is not increased, diminished, abrogated, — there is such an unknown X which makes existence a problem, our own self a mystery, the universe a riddle. If we were only what we seem to be to our normal self-awareness, there would be no mystery; if the world were only what it can be made out to be by the perceptions of the senses and their strict analysis in the reason, there would be no riddle; and if to take our life as it is now and the world as it has so far developed to our experience were the whole possibility of our knowing and doing, there would be no problem. Or at best there would be but a shallow mystery, an easily solved riddle, the problem only of a child's puzzle. But there is more, and that more is the hidden head of the Infinite and the secret heart of the Eternal. It is the highest and this highest is the all; there is none beyond and there

is none other than it. To know it is to know the highest and by knowing the highest to know all. For as it is the beginning and source of all things, so everything else is its consequence; as it is the support and constituent of all things, so the secret of everything else is explained by its secret; as it is the sum and end of all things, so everything else amounts to it and by throwing itself into it achieves the sense of its own existence.

This is the Brahman.

**

If this unknown be solely an indecipherable, only indefinable *X*, always unknown and unknowable, the hidden never revealed, the secret never opened to us, then our mystery would for ever remain a mystery, our riddle insoluble, our problem intangible. Its existence, even while it determines all we are, know and do, could yet make no practical difference to us; for our relation to it would then be a blind and helpless dependence, a relation binding us to ignorance and maintainable only by that ignorance. Or again, if it be in some way knowable, but the sole result of knowledge were an extinction or cessation of our being, then within our being it could have no consequences; the very act and fructuation of knowledge would bring the annihilation of all that we now are, not its completion or fulfilment. The mystery, riddle, problem would not be so much solved as abolished, for it would lose all its data. In effect we should have to suppose that there is an eternal and irreconcilable opposition between Brahman and what we now are, between the supreme cause and all its effects or between the supreme source and all its derivations. And it would then seem that all that the Eternal originates, all he supports, all he takes back to himself is a denial or contradiction of his being which, though in itself a negative of that which alone is, has yet in some way become a positive. The two could not coexist in consciousness; if he allowed the world to know him, it would disappear from being.

But the Eternal is knowable, He defines himself so that we may seize him, and man can become, even while he exists as man and in this world and in this body, a knower of the Brahman.

The knowledge of the Brahman is not a thing luminous but otiose, informing to the intellectual view of things but without consequence to the soul of the individual or his living; it is a knowledge that is a power and a divine compulsion to change; by it his existence gains something that now he does not possess in consciousness. What is this gain? It is this that he is conscious now in a lower state only of his being, but by knowledge he gains his highest being.

The highest state of our being is not a denial, contradiction and annihilation of all that we now are; it is a supreme accomplishment of all things that our present existence means and aims at, but in their highest sense and in the eternal values.

*
**

To live in our present state of self-consciousness is to live and to act in ignorance. We are ignorant of ourselves, because we know as yet only that in us which changes always, from moment to moment, from hour to hour, from period to period, from life to life, and not that in us which is eternal. We are ignorant of the world because we do not know God; we are aware of the law of appearances, but not of the law and truth of being.

Our highest wisdom, our minutest most accurate science, our most effective application of knowledge can be at most a thinning of the veil of ignorance, but not a going beyond it, so long as we do not get at the fundamental knowledge and the consciousness to which that is native. The rest are effective for their own temporal purposes, but prove ineffective in the end, because they do not bring to the highest good; they lead to no permanent solution of the problem of existence.

The ignorance in which we live is not a baseless and wholesale falsehood, but at its lowest the misrepresentation of a Truth, at its highest an imperfect representation and translation into inferior and to that extent misleading values. It is a knowledge of the superficial only and therefore a missing of the secret essential which is the key to all that the superficial is striving for; a knowledge of the finite and apparent, but a missing of all that the apparent symbolises and the finite suggests; a knowledge of inferior forms, but a missing of all that our inferior life and being has above it and to which it must aspire if it is to fulfil its greatest possibilities. The true knowledge is that of the highest, the inmost, the infinite. The knower of the Brahman sees all these lower things in the light of the Highest, the external and superficial as a translation of the internal and essential, the finite from the view of the Infinite. He begins to see and know existence no longer as the thinking animal, but as the Eternal sees and knows it. Therefore he is glad and rich in being, luminous in joy, satisfied of existence.

*
**

Knowledge does not end with knowing, nor is it pursued and found for the sake of knowing alone. It has its full value only when it leads to some greater gain than itself, some gain of being. Simply to know the eternal and to remain in the pain, struggle and inferiority of our present way of being, would be a poor and lame advantage.

A greater knowledge opens the possibility and, if really possessed, brings the actuality of a greater being. To be is the first verb which contains all the others; knowledge, action, creation, enjoyment are only a fulfilment of being. Since we are incomplete in being, to grow is our aim, and that knowledge, action, creation, enjoyment are the best which most help us to expand, grow, feel our existence.

Mere existence is not fullness of being. Being knows itself as power, consciousness, delight; a greater being means a greater power, consciousness and delight.

If by greater being we incurred only a greater pain and suffering, this good would not be worth having. Those who say that it is, mean simply that we get by it a greater sense of fulfilment which brings of itself a greater joy of the power of existence, and an extension of suffering or a loss of other enjoyment is worth having as a price for this greater sense of wideness, height and power. But this could not be the perfection of being or the highest height of its fulfilment; suffering is the seal of a lower status. The highest consciousness is integrally fulfilled in wideness and power of its existence, but also it is integrally fulfilled in delight.

The knower of Brahman has not only the joy of light, but gains something immense as the result of his knowledge, *brahmavid āpnoti*.

What he gains is that highest, that which is supreme; he gains the highest being, the highest consciousness, the highest wideness and power of being, the highest delight; *brahmavid āpnoti param*.

*
**

The Supreme is not something aloof and shut up in itself. It is not a mere indefinable, prisoner of its own featureless absoluteness, impotent to define, create, know itself variously, eternally buried in a sleep or a swoon of self-absorption. The Highest is the Infinite and the Infinite contains the All. Whoever attains the highest consciousness, becomes infinite in being and embraces the All.

To make this clear the Upanishad has defined the Brahman as the Truth, Knowledge, Infinity and has defined the result of the knowledge of Him in the secrecy, in the cave of being, in the supreme ether as the enjoyment of all its desires by the soul of the individual in the attainment of its highest self-existence.

Our highest state of being is indeed a becoming one with Brahman in his eternity and infinity, but it is also an association with him in delight of self-fulfilment, *aśnute saha brahmaṇā*. And that principle of the Eternal by which this association is possible, is the principle of his knowledge, his self-discernment and all-discernment, the wisdom by which he knows himself perfectly in all the world and all beings, *brahmaṇā vipaścitā*.

Delight of being is the continent of all the fulfilled values of existence which we now seek after in the forms of desire. To know its conditions and possess it purely and perfectly is the infinite privilege of the eternal Wisdom.

Truth, Knowledge, Infinity

TRUTH, Knowledge, Infinity, not as three separate things, but in their inseparable unity, are the supernal conscious being of the Eternal. It is an infinite being, an infinite truth of being, an infinite self-knowledge of self-being. Take one of these away and the idea of the Eternal fails us; we land ourselves in half-lights, in dark or shining paradoxes without issue or in a vain exaggeration and apotheosis of isolated intellectual conceptions.

Infinity is the timeless and spaceless and causeless infinity of the eternal containing all the infinities of space and time and the endless succession which humanly we call causality. But in fact causality is only an inferior aspect and translation into mental and vital terms of something which is not mechanical causality, but the harmonies of a free self-determination of the being of the Eternal.

Truth is truth of the infinite and eternal, truth of being, and truth of becoming only as a self-expression of the being. The circumstances of the self-expression appear to the mind as the finite, but nothing is really finite except the way the mind has of experiencing all that appears to its view. All things are, each thing is the Brahman.

Knowledge is the Eternal's inalienable self-knowledge of his infinite self-existence and of all its truth and reality and, in that truth, of all things as seen not by the mind, but by the self-view of the Spirit. This knowledge is not possible to the mind; it can only be reflected inadequately by it when it is touched by a ray from the secret luminous cavern of our superconscient being; yet of that ray we can make a shining ladder to climb into the source of this supreme self-viewing wisdom.

To know the eternal Truth, Knowledge, Infinity is to know the Brahman.

SECTION TWO

Translations Done before 1910

TAITTIRIYA UPANISHAD

Taittiriya Upanishad

SHIKSHAVALLI

CHAPTER ONE

हरिः ॐ ॥ शं नो मित्रः शं वरुणः । शं नो भवत्वर्यमा । शं न इन्द्रो
बृहस्पतिः । शं नो विष्णुरुरुक्रमः ॥ नमो ब्रह्मणे । नमस्ते वायो । त्वमेव
प्रत्यक्षं ब्रह्मासि । त्वामेव प्रत्यक्षं ब्रह्म वदिष्यामि । ऋतं वदिष्यामि ।
सत्यं वदिष्यामि । तन्मामवतु । तद्वक्तारमवतु । अवतु माम् । अवतु
वक्तारम् । ॐ शान्तिः शान्तिः शान्तिः ॥

Hari OM. Be peace to us Mitra. Be peace to us Varuna. Be
peace to us Aryaman. Be peace to us Indra and Brihaspati. May
far-striding Vishnu be peace to us. Adoration to the Eternal.
Adoration to thee, O Vayu. Thou, thou art the visible Eternal
and as the visible Eternal I will declare thee. I will declare
Righteousness! I will declare Truth! May that protect me! May
that protect the speaker! Yea, may it protect me! May it protect
the speaker! OM! Peace! Peace! Peace!

CHAPTER TWO

ॐ शीक्षां व्याख्यास्यामः । वर्णः स्वरः । मात्रा बलम् । साम सन्तानः ।
इत्युक्तः शीक्षाध्यायः ॥

OM. We will expound Shiksha, the elements. Syllable and
Accent, Pitch and Effort, Even Tone and Continuity: in these
six we have declared the chapter of the elements.

CHAPTER THREE

सह नौ यशः। सह नौ ब्रह्मवर्चसम्। अथातः संहितायाः उपनिषदं व्या-
ख्यास्यामः। पञ्चस्वधिकरणेषु। अधिलोकमधिज्यौतिषमधिविद्यमधिप्रज-
मध्यात्मम्। ता महासंहिता इत्याचक्षते।

अथाधिलोकम्। पृथिवी पूर्वरूपम्। द्यौरुत्तररूपम्। आकाशः सन्धिः।
वायुः सन्धानम्। इत्यधिलोकम्॥

अथाधिज्यौतिषम्। अग्निः पूर्वरूपम्। आदित्य उत्तररूपम्। आपः
सन्धिः। वैद्युतः सन्धानम्। इत्यधिज्यौतिषम्।

अथाधिविद्यम्। आचार्यः पूर्वरूपम्। अन्तेवास्युत्तररूपम्। विद्या
सन्धिः। प्रवचनं सन्धानम्। इत्यधिविद्यम्।

अथाधिप्रजम्। माता पूर्वरूपम्। पितोत्तररूपम्। प्रजा सन्धिः।
प्रजननं सन्धानम्। इत्यधिप्रजम्।

अथाध्यात्मम्। अधरा हनुः पूर्वरूपम्। उत्तरा हनुरुत्तररूपम्। वाक्
सन्धिः। जिह्वा सन्धानम्। इत्यध्यात्मम्।

इतीमा महासंहिताः। य एवमेता महासंहिता व्याख्याता वेद। सन्धीयते
प्रजया पशुभिः। ब्रह्मवर्चसेनान्नाद्येन सुवर्ग्येण लोकेन॥

Together may we attain glory, together to the radiance of holi-
ness. Hereupon we will expound next the secret meaning of
Sanhita whereof there are five capitals; Concerning the Worlds:
Concerning the Shining Fires: Concerning the Knowledge:
Concerning Progeny: Concerning Self. These are called the
great Sanhitas.

Now concerning the Worlds. Earth is the first form; the
heavens are the second form; ether is the linking; air is the joint
of the linking. Thus far concerning the Worlds.

Next concerning the Shining Fires. Fire is the first form; the
Sun is the latter form; the waters are the linking; electricity is the
joint of the linking. Thus far concerning the Shining Fires.

Next concerning the Knowledge. The Master is the first
form; the disciple is the latter form; Knowledge is the linking;
exposition is the joint of the linking. Thus far concerning the
Knowledge.

Next concerning Progeny. The mother is the first form; the
father is the latter form; Progeny is the linking; act of procreation
is the joint of the linking. Thus far concerning Progeny.

Next concerning Self. The upper jaw is the first form; the lower jaw is the latter form; speech is the linking; the tongue is the joint of the linking. Thus far concerning Self.

These are the great Sanhitas. He who knoweth thus the great Sanhitas as we have expounded them, to him are linked progeny and wealth of cattle and the radiance of holiness and food and all that is of food and the world of his high estate in heaven.

CHAPTER FOUR

यश्छन्दसामृषभो विश्वरूपः। छन्दोभ्योऽध्यमृतात्सम्बभूव। स मेन्द्रो मेधया
स्पृणोतु। अमृतस्य देव धारणो भूयासम्। शरीरं मे विचर्षणम्। जिह्वा
मे मधुमत्तमा। कर्णाभ्यां भूरि विश्रुवम्। ब्रह्मणः कोशोऽसि मेधया
पिहितः। श्रुतं मे गोपाय।

आवहन्ती वितन्वाना। कुर्वाणा चीरमात्मनः। वासांसि मम गावश्च।
अन्नपाने च सर्ववा। ततो मे श्रियमावह। लोमशां पशुभिः सह स्वाहा।

आ मा यन्तु ब्रह्मचारिणः स्वाहा।
वि मा यन्तु ब्रह्मचारिणः स्वाहा।
प्र मा यन्तु ब्रह्मचारिणः स्वाहा।
दमायन्तु ब्रह्मचारिणः स्वाहा।
शमायन्तु ब्रह्मचारिणः स्वाहा।
यशो जनेऽसानि स्वाहा।
श्रेयान् वस्यसोऽसानि स्वाहा।
तं त्वा भग प्रविशानि स्वाहा।
स मा भग प्रविश स्वाहा।
तस्मिन् सहस्रशाखे। नि भगाहं त्वयि मृजे स्वाहा।
यथापः प्रवता यन्ति। यथा मासा अहर्जरम्। एवं मां ब्रह्मचारिणो
धातरायन्तु सर्वतः स्वाहा।
प्रतिवेशोऽसि। प्र मा भाहि। प्र मा पद्यस्व॥

The bull of the hymns of Veda whose visible form is all this Universe, he above the Vedas who sprang from that which is deathless, may Indra increase intellect unto me for my strengthening. O God, may I become a vessel of immortality. May my body be swift to all works, may my tongue drop pure honey. May I hear vast and manifold lore with my ears. O Indra, thou art the sheath of the Eternal and the veil that the workings of brain have drawn over Him; preserve whole unto me the sacred lore that I have studied.

She bringeth unto me wealth and extendeth it, yea, she maketh speedily my own raiment and cattle and drink and food now and always; therefore carry to me Fortune of much fleecy wealth and cattle with her. Swaha!

May the Brahmacharins come unto me. Swaha!

From here and there may the Brahmacharins come unto me. Swaha!

May the Brahmacharins set forth unto me. Swaha!

May the Brahmacharins attain self-mastery. Swaha!

May the Brahmacharins attain to peace of soul. Swaha!

May I be a name among the folk! Swaha!

May I be the first of the wealthy! Swaha!

O Glorious Lord, into That which is Thou may I enter. Swaha!

Do thou also enter into me, O Shining One. Swaha!

Thou art a river with a hundred branching streams, O Lord of Grace, in thee may I wash me clean. Swaha!

As the waters of a river pour down the steep, as the months of the year hasten to the old age of days, O Lord that cherisheth, so may the Brahmacharins come to me from all the regions. Swaha!

O Lord, thou art my neighbour, thou dwellest very near me. Come to me, be my light and sun.

CHAPTER FIVE

भूर्भुवः सुवरिति वा एतास्तिस्रो व्याहृतयः । तासामु ह स्मैतां चतुर्थीं
माहाचमस्यः प्रवेदयते । मह इति । तद् ब्रह्म । स आत्मा । अङ्गान्यन्या
देवताः ।

भूरिति वा अयं लोकः । भुव इत्यन्तरिक्षम् । सुवरित्यसौ लोकः ।
मह इत्यादित्यः । आदित्येन वाव सर्वे लोका महीयन्ते ।

भूरिति वा अग्निः । भुव इति वायुः । सुवरित्यादित्यः । मह इति
चन्द्रमाः । चन्द्रमसा वाव सर्वाणि ज्योतींषि महीयन्ते ।

भूरिति वा ऋचः । भुव इति सामानि । सुवरिति यजूंषि । मह इति
ब्रह्म । ब्रह्मणा वाव सर्वे वेदा महीयन्ते ।

भूरिति वै प्राणः । भुव इत्यपानः । सुवरिति व्यानः । मह इत्यन्नम् ।
अन्नेन वाव सर्वे प्राणा महीयन्ते ।

ता वा एतास्चतस्रश्चतुर्धा । चतस्रश्चतस्रो व्याहृतयः । ता यो वेद ।
स वेद ब्रह्म । सर्वेऽस्मै देवा बलिमावहन्ति ॥

Bhur, Bhuvar and Suvar, these are the three Words of His
naming. Verily the Rishi Mahachamasya made known a fourth
to these, which is Mahas. It is Brahman, it is the Self, and the
other gods are his members.

Bhur, it is this world; Bhuvar, it is the sky; Suvar, it is the
other world: but Mahas is the Sun. By the Sun all these worlds
increase and prosper.

Bhur, it is Fire; Bhuvar, it is Air; Suvar, it is the Sun: but
Mahas is the Moon. By the Moon all these shining fires[1] increase and prosper.

Bhur, it is the hymns of the Rig-veda; Bhuvar, it is the hymns
of the Sama; Suvar, it is the hymns of the Yajur: but Mahas is
the Eternal. By the Eternal all these Vedas increase and prosper.

Bhur, it is the main breath; Bhuvar, it is the lower breath;
Suvar, it is the breath pervasor: but Mahas is food. By food all
these breaths increase and prosper.

These are the four and they are fourfold; — four Words of
His naming and each is four again. He who knoweth these
knoweth the Eternal, and to him all the Gods carry the offering.

---

[1] *Or*, lights of heaven.

CHAPTER SIX

स य एषोऽन्तर्हृदय आकाशः। तस्मिन्नयं पुरुषो मनोमयः। अमृतो
हिरण्मयः। अन्तरेण तालुके। य एष स्तन इवावलम्बते। सेन्द्रयोनिः।
यत्रासौ केशान्तो विवर्तते। व्यपोह्य शीर्षकपाले।

भूरित्यग्नौ प्रतितिष्ठति। भुव इति वायौ। सुवरित्यादित्ये। मह
इति ब्रह्मणि। आप्नोति स्वाराज्यम्। आप्नोति मनसस्पतिम्। वा-
क्पतिश्चक्षुष्पतिः। श्रोत्रपतिर्विज्ञानपतिः। एतत्ततो भवति। आकाश-
शरीरं ब्रह्म। सत्यात्म प्राणारामं मनआनन्दम्। शान्तिसमृद्धममृतम्।
इति प्राचीनयोग्योपास्स्व॥

Lo, this heaven of ether which is in the heart within, there dwelleth the Being who is all Mind, the radiant and golden Immortal.
Between the two palates, this that hangeth down like the breast
of a woman, is the womb of Indra; yea, where the hair at its
end whirleth round like an eddy, there it divideth the skull and
pusheth through it.

As Bhur He is established in Agni, as Bhuvar in Vayu, as
Suvar in the Sun, as Mahas in the Eternal. He attaineth to the
kingdom of Himself; He attaineth to be the Lord of Mind; He
becometh Lord of Speech, Lord of Sight, Lord of Hearing, Lord
of the Knowledge. Thereafter this too He becometh, — the Eternal
whose body is all ethereal space, whose soul is Truth, whose bliss
is in Mind, who taketh His ease in Prana, the Rich in Peace, the
Immortal. As such, O son of the ancient Yoga, do thou adore
Him.

CHAPTER SEVEN

पृथिव्यन्तरिक्षं द्यौर्दिशोऽवान्तरदिशः । अग्निर्वायुरादित्यश्चन्द्रमा नक्षत्राणि ।
आप ओषधयो वनस्पतय आकाश आत्मा । इत्यधिभूतम् ।

अथाध्यात्मम् । प्राणो व्यानोऽपान उदानः समानः ।

चक्षुः श्रोत्रं मनो वाक्त्वक् । चर्म माꣳसꣳ स्नावास्थि मज्जा । एतदधि-
विधाय ऋषिरवोचत् । पाङ्क्तं वा इदꣳ सर्वम् । पाङ्क्तेनैव पाङ्क्तं
स्पृणोतीति ॥

Earth, sky, heaven, the quarters and the lesser quarters; Fire,
Air, Sun, Moon and the Constellations; Waters, herbs of healing,
trees of the forest, ether and the Self in all; these three concerning this outer creation.

Then concerning the Self. The main breath, the middle
breath, the nether breath, the upper breath and the breath
pervasor; eye, ear, mind, speech and the skin; hide, flesh, muscle,
bone and marrow. Thus the Rishi divided them and said, "In sets
of five is this universe; five and five with five and five He relateth."

CHAPTER EIGHT

ओमिति ब्रह्म । ओमितीदꣳ सर्वम् । ओमित्येतदनुकृति हं स्म वा अप्यो
श्रावयेत्याश्रावयन्ति । ओमिति सामानि गायन्ति । ओम् शोमिति
शस्त्राणि शंसन्ति । ओमित्यध्वर्युः प्रतिगरं प्रतिगृणाति । ओमिति ब्रह्मा
प्रसौति । ओमित्यग्निहोत्रमनुजानाति । ओमिति ब्राह्मणः प्रवक्ष्य-
न्नाह ब्रह्मोपाप्नवानीति । ब्रह्मैवोपाप्नोति ॥

OM is the Eternal, OM is all this universe. OM is the syllable
of assent: saying OM! let us hear, they begin the citation. With
OM they sing the hymns of the Sama; with OM SHOM they
pronounce the Shastra. With OM the priest officiating at the
sacrifice sayeth the response. With OM Brahma beginneth creation (or, With OM the chief priest giveth sanction). With OM
one sanctioneth the burnt offering. With OM the Brahmin ere
he expound the Knowledge, crieth "May I attain the Eternal."
The Eternal verily he attaineth.

CHAPTER NINE

ऋतं च स्वाध्यायप्रवचने च । सत्यं च स्वाध्यायप्रवचने च । तपश्च
स्वाध्यायप्रवचने च । दमश्च स्वाध्यायप्रवचने च । शमश्च स्वाध्याय-
प्रवचने च । अग्नयश्च स्वाध्यायप्रवचने च । अग्निहोत्रं च स्वाध्यायप्रवचने
च । अतिथयश्च स्वाध्यायप्रवचने च । मानुषं च स्वाध्यायप्रवचने च ।
प्रजा च स्वाध्यायप्रवचने च । प्रजनश्च स्वाध्यायप्रवचने च । प्रजातिश्च
स्वाध्यायप्रवचने च । सत्यमिति सत्यवचा राथीतरः । तप इति तपोनित्यः
पौरुशिष्टिः । स्वाध्यायप्रवचने एवेति नाको मौद्गल्यः । तद्धि तपस्तद्धि तपः ॥

Righteousness with the study and teaching of Veda; Truth
with the study and teaching of Veda; askesis with the study and
teaching of Veda; self-mastery with the study and teaching of
Veda. Peace of soul with the study and teaching of Veda.
The household fires with the study and teaching of Veda. The
burnt offering with the study and teaching of Veda. Progeny with
the study and teaching of Veda. Act of procreation[1] with the
study and teaching of Veda. Children of thy children with the
study and teaching of Veda — *these duties*. "Truth is first," said
the truth-speaker, the Rishi, son of Rathitara. "Askesis is first,"
said the constant in austerity, the Rishi, son of Purushishta.
"Study and teaching of Veda is first," said Naka, son of Mudgala.
For this too is austerity and this too is askesis.

CHAPTER TEN

अहं वृक्षस्य रेरिवा । कीर्तिः पृष्ठं गिरेरिव । ऊर्ध्वपवित्रो वाजिनीव
स्वमृतमस्मि । द्रविणं सवर्चसम् । सुमेधा अमृतोक्षितः । इति त्रिशङ्को-
र्वेदानुवचनम् ॥

"I am He that moveth the Tree of the Universe and my glory
is like the shoulders of a high mountain. I am lofty and pure like
sweet nectar in the strong, I am the shining riches of the world,
I am the deep thinker, the deathless One who decayeth not from
the beginning. "This is Trishanku's voicing of Veda and the
hymn of his self-knowledge.

[1] *Or*, Joy of thy child's mother.

CHAPTER ELEVEN

वेदमनूच्याचार्योऽन्तेवासिनमनुशास्ति ।

सत्यं वद । धर्मं चर । स्वाध्यायान्मा प्रमदः । आचार्याय प्रियं धनमाहृत्य प्रजातन्तुं मा व्यवच्छेत्सीः । सत्यान्न प्रमदितव्यम् । धर्मान्न प्रमदितव्यम् । कुशलान्न प्रमदितव्यम् । भूत्यै न प्रमदितव्यम् । स्वाध्यायप्रवचनाभ्यां न प्रमदितव्यम् ।

देवपितृकार्याभ्यां न प्रमदितव्यम् । मातृदेवो भव । पितृदेवो भव । आचार्यदेवो भव । अतिथिदेवो भव । यान्यनवद्यानि कर्माणि । तानि सेवितव्यानि । नो इतराणि । यान्यस्माकꣳ सुचरितानि । तानि त्वयो-पास्यानि । नो इतराणि ।

ये के चास्मच्छ्रेयाꣳसो ब्राह्मणाः । तेषां त्वयासनेन प्रश्वसितव्यम् । श्रद्धया देयम् । अश्रद्धयाऽदेयम् । श्रिया देयम् । ह्रिया देयम् । भिया देयम् । संविदा देयम् ।

अथ यदि ते कर्मविचिकित्सा वा वृत्तविचिकित्सा वा स्यात् । ये तत्र ब्राह्मणाः सम्मर्शिनः । युक्ता आयुक्ताः । अलूक्षा धर्मकामाः स्युः । यथा ते तत्र वर्तेरन् । तथा तत्र वर्तेथाः । अथाभ्याख्यातेषु । ये तत्र ब्राह्मणाः सम्मर्शिनः । युक्ता आयुक्ताः । अलूक्षा धर्मकामाः स्युः । यथा ते तेषु वर्तेरन् । तथा तेषु वर्तेथाः ।

एष आदेशः । एष उपदेशः । एषा वेदोपनिषत् । एतदनुशासनम् । एवमुपासितव्यम् । एवमु चैतदुपास्यम् ॥

When the Master hath declared Veda, then he giveth the commandments to his disciple.

Speak truth, walk in the way of thy duty, neglect not the study of Veda. When thou hast brought to the Master the wealth that he desireth, thou shalt not cut short the long thread of thy race. Thou shalt not be negligent of truth; thou shalt not be negligent of thy duty; thou shalt not be negligent of welfare; thou shalt not be negligent towards thy increase and thy thriving; thou shalt not be negligent of the study and teaching of Veda.

Thou shalt not be negligent of thy works unto the Gods or thy works unto the Fathers. Let thy father be unto thee as thy God and thy mother as thy Goddess whom thou adorest. Serve the Master as a God and as a God the stranger within thy dwelling. The works that are without blame before the people, thou shalt do these with diligence and no others. The deeds we have done that are good and righteous, thou shalt practise these as a religion and no others.

Whosoever are better and nobler than we among the Brahmins, thou shalt refresh with a seat to honour them. Thou shalt give with faith and reverence; without faith thou shalt not give. Thou shalt give with shame, thou shalt give with fear; thou shalt give with fellow-feeling.

Moreover if thou doubt of thy course or of thy action, then whatsoever Brahmins be there who are careful thinkers, devout, not moved by others, lovers of virtue, not severe or cruel, even as they do in that thing, so do thou. Then as to men accused and arraigned by their fellows, whatsoever Brahmins be there who are careful thinkers, devout, not moved by others, lovers of virtue, not severe or cruel, even as they are towards these, so be thou.

This is the law and the teaching. These are the commandments. In such wise shalt thou practise religion, yea, verily in such wise do ever religiously.

CHAPTER TWELVE

शं नो मित्रः शं वरुणः। शं नो भवत्वर्यमा। शं न इन्द्रो बृहस्पतिः। शं नो विष्णुरुरुक्रमः। नमो ब्रह्मणे। नमस्ते वायो। त्वमेव प्रत्यक्षं ब्रह्मासि। त्वामेव प्रत्यक्षं ब्रह्मावादिषम्। ऋतमवादिषम्। सत्यमवा- दिषम्। तन्मामावीत्। तद्वक्तारमावीत्। आवीन्माम्। आवीद्वक्तारम्। ॐ शान्तिः शान्तिः शान्तिः॥

Be peace to us Mitra. Be peace to us Varuna. Be peace to us Aryaman. Be peace to us Indra and Brihaspati. May far-striding Vishnu be peace to us. Adoration to the Eternal. Adoration to thee, O Vayu. Thou, thou art the visible Eternal and as the visible Eternal I have declared thee. I have declared Righteousness; I have declared Truth. That has protected me. That has protected the speaker. Yea, it protected me; it protected the speaker. OM! Peace! Peace! Peace!

BRAHMANADAVALLI

CHAPTER ONE

हरिः ॐ । सह नाववतु । सह नौ भुनक्तु । सह वीर्यं करवावहै ।
तेजस्वि नावधीतमस्तु । मा विद्विषावहै । ॐ शान्तिः शान्तिः शान्तिः ॥

ॐ ब्रह्माविदाप्नोति परम् । तदेषाभ्युक्ता । सत्यं ज्ञानमनन्तं ब्रह्म ।
यो वेद निहितं गुहायां परमे व्योमन् । सोऽश्नुते सर्वान् कामान्
सह ब्रह्मणा विपश्चितेति ।

तस्माद्वा एतस्मादात्मन आकाशः सम्भूतः । आकाशाद्वायुः । वायोरग्निः ।
अग्नेरापः । अद्भ्यः पृथिवी । पृथिव्या ओषधयः । ओषधीभ्योऽन्नम् ।
अन्नात्पुरुषः । स वा एष पुरुषोऽन्नरसमयः । तस्येदमेव शिरः । अयं
दक्षिणः पक्षः । अयमुत्तरः पक्षः । अयमात्मा । इदं पुच्छं प्रतिष्ठा ।
तदप्येष श्लोको भवति ॥

Hari OM. Together may He protect us, together may He
possess us, together may we make unto us strength and virility!
May our study be full to us of light and power! May we never
hate! OM! Peace! Peace! Peace!

OM. The knower of Brahman attaineth the Highest; for this
is the verse that was declared of old, "Brahman is Truth, Brahman is Knowledge, Brahman is the Infinite, he that findeth Him
hidden in the cavern heart of being; in the highest heaven of
His creatures, lo, he enjoyeth all desire and he abideth with the
Eternal, even with that cognisant and understanding Spirit."

This is the Self, the Spirit, and from the Spirit ether was
born; and from the ether, air; and from the air, fire; and from
the fire, the waters; and from the waters, earth; and from the
earth, herbs and plants; and from the herbs and plants, food;
and from food man was born. Verily man, this human being,
is made of the essential substance of food. And this that we see
is the head of him, and this is his right side and this is his left;
and this is his spirit and the self of him; and this is his lower
member whereon he resteth abidingly. Whereof this is the Scripture.

CHAPTER TWO

अन्नाद्धै प्रजाः प्रजायन्ते । याः काश्च पृथिवीं श्रिताः । अथो अन्नेनैव
जीवन्ति । अथैनदपि यन्त्यन्ततः । अन्नं हि भूतानां ज्येष्ठम् । तस्मात्
सर्वौषधमुच्यते । सर्वं वै तेऽन्नमाप्नुवन्ति येऽन्नं ब्रह्मोपासते । अन्नं
हि भूतानां ज्येष्ठम् । तस्मात्सर्वौषधमुच्यते । अन्नाद् भूतानि जायन्ते ।
जातान्यन्नेन वर्धन्ते । अद्यतेऽत्ति च भूतानि । तस्मादन्नं तदुच्यत इति ।

तस्माद्वा एतस्मादन्नरसमयात् । अन्योऽन्तर आत्मा प्राणमयः । तेनैव
पूर्णः । स वा एष पुरुषविध एव । तस्य पुरुषविधताम् । अन्वयं
पुरुषविधः । तस्य प्राण एव शिरः । व्यानो दक्षिणः पक्षः । अपान
उत्तरः पक्षः । आकाश आत्मा । पृथिवी पुच्छं प्रतिष्ठा । तदप्येष
श्लोको भवति ॥

Verily all sorts and races of creatures that have their refuge
upon earth, are begotten from food; thereafter they live also by
food and 'tis to food again that they return at the end and last.
For food is the eldest of created things and therefore they name it
the Green Stuff of the Universe. Verily they who worship the
Eternal as food, attain the mastery of food to the uttermost; for
food is the eldest of created things and therefore they name it
the Green Stuff of the Universe. From food all creatures are born
and being born they increase[1] by food. Lo, it is eaten and it
eateth; yea, it devoureth the creatures that feed upon it, therefore
it is called food from the eating.

Now there is a second and inner Self which is other than this
that is of the substance of food; and it is made of the vital stuff
called Prana. And the Self of Prana filleth the Self of food. Now
the Self of Prana is made in the image of a man; according as is
the human image of the other, so is it in the image of the man.
The main Breath is the head of him, the breath pervasor is his
right side and the lower breath is his left side; ether is his spirit
which is the self of him, earth is his lower member whereon he
resteth abidingly. Whereof this is the Scripture.

[1] *Or*, grow.

CHAPTER THREE

प्राणं देवा अनु प्राणन्ति । मनुष्याः पशवश्च ये । प्राणो हि भूतानामायुः ।
तस्मात्सर्वायुषमुच्यते । सर्वमेव त आयुर्यन्ति ये प्राणं ब्रह्मोपासते ।
प्राणो हि भूतानामायुः । तस्मात्सर्वायुषमुच्यत इति । तस्यैष एव शारीर
आत्मा यः पूर्वस्य ।

तस्माद्वा एतस्मात्प्राणमयात् । अन्योऽन्तर आत्मा मनोमयः । तेनैष
पूर्णः । स वा एष पुरुषविध एव । तस्य पुरुषविधताम् । अन्वयं पुरुष-
विधः । तस्य यजुरेव शिरः । ऋग् दक्षिणः पक्षः । सामोत्तरः पक्षः ।
आदेश आत्मा । अथर्वाङ्गिरसः पुच्छं प्रतिष्ठा । तदप्येष श्लोको भवति ॥

The Gods live and breathe under the dominion of Prana and
men and all these that are beasts; for Prana is the life of created
things and therefore they name it the Life-Stuff of the All. Verily
they who worship the Eternal as Prana attain mastery of[1] Life
to the uttermost; for Prana is the life of created things and therefore they name it the Life-Stuff of the All. And this Self of Prana
is the soul in the body of the former one which was of food.

Now there is yet a second and inner Self which is other than
this that is of Prana, and it is made of Mind. And the Self of
Mind filleth the Self of Prana. Now the Self of Mind is made in
the image of a man; according as is the human image of the
other, so is it in the image of the man. Yajur is the head of him
and the Rig-veda is his right side and the Sama-veda is his left
side: the Commandment is his spirit which is the self of him,
Atharvan Angiras is his lower member whereon he resteth
abidingly. Whereof this is the Scripture.

---

[1] *Or*, reach.

CHAPTER FOUR

यतो वाचो निवर्तन्ते । अप्राप्य मनसा सह । आनन्दं ब्रह्मणो विद्वान् ।
न बिभेति कदाचनेति । तस्यैष एव शारीर आत्मा यः पूर्वस्य ।
तस्माद्वा एतस्मान्मनोमयात् । अन्योऽन्तर आत्मा विज्ञानमयः । तेनेष
पूर्णः । स वा एष पुरुषविध एव । तस्य पुरुषविधताम् । अन्वयं
पुरुषविधः । तस्य श्रद्धैव शिरः । ऋतं दक्षिणः पक्षः । सत्यमुत्तरः
पक्षः । योग आत्मा । महः पुच्छं प्रतिष्ठा । तदप्येष श्लोको भवति ॥

The delight of the Eternal from which words turn away without
attaining and the mind also returneth baffled, who knoweth the
delight of the Eternal? He shall fear nought now or hereafter.
And this Self of Mind is the soul in the body to the former one
which was of Prana.

Now there is yet a second and inner self which is other
than this which is of Mind and it is made of Knowledge. And
the Self of Knowledge filleth the Self of Mind. Now the Know-
ledge-Self is made in the image of a man; according as is the
human image of the other, so is it in the image of the man. Faith
is the head of him, Law is his right side, Truth is his left side;
Yoga is his spirit which is the self of him; Mahas (the material
world) is his lower member whereon he resteth abidingly. Whereof this is the Scripture.

CHAPTER FIVE

विज्ञानं यज्ञं तनुते । कर्माणि तनुतेऽपि च । विज्ञानं देवाः सर्वे । ब्रह्म
ज्येष्ठमुपासते । विज्ञानं ब्रह्म चेद्वेद । तस्माच्चेन्न प्रमाद्यति । शरीरे
पाप्मनो हित्वा । सर्वान् कामान् समश्नुत इति । तस्यैष एव शारीर
आत्मा यः पूर्वस्य ।

तस्माद्वा एतस्माद्विज्ञानमयात् । अन्योऽन्तर आत्माऽऽनन्दमयः । तेनैष
पूर्णः । स वा एष पुरुषविध एव । तस्य पुरुषविधताम् । अन्वयं पुरुष-
विधः । तस्य प्रियमेव शिरः । मोदो दक्षिणः पक्षः । प्रमोद उत्तरः
पक्षः । आनन्द आत्मा । ब्रह्म पुच्छं प्रतिष्ठा । तदप्येष श्लोको भवति ॥

Knowledge spreadeth the feast of sacrifice and knowledge spreadeth also the feast of works; all the gods offer adoration to him
as to Brahman and the Elder of the Universe. For if one worship
Brahman as the knowledge and if one swerve not from it neither
falter, then he casteth sin from him in this body and tasteth all
desire. And this Self of Knowledge is the soul in the body to the
former one which was of Mind.

Now there is yet a second and inner self which is other than
this which is of Knowledge and it is fashioned out of Bliss. And
the Self of Bliss filleth the Self of Knowledge. Now the Bliss-Self
is made in the image of a man; according as is the human image
of the other, so is it made in the image of the man. Love is the
head of Him, Joy is His right side, pleasure is His left side; Bliss
is His spirit which is the self of Him; the Eternal is His lower
member wherein He resteth abidingly. Whereof this is the Scripture.

CHAPTER SIX

असन्नेव स भवति। असद् ब्रह्मेति वेद चेत्। अस्ति ब्रह्मेति चेद्वेद।
सन्तमेनं ततो विदुरिति॥ तस्यैष एव शारीर आत्मा यः पूर्वस्य।
अथातोऽनुप्रश्नाः। उताविद्वानमुं लोकं प्रेत्य। कश्चन गच्छती ३। आहो
विद्वानमुं लोकं प्रेत्य। कश्चित्समश्नुता३ उ।

सोऽकामयत। बहु स्यां प्रजायेयेति। स तपोऽतप्यत। स तपस्तप्त्वा।
इद॰ सर्वमसृजत। यदिदं किंच। तत् सृष्ट्वा तदेवानुप्राविशत्। तदनु-
प्रविश्य। सच्च त्यच्चाभवत्। निरुक्तं चानिरुक्तं च। निलयनं चानि-
लयनं च। विज्ञानं चाविज्ञानं च। सत्यं चानृतं च सत्यमभवत्। यदिदं
किंच। तत्सत्यमित्याचक्षते। तदप्येष श्लोको भवति॥

One becometh as the unexisting, if he know the Eternal as negation; but if one knoweth of the Eternal that He is, then men know
him for the saint and the one reality. And this Self of Bliss is
the soul in the body to the former one which was of Knowledge.
And thereupon there arise these questions. "When one who hath
not the Knowledge, passeth over to that other world, doth any
such travel farther? Or when one who knoweth, hath passed over
to the other world, doth any such enjoy possession?"

The Spirit desired of old, "I would be manifold for the birth
of peoples." Therefore He concentrated all Himself[1] in thought,
and by the force of His brooding He created all this universe, yea,
all whatsoever existeth. Now when He had brought it forth, He
entered into that He had created, He entering in became the Is
here and the May Be there; He became that which is defined and
that which hath no feature; He became this housèd thing and
that houseless; He became Knowledge and He became Ignorance; He became Truth and He became falsehood. Yea, He
became all truth, even whatsoever here existeth. Therefore they
say of Him that He is Truth. Whereof this is the Scripture.

[1] *Or,* strength.

CHAPTER SEVEN

असद् वा इदमग्र आसीत् । ततो वै सदजायत । तदात्मानꣳ स्वयमकुरुत ।
तस्मात् तत्सुकृतमुच्यत इति । यद् वै तत् सुकृतम् । रसो वै सः । रसꣳ
ह्येवायं लब्ध्वानन्दी भवति । को ह्येवान्यात् कः प्राण्यात् । यदेष आकाश
आनन्दो न स्यात् । एष ह्येवानन्दयाति । यदा ह्येवैष एतस्मिन्नदृश्ये-
ऽनात्म्येऽनिरुक्तेऽनिलयनेऽभयं प्रतिष्ठां विन्दते । अथ सोऽभयं गतो भवति ।
यदा ह्येवैष एतस्मिन्नुदरमन्तरं कुरुते । अथ तस्य भयं भवति । तत्त्वेव
भयं विदुषो मन्वानस्य । तदप्येष श्लोको भवति ॥

In the beginning all this Universe was Non-Existent and Unmanifest, from which this manifest Existence was born. Itself
created itself; none other created it. Therefore they say of it
the well and beautifully made. Lo, this that is well and beautifully made, verily it is no other than the delight behind existence.
When he hath gotten him this delight, then it is that this creature
becometh a thing of bliss; for who could labour to draw in the
breath or who could have strength to breathe it out, if there were
not that Bliss in the heaven of his heart, the ether within his
being? It is He that is the fountain of bliss; for when the Spirit
that is within us findeth his refuge and firm foundation in the
Invisible, Bodiless, Undefinable and Unhoused Eternal, then he
hath passed beyond the reach of Fear. But when the Spirit that
is within us maketh for himself even a little difference in the
Eternal, then he hath fear, yea, the Eternal himself becometh a
terror to such a knower who thinketh not. Whereof this is the
Scripture.

CHAPTER EIGHT

भीषाऽस्माद्वातः पवते । भीषोदेति सूर्यः । भीषाऽस्मादग्निश्चेन्द्रश्च ।
मृत्युर्धावति पञ्चम इति ॥ सैषाऽऽनन्दस्य मीमांसा भवति । युवा स्यात्
साधुयुवाऽध्यायकः । आशिष्ठो द्रढिष्ठो बलिष्ठः । तस्येयं पृथिवी सर्वा
वित्तस्य पूर्णा स्यात् । स एको मानुष आनन्दः । ते ये शतं
मानुषा आनन्दाः । स एको मनुष्यगन्धर्वाणामानन्दः । श्रोत्रियस्य चाकाम-
हतस्य । ते ये शतं मनुष्यगन्धर्वाणामानन्दाः । स एको देवगन्धर्वा-
णामानन्दः । श्रोत्रियस्य चाकामहतस्य । ते ये शतं देवगन्धर्वाणामानन्दाः ।
स एकः पितॄणां चिरलोकलोकानामानन्दः । श्रोत्रियस्य चाकामहतस्य ।
ते ये शतं पितॄणां चिरलोकलोकानामानन्दाः । स एक आजानजानां देवा-
नामानन्दः । श्रोत्रियस्य चाकामहतस्य । ते ये शतमाजानजानां देवा-
नामानन्दाः । स एकः कर्मदेवानां देवानामानन्दः । ये कर्मणा देवानपि-
यन्ति । श्रोत्रियस्य चाकामहतस्य । ते ये शतं कर्मदेवानां देवानामा-
नन्दाः । स एको देवानामानन्दः । श्रोत्रियस्य चाकामहतस्य । ते ये शतं
देवानामानन्दाः । स एक इन्द्रस्यानन्दः । श्रोत्रियस्य चाकामहतस्य । ते
ये शतमिन्द्रस्यानन्दाः । स एको बृहस्पतेरानन्दः । श्रोत्रियस्य चाकाम-
हतस्य । ते ये शतं बृहस्पतेरानन्दाः । स एकः प्रजापतेरानन्दः ।
श्रोत्रियस्य चाकामहतस्य । ते ये शतं प्रजापतेरानन्दाः । स एको ब्रह्मण
आनन्दः । श्रोत्रियस्य चाकामहतस्य ।

स यश्चायं पुरुषे । यश्चासावादित्ये । स एकः । स य एवंवित् ।
अस्माल्लोकात् प्रेत्य । एतमन्नमयमात्मानमुपसङ्क्रामति । एतं प्राणमय-
मात्मानमुपसङ्क्रामति । एतं मनोमयमात्मानमुपसङ्क्रामति । एतं
विज्ञानमयमात्मानमुपसङ्क्रामति । एतमानन्दमयमात्मानमुपसङ्क्रामति ।
तदप्येष श्लोको भवति ॥

Through the fear of Him the Wind bloweth; through the fear of
Him the Sun riseth; through the fear of Him Indra and Agni and
Death hasten in their courses. Behold this exposition of the Bliss
to which ye shall hearken. Let there be a young man, excellent
and lovely in his youth, a great student; let him have fair
manners and a most firm heart and great strength of body, and
let all this wide earth be full of wealth for his enjoying. That is
the measure of bliss of one human being. Now a hundred and
a hundredfold of the human measure of bliss, is one bliss of
men that have become angels in heaven. And this is the bliss of
the Vedawise whose soul the blight of desire not toucheth. A

hundred and a hundredfold of this measure of angelic bliss is one bliss of Gods that are angels in heaven. And this is the bliss of the Vedawise whose soul the blight of desire not toucheth. A hundred and a hundredfold of this measure of divine angelic bliss is one bliss of the Fathers whose world of heaven is their world for ever. And this is the bliss of the Vedawise whose soul the blight of desire not toucheth. A hundred and a hundredfold of this measure of bliss of the Fathers whose worlds are for ever, is one bliss of the Gods who are born as Gods in heaven. And this is the bliss of the Vedawise whose soul the blight of desire not toucheth. A hundred and a hundredfold of this measure of bliss of the firstborn in heaven, is one bliss of the Gods of work who are Gods, for by the strength of their deeds they depart and are Gods in heaven. And this is the bliss of the Vedawise whose soul the blight of desire not toucheth. A hundred and a hundredfold of this measure of bliss of the Gods of work, is one bliss of the great Gods who are Gods for ever. And this is the bliss of the Vedawise whose soul the blight of desire not toucheth. A hundred and a hundredfold of this measure of divine bliss, is one bliss of Indra, the King in Heaven. And this is the bliss of the Vedawise whose soul the blight of desire not toucheth. A hundred and a hundredfold of this measure of Indra's bliss is one bliss of Brihaspati, who taught the Gods in heaven. And this is the bliss of the Vedawise whose soul the blight of desire not toucheth. A hundred and a hundredfold of this measure of Brihaspati's bliss, is one bliss of Prajapati, the Almighty Father. And this is the bliss of the Vedawise whose soul the blight of desire not toucheth. A hundred and a hundredfold of this measure of Prajapati's bliss, is one bliss of the Eternal Spirit. And this is the bliss of the Vedawise whose soul the blight of desire not toucheth.

The Spirit who is here in a man and the Spirit who is there in the Sun, it is one Spirit and there is no other. He who knoweth this, when he hath gone away from this world, passeth to this Self which is of food; he passeth to this Self which is of Prana; he passeth to this Self which is of Mind; he passeth to this Self which is of Knowledge; he passeth to this Self which is of Bliss. Whereof this is the Scripture.

CHAPTER NINE

यतो वाचो निवर्तन्ते । अप्राप्य मनसा सह । आनन्दं ब्रह्मणो विद्वान् ।
न बिभेति कुतश्चनेति । एतं ह वाव न तपति । किमहं साधु नाकर-
वम् । किमहं पापमकरवमिति । स य एवं विद्वानेते आत्मानं स्पृणुते ।
उभे ह्येवैष एते आत्मानं स्पृणुते । य एवं वेद । इत्युपनिषत् ।
        सह नाववतु । सह नौ भुनक्तु । सह वीर्यं करवावहै । तेजस्वि
नावधीतमस्तु । मा विद्विषावहै ॥ ॐ शान्तिः शान्तिः शान्तिः ॥

The Bliss of the Eternal from which words turn back without
attaining and mind also returneth baffled, who knoweth the Bliss
of the Eternal? He feareth not for aught in this world or elsewhere. Verily to him cometh not remorse and her torment saying, "Why have I left undone the good and why have I done that
which was evil?" For he who knoweth the Eternal, knoweth these
that they are alike, and delivereth from them his Spirit; yea,
he knoweth both evil and good for what they are and delivereth
his Spirit, who knoweth the Eternal. And this is Upanishad, the
secret of the Veda.

Together may He protect us, together may He possess us,
together may we make unto us strength and virility! May our
reading be full of light and power! May we never hate! OM!
Peace! Peace! Peace!

BHRIGUVALLI

हरिः ॐ। सह नाववतु। सह नौ भुनक्तु। सह वीर्यं करवावहै।
तेजस्वि नावधीतमस्तु। मा विद्विषावहै॥ ॐ शान्तिः शान्तिः शान्तिः॥

Hari OM. Together may He protect us, together may He possess
us, together may we make unto us force and virility! May our
reading be full of light and power! May we never hate! OM!
Peace! Peace! Peace!

CHAPTER ONE

भृगुर्वै वारुणिः। वरुणं पितरमुपससार। अधीहि भगवो ब्रह्मेति। तस्मा
एतत् प्रोवाच। अन्नं प्राणं चक्षुः श्रोत्रं मनो वाचमिति। तं होवाच।
यतो वा इमानि भूतानि जायन्ते। येन जातानि जीवन्ति। यत् प्रयन्त्यभि-
संविशन्ति। तद् विजिज्ञासस्व। तद् ब्रह्मेति। स तपोऽतप्यत। स
तपस्तप्त्वा॥

Bhrigu, Varuna's son, came unto his father Varuna and said,
"Lord, teach me the Eternal." And his father declared it unto
him thus, "Food and Prana and Eye and Ear and Mind — even
these." Verily he said unto him, "Seek thou to know that from
which these creatures are born, whereby being born they live
and to which they go hence and enter again; for that is the Eternal." And Bhrigu concentrated himself in thought and by the
askesis of his brooding

CHAPTER TWO

अन्नं ब्रह्मेति व्यजानात्। अन्नाद्ध्येव खल्विमानि भूतानि जायन्ते। अन्नेन
जातानि जीवन्ति। अन्नं प्रयन्त्यभिसंविशन्तीति॥ तद्विज्ञाय। पुनरेव
वरुणं पितरमुपससार। अधीहि भगवो ब्रह्मेति। तं होवाच। तपसा
ब्रह्म विजिज्ञासस्व। तपो ब्रह्मेति। स तपोऽतप्यत॥ स तपस्तप्त्वा॥

He knew food for the Eternal. For from food alone, it appeareth,
are these creatures born and being born they live by food, and
into food they depart and enter again. And when he had known
this, he came again to Varuna his father and said, "Lord, teach
me the Eternal." And his father said to him, "By askesis do thou
seek to know the Eternal, for askesis[1] is the Eternal." He concentrated himself in thought and by the energy of his brooding

CHAPTER THREE

प्राणो ब्रह्मेति व्यजानात्। प्राणाद्ध्येव खल्विमानि भूतानि जायन्ते।
प्राणेन जातानि जीवन्ति। प्राणं प्रयन्त्यभिसंविशन्तीति॥ तद्विज्ञाय।
पुनरेव वरुणं पितरमुपससार। अधीहि भगवो ब्रह्मेति। तं होवाच।
तपसा ब्रह्म विजिज्ञासस्व। तपो ब्रह्मेति। स तपोऽतप्यत। स तपस्तप्त्वा॥

He knew Prana for the Eternal. For from Prana alone, it
appeareth, are these creatures born and being born they live by
Prana and to Prana they go hence and return. And when he
had known this, he came again to Varuna his father and said,
"Lord, teach me the Eternal." But his father said to him, "By
askesis do thou seek to know the Eternal, for askesis is the
Eternal." He concentrated himself in thought and by the energy
of his brooding

---

[1] *Or*, concentration in thought.

CHAPTER FOUR

मनो ब्रह्मेति व्यजानात् । मनसो ह्येव खल्विमानि भूतानि जायन्ते । मनसा
जातानि जीवन्ति । मनः प्रयन्त्यभिसंविशन्तीति ॥ तद्विज्ञाय । पुनरेव
वरुणं पितरमुपससार । अधीहि भगवो ब्रह्मेति । तं होवाच । तपसा
ब्रह्म विजिज्ञासस्व । तपो ब्रह्मेति । स तपोऽतप्यत । स तपस्तप्त्वा ॥

He knew mind for the Eternal. For from mind alone, it appeareth,
are these creatures born and being born they live by mind, and
to mind they go hence and return. And when he had known this,
he came again to Varuna his father and said, "Lord, teach me
the Eternal." But his father said to him, "By askesis do thou seek
to know the Eternal, for concentration in thought[1] is the Eternal." He concentrated himself in thought and by the energy of
his brooding

CHAPTER FIVE

विज्ञानं ब्रह्मेति व्यजानात् । विज्ञानाद्ध्येव खल्विमानि भूतानि जायन्ते ।
विज्ञानेन जातानि जीवन्ति । विज्ञानं प्रयन्त्यभिसंविशन्तीति ॥ तद्विज्ञाय ।
पुनरेव वरुणं पितरमुपससार । अधीहि भगवो ब्रह्मेति । तं होवाच ।
तपसा ब्रह्म विजिज्ञासस्व । तपो ब्रह्मेति । स तपोऽतप्यत । स तप-
स्तप्त्वा ॥

He knew Knowledge for the Eternal. For from Knowledge
alone, it appeareth, are these creatures born and being born they
live by Knowledge and to Knowledge they go hence and return.
And when he had known this, he came again to Varuna his father
and said, "Lord, teach me the Eternal." But his father said to
him, "By askesis do thou seek to know the Eternal, for concentration of force is the Eternal." He concentrated himself in
thought and by the energy of his brooding

---

[1] *Or*, concentration of force.

CHAPTER SIX

आनन्दो ब्रह्मेति व्यजानात् । आनन्दाद्धचेव खल्विमानि भूतानि जायन्ते ।
आनन्देन जातानि जीवन्ति । आनन्दं प्रयन्त्यभिसंविशन्तीति ॥ सैषा
भार्गवी वारुणी विद्या । परमे व्योमन्प्रतिष्ठिता । स य एवं वेद प्रति-
तिष्ठति । अन्नवानन्नादो भवति । महान् भवति प्रजया पशुभिर्ब्रह्म-
वर्चसेन । महान् कीर्त्या ॥

He knew Bliss for the Eternal. For from Bliss alone, it appeareth,
are these creatures born and being born they live by Bliss and
to Bliss they go hence and return. This is the lore of Bhrigu, the
lore of Varuna, which hath its firm base in the highest heaven.
Who knoweth, getteth his firm base, he becometh the master of
food and its eater, great in progeny, great in cattle, great in the
splendour of holiness, great in glory.

CHAPTER SEVEN

अन्नं न निन्द्यात् । तद् व्रतम् । प्राणो वा अन्नम् । शरीरमन्नादम् ।
प्राणे शरीरं प्रतिष्ठितम् । शरीरे प्राणः प्रतिष्ठितः । तदेतदन्नमन्ने प्रति-
ष्ठितम् । स य एतदन्नमन्ने प्रतिष्ठितं वेद प्रतितिष्ठति । अन्नवानन्नादो
भवति । महान् भवति प्रजया पशुभिर्ब्रह्मवर्चसेन । महान् कीर्त्या ॥

Thou shalt not blame food; for that is thy commandment unto
labour. Verily Prana also is food, and the body is the eater.
The body is established upon Prana and Prana is established
upon the body. Therefore food here is established upon food.
He who knoweth this food that is established upon food, getteth
his firm base, he becometh the master of food and its eater, great
in progeny, great in cattle, great in the radiance of holiness, great
in glory.

CHAPTER EIGHT

अन्नं न परिचक्षीत। तद् व्रतम्। आपो वा अन्नम्। ज्योतिरन्नादम्।
अप्सु ज्योतिः प्रतिष्ठितम्। ज्योतिष्यापः प्रतिष्ठिताः। तदेतदन्नमन्ने
प्रतिष्ठितम्। स य एतदन्नमन्ने प्रतिष्ठितं वेद प्रतितिष्ठति। अन्नवानन्नादो
भवति। महान् भवति प्रजया पशुभिर्ब्रह्मवर्चसेन। महान् कीर्त्या॥

Thou shalt not reject food; for that too is the vow of thy labour.
Verily the waters also are food, and the bright fire is the eater.
The fire is established upon the waters and the waters are established upon the fires. Here too is food established upon food.
He who knoweth this food that is established upon food, getteth
his firm base, he becometh the master of food and its eater, great in
progeny, great in cattle, great in the radiance of holiness, great
in glory.

CHAPTER NINE

अन्नं बहु कुर्वीत। तद् व्रतम्। पृथिवी वा अन्नम्। आकाशोऽन्नादः।
पृथिव्यामाकाशः प्रतिष्ठितः। आकाशे पृथिवी प्रतिष्ठिता। तदेतदन्नमन्ने
प्रतिष्ठितम्। स य एतदन्नमन्ने प्रतिष्ठितं वेद प्रतितिष्ठति। अन्नवानन्नादो
भवति। महान् भवति प्रजया पशुभिर्ब्रह्मवर्चसेन। महान् कीर्त्या॥

Thou shalt increase and amass food; for that too is thy commandment unto labour. Verily earth also is food and ether is
the eater. Ether is established upon earth and earth is established
upon ether. Here too is food established upon food. He who knoweth this food that is established upon food, getteth his firm base.
He becometh the master of food and its eater, great in progeny,
great in cattle, great in the radiance of holiness, great in glory.

CHAPTER TEN

न कञ्चन वसतौ प्रत्याचक्षीत। तद् व्रतम्। तस्माद् यया कया च
विधया बह्वन्नं प्राप्नुयात्। अराध्यस्मा अन्नमित्याचक्षते। एतद् वै मुखतो-
ऽन्नं राद्धम्। मुखतोऽस्मा अन्नं राध्यते। एतद् वै मध्यतोऽन्नं राद्धम्।
मध्यतोऽस्मा अन्नं राध्यते। एतद् वा अन्ततोऽन्नं राद्धम्। अन्ततोऽस्मा
अन्नं राध्यते। य एवं वेद। क्षेम इति वाचि। योगक्षेम इति प्राणा-
पानयोः। कर्मेति हस्तयोः। गतिरिति पादयोः। विमुक्तिरिति पायौ।
इति मानुषीः समाज्ञाः॥ अथ दैवीः। तृप्तिरिति वृष्टौ। बलमिति
विद्युति। यश इति पशुषु। ज्योतिरिति नक्षत्रेषु। प्रजातिरमृतमानन्द
इत्युपस्थे। सर्वमित्याकाशे। तत्प्रतिष्ठेत्युपासीत। प्रतिष्ठावान् भवति।
तन्मह इत्युपासीत। महान् भवति। तन्मन इत्युपासीत। मानवान्
भवति। तन्नम इत्युपासीत। नम्यन्तेऽस्मै कामाः। तद् ब्रह्मेत्युपासीत।
ब्रह्मवान् भवति। तद् ब्रह्मणः परिमर इत्युपासीत। पर्येणं म्रियन्ते
द्विषन्तः सपत्नाः। परि येऽप्रिया भ्रातृव्याः। स यश्चायं पुरुषे। य-
श्चासावादित्ये। स एकः। स य एवंवित्। अस्माल्लोकात् प्रेत्य।
एतमन्नमयमात्मानमुपसङ्क्रम्य। एतं प्राणमयमात्मानमुपसङ्क्रम्य।
एतं मनोमयमात्मानमुपसङ्क्रम्य। एतं विज्ञानमयमात्मानमुपसङ्क्रम्य।
एतमानन्दमयमात्मानमुपसङ्क्रम्य। इमाँल्लोकान् कामान्नी कामरूप्यनु-
सञ्चरन्। एतत् साम गायन्नास्ते। हा३वु हा३वु हा३वु। अहमन्न-
महमन्नमहमन्नम्। अहमन्नादो३ऽहमन्नादो३ऽहमन्नादः। अहं श्लोककृदहं
श्लोककृदहं श्लोककृत्। अहमस्मि प्रथमजा ऋता३स्य। पूर्वं देवेभ्यो-
ऽमृतस्य ना३भायि। यो मा ददाति स इदेव मा३ऽवाः। अहमन्नमन्न-
मदन्तमा३द्मि। अहं विश्वं भुवनमभ्यभवा३म्। सुवर्णं ज्योतीः। य
एवं वेद। इत्युपनिषत्॥

सह नाववतु। सह नौ भुनक्तु। सह वीर्यं करवावहै। तेजस्वि
नावधीतमस्तु। मा विद्विषावहै। ॐ शान्तिः शान्तिः शान्तिः॥

Thou shalt not reject any man in thy habitation, for that too is
thy commandment unto labour. Therefore in whatsoever sort
do thou get thee great store of food. They say unto the stranger
in their dwelling, "Arise, the food is ready." Was the food made
ready at the beginning? To him also is food made ready in the
beginning. Was the food made ready in the middle? To him also
is food made ready in the middle. Was the food made ready at
the end and last? To him also is the food made ready at the end
and last, who hath this knowledge As prosperity in speech, as

getting and having in the main breath and the nether, as work in the hands, as movement in the feet, as discharge in the anus, these are the cognitions in the human. Then in the divine; as satisfaction in the rain, as force in the lightning, as splendour in the beasts, as brightness in the constellations, as procreation and bliss and death conquered in the organ of pleasure, as the All in Ether. Pursue thou Him as the firm foundation of things and thou shalt get thee firm foundation; pursue Him as Mahas, thou shalt become Mighty; pursue Him as Mind, thou shalt become full of mind; pursue Him as adoration, thy desires shall bow down before thee; pursue Him as the Eternal, thou shalt become full of the Spirit; pursue Him as the destruction of the Eternal that rangeth abroad, thy rivals and thy haters shall perish thick around thee and thy kin who loved thee not. The Spirit who is here in man and the Spirit who is there in the Sun, lo, it is One Spirit and there is no other. He who hath this knowledge, when he goeth from this world having passed to the Self which is of food; having passed to the Self which is of Prana; having passed to the Self which is of Mind; having passed to the Self which is of Knowledge; having passed to the Self which is of Bliss, lo, he rangeth about the worlds, and eateth what he will and taketh what shape he will and ever he singeth the mighty Sama. "Ho! ho! ho! I am food! I am food! I am food! I am the eater of food! I am the eater! I am the eater! I am he who maketh Scripture! I am he who maketh! I am he who maketh! I am the firstborn of the Law; before the gods were, I am, yea, at the very heart of immortality. He who giveth me, verily he preserveth me; for I being food, eat him that eateth. I have conquered the whole world and possessed it, my light is as the sun in its glory." Thus he singeth, who hath the knowledge. This verily is Upanishad, the secret of the Veda.

Together may He protect us, together may He possess us, together may we make unto us strength and virility! May our study be full of light and power! May we never hate! OM! Peace! Peace! Peace!

AITAREYA UPANISHAD

Aitareya Upanishad

CHAPTER ONE: SECTION I

हरिः ॐ ॥ आत्मा वा इदमेक एवाग्र आसीन्नान्यत्किञ्चन मिषत्;
स ईक्षत लोकान्नु सृजा इति ॥१॥

1. Hari OM. In the beginning the Spirit was One and all this
(universe) was the Spirit; there was nought else that saw.[1]
The Spirit thought, "Lo, I will make me worlds from out
my being."

स इमाँल्लोकानसृजत —अम्भो मरीचीमँरमापोऽदोऽम्भः परेण दिवं
द्यौः प्रतिष्ठाऽन्तरिक्षं मरीचयः। पृथिवी मरो या अधस्तात्ता
आपः ॥२॥

2. These were the worlds he made; *ambhaḥ*, of the ethereal
waters, *marīcīḥ*, of light, *mara*, of death and mortal things,
āpaḥ, of the lower waters. Beyond the shining firmament
are the ethereal waters and the firmament is their base and
resting-place; Space is the world of light; the earth is the
world mortal; and below the earth are the lower waters.

स ईक्षतेमे नु लोका लोकपालान्नु सृजा इति। सोऽद्भ्य एव पुरुषं
समुद्धृत्यामूर्छयत् ॥३॥

3. The Spirit thought, "Lo, these are the worlds; and now will
I make me guardians for my worlds." Therefore he gathered
the Purusha out of the waters and gave Him shape and
substance.

तमभ्यतपत्तस्याभितप्तस्य मुखं निरभिद्यत, यथाण्डं; मुखाद्वाग्वा-
ग्निग्निर्नासिके निरभिद्येतां, नासिकाभ्यां प्राणः। प्राणाद्वायुरक्षिणी
निरभिद्येतामक्षिभ्यां चक्षुश्चक्षुष आदित्यः कर्णौ निरभिद्येतां, कर्णा-
भ्यां श्रोत्रं श्रोत्राद्दिशस्त्वङ निरभिद्यत, त्वचो लोमानि लोमभ्य

[1] Or, moving.

ओषधिवनस्पतयो हृदयं निरभिद्यत, हृदयान्मनो मनसश्चन्द्रमा
नाभिर्निरभिद्यत नाभ्या अपानोऽपानान्मृत्युः शिश्नं निरभिद्यत,
शिश्नाद्रेतो रेतस आपः ॥४॥

4. Yea, the Spirit brooded over Him and of Him thus brooded
over the mouth broke forth, as when an egg is hatched and
breaketh; from the mouth brake Speech and of Speech fire
was born. The nostrils brake forth and from the nostrils
Breath and of Breath air was born. The eyes brake forth
and from the eyes Sight and of Sight the Sun was born. The
ears brake forth and from the ears Hearing and of Hearing
the regions were born. The Skin brake forth and from the
Skin hairs and from the hairs herbs of healing and all trees
and plants were born. The heart brake forth and from the
heart Mind and of Mind the moon was born. The navel
brake forth and from the navel *apāna* and of *apāna* Death
was born. The organ of pleasure brake forth and from the
organ seed and of seed the waters were born.

CHAPTER ONE: SECTION II

ता एता देवताः सृष्टा अस्मिन्महत्यर्णवे प्रापतंस्तमशनायापिपासाभ्या-
मन्ववार्जत् । ता एनमब्रुवन्नायतनं नः प्रजानीहि, यस्मिन् प्रतिष्ठिता
अन्नमवामेति ॥१॥

1. These were the Gods that He created; they fell into this
great Ocean, and Hunger and Thirst leaped upon them.
Then they said to Him, "Command unto us an habitation
that we may dwell secure and eat of food."

ताभ्यो गामानयत्ता अब्रुवन्न वै नोऽयमलमिति ताभ्योऽश्वमानयत्ता
अब्रुवन्न वै नोऽयमलमिति ॥२॥

2. He brought unto them the cow, but they said, "Verily, it is
not sufficient for us." He brought unto them the horse,
but they said, "Verily, it is not enough for us."

ताभ्यः पुरुषमानयत्ता अब्रुवन् सुकृतं बतेति; पुरुषो वाव सुकृतम् ।
ता अब्रवीद्ययातनं प्रविशतेति ॥३॥

3. He brought unto them Man, and they said, "O well
fashioned truly! Man indeed is well and beautifully made."
Then the Spirit said unto them, "Enter ye in each according
to his habitation."

अग्निर्वाग्भूत्वा मुखं प्राविशद्वायुः प्राणो भूत्वा नासिके प्राविशदादि-
त्यश्चक्षुर्भूत्वाऽक्षिणी प्राविशद्दिशः श्रोत्रं भूत्वा कर्णौ प्राविशन्नोषधि-
वनस्पतयो लोमानि भूत्वा त्वचं प्राविशंश्चन्द्रमा मनो भूत्वा हृदयं
प्राविशन्मृत्युरपानो भूत्वा नाभिं प्राविशदापो रेतो भूत्वा शिश्नं
प्राविशन् ॥४॥

4. Fire became Speech and entered into the mouth; Air became Breath and entered into the nostrils; the Sun became
Sight and entered into the eyes; the Quarters became Hearing and entered into the ears; Herbs of healing and the
plants and trees became Hairs and entered into the skin;
the Moon became Mind and entered into the heart; Death
became *apāna*, the lower breathing, and entered into the
navel; the Waters became Seed and entered into the organ.

तमशनापिपासे अब्रूतामावाभ्यामभिप्रजानीहीति । ते अब्रवीदेता-
स्वेव वां देवतास्वाभजाम्येतासु भागिन्यौ करोमीति । तस्मादस्यं
कस्यं च देवतायै हविर्गृह्यते भागिन्यावेवास्यामशनापिपासे भवतः ॥५॥

5. Then Hunger and Thirst said unto the Spirit, "Unto us too
command an habitation." But He said unto them, "Even
among these gods do I apportion you; lo! I have made
you sharers in their godhead." Therefore to whatever god
the oblation is offered, Hunger and Thirst surely have their
share in the offering.

CHAPTER ONE : SECTION III

स ईक्षतेमे नु लोकाश्च लोकपालाश्चान्नमेभ्यः सृजा इति ॥१॥

1. The Spirit thought, "These verily are my worlds and their guardians; and now will I make me food for these."

सोऽपोऽभ्यतपत्; ताभ्योऽभितप्ताभ्यो मूर्तिरजायत। या वै सा मूर्तिरजायताशं वै तत् ॥२॥

2. The Spirit brooded in might upon the waters and from the waters brooded mightily over, Form was born. Lo, all this that was born as form, is no other than Food.

तदेनदभिसृष्टं पराङत्यजिघांसत्। तद्वाचाजिघृक्षत्, तन्नाशक्नोद्वाचा ग्रहीतुम्। स यद्धैनद्वाचाग्रहैष्यदभिव्याहृत्य हैवान्नमत्रप्स्यत् ॥३॥

3. Food being created fled back from His grasp. By speech He would have seized it, but He could not seize it by speech. Had He seized it by speech, then would a man be satisfied by merely speaking food.

तत् प्राणेनाजिघृक्षत्, तन्नाशक्नोत् प्राणेन ग्रहीतुम्। स यद्धैनत् प्राणेनाग्रहैष्यदभिप्राण्य हैवान्नमत्रप्स्यत् ॥४॥

4. By the breath He would have seized it, but He could not seize it by the breath. Had He seized it by the breath, then would a man be satisfied by merely breathing food.

तच्चक्षुषाजिघृक्षत्, तन्नाशक्नोच्चक्षुषा ग्रहीतुम्। स यद्धैनच्चक्षुषाप्रह-ष्यद् दृष्ट्वा हैवान्नमत्रप्स्यत् ॥५॥

5. By the eye He would have seized it, but He could not seize it by the eye. Had He seized it by the eye, then would a man be satisfied by merely seeing food.

तच्छ्रोत्रेणाजिघृक्षत्, तन्नाशक्नोच्छ्रोत्रेण ग्रहीतुम्। स यद्धैनच्छ्रोत्रे-णाग्रहैष्यच्छ्रुत्वा हैवान्नमत्रप्स्यत् ॥६॥

6. By the ear He would have seized it, but He could not seize it by the ear. Had He seized it by the ear, then would a man be satisfied by merely hearing food.

तत्त्वचाजिघृक्षत्, तन्नाशक्नोत्त्वचा प्रहीतुम् । स यद्धैनत्त्वचाप्रहे-
ष्यत्स्पृष्ट्वा हैवान्नमत्रप्स्यत् ॥७॥

7. By the skin He would have seized it, but He could not seize it by the skin. Had He seized it by the skin, then would a man be satisfied by merely touching food.

तन्मनसाजिघृक्षत्, तन्नाशक्नोन्मनसा प्रहीतुम् । स यद्धैनन्मनसा-
प्रहैष्यद्, ध्यात्वा हैवान्नमत्रप्स्यत् ॥८॥

8. By the Mind He would have seized it, but He could not seize it by the mind. Had He seized it by the mind, then would a man be satisfied by merely thinking food.

तच्छिश्नेनाजिघृक्षत्, तन्नाशक्नोच्छिश्नेन प्रहीतुम् । स यद्धैन-
च्छिश्नेनाप्रहैष्यद्विसृज्य हैवान्नमत्रप्स्यत् ॥९॥

9. By the organ He would have seized it, but He could not seize it by the organ. Had He seized it by the organ, then would a man be satisfied by merely emitting food.

तदपानेनाजिघृक्षत्, तदावयत् । सैषोऽन्नस्य ग्रहो यद्वायुरन्नायुर्वा एष
यद्वायुः ॥१०॥

10. By the *apāna* He would have seized it, and it was seized. Lo, this is the seizer of food which is also Breath of the Life, and therefore all that is Breath hath its life in food.

स ईक्षत कथं न्विदं मदृते स्यादिति । स ईक्षत कतरेण प्रपद्या
इति । स ईक्षत यदि वाचाभिव्याहृतं, यदि प्राणेनाभिप्राणितं,
यदि चक्षुषा दृष्टं, यदि श्रोत्रेण श्रुतं, यदि त्वचा स्पृष्टं, यदि मनसा
ध्यातं, यद्यपानेनाभ्यपानितं, यदि शिश्नेन विसृष्टमथ
कोऽहमिति ॥११॥

11. The Spirit thought, "Without Me how should all this be?" and He thought, "By what way shall I enter in?" He thought also, "If utterance is by Speech, if breathing is by the Breath, if sight is by the Eye, if hearing is by the Ear, if

thought is by the Mind, if the lower workings are by *apāna*,
if emission is by the organ, who then am I?"

स एतमेव सीमानं विदार्यैतया द्वारा प्रापद्यत। सैषा विदृतिर्नाम
द्वास्तदेतन्नान्दनम्। तस्य त्रय आवसथास्त्रयः स्वप्नाः। अयमा-
वसथोऽयमावसथोऽयमावसथ इति ॥१२॥

12. It was this bound that He cleft, it was by this door that He
    entered in. 'Tis this that is called the gate of the cleaving;
    this is the door of His coming and here is the place of His
    delight. He hath three mansions in His city, three dreams
    wherein He dwelleth, and of each in turn He saith, "Lo, this
    is my habitation" and "This is my habitation" and "This is
    my habitation."

स जातो भूतान्यभिव्यैख्यत्, किमिहान्यं वावदिषदिति। स एतमेव
पुरुषं ब्रह्म ततममपश्यदिदमदर्शमिती३ ॥१३॥

13. Now when He was born, He thought and spoke only of
    Nature and her creations; in this world of matter of what
    else should He speak or reason? Thereafter He beheld that
    Being who is the Brahman and the last Essence. He said,
    "Yea, this is He; verily, I have beheld Him."

तस्मादिदन्द्रो नामेदन्द्रो ह वै नाम। तमिदन्द्रं सन्तमिन्द्र इत्या-
चक्षते परोक्षेण। परोक्षप्रिया इव हि देवाः, परोक्षप्रिया इव हि
देवाः ॥१४॥

14. Therefore is He Idandra; for Idandra is the true name of
    Him. But though He is Idandra, they call Him Indra be-
    cause of the veil of the Unrevelation; for the gods love the
    veil of the Unrevelation, yea, verily, the gods love the
    Unrevelation.

CHAPTER TWO

पुरुषे ह वा अयमादितो गर्भो भवति । यदेतद्रेतः तदेतत्सर्वेभ्यो-
ऽङ्गेभ्यस्तेजः सम्भूतमात्मन्येवात्मानं बिभर्ति; तद्यदा स्त्रियां सिञ्च-
त्यथैनज्जनयति; तदस्य प्रथमं जन्म ॥१॥

1. In the male first the unborn child becometh. This which is
    seed is the force and heat of him that from all parts of the
    creature draweth together for becoming; therefore he beareth
    himself in himself, and when he casteth it into the woman, 'tis
    himself he begetteth. And this is the first birth of the Spirit.

तत् स्त्रिया आत्मभूयं गच्छति, यथा स्वमङ्गं तथा; तस्मादेनां
न हिनस्ति; सास्यैतमात्मानमत्र गतं भावयति ॥२॥

2. It becometh one self with the woman, therefore it doeth her
    no hurt and she cherisheth this self of her husband that hath
    got into her womb.

सा भावयित्री भावयितव्या भवति । तं स्त्री गर्भं बिभर्ति; सोऽग्र
एव कुमारं जन्मनोऽग्रेऽधिभावयति । स यत् कुमारं जन्मनोऽग्रे-
ऽधिभावयति, आत्मानमेव तद् भावयति, एषां लोकानां सन्तत्या ।
एवं सन्तता हीमे लोकास्तदस्य द्वितीयं जन्म ॥३॥

3. She the cherisher must be cherished. So the woman beareth
    the unborn child and the man cherisheth the boy even from
    the beginning ere it is born. And whereas he cherisheth
    the boy ere it is born, 'tis verily himself that he cherisheth
    for the continuance of these worlds and their peoples; for 'tis
    even thus the thread of these worlds spinneth on unbroken.
    And this is the second birth of the Spirit.

सोऽस्यायमात्मा पुण्येभ्यः कर्मभ्यः प्रतिधीयते । अथास्यायमितर
आत्मा कृतकृत्यो वयोगतः प्रैति, स इतः प्रयन्नेव पुनर्जायते; तदस्य
तृतीयं जन्म ॥४॥

4. Lo, this is the spirit and self of him and he maketh it his

vicegerent for the works of righteousness. Now this his
other self when it hath done the works it came to do and hath
reached its age, lo! it goeth hence, and even as it departeth,
it is born again. And this is the third birth of the Spirit.

तदुक्तमृषिणा — गर्भे नु सन्नन्वेषामवेदमहं देवानां जनिमानि विश्वा ।
शतं मा पुर आयसीररक्षन्नधः श्येनो जवसा निरदीयमिति; गर्भे
एवैतच्छयानो वामदेव एवमुवाच ॥५॥

5. Therefore it was said by the sage Vamadeva, "I, Vamadeva,
being yet in the womb, knew all the births of these gods
and their causes. In a hundred cities of iron they held me
down and kept me; I broke through them all with might[1]
and violence, like a hawk I soared up into my heavens."
While yet he lay in the womb, thus said Vamadeva.

स एवं विद्वानस्माच्छरीरभेदादूर्ध्वं उत्क्रम्यामुष्मिन् त्स्वर्गे लोके सर्वान्
कामानाप्त्वाऽमृतः समभवदमृतः समभवत् ॥६॥

6. And because he knew this, therefore when the strings of the
body were snapped asunder, lo, he soared forth into yonder
world of Paradise and there having possessed all desires, put
death behind him, yea, he put death behind him.

---

[1] *Or,* speed.

CHAPTER THREE

कोऽयमात्मेति वयमुपास्महे ? कतरः स आत्मा येन वा पश्यति,
येन वा शृणोति, येन वा गन्धानाजिघ्रति, येन वा वाचं व्याकरोति,
येन वा स्वादु चास्वादु च विजानाति ॥१॥

1. Who is this Spirit that we may adore Him? and which of
all these is the Spirit? By whom one seeth or by whom one
heareth or by whom one smelleth all kinds of perfume or by
whom one uttereth clearness of speech or by whom one
knoweth the sweet and bitter.

यदेतद्धृदयं मनश्चैतत् । संज्ञानमाज्ञानं विज्ञानं प्रज्ञानं मेधा दृष्टि-
र्धृतिर्मतिर्मनीषा जूतिः स्मृतिः संकल्पः ऋतुरसुः कामो वश इति सर्वा-
ण्येवैतानि प्रज्ञानस्य नामधेयानि भवन्ति ॥२॥

2. This which is the heart, is mind also. Concept and will and
analysis and wisdom and intellect and vision and continuity
of purpose and feeling and understanding, pain and memory
and volition and operation[1] of thought and vitality and
desire and passion, all these, yea all, are but names of the
Eternal Wisdom.

एष ब्रह्मैष इन्द्र एष प्रजापतिरेते सर्वं देवाः, इमानि च पञ्च महा-
भूतानि — पृथिवी वायुराकाश आपो ज्योतींषीत्येतानि, इमानि च
क्षुद्रमिश्राणीव बीजानि, इतराणि चेतराणि चाण्डजानि च जारुजानि
च, स्वेदजानि चोद्भिज्जानि चाश्वा गावः पुरुषा हस्तिनः, यत्किञ्चेदं
प्राणि जङ्गमं च पतत्रि च यच्च स्थावरं; सर्वं तत् प्रज्ञानेत्रं प्रज्ञाने
प्रतिष्ठितं प्रज्ञानेत्रो लोकः, प्रज्ञा प्रतिष्ठा, प्रज्ञानं ब्रह्म ॥३॥

3. This creating Brahma; this ruling Indra; this Prajapati,
Father of his peoples; all these Gods and these five elemental substances, even earth, air, ether, water and the
shining principles; and these great creatures and those
small; and seeds of either sort; and things egg-born and
things sweat-born and things born of the womb and plants

[1] Or, application.

that sprout; and horses and cattle and men and elephants;
yea, whatsoever thing here breatheth and all that moveth
and everything that hath wings and whatso moveth not; by
Wisdom all these are guided and have their firm abiding in
Wisdom. For Wisdom is the eye of the world, Wisdom is
the sure foundation, Wisdom is Brahman Eternal.

स एतेन प्रज्ञेनात्मनास्माल्लोकादुत्क्रम्यामुष्मिन् स्वर्गे लोके सर्वान्
कामानाप्त्वाऽमृतः समभवदमृतः समभवत् ॥४॥

4.　By the strength of the wise and seeing Self, the sage having
soared up from this world, mounted[1] into this other world
of Paradise; and there having possessed desire, put death
behind him, yea, he put death behind him.

---

[1] *Or,* ascended.

PRASHNA UPANISHAD

Prashna Upanishad

(Being the Upanishad of the Six Questions)

FIRST QUESTION

ॐ नमः परमात्मने । हरिः ॐ ॥ सुकेशा च भारद्वाजः, शैब्यश्च
सत्यकामः, सौर्यायणी च गार्ग्यः, कौसल्यश्चाश्वलायनः, भार्गवो
वैदर्भिः, कबन्धी कात्यायनस्ते हैते ब्रह्मपरा ब्रह्मनिष्ठाः परं ब्रह्मान्वेष-
माणा एष ह वै तत्सर्वं वक्ष्यतीति, ते ह समित्पाणयो भगवन्तं
पिप्पलादमुपसन्नाः ॥१॥

1. OM! Salutation to the Supreme Spirit. The Supreme is
    OM.
        Sukesha the Bharadwaja; the Shaibya, Satyakama;
    Gargya, son of the Solar race; the Koshalan, son of
    Ashwala; the Bhargava of Vidarbha; and Kabandhi Katya-
    yana; — these sought the Most High God, believing in the
    Supreme and to the Supreme devoted. Therefore they came
    to the Lord Pippalada, for they said: "This is he that shall
    tell us of that Universal."

तान् ह स ऋषिरुवाच, — भूय एव तपसा ब्रह्मचर्येण श्रद्धया
संवत्सरं संवत्स्यथ, यथाकामं प्रश्नान् पृच्छत, यदि विज्ञास्यामः सर्वं
ह वो वक्ष्याम इति ॥२॥

2. The Rishi said to them: "Another year do ye dwell in
    holiness and faith and askesis: then ask what ye will, and if
    I know, surely I will conceal nothing."

अथ कबन्धी कात्यायन उपेत्य पप्रच्छ, भगवन् कुतो ह वा इमाः
प्रजाः प्रजायन्त इति ॥३॥

3. Then came Kabandhi, son of Katya, to him and asked:
    "Lord, whence are all these creatures born?"

तस्मे स होवाच—प्रजाकामो वै प्रजापति:, स तपोऽतप्यत, स
तपस्तप्त्वा, स मिथुनमुत्पादयते रयिश्च प्राणश्चेति, एतौ मे बहुधा
प्रजाः करिष्यत इति ॥४॥

4.   To him answered the Rishi Pippalada : "The Eternal Father
     desired children, therefore he put forth his energy and by
     the heat of his energy produced twin creatures, Prana the
     Life, who is Male, and Rayi the Matter, who is Female.
     'These,' said he, 'shall make for me children of many
     natures.'

आदित्यो ह वै प्राण:, रयिरेव चन्द्रमाः, रयिर्वा एतत् सर्वं यन्मूर्तं
चामूर्तं च, तस्मान्मूर्तिरेव रयिः ॥५॥

5.   "The Sun verily is Life and the Moon is no more than
     Matter : yet truly all this Universe formed and formless is
     Matter : therefore Form and Matter are One.

अथादित्य उदयन् यत् प्राचीं दिशं प्रविशति तेन प्राच्यान् प्राणान्
रश्मिषु सन्निधत्ते । यद्दक्षिणां यत्प्रतीचीं यदुदीचीं यदधो यदूर्ध्वं
यदन्तरा दिशो यत्सर्वं प्रकाशयति तेन सर्वान् प्राणान् रश्मिषु
सन्निधत्ते ॥६॥

6.   "Now when the Sun rising entereth the East, then absorbeth
     he the eastern breaths into his rays. But when he illumineth
     the south and west and north, and below and above and all
     the angles of space, yea, all that is, then he taketh all the
     breaths into his rays.

स एष वैश्वानरो विश्वरूपः प्राणोऽग्निरुदयते ।
तदेतदृचाभ्युक्तम् ॥७॥

7.   "Therefore is this fire that riseth, this Universal Male, of
     whom all things are the bodies, Prana the breath of exis-
     tence. This is that which was said in the Rig-veda :

विश्वरूपं हरिणं जातवेदसं परायणं ज्योतिरेकं तपन्तम् । सहस्ररश्मिः
शतधा वर्तमानः प्राणः प्रजानामुदयत्येष सूर्यः ॥८॥

8. " 'Fire is this burning and radiant Sun, he is the One lustre and all-knowing Light, he is the highest heaven of spirits. With a thousand rays he burneth and existeth in a hundred existences: lo this Sun that riseth, he is the Life of all his creatures.'

संवत्सरो वै प्रजापतिः, तस्यायने दक्षिणञ्चोत्तरं च। तद्ये ह वै तद्विष्टापूर्त्तं कृतमित्युपासते, ते चान्द्रमसमेव लोकमभिजयन्ते, त एव पुनरावर्त्तन्ते। तस्मादेत ऋषयः प्रजाकामा दक्षिणं प्रतिपद्यन्ते। एष ह वै रयिर्यः पितृयाणः ॥९॥

9. "The year also is that Eternal Father and of the year there are two paths, the northern solstice and the southern. Now they who worship God with the well dug and the oblation offered, deeming these to be righteousness, conquer their heavens of the Moon: these return again to the world of birth. Therefore do the souls of sages who have not yet put from them the desire of offspring, take the way of the southern solstice which is the road of the Fathers. And this also is Matter, the Female.

अथोत्तरेण तपसा ब्रह्मचर्येण श्रद्धया विद्ययात्मानमन्विष्यादित्यमभि-जयन्ते। एतद्वै प्राणानामायतनमेतदमृतमभयमेतत् परायणमेतस्मान्न पुनरावर्त्तन्त इत्येष निरोधः। तदेष श्लोकः ॥१०॥

10. "But by the way of the northern solstice go the souls that have sought the Spirit through holiness and knowledge and faith and askesis: for they conquer their heavens of the Sun. There is the resting place of the breaths, there immortality casteth out fear, there is the highest heaven of spirits: thence no soul returneth: therefore is the wall and barrier. Whereof this is the Scripture:

पञ्चपादं पितरं द्वादशाकृतिं दिव आहुः परे अर्धे पुरीषिणम्। अथेमे अन्य उ परे विचक्षणं सप्तचक्रे षडर आहुरर्पितमिति ॥११॥

11. " 'Five-portioned, some say, is the Father and hath twelve figures and he floweth in the upper hemisphere beyond the

heavens: but others speak of him as the Wisdom who
standeth in a chariot of six spokes and seven wheels.'

मासो वै प्रजापतिस्तस्य कृष्णपक्ष एव रयि: शुक्ल: प्राणस्तस्मादेत
ऋषय: शुक्ल इष्टं कुर्वन्तीतर इतरस्मिन् ॥१२॥

12. "The month also is that Eternal Father, whereof the dark
fortnight is Matter the Female and the bright fortnight
is Life the Male. Therefore do one manner of sages offer
sacrifice in the bright fortnight and another in the dark.

अहोरात्रौ वै प्रजापतिस्तस्याहरेव प्राणो रात्रिरेव रयि: । प्राणं वा
एते प्रस्कन्दन्ति ये दिवा रत्या संयुज्यन्ते, ब्रह्मचर्यमेव तद्यद्रात्रौ रत्या
संयुज्यन्ते ॥१३॥

13. "Day and night also are the Eternal Father, whereof the
day is Life and the night is Matter. Therefore do they
offend against their own life who take joy with woman by
day: by night who take joy, enact holiness.

अन्नं वै प्रजापतिस्ततो ह वै तद्रेतस्तस्मादिमा: प्रजा: प्रजायन्त
इति ॥१४॥

14. "Food is the Eternal Father: for of this came the seed and
of the seed is the world of creatures born.

तद्ये ह वै तत्प्रजापतिव्रतं चरन्ति ते मिथुनमुत्पादयन्ते । तेषामेवैष
ब्रह्मलोको येषां तपो ब्रह्मचर्यं येषु सत्यं प्रतिष्ठितम् ॥१५॥

15. "They therefore who perform the vow of the Eternal Father
produce the twin creature. But theirs is the heaven of the
spirit in whom are established askesis and holiness and in
whom Truth has her dwelling.

तेषामसौ विरजो ब्रह्मलोको न येषु जिह्ममनृतं न माया चेति ॥१६॥

16. "Theirs is the heaven of the Spirit, the world all spotless,
in whom there is neither crookedness nor lying nor any
illusion."

अथ हैनं भार्गवो वैदर्भिः पप्रच्छ । भगवन् कत्येव देवाः प्रजां
विधारयन्ते ? कतर एतत्प्रकाशयन्ते ? कः पुनरेषां वरिष्ठः ? इति ॥१॥

1. Then the Bhargava, the Vidarbhan, asked him: "Lord, how
   many Gods maintain this creature, and how many illumine
   it, and which of these again is the mightiest?"

तस्मै स होवाचाकाशो ह वा एष देवो वायुरग्निरापः पृथिवी वाङ्-
मनश्चक्षुः श्रोत्रं च । ते प्रकाश्याभिवदन्ति वयमेतद्बाणमवष्टभ्य
विधारयामः ॥२॥

2. To him answered the Rishi Pippalada: "These are the
   Gods, even Ether and Wind and Fire and Water and Earth
   and Speech and Mind and Sight and Hearing. These nine
   illumine the creature: therefore they vaunted themselves,
   'We, even we, support this harp of God and we are the pre-
   servers.'

तान् वरिष्ठः प्राण उवाच । मा मोहमापद्यथ अहमेवैतत्पञ्चधा-
त्मानं प्रविभज्यैतद्बाणमवष्टभ्य विधारयामीति; तेऽश्रद्दधाना
बभूवुः ॥३॥

3. "Then answered Breath, their mightiest: 'Yield not unto
   delusion: I dividing myself into this fivefold support this
   harp of God, I am its preserver.' But they believed him not.

सोऽभिमानादूर्ध्वमुत्क्रमत इव; तस्मिन्नुत्क्रामत्यथेतरे सर्व एवोत्क्रामन्ते,
तस्मिंश्च प्रतिष्ठमाने सर्व एव प्रातिष्ठन्ते । तद्यथा मक्षिका मधु-
करराजानमुत्क्रामन्तं सर्वा एवोत्क्रामन्ते, तस्मिंश्च प्रतिष्ठमाने सर्वा
एव प्रातिष्ठन्त एवं वाङ्मनश्चक्षुःश्रोत्रं च, ते प्रीताः प्राणं स्तुन्वन्ति ॥४॥

4. "Therefore offended he rose up, he was issuing out from
   the body. But when the Breath goeth out, then go all the
   others with him, and when the Breath abideth all the others
   abide: therefore as bees with the king-bee: when he goeth

out all go out with him, and when he abideth all abide, even so was it with Speech and Mind and Sight and Hearing: then were they well-pleased and hymned the Breath to adore him.

एषोऽग्निस्तपत्येष सूर्य एष पर्जन्यो मघवानेष वायुः ।
एष पृथिवी रयिर्देवः सदसच्चामृतं च यत् ॥५॥

5. " 'Lo, this is he that is Fire and the Sun that burneth, Rain and Indra and Earth and Air, Matter and Deity, Form and Formless, and Immortality.

अरा इव रथनाभौ प्राणे सर्वं प्रतिष्ठितम् ।
ऋचो यजूंषि सामानि यज्ञः क्षत्रं ब्रह्म च ॥६॥

6. " 'As the spokes meet in the nave of a wheel, so are all things in the Breath established, the Rig-veda and the Yajur and the Sama, and Sacrifice and Brahminhood and Kshatriyahood.

प्रजापतिश्चरसि गर्भे त्वमेव प्रतिजायसे । तुभ्यं प्राण प्रजास्त्विमा
बलिं हरन्ति यः प्राणैः प्रतितिष्ठसि ॥७॥

7. " 'As the Eternal Father thou movest in the womb and art born in the likeness of the parents. To thee, O Life, the world of creatures offer the burnt offering, who by the breaths abidest.

देवानामसि वह्नितमः पितॄणां प्रथमा स्वधा ।
ऋषीणां चरितं सत्यमथर्वाङ्गिरसामसि ॥८॥

8. " 'Of all the Gods thou art the strongest and fiercest and to the fathers thou art the first oblation: thou art the truth and virtue of the sages and thou art Atharvan among the sons of Angiras.

इन्द्रस्त्वं प्राण तेजसा रुद्रोऽसि परिरक्षिता ।
त्वमन्तरिक्षे चरसि सूर्यस्त्वं ज्योतिषां पतिः ॥९॥

9. " 'Thou art Indra, O Breath, by thy splendour and energy and Rudra because thou preservest: thou walkest in the welkin as the Sun, that imperial lustre.

यदा त्वमभिवर्षस्यथेमाः प्राण ते प्रजाः ।
आनन्दरूपास्तिष्ठन्ति कामायान्नं भविष्यतीति ॥१०॥

10. " 'When thou, O Breath, rainest, thy creatures stand all joy because there shall be grain to the heart's desire.

व्रात्यस्त्वं प्राणैकर्षिरत्ता विश्वस्य सत्पतिः ।
वयमाद्यस्य दातारः पिता त्वं मातरिश्व नः ॥११॥

11. " 'Thou art, O Breath, the unpurified and thou art Fire, the only purity, the devourer of all and the lord of existences. We are the givers to thee of thy eating: for thou, O Matarishwan, art our Father.

या ते तनूर्वाचि प्रतिष्ठिता या श्रोत्रे या च चक्षुषि ।
या च मनसि सन्तता शिवां तां कुरु मोत्क्रमीः ॥१२॥

12. " 'That body of thine which is established in the speech, sight and hearing, and in the mind is extended, that make propitious: O Life, go not out from our midst!

प्राणस्येवं वशे सर्वं त्रिदिवे यत् प्रतिष्ठितम् ।
मातेव पुत्रान् रक्षस्व श्रीश्च प्रज्ञां च विधेहि न इति ॥१३॥

13. " 'For all this Universe, yea, all that is established in the heavens to the Breath is subject: guard us as a mother watcheth over her little children: give us fortune and beauty, give us Wisdom.' "

अथ हैनं कौसल्यश्चाश्वलायनः पप्रच्छ। भगवन् कुत एष प्राणो
जायते कथमायात्यस्मिञ्छरीरे, आत्मानं वा प्रविभज्य कथं प्रातिष्ठते
केनोत्क्रमते कथं बाह्यमभिधत्ते कथमध्यात्ममिति ॥१॥

1. Then the Koshalan, the son of Ashwala, asked him: "Lord, whence is this Life born? How cometh it in this body or how standeth by self-division? By what departeth, or how maintaineth the outward and how the inward spiritual?"

तस्मै स होवाचातिप्रश्नान् पृच्छसि ब्रह्मिष्ठोऽसीति तस्मात्तेऽहं
ब्रवीमि ॥२॥

2. To him answered the Rishi Pippalada: "Many and difficult things thou askest: but because thou art very holy, therefore will I tell thee.

आत्मन एष प्राणो जायते। यथैषा पुरुषे छायैतस्मिन्नेतदाततं
मनोकृतेनायात्यस्मिञ्छरीरे ॥३॥

3. "Of the Spirit is this breath of Life born: even as a shadow is cast by a man, so is this Life extended in the Spirit and by the action of the Mind it entereth into this body.

यथा सम्राडेवाधिकृतान् विनियुङ्क्ते। एतान् ग्रामानेतान् ग्रामानधि-
तिष्ठस्वेत्येवमेवैष प्राण इतरान् प्राणान् पृथक्पृथगेव सन्निधत्ते ॥४॥

4. "As an Emperor commandeth his officers, and he sayeth to one, 'Govern for me these villages,' and to another, 'Govern for me these others,' so this breath, the Life, appointeth the other breaths each in his province.

पायूपस्थेऽपानं चक्षुःश्रोत्रे मुखनासिकाभ्यां प्राणः स्वयं प्रातिष्ठते
मध्ये तु समानः। एष ह्येतद्धुतमन्नं समं नयति तस्मादेताः सप्ता-
र्चिषो भवन्ति ॥५॥

5. "In the anus and the organ of pleasure is the lower breath, and in the eyes and the ears, the mouth and the nose, the main breath itself is seated: but the medial breath is in the middle. This is he that equally distributeth the burnt offering of food: for from this are the seven fires born.

हृदि ह्येष आत्मा । अत्रैतदेकशतं नाडीतां तासां शतं शतमेकैकस्यां द्वासप्ततिर्द्वासप्ततिः प्रतिशाखानाडीसहस्राणि भवन्त्यासु व्यान-श्चरति ॥६॥

6. "The Spirit in the heart abideth, and in the heart there are one hundred and one nerves, and each nerve hath a hundred branch-nerves and each branch-nerve hath seventy-two thousand sub-branch-nerves: through these the breath pervasor moveth.

अथैकयोर्ध्वं उदानः पुण्येन पुण्यं लोकं नयति । पापेन पापमुभाभ्यामेव मनुष्यलोकम् ॥७॥

7. "Of these many there is one by which the upper breath departeth that by virtue taketh to the heaven of virtue, by sin to the hell of sin, and by mingled sin and righteousness back to the world of men restoreth.

आदित्यो ह वै बाह्यः प्राण उदयत्येष ह्येनं चाक्षुषं प्राणमनुगृह्णानः । पृथिव्यां या देवता सैषा पुरुष्यापानमवष्टभ्यान्तरा यदाकाशः स समानो वायुर्व्यानः ॥८॥

8. "The Sun is the main breath outside this body, for it cherisheth the eye in its rising. The divinity in the earth, she attracteth the lower breath of man, and the ether between is the medial breath: air is the breath pervasor.

तेजो ह वा उदानस्तस्मादुपशान्ततेजाः पुनर्भवमिन्द्रियैर्मनसि सम्पद्य-मानैः ॥९॥

9. "Light, the primal energy, is the upper breath: therefore when the light and heat in a man hath dwindled, his senses

retire into the mind and with these he departeth into another
birth.

यच्चित्तस्तेनैष प्राणमायाति प्राणस्तेजसा युक्तः।   सहात्मना यथा-
सङ्कल्पितं लोकं नयति ॥१०॥

10. "Whatsoever be the mind of a man, with that mind he seek-
     eth refuge with the breath when he dieth, and the breath
     and the upper breath lead him with the Spirit within him to
     the world of his imaginings.

य एवं विद्वान् प्राणं वेद।   न ह्यास्य प्रजा हीयतेऽमृतो भवति तदेष
श्लोकः ॥११॥

11. "The wise man that knoweth thus of the breath, his progeny
     wasteth not and he becometh immortal. Whereof this is
     the Scripture:

उत्पत्तिमायाति स्थानं विभुत्वं चैव पञ्चधा।
अध्यात्मं चैव प्राणस्य विज्ञायामृतमश्नुते विज्ञायामृतमश्नुत इति ॥१२॥

12. " 'By knowing the origin of the Breath, his coming and his
     staying and his lordship in the five provinces, likewise his
     relation to the Spirit, one shall taste immortality.' "

अथ हैनं सौर्यायणी गार्ग्यः पप्रच्छ। भगवन्नेतस्मिन् पुरुषे कानि
स्वपन्ति? कान्यस्मिञ्जाग्रति? कतर एष देवः स्वप्नान् पश्यति?
कस्यैतत्सुखं भवति? कस्मिन्नु सर्वे संप्रतिष्ठिता भवन्तीति॥१॥

1. Then Gargya of the Solar race asked him: "Lord, what are
   they that slumber in this Existing and what that keep vigil?
   Who is this god who seeth dreams or whose is this felicity?
   Into whom do all they vanish?"

तस्मै स होवाच। यथा गार्ग्य मरीचयोऽर्कस्यास्तं गच्छतः सर्वा
एतस्मिंस्तेजोमण्डल एकीभवन्ति। ताः पुनः पुनरुदयतः प्रचरन्त्येवं
ह वै तत् सर्वं परे देवे मनस्येकीभवति। तेन तर्ह्येष पुरुषो न
शृणोति न पश्यति न जिघ्रति न रसयते न स्पृशते नाभिवदते नादत्ते
नानन्दयते न विसृजते नेयायते स्वपितीत्याचक्षते॥२॥

2. To him answered the Rishi Pippalada: "O Gargya, as are
   the rays of the sun in its setting, for they retire and all
   become one in yonder circle of splendour, but when he
   riseth again once more they walk abroad, so all the man
   becometh one in the highest god, even the mind. Then
   indeed this being seeth not, neither heareth, nor doth he
   smell, nor taste, nor touch, nor speaketh he aught, nor taketh
   in or giveth out, nor cometh nor goeth: he feeleth not any
   felicity. Then they say of him, 'He sleepeth.'

प्राणाग्नय एवैतस्मिन् पुरे जाग्रति। गार्हपत्यो ह वा एषोऽपानो
व्यानोऽन्वाहार्यपचनो यद् गार्हपत्यात् प्रणीयते प्रणयनादाहवनीयः
प्राणः॥३॥

3. "But the fires of the breath keep watch in that sleeping city.
   The lower breath is the householder's fire and the breath
   pervasor the fire of the Lares that burneth to the southward.
   The main breath is the orient fire of the sacrifice: and even
   as the eastern fire taketh its fuel from the western, so in the

slumber of a man the main breath taketh from the lower.

यदुच्छ्वासनिःश्वासावेतावाहुती समं नयतीति स समानः।   मनो
ह वाव यजमानः इष्टफलमेवोदानः स एनं यजमानमहरहर्ब्रह्म
गमयति ॥४॥

4.   "But the medial breath is the priest, the sacrificant: for he
equaliseth the offering of the inbreath and the offering of the
outbreath. The Mind is the giver of the sacrifice and the
upper breath is the fruit of the sacrifice, for it taketh the
sacrificer day by day into the presence of the Eternal.

अत्रैष देवः स्वप्ने महिमानमनुभवति।   यद् दृष्टं दृष्टमनुपश्यति
श्रुतं श्रुतमेवार्थमनुशृणोति देशदिगन्तरैश्च प्रत्यनुभूतं पुनः पुनः प्रत्यनु-
भवति, दृष्टं चादृष्टं च श्रुतं चाश्रुतं चानुभूतं चाननुभूतं च सच्चा-
सच्च सर्वं पश्यति सर्वः पश्यति ॥५॥

5.   "Now the Mind in dream revelleth in the glory of his ima-
ginings. All that it has seen it seemeth to see over again, and
of all that it hath heard it repeateth the hearing: yea, all
that it hath felt and thought and known in many lands and
in various regions, these it liveth over again in its dreaming.
What it hath seen and what it hath not seen, what it hath
heard and what it hath not heard, what it hath known and
what it hath not known, what is and what is not, all, all it
seeth: for the Mind is the Universe.

स यदा तेजसाभिभूतो भवत्यत्रैष देवः स्वप्नान् न पश्यत्यथ तदै-
तस्मिञ्छरीर एतत्सुखं भवति ॥६॥

6.   "But when he is overwhelmed with light, then Mind, the
God, dreameth no longer: then in this body he hath felicity.

स यथा सोम्य वयांसि वासोवृक्षं संप्रतिष्ठन्ते, एवं ह वै तत् सर्वं
पर आत्मनि संप्रतिष्ठते ॥७॥

7. "O fair son, as birds wing towards their resting tree, so do all these depart into the Supreme Spirit:

पृथिवी च पृथिवीमात्रा चापश्चापोमात्रा च, तेजश्च तेजोमात्रा च
वायुश्च वायुमात्रा चाकाशश्चाकाशमात्रा च चक्षुश्च द्रष्टव्यं च
श्रोत्रं च श्रोतव्यं च घ्राणं च घ्रातव्यं च रसश्च रसयितव्यं च
त्वक्च स्पर्शयितव्यं च वाक्च वक्तव्यं च हस्तौ चादातव्यं चोपस्थश्चा-
नन्दयितव्यं च पायुश्च विसर्जयितव्यं च पादौ च गन्तव्यं च मनश्च
मन्तव्यं च बुद्धिश्च बोद्धव्यं चाहंकारश्चाहंकर्त्तव्यं च, चित्तं
च चेतयितव्यं च तेजश्च विद्योतयितव्यं च प्राणश्च विधारयितव्यं
च ॥८॥

8. "Earth and the inner things of earth: water and the inner things of water: light and the inner things of light: air and the inner things of air: ether and the inner things of ether: the eye and its seeings: the ear and its hearings: smell and the objects of smell: taste and the objects of taste: the skin and the objects of touch: speech and the things to be spoken: the two hands and their takings: the organ of pleasure and its enjoyings: the anus and its excretions: the feet and their goings: the mind and its feelings: the intelligence and what it understandeth: the sense of Ego and that which is felt to be Ego: the conscious heart and that of which it is conscious: light and what it lightens: Life and the things it maintaineth.

एष हि द्रष्टा स्प्रष्टा श्रोता घ्राता रसयिता मन्ता बोद्धा कर्त्ता
विज्ञानात्मा पुरुषः। स परेऽक्षर आत्मनि सम्प्रतिष्ठते ॥९॥

9. "For this that seeth and toucheth, heareth, smelleth, tasteth, feeleth, understandeth, acteth, is the reasoning self, the Male within. This too departeth into the Higher Self which is Imperishable.

परमेवाक्षरं प्रतिपद्यते स यो ह वै तदच्छायमशरीरमलोहितं शुभ्र-
मक्षरं वेदयते यस्तु सोम्य स सर्वज्ञः सर्वो भवति तदेष श्लोकः ॥१०॥

10. "He that knoweth the shadowless, colourless, bodiless, lumi-

nous and imperishable Spirit, attaineth to the Imperishable,
even to the Most High. O fair son, he knoweth the All and
becometh the All. Whereof this is the Scripture:

विज्ञानात्मा सह देवैश्च सर्वें: प्राणा भूतानि संप्रतिष्ठन्ति यत्र ।
तदक्षरं वेदयते यस्तु सोम्य स सर्वज्ञ: सर्वमेवाविवेशोति ॥११॥

11.   " 'He, O fair son, that knoweth the Imperishable into whom
       the understanding self departeth, and all the Gods, and the
       life-breaths and the elements, he knoweth the Universe!' "

अथ हैनं शैब्यः सत्यकामः पप्रच्छ — स यो ह वै तद् भगवन्
मनुष्येषु प्रायणान्तमोङ्कारमभिध्यायीत कतमं वाव स तेन लोकं
जयतीति ॥१॥

1. Then the Shaibya Satyakama asked him: "Lord, he among
   men that meditate unto death on OM the syllable, which
   of the worlds doth he conquer by its puissance?"

तस्मै स होवाच एतद् वै सत्यकाम परं चापरं च ब्रह्म यदोङ्कारः ।
तस्माद् विद्वानेतेनैवायतनेनैकतरमन्वेति ॥२॥

2. To him answered the Rishi Pippalada: "This imperishable
   Word that is OM, O Satyakama, is the Higher Brahman and
   also the Lower. Therefore the wise man by making his
   home in the Word, winneth to one of these.

स यद्येकमात्रमभिध्यायीत स तेनैव संवेदितस्तूर्णमेव जगत्यामभि-
सम्पद्यते । तमृचो मनुष्यलोकमुपनयन्ते, स तत्र तपसा ब्रह्मचर्येण
श्रद्धया सम्पन्नो महिमानमनुभवति ॥३॥

3. "If he meditate on the one letter of OM the syllable, by
   that enlightened he attaineth swiftly in the material universe,
   and the hymns of the Rig-veda escort him to the world of
   men: there endowed with askesis and faith and holiness
   he experienceth majesty.

अथ यदि द्विमात्रेण मनसि सम्पद्यते सोऽन्तरिक्षं यजुर्भिरुन्नीयते
सोमलोकम् । स सोमलोके विभूतिमनुभूय पुनरावर्तते ॥४॥

4. "Now if by the two letters of the syllable he in the mind attaineth, to the skies he is exalted and the hymns of the Yajur
   escort him to the Lunar World. In the heavens of the Moon
   he feeleth his soul's majesty: then once more he returneth.

यः पुनरेतं त्रिमात्रेणौमित्येतेनैवाक्षरेण परं पुरुषमभिध्यायीत स तेजसि
सूर्ये सम्पन्नः। यथा पादोदरस्त्वचा विनिर्मुच्यत एवं ह वै स
पाप्मना विनिर्मुक्तः स सामभिरुन्नीयते ब्रह्मलोकं स एतस्माज्जीव-
घनात्परात्परं पुरिशयं पुरुषमीक्षते तदेतौ श्लोकौ भवतः ॥५॥

5. "But he who by all the three letters meditateth by this syllable, even by OM on the Most High Being, he in the Solar World of light and energy is secured in his attainings: as a snake casteth off its slough: so he casteth off sin, and the hymns of the Sama-veda escort him to the heaven of the Spirit. He from that Lower who is the density of existence beholdeth the Higher than the Highest of whom every form is one city. Whereof these are the verses:

तिस्रो मात्रा मृत्युमत्यः प्रयुक्ता अन्योन्यसक्ता अनविप्रयुक्ताः।
क्रियासु बाह्यान्तरमध्यमासु सम्यक्प्रयुक्तासु न कम्पते ज्ञः ॥६॥

6. " "Children of death are the letters when they are used as three, the embracing and the inseparable letters: but the wise man is not shaken: for there are three kinds of works, outward deed and inward action and another which is blended of the two, and all these he doeth rightly without fear and without trembling.

ऋग्भिरेतं यजुर्भिरन्तरिक्षं सामभिर्यत्तत्कवयो वेदयन्ते।
तमोङ्कारेणैवायतनेनान्वेति विद्वान् यत्तच्छान्तमजरममृतमभयं परं
चेति ॥७॥

7. " "To the earth the Rig-veda leadeth, to the skies the Yajur, but the Sama to That of which the sages know. Thither the wise man by resting on OM the syllable attaineth, even to that Supreme Quietude where age is not and fear is cast out by immortality.' "

अथ हैनं सुकेशा भारद्वाजः पप्रच्छ । भगवन् हिरण्यनाभः कौसल्यो
राजपुत्रो मामुपेत्येतं प्रश्नमपृच्छत — षोडशकलं भारद्वाज पुरुषं
वेत्थ ? तमहं कुमारमब्रुवं नाहमिमं वेद यद्यहमिममवेदिषं कथं ते
नावक्ष्यमिति । समूलो वा एष परिशुष्यति योऽनृतमभिवदति ।
तस्मान्नार्हाम्यनृतं वक्तुम् । स तूष्णीं रथमारुह्य प्रवव्राज । तं
त्वा पृच्छामि क्वासौ पुरुष इति ॥१॥

1. Then Sukesha the Bharadwaja asked him: "Lord, Hiranya-
   nabha of Koshala, the king's son, came to me and put me
   this question, 'O Bharadwaja, knowest thou the Being and
   the sixteen parts of Him?' and I answered the boy, 'I know
   Him not: for if I knew Him, surely I should tell thee of
   Him: but I cannot tell thee a lie: for from the roots he shall
   wither who speaketh falsehood.' But he mounted his chariot
   in silence and departed from me. Of Him I ask thee, who is
   the Being?"

तस्मै स होवाच । इहैवान्तःशरीरे सोम्य स पुरुषो यस्मिन्नेताः
षोडश कलाः प्रभवन्तीति ॥२॥

2. To him answered the Rishi Pippalada: "O fair son, even
   here is that Being, in the inner body of every creature, for in
   Him are the sixteen members born.

स ईक्षांचक्रे । कस्मिन्नहमुत्क्रान्त उत्क्रान्तो भविष्यामि कस्मिन्
वा प्रतिष्ठिते प्रतिष्ठास्यामीति ॥३॥

3. "He bethought Him: 'What shall that be in whose issuing
   forth I shall issue forth from the body and in his abiding
   I shall abide?'

स प्राणमसृजत । प्राणाच्छ्रद्धां खं वायुर्ज्योतिरापः पृथिवीन्द्रियं मनो-
ऽन्नमन्नाद्वीर्यं तपो मन्त्राः कर्म लोका लोकेषु च नाम च ॥४॥

4. "Then he put forth the Life, and from the Life faith, next
ether and then air, and then light, and then water, and then
earth, the senses and mind and food, and from food virility
and from virility askesis, and from askesis the mighty verses,
and from these action, and the worlds from action and name
in the worlds: in this wise were all things born from the
Spirit.

स यथेमा नद्यः स्यन्दमानाः समुद्रायणाः समुद्रं प्राप्यास्तं गच्छन्ति
भिद्येते तासां नामरूपे समुद्र इत्येवं प्रोच्यते । एवमेवास्य परिद्रष्टु-
रिमाः षोडश कलाः पुरुषायणाः पुरुषं प्राप्यास्तं गच्छन्ति; भिद्येते
चासां नामरूपे पुरुष इत्येवं प्रोच्यते स एषोऽकलोऽमृतो भवति तदेष
श्लोकः ॥५॥

5. "Therefore as all these flowing rivers move towards the sea,
but when they reach the sea they are lost in it and name
and form break away from them and all is called only the
sea, so all the sixteen members of the silent witnessing Spirit
move towards the Being, and when they have attained the
Being they are lost in Him and name and form break away
from them and all is called only the Being: then is He
without members and immortal. Whereof this is the
Scripture:

अरा इव रथनाभौ कला यस्मिन् प्रतिष्ठिताः ।
तं वेद्यं पुरुषं वेद यथा मा वो मृत्युः परिव्यथा इति ॥६॥

6. "'He in whom the members are set as the spokes of a wheel
are set in its nave, Him know for the Being who is the goal
of knowledge, so shall death pass away from you and his
anguish.'"

तान् होवाचैतावदेवाहमेतत् परं ब्रह्म वेद । नातः परमस्तीति ॥७॥

7. And Pippalada said to them: "Thus far do I know the Most
High God: than He there is none Higher."

ते तमर्चयन्तस्तवं हि नः पिता योऽस्माकमविद्यायाः परं पारं तारय-
सीति ।   नमः परमऋषिभ्यो नमः परमऋषिभ्यः ॥८॥

8. And they worshipping him: "For thou art our father who
hast carried us over to the other side of the Ignorance."
Salutation to the mighty sages, salutation!

MUNDAKA UPANISHAD

Mandukya Upanishad

ओमित्येतदक्षरमिदꣳ सर्वं तस्योपव्याख्यानं, भूतं भवद् भविष्यदिति
सर्वमोङ्कार एव । यच्चान्यत् त्रिकालातीतं तदप्योङ्कार एव ॥१॥

1. OM is this imperishable Word, OM is the Universe, and this
   is the exposition of OM. The past, the present and the
   future, all that was, all that is, all that will be, is OM. Likewise all else that may exist beyond the bounds of Time,
   that too is OM.

सर्वꣳ ह्येतद् ब्रह्म, अयमात्मा ब्रह्म, सोऽयमात्मा चतुष्पात् ॥२॥

2. All this Universe is the Eternal Brahman, this Self is the
   Eternal, and the Self is fourfold.

जागरितस्थानो बहिष्प्रज्ञः सप्ताङ्ग एकोनर्विंशतिमुखः स्थूलभुग् वैश्वा-
नरः प्रथमः पादः ॥३॥

3. He whose place is the wakefulness, who is wise of the outward, who hath seven limbs, to whom there are nineteen
   doors, who feeleth and enjoyeth gross objects, Vaishwanara,
   the Universal Male, He is the first.

स्वप्नस्थानोऽन्तःप्रज्ञः सप्ताङ्ग एकोनर्विंशतिमुखः प्रविविक्तभुक् तैजसो
द्वितीयः पादः ॥४॥

4. He whose place is the dream, who is wise of the inward,
   who hath seven limbs, to whom there are nineteen doors, who
   feeleth and enjoyeth subtle objects, Taijasa, the Inhabitant
   in Luminous Mind, He is the second.

यत्र सुप्तो न कञ्चन कामं कामयते, न कञ्चन स्वप्नं पश्यति, तत्
सुषुप्तम् । सुषुप्तस्थान एकीभूतः प्रज्ञानघन एवानन्दमयो ह्यानन्द-
भुक् चेतोमुखः प्राज्ञस्तृतीयः पादः ॥५॥

5. When one sleepeth and yearneth not with any desire, nor
seeth any dream, that is the perfect slumber. He whose place
is the perfect slumber, who is become Oneness, who is wisdom gathered into itself, who is made of mere delight, who
enjoyeth delight unrelated, to whom conscious mind is the
door, Prajna, the Lord of Wisdom, He is the third.

एष सर्वेश्वर एष सर्वज्ञ एषोऽन्तर्याम्येष योनिः सर्वस्य प्रभवाप्ययौ
हि भूतानाम् ॥६॥

6. This is the Almighty, this is the Omniscient, this is the Inner
Soul, this is the Womb of the Universe, this is the Birth and
Destruction of creatures.

नान्तःप्रज्ञं न बहिष्प्रज्ञं नोभयतःप्रज्ञं न प्रज्ञानघनं न प्रज्ञं नाप्रज्ञम् ।
अदृष्टमव्यवहार्यमग्राह्यमलक्षणमचिन्त्यमव्यपदेश्यमेकात्मप्रत्ययसारं
प्रपञ्चोपशमं शान्तं शिवमद्वैतं चतुर्थं मन्यन्ते स आत्मा स विज्ञेयः ॥७॥

7. He who is neither inward-wise, nor outward-wise, nor both
inward- and outward-wise, nor wisdom self-gathered, nor
possessed of wisdom, nor unpossessed of wisdom, He Who
is unseen and incommunicable, unseizable, featureless, unthinkable, and unnameable, Whose essentiality is awareness of the Self in its single existence, in Whom all phenomena dissolve, Who is Calm, Who is Good, Who is the One
than Whom there is no other, Him they deem the fourth:
He is the Self, He is the object of Knowledge.

सोऽयमात्माध्यक्षरमोङ्कारोऽधिमात्रं पादा मात्रा मात्राश्च पादा अकार
उकारो मकार इति ॥८॥

8. Now this the Self, as to the imperishable Word, is OM:
and as to the letters, His parts are the letters and the letters
are His parts, namely, A U M.

जागरितस्थानो वैश्वानरोऽङ्कारः प्रथमा मात्रा, आप्तेरादिमत्त्वाद् वा,
आप्नोति ह वै सर्वान् कामानादिश्च भवति य एवं वेद ॥९॥

9. The Waker, Vaishwanara, the Universal Male, He is A, the first letter, because of Initiality and Pervasiveness: he that knoweth Him for such pervadeth and attaineth all his desires: he becometh the source and first.

स्वप्नस्थानस्तैजस उकारो द्वितीया मात्रा, उत्कर्षादुभयत्वाद् वा,
उत्कर्षति ह वै ज्ञानसन्ततिं समानश्च भवति; नास्याब्रह्मवित् कुले
भवति य एवं वेद ॥१०॥

10. The Dreamer, Taijasa, the Inhabitant in Luminous Mind, He is U, the second letter, because of Advance and Centrality: he that knoweth Him for such, advanceth the bounds of his knowledge and riseth above difference: nor of his seed is any born that knoweth not the Eternal.

सुषुप्तस्थानः प्राज्ञो मकारस्तृतीया मात्रा, मितेरपीतेर्वा, मिनोति ह
वा इदं सर्वमपीतिश्च भवति य एवं वेद ॥११॥

11. The Sleeper, Prajna, the Lord of Wisdom, He is M, the third letter, because of Measure and Finality: he that knoweth Him for such measureth with himself the Universe and becometh the departure into the Eternal.

अमात्रश्चतुर्थोऽव्यवहार्यः प्रपञ्चोपशमः शिवोऽद्वैत एवमोङ्कार आत्मैव,
संविशत्यात्मनात्मानं य एवं वेद य एवं वेद ॥१२॥

12. Letterless is the fourth, the Incommunicable, the end of phenomena, the Good, the One than Whom there is no other: thus is OM. He that knoweth is the Self and entereth by his self into the Self, he that knoweth, he that knoweth.

SECTION THREE

Incomplete and Fragmentary Translations and Commentaries

BRIHADARANYAKA UPANISHAD

Chapter One, Sections 1, 2 and part of 3

Brihadaranyaka Upanishad

CHAPTER ONE: SECTION 1

ॐ । उषा वा अश्वस्य मेध्यस्य शिरः । सूर्यश्चक्षुर्वातः प्राणो
व्यात्तमग्निर्वैश्वानरः संवत्सर आत्माऽश्वस्य मेध्यस्य । द्यौः पृष्ठ-
मन्तरिक्षमुदरं पृथिवी पाजस्यं दिशः पार्श्वे अवान्तरदिशः पर्शव
ऋतवोऽङ्गानि मासाश्चार्धमासाश्च पर्वाण्यहोरात्राणि प्रतिष्ठा
नक्षत्राण्यस्थीनि नभो माꣳसानि । ऊवध्यꣳ सिकताः सिन्धवो
गुदा यकृच्च क्लोमानश्च पर्वता ओषधयश्च वनस्पतयश्च लोमा-
न्युद्यन्पूर्वार्धो निम्लोचञ्जघनार्धो यद्विजृम्भते तद्विद्योतते यद्विधूनुते
तत्स्तनयति यन्मेहति तद्वर्षति वागेवास्य वाक् ॥१॥

1.   OM. Dawn is the head[1] of the horse sacrificial.[2] The sun is
his eye,[3] his breath is the wind, his wide open mouth is Fire,
the master might universal.[4] Time is the self of the horse
sacrificial.[5] Heaven is his back and the midworld his belly,
earth is his footing, — the regions are his flanks and the
lesser regions their ribs, the seasons his members, the months
and the half months are their joints, the days and nights are
his standing place, the stars his bones and the sky is the flesh
of his body. The strands are the food in his belly, the rivers
are his veins, his liver and his lungs are the mountains, herbs
and plants are his hairs, the rising is his front and the setting
his hinder portion, when he stretches himself, then it
lightens, when he shakes his frame, then it thunders, when he
urines, then it rains. Speech, verily, is the sound of him.

---

[1] Because it is the front and beginning.

[2] Ashwa meant originally "being, existence, substance". From the sense of speed and
strength it came to mean "horse". The word is therefore used to indicate material existence
and the horse (the image usually conveyed by this name) is taken as the symbol of universal
existence in *annam*.

The horse is symbolic and the sacrifice is symbolic. We have in it an image of the Virat
Purusha, of Yajniya Purusha, God expressing himself in the material universe.

[3] Because the sun is the master of sight.

[4] Air is the basis of life, Fire of strength and expansion.

[5] Time is that which upholds existence in material space and is the soul of it.

अह्वां अश्वं पुरस्तान्महिमाऽन्वजायत तस्य पूर्वे समुद्रे योनी रात्रि-
रेनं पश्चाःमहिमाऽन्वजायत तस्यापरे समुद्रे योनिरेतौ वा अश्वं
महिमानावभितः संबभूवतुः । हयो भूत्वा देवानवहद्वाजी गन्धर्वा-
नर्वाऽ्डुरानइवो मनुष्यान्समुद्र एवास्य बन्धुः समुद्रो योनिः ॥२॥

2. Day was the grandeur that was borne before the horse as he
   galloped, the eastern ocean gave it birth; night was the grandeur that was borne behind him and its birth was from the
   other waters. These are the grandeurs that came into being
   on either side of the horse. He became Haya and bore the
   gods, Vaja and bore the Gandharvas, Arvan and bore the
   Titans, Ashwa and bore mankind. The sea was his brother
   and the sea was his birthplace.

नंवेह किञ्चनाग्र आसीन्मृत्युनैवेदमावृतमासीत्। अशनाययाऽ
ऽशनाया हि मृत्युस्तन्मनोऽकुरुताऽऽत्मन्वी स्यामिति। सोऽर्चं-
न्नचरत्स्यार्चत आपोऽजायन्तार्चते वै मे कमभूदिति तदेवार्कस्या-
र्कत्वं कऽह वा अस्मै भवति य एवमेतदर्कस्यार्कत्वं वेद ॥१॥

1. Formerly there was nothing here; this was concealed by
Death — by Hunger, for it is Hunger that is Death. That
created Mind, and he said, "Let me have substance." He
moved about working and as he worked the waters were
born and he said, "Felicity was born to me as I worked."
This verily is the activity in action. Therefore felicity cometh
to him who thus knoweth this soul of activity in action.

आपो वा अर्कस्तद्यदपाश्शर आसीत्तत्समहृन्यत। सा पृथिव्यभव-
त्तस्यामश्राम्यत्तस्य श्रान्तस्य तप्तस्य तेजोरसो निरवर्तताग्निः ॥२॥

2. The waters verily (in their movement) are action; that which
was a lake of waters was contracted and became compact.
This became earth; upon earth he grew weary; in his weari-
ness he was heated and the Essence of energy went out from
him, even Fire.

स त्रेधाऽत्मानं व्यकुरुताऽऽदित्यं तृतीयं वायुं तृतीयꣳ स एष प्राण-
स्त्रेधा विहितः। तस्य प्राची दिक्शिरोऽसौ चासौ चेर्मौ।
अथास्य प्रतीची दिक्पुच्छमसौ चासौ च सक्थ्यौ दक्षिणा चोदीची
च पार्श्वे द्यौः पृष्ठमन्तरिक्षमुदरमियमुरः स एषोऽप्सु प्रतिष्ठितो
यत्र क्व चैति तदेव प्रतितिष्ठत्येवं विद्वान् ॥३॥

3. Fire divided himself into three — the sun one of the three
and Vayu one of the three; this is that force of life arranged
triply. The east is his head and the northeast and the south-
east are his arms. Now the west is his seat and the southwest
and the northwest are his thighs; his sides are the south and
the north; heaven is his back and the middle region is his
belly; this earth is his bosom. This is he that is established

in the waters wheresoever thou turn. And as that is he
established who thus knoweth.

> सोऽकामयत द्वितीयो म आत्मा जायेतेति स मनसा वाचं मिथुन॒
> समभवदशनाया मृत्युस्तद्यद्रेत आसीत्स संवत्सरोऽभवत्। न ह पुरा
> ततः संवत्सर आस तमेतावन्तं कालमबिभः। यावान्संवत्सरस्तमेता-
> वतः कालस्य परस्तादसृजत। तं जातमभिव्याददात्स भाणकरोत्सैव
> वागभवत् ॥४॥

4.	He desired, "Let a second self be born to me." He by mind
had intercourse with speech, even Hunger that is Death; the
seed that was of that union became Time. For before this
Time was not (period of Time) but so long He had borne him
in Himself. So long as is Time's period, after so long He gave
it birth. He yearned upon him as soon as it was born; it
cried out and that became speech.

> स ऐक्षत यदि वा इममभिम॒स्ये कनीयोऽन्नं करिष्य इति स तया
> वाचा तेनाऽऽत्मनेद॒ सर्वमसृजत यदिदं किञ्चर्चो यजू॒ष्षि सामानि
> च्छन्दा॒ष्सि यज्ञान्प्रजाः पशून्। स यद्यदेवासृजत तत्तदत्तुमध्रियत
> सर्वं वा अत्तीति तददितेरदितित्व॒ सर्वस्यैतस्यात्ता भवति सर्व-
> मस्यान्नं भवति य एवमेतददितेरदितित्वं वेद ॥५॥

5.	He saw, "If I devour this, I shall diminish food"; therefore
by that speech and by that self he created all this that we see,
the Riks and the Yajus and the Samas and the rhythms and
sacrifices and animals and these nations. Whatsoever he
created, that he set about devouring, verily he devoureth all;
this is the substantiality of being in substance (that it can be
destroyed[1]). He becometh the Eater of all the world and
everything becometh his food who thus knoweth the substantiality of being in substance.

> सोऽकामयत भूयसा यज्ञेन भूयो यजेयेति। सोऽश्राम्यत्स तपो-
> ऽतप्यत तस्य श्रान्तस्य तप्तस्य यशो वीर्यमुदक्रामत्। प्राणा वै
> यशो वीर्यं तत्प्राणेषूत्क्रान्तेषु शरीर॒ श्वयितुमध्रियत तस्य शरीर
> एव मन आसीत् ॥६॥

---
[1] Destroyed, i.e. enjoyed by absorption.

6. He desired, "Let me sacrifice more richly with richer sacrifice." He laboured and put forth heat of force, and of him thus laboured and heated splendour and strength came forth. The life-forces are that splendour and strength, therefore when the life-forces go forth, the body sets about to rot, yet in his body even so mind was.

सोऽकामयत मेध्यं म इदꣳ स्यादात्मन्व्यनेन स्यामिति । ततो-
ऽश्व: समभवद्यदश्वत्तन्मेध्यमभूदिति तदेवाश्वमेधस्याश्वमेधत्वम् ।
एष ह वा अश्वमेधं वेद य एनमेवं वेद । तमनवरुध्यैवामन्यत ।
तꣳ संवत्सरस्य परस्तादात्मन आलभत । . . .॥७॥

7. He desired, "Let this have sacrificial capacity for me, by this let me be provided with a body. That which has expressed power and being, that is fit for the sacrifice. This verily is the secret of the Ashwamedha and he knoweth indeed the Ashwamedha who thus knoweth it. He gave him free course and thought, then after a year (a fixed period of time) he dedicated him to the self. [...]¹

¹ Rest of passage not translated.

द्वया ह प्राजापत्या देवाश्चासुराश्च । ततः कानीयसा एव देवा
ज्यायसा असुरास्त एषु लोकेष्वस्पर्धन्त ते ह देवा ऊचुर्हन्तासुरा-
न्यज्ञ उद्गीथेनात्ययामेति ॥१॥

1. Two were the races of the Sons of God, the gods and the
    Titans. Thereafter the gods were weaker, mightier the Ti-
    tans. They in these worlds strove together, and the gods
    said, "Let us by this *udgitha* overpass the Titans in the
    Yajna."

ते ह वाचमूचुस्त्वं न उद्गायेति तथेति तेभ्यो वागुद्गायत् । यो
वाचि भोगस्तं देवेभ्य आगायद्यत्कल्याणं वदति तदात्मने । ते
विदुरनेन वै न उद्गात्राऽत्येष्यन्तीति तमभिद्रुत्य पाप्मनाऽविध्यन्स
यः स पाप्मा यदेवेदमप्रतिरूपं वदति स एव स पाप्मा ॥२॥

2. They said to Speech, "Do thou go upward (by the *udgitha*)
    for us." "So be it", said Speech and he went upward for
    them; the enjoyment that is in speech, he reached for the
    gods, the good that it speaks, he reached for the self. They
    thought it was by this singer they would overpass them, but
    they ran at him and penetrated him with evil. The evil that
    one speaketh, this that hath no correspondence (to the thing
    in fact to be expressed), — this is that evil.

Incomplete

The Great Aranyaka

A COMMENTARY ON THE BRIHADARANYAKA UPANISHAD

FOREWORD

THE Brihadaranyaka Upanishad, at once the most obscure and the profoundest of the Upanishads, offers peculiar difficulties to the modern mind. If its ideas are remote from us, its language is still more remote. Profound, subtle, extraordinarily rich in rare philosophical suggestions and delicate psychology, it has preferred to couch its ideas in a highly figurative and symbolical language, which to its contemporaries, accustomed to this suggestive dialect, must have seemed a noble frame for its riches, but meets us rather as an obscuring veil. To draw aside this curtain, to translate the old Vedic language and figures into the form contemporary thought prefers to give to its ideas is the sole object of this commentary. The task is necessarily a little hazardous. It would have been easy merely to reproduce the thoughts and interpretations of Shankara in the modern tongue; if there were an error, one could afford to err with so supreme an authority. But it seems to me that both the demands of truth and the spiritual need of mankind in this age call for a restoration of old Vedantic truth rather than for the prolonged dominion of that single side of it systematised by the mediaeval thinker. The great Shankaracharya needs no modern praise and can be hurt by no modern disagreement. Easily the first of metaphysical thinkers, the greatest genius in the history of philosophy, his commentary has also done an incalculable service to our race by bridging the intellectual gulf between the sages of the Upanishads and ourselves. It has protected them from the practical oblivion in which our ignorance and inertia have allowed the Veda to rest for so many centuries — only to be dragged out by the rude hands of the daringly speculative Teuton. It has kept these ancient grandeurs of thought, these high repositories of spirituality under the safeguard of that temple of metaphysics, the Adwaita philosophy — a little in the

background, a little too much veiled and shrouded, but nevertheless safe from the iconoclasm and the restless ingenuities
of modern scholarship. Nevertheless, it remains true that
Shankara's commentary is interesting not so much for the light
it sheds on the Upanishad as for its digressions into his own
philosophy. I do not think that Shankara's rational intellect,
subtle indeed to the extreme, but avid of logical clearness and
consistency, could penetrate far into that mystic symbolism and
that deep and elusive flexibility which is characteristic of all the
Upanishads, but rises to an almost unattainable height in the
Brihadaranyaka. He has done much, has shown often a readi-
ness and quickness astonishing in so different a type of intellec-
tuality, but more is possible and needed. The time is fast coming
when the human intellect, aware of the mighty complexity of the
universe, will be more ready to learn and less prone to dispute
and dictate; we shall be willing then to read ancient documents
of knowledge for what they contain instead of attempting to
force into them our own truth or get them to serve our philos-
phic or scholastic purposes. To enter passively into the thoughts
of the old Rishis, allow their words to sink into our souls, mould
them and create their own reverberations in a sympathetic and
responsive material — submissiveness, in short, to the Sruti —
was the theory the ancients themselves had of their method of
Vedic knowledge — *girām upaśrutiṁ cara, stomān abhi svara,
abhi gṛṇīhi, ā ruva* — to listen in soul to the old voices and allow
the Sruti in the soul to respond, to vibrate, first obscurely, in
answer to the Vedantic hymn of knowledge, to give the response,
the echo and last to let that response gain in clarity, intensity and
fullness. This is the principle of interpretation that I have
followed — mystical perhaps, but not necessarily more unsound
than the insistence and equally personal standards of the logician
and the scholar. And for the rest, where no inner experience of
truth sheds light on the text, to abide faithfully by the wording
of the Upanishad and trust my intuitions. For I hold it right to
follow the intuitions especially in interpreting the Upanishad,
even at the risk of being accused of reading mysticism into the
Vedanta, because the early Vedantists, it seems to me, were mys-
tics not in the sense of being vague and loose-thoughted

visionaries, but in the sense of being intuitional symbolists —
who regarded the world as a movement of consciousness and
all material forms and energies as external symbols and shadows
of deeper and ever deeper internal realities. It is not my intention here nor is it in my limits possible to develop the philosophy
of the Great Aranyaka Upanishad, but only to develop with just
sufficient amplitude for entire clearness the ideas contained in
its language and involved in its figures. The business of my
commentary is to lay a foundation; it is for the thinker to build
the superstructure.

THE HORSE OF THE WORLDS

The Upanishad begins with a grandiose abruptness in an impe-
tuous figure of the Horse of the Ashwamedha. "OM," it begins,
"Dawn is the head of the Horse sacrificial. The sun is his eye,
his breath is the wind, his wide-open mouth is Fire, the universal
energy; Time is the self of the Horse sacrificial. Heaven is his
back and the mid-region is his belly, earth is his footing, —
the quarters are his flanks and their intermediate regions are his
ribs; the seasons are his members, the months and the half
months are[1] that on which he stands, the stars are his bones and
the sky is the flesh of his body. The strands are the food in his
belly, the rivers are his veins, the mountains are his liver and
lungs, herbs and plants are the hairs of his body; the rising day
is his front portion and the setting day is his hinder portion.
When he stretches himself, then it lightens; when he shakes
himself, then it thunders; when he urines, then it rains. Speech
verily is the voice of him. Day was the grandeur that was born
before the Horse as he galloped, the eastern ocean gave it birth.
Night was the grandeur that was born in his rear and its birth
was in the western waters. These were the grandeurs that arose
into being on either side of the Horse. He became Haya and
carried the gods, — Vajin and bore the Gandharvas, — Arvan
and bore the Titans, — Ashwa and carried mankind. The sea

---

[1] *The following words were omitted when Sri Aurobindo copied his translation here:* their
joints, the days and nights are...

was his brother and the sea his birthplace."

This passage, full of a gigantic imagery, sets the key to the
Upanishad and only by entering into the meaning of its symbolism can we command the gates of this many-mansioned city of
Vedantic thought. There is never anything merely poetic or orna-
mental in the language of the Upanishads. Even in this passage
which would at first sight seem to be sheer imagery, there is a
choice, a selecting eye, an intention in the images. They are all
dependent not on the author's unfettered fancy, but on the common ideas of the early Vedantic theosophy. It is fortunate, also,
that the attitude of the Upanishad to the Vedic sacrifices is perfectly plain from this opening. We shall not stand in danger of
being accused of reading modern subtleties into primitive minds
or of replacing barbarous superstitions by civilised mysticism.
The Ashwamedha or Horse-Sacrifice is, as we shall see, taken
as the symbol of a great spiritual advance, an evolutionary
movement, almost, out of the dominion of apparently material
forces into a higher spiritual freedom. The Horse of the Ashwamedha is, to the author, a physical figure representing, like some
algebraical symbol, an unknown quantity of force and speed.
From the imagery it is evident that this force, this speed, is something worldwide, something universal; it fills the regions with
its being, it occupies Time, it gallops through Space, it bears on
in its speed men and gods and the Titans. It is the Horse of the
Worlds, — and yet the Horse sacrificial.

Let us regard first the word *aśva* and consider whether it
throws any light on the secret of this image. For we know that
the early Vedantins attached great importance to words in both
their apparent and their hidden meaning and no one who does
not follow them in this path, can hope to enter into the associations with which their minds were full. Yet the importance of
associations in colouring and often in determining our thoughts,
determining even philosophic and scientific thought when it is
most careful to be exact and free, should be obvious to the most
superficial psychologist. Swami Dayananda's method with the
Vedas, although it may have been too vigorously applied and
more often out of the powerful mind ·of the modern Indian
thinker than out of the recovered mentality of the old Aryan

Rishis, would nevertheless, in its principle have been approved by these Vedantins. Now the word *aśva* must originally have implied strength or speed or both before it came to be applied to a horse. In its first or root significance it means to exist pervadingly and so to possess, have, obtain or enjoy. It is the Greek *ekhō* (old Sanskrit *aśā*), the ordinary word in Greek for "I have". It means, also and even more commonly, to eat or enjoy. Beside this original sense inherent in the roots of its family it has its own peculiar significance of existence in force — strength, solidity, sharpness, speed, — in *aśan* and *aśma*, a stone, *aśani*, a thunderbolt, *aśri*, a sharp edge or corner (Latin *acer, acris*, sharp, *acus*, point etc.) and finally *aśva*, the strong, swift horse. Its fundamental meanings are, therefore, pervading existence, enjoyment, strength, solidity, speed. Shall we not say, therefore, that *aśva* to the Rishis meant the unknown power made up of force, strength, solidity, speed and enjoyment that pervades and constitutes the material world?

But there is a danger that etymological fancies may mislead us. It is necessary, therefore, to test our provisional conclusion from philology by a careful examination of the images of this parable. Yet before we proceed to this enquiry, it is as well to note that in the very opening of his second Brahmana, the Rishi passes on immediately from Ashwa the horse to *aśanāyā mṛtyuḥ*, Hunger that is death and assigns this Hunger that is death as the characteristic, indeed the very nature of the Force that has arranged and developed — evolved, as the moderns would say — the material worlds.

"Dawn," says the Rishi, "is the head of the Horse sacrificial." Now the head is the front, the part of us that faces and looks out upon our world, — and Dawn is that part to the Horse of the Worlds. This goddess must therefore be the opening out of the world to the eye of being — for as day is the symbol of a time of activity, night of a time of inactivity, so dawn images the imperfect but pregnant beginnings of regular cosmic action; it is the Being's movement forward, it is its impulse to look out at the universe in which it finds itself and looking towards it, to yearn, to desire to enter upon possession of a world which looks so bright because of the brightness of the gaze that

is turned upon it. The word Ushas means etymologically coming
into manifested being; and it could mean also desire or yearning.
Ushas or Dawn to the early thinkers was the impulse towards
manifest existence, no longer a vague movement in the depths
of the Unmanifest, but already emerging and on the brink of
its satisfaction. For we must remember that we are dealing with
a book full of mystical imagery which starts with and looks on
psychological and philosophical truths in the most material
things and we shall miss its meaning altogether, if in our interpretation we are afraid of mysticism.

The sun is the eye of this great Force, the wind is its life-
breath or vital energy, Fire is its open mouth. We are here in
the company of very familiar symbols. We shall have to return
to them hereafter but they are, in their surface application, obvious and lucid. By themselves they are almost sufficient to reveal the meaning of the symbol, — yet not altogether sufficient.
For, taken by themselves, they might mislead us into supposing
the Horse of the Worlds to be an image of the material universe
only, a figure for those movements of matter and in matter with
which modern Science is so exclusively preoccupied. But the
next image delivers us from passing by this side-gate into mate-
rialism. "Time in its period is the self of the Horse sacrificial."
If we accept for the word *ātmā* a significance which is also common and is, indeed, used in the next chapter, if we understand by
it, as I think we ought here to understand by it, "substance" or
"body", the expression, in itself remarkable, will become even
more luminous and striking. Not Matter then, but Time, a mental circumstance, is the body of this force of the material universe whose eye is the sun and his breath the wind. Are we
then to infer that the Seer denies the essential materiality of
matter? does he assert it to be, as Huxley admitted it to be, "a
state of consciousness"? We shall see. Meanwhile it is evident
already that this Horse of the Worlds is not an image merely of
matter or material force, but, as we had already supposed it to
be, an image of the power which pervades and constitutes the
material universe. We get also from this image about Time
the idea of it as an unknown power — for Time which is its self
or body, is itself an unknown quantity. The reality which

expresses itself to us through Time — its body —, but remains itself ungrasped, must be still what men have always felt it to be, the unknown God.

In the images that immediately follow we have the conception of Space added to the conception of Time and both are brought together side by side as constituents of the being of the Horse. For the sky is the flesh of his body, the quarters his flanks and the intermediate regions his ribs — the sky, *nabhas*, the ether above us in which the stellar systems are placed; and these stellar systems themselves, concentrations of ether, are the bones which support the flesh and of which life in this spatial infinity takes advantage in order more firmly to place and organise itself in matter. But side by side with this spatial image is that of the seasons reminding us immediately and intentionally of the connection of Time to Space. The seasons, determined for us by the movements of the sun and stars, are the flanks of the Horse and he stands upon the months and the fortnights — the lunar divisions. Space, then, is the flesh constituting materially this body of Time which the sage attributes to his Horse of the Worlds, — by movement in Space its periods are shaped and determined. Therefore we return always to the full idea of the Horse — not as an image of matter, not as a symbol of the unknown supramaterial Power in its supramaterial reality, but of that Power expressing itself in matter — materially, we might almost say, pervading and constituting the universe. Time is its body, — yes, but *samvatsara* not *kāla*, Time in its periods determined by movement in Space, not Time in its essentiality.

Moreover, it is that Power imaging itself in Cosmos, it is the Horse of the Worlds. For, we read, "Heaven is its back, the mid-region is its belly, earth is its footing" — *pājasyam*, the four feet upon which it stands. We must be careful not to confuse the ancient Seer's conception of the universe with our modern conception. To us nothing exists except this system of gross material worlds — *annamayam jagat*, — this earth, this moon, this sun and its planets, these myriad suns and their systems. But to the Vedantic thinkers the universe, the manifest Brahman, was a harmony of worlds within worlds; they beheld a space within our space but, linked with it, they were aware of a Time

connected with our Time but different from it. This earth was
Bhur. Rising in soul into the air above the earth, the *antariksam*,
they thought they came into contact with other sevenfold earths
in which just as here matter is the predominant principle, so there
nervous or vital energy is the main principle or else *manas*, still
dependent on matter and vital energy; these earths they called
Bhuvar. And rising beyond this atmosphere into the ethereal
void they believed themselves to be aware of other worlds which
they called Swar or heaven, where again, in its turn, mind, free,
blithe, delivered from its struggle to impose itself in a world not
its own upon matter and nerve-life, is the medium of existence
and the governing Force. If we keep in mind these ideas, we shall
easily understand why the images are thus distributed in the
sentence I have last quoted. Heaven is the back of the Horse,
because it is on mind that we rest, mind that bears up the Gods
and Gandharvas, Titans and men; — the mid-region is the belly
because vital energy is that which hungers and devours, moves
restlessly everywhere seizing everything and turning it into food
or else because mind is the womb of all our higher consciousness
here; — earth is the footing because matter, outward form, is
the fundamental condition for the manifestation of life, mind
and all higher forces. On Matter we rest and have our firm
stand; out of Matter we rise to our fulfilment in Spirit.

Then once again, after these higher and more remote
suggestions, we are reminded that it is some Force manifesting
in matter which the Horse symbolises; the material manifestation constitutes the essence of its symbolism. The images used
are of an almost gross materiality. Some of them are at the same
time of a striking interest to the practical student of Yoga, for
he recognises in them allusions to certain obscure but exceedingly common Yogic phenomena. The strands of the rivers are
imaged as the undigested food in the Horse's belly — earth not
yet assimilated or of sufficient consistency for the habitual
works of life; the rivers, distributing the water that is the life-
blood of earth's activities, are his veins; the mountains, breathing in health for us from the rarer altitudes and supporting by
the streams born from them the works of life, are his lungs and
liver; herbs and plants, springing up out of the sap of earth, are

the hairs covering and clothing his body. All that is clear enough and designedly superficial. But then the Upanishad goes on to speak no longer of superficial circumstances but of the powers of the Horse. Some of these are material powers, the thunder, the lightning, the rain. "When he stretches himself, then it lightens; when he shakes himself, then it thunders; when he urines, then it rains." *Vijṛmbhate*, extends himself by intensity, makes the most of his physical bulk and force; *vidhūnute*, throws himself out by energy, converts his whole body into a motion and force; these two words are of a great impetuosity and vehemence, and taken in conjunction with the images extremely significant. The Yogin will at once recognise the reference to the electrical manifestations, visible or felt, which accompany so often the increase of concentration, thought and inner activity in this waking condition — electricity, *vidyutas*, the material symbol, medium and basis of all activities of knowledge, *sarvāṇi vijñānavijṛmbhitāni*. He will recognise also the *meghadhvani*, one of the characteristic sounds heard in the concentration of Yoga, symbolical of *kṣātratejas* and physically indicative of force gathering itself for action. The first image is therefore an image of knowledge expressing itself in matter, the second is an image of power expressing itself in matter. The third, the image of the rain, suggests that it is from the mere waste matter of his body that this great Power is able to fertilise the world and produce sustenance for the myriad nations of his creatures. "Speech verily is the voice of him." *Vāgevāsya vāk*. Speech with its burden of definite thought is the neighing of this mighty Horse of sacrifice; by that this great Power in matter expresses materially the uprush of his thought and yearning and emotion, the visible sparks of the secret universal fire that is in him — *guhāhitam*.

But the real powers, the wonderful fundamental greatnesses of the Horse are, the sage would have us remember, not the material. What are they then? The sunrise and sunset, day and night are their symbols, not the magnitudes of Space, but the magnitudes of Time, — Time, that mysterious condition of universal mind which alone makes the ordering of the universe in Space possible, although its own particular relations to matter are necessarily determined by material events and movements — for itself subtle as well as infinite it offers no means by which it can be materially measured. Sunrise and sunset, that is to say birth and death, are the front and hind part of the body of the Horse, Time expressed in matter. But on Day and Night the sage fixes a deeper significance. Day is the symbol of the continual manifestation of material things in *vyakta*, the manifest or fundamentally in Sat, in infinite being; Night is the symbol of their continual disappearance into *avyakta*, the unmanifest or finally into Asat, into infinite non-being. They appear according to the swift movement of this Horse of the Worlds, *anu ajāyata*, or, as I have written, translating the idea and rhythm of the Upanishads rather than the exact words, as he gallops. Day is the greatness that appears in his front, Night is the greatness that appears in his rear, — whatever this Time-Spirit, this Zeitgeist, turns his face towards or arrives at as he gallops through Time, that appears or, as we say, comes into being, whatever he passes away from and so leaves, that disappears out of being or, as we say, perishes. Not that things are really destroyed, for nothing that is can be destroyed, *na abhāvo vidyate satah*, but they no longer appear, they are swallowed up in this darkness of his refusal of consciousness; for the purposes of manifestation they cease to exist. All things exist already in Parabrahman, but all are not here manifest. They are already there in Being, not in Time. The universal Thought expressing itself as Time reaches them, they seem to be born; It passes away from them, they seem to perish; but there they still are, in Being, but not in Time. These two greatnesses of the appearance of things in Time and Space and their disappearance in Time and Space act always and continuously so long as the Horse is galloping, and they are his essential greatnesses. *Etau vai mahimānau*. The birth of one is in the eastern ocean, of the other in the western, that is to say in Sat and Asat, in the ocean of Being and the ocean of denial of Being or else in *vyākṛta prakṛti* and *avyākṛta prakṛti*, occult sea of Chaos, manifest sea of Cosmos.

Then the sage throws out briefly a description, not exhaustive but typical, of the relations of the Horse to the different natural types of being that seem to possess this universe. For all of them He is the *vāhana*, He bears them up on His infinite strength and speed and motion. He bears all of them without respect of differences, *samabhāvena*, with the divine impartiality and equality of soul — *samam hi brahma*. To the type of each individual being this Universal Might adapts himself; He seems to take upon himself their image. He is Haya to the Gods, Arvan to the Asura, Vajin to the Gandharvas, Ashwa to men. *Ye yathā mām prapadyante tams tathaiva bhajāmyaham. Mama vartmānuvartante manuṣyāḥ pārtha sarvaśaḥ.* In reality, they are made in His image, not He in theirs and though He seems to obey them and follow their needs and impulses, though they handle the whip, ply the spur and tug the reins, it is He who bears them on in the courses of Time that are marked out for Him by His hidden Self; He is free and exults in the swiftness of His galloping.

But what are these names, Haya, Vajin, Arvan, Ashwa? Certainly, they must suggest qualities which fit the Horse in each case to the peculiar type of its rider; but the meaning depends on associations and an etymology which in modern Sanskrit have gone below the surface and are no longer easily seizable. Haya is especially difficult. For this reason Shankara, relying too much on scholarship and intellectual inference and too little on his intuitions, is openly at a loss in this passage. He sees that the word *haya* for horse must arise from the radical sense of motion born by the root *hi*; but every horse has motion for his chief characteristic and utility, Arvan and Vajin no less than Haya. Why then should Haya alone be suitable for riding by the gods, why Arvan for the Asuras? He has, I think, the right intuition when he suggests that it is some peculiar and excelling kind of motion (*viśiṣṭagati*) which is the characteristic of Haya. But then, unable to fix on that peculiarity, unable to read any characteristic meaning in the names that follow, he draws back from his intuition and adds that after all, these names may have merely indicated particular kinds of horses attributed mythologically to these various families of riders. But this suggestion would make the passage mere mythology; but the Upanishads, always intent on their deeper object, never waste time over mere mythology. We must therefore go deeper than Shankara and follow out the intuition he himself has abandoned.

I am dwelling on this passage at a length disproportionate
to its immediate importance, not only because Shankara's failure
in handling it shows the necessity and fruitfulness of trusting our
intuitions when in contact with the Upanishads, but because the
passage serves two other important uses. It illustrates the Vedantic use of the etymology of words and it throws light on the
precise notions of the old thinkers about those super-terrestrial
beings with whom the vision of the ancient Hindus peopled the
universe. The Vedantic writers, we continually find, dwelt deeply
and curiously on the innate and on the concealed meaning of
words; *vyākaraṇa*, always considered essential to the inter-
prétation of the Vedas, they used not merely as scholars, but
much more as intuitive thinkers. It was not only the actual etymological sense or the actual sense in use but the suggestions of
the sound and syllables of the words which attracted them; for
they found that by dwelling on them new and deep truths arose
into their understandings. Let us see how they use this method
in assigning the names assumed by the sacrificial Horse.

Here modern philology comes to our help, for, by the clue
it has given, we can revive in its principle the Nirukta of our
ancestors and discover by induction and inference the old
meaning of the Vedic vocables. I will leave *haya* alone for the
present; because philology unaided does not help us very much
in getting at the sense of its application, — in discovering the
viśiṣṭagati which the word conveyed to the mind of the sage.
But *vājin* and *arvan* are very illuminative. *Vāja* and *vājin* are common Vedic words; they recur perpetually in the Rig-veda. The
sense of *vāja* is essentially substantiality of being attended with
plenty, from which it came to signify full force, copiousness,
strength, and by an easy transition, substance and plenty in the
sense of wealth and possessions. There can be no doubt about
vājin. But European scholarship has confused for us the approach to the sense of *arvan*. *Ar* is a common Sanskrit root, the
basis of *ari*, *ārya*, *aryamā* and a number of well-known words.
But the scholars tell us that it means to till or plough and the
Aryans so called themselves because they were agriculturists and
not nomads and hunters. Starting from this premise one may see
in *arvan* a horse for ploughing as opposed to a draught-animal

or a war-horse, and support the derivation by instancing the Latin *arvum*, a tilled field. But even if the Aryans were plough-men, the Titans surely were not — Hiranyakashipu and Prahlada did not pride themselves on the breaking of the glebe and the honest sweat of their brow! There is no trace of such an association in *arvan* here, — I know not whether there is any elsewhere in the Vedas. Indeed, this agriculturist theory of the Aryans seems one of the worst of the many irresponsible freaks which scholastic fancifulness has perpetrated in the field of Sanskrit learning. No ancient race would be likely so to designate itself. *Ar* signifies essentially any kind of pre-eminence in fact or force in act. It means therefore to be strong, high, swift or active, pre-eminent, noble, excellent, or first; to raise, lead, begin or rule; it means also to struggle, fight, to drive, to labour, to plough. The sense of struggle and combat appears in *ari*, an enemy; the Greek Ares, the war-god, *aretē*, virtue, meaning originally like the Latin *virtus*, valour; the Latin *arma*, weapons. Arya means strong, high, noble or warlike, as indeed its use in literature constantly indicates. We can now discover the true force of Arvan, — it is the strong one in command, it is the stallion, or the bull, i.e. master of the herd, the leader, master or fighter. The word *asura* also means the strong or mighty one. The Gandharvas are listed[1] here briefly, so as to suit the rapidity of the passage, as the type of a particular class of beings, Gandharvas, Yakshas, Kinnaras, whose unifying characteristic is material ease, prosperity and a beautiful, happy and undisturbed self-indulgence; they are angels of joy, ease, art, beauty and pleasure. For them the Horse becomes full of ease and plenty, the support of these qualities, the *vāhana* of the Gandharvas. The Asuras are, similarly, angels of might and force and violent struggle, — self-will is their characteristic, just as an undisciplined fury of self-indulgence is the characteristic of their kindred Rakshasas. It is a self-will capable of discipline, but always huge and impe-tuous even in discipline, always based on a colossal egoism. They struggle gigantically to impose that egoism on their sur-roundings. It is for these mighty but imperfect beings that the Horse adapts himself to their needs, becomes full of force and

---

[1] *Doubtful reading.*

might and bears up their gigantic struggle, their unceasing effort. And Haya? In the light of these examples we can hazard a suggestion. The root meaning is motion; but from certain kindred words, *hil*, to swing, *hind*, to swing, *hiṇḍ*, to roam about freely and from another sense of *hi*, to exhilarate or gladden, we may, perhaps, infer that *haya* indicated to the sage a swift, free and joyous, bounding motion, fit movement for the bearer of the gods. For the Aryan gods were *devas*, angels of joy and brightness, fulfilled in being, in harmony with their functions and surroundings, not like the Titans imperfect, dispossessed, struggling. Firmly seated on the bounding joy of the Horse, they deliver themselves confidently to the exultation of his movements. The sense here is not so plain and certain as with Vajin and Arvan; but Haya must certainly have been one in character with the Deva in order to be his *vāhana*; the sense I have given certainly belongs to the word "the Deva", is discoverable in *haya* from its roots,[1] and that this brightness and joyousness was the character of the Aryan gods, I think every reader of Veda and Purana must feel and admit. Last of all, the Horse becomes Ashwa for men. But is he not Ashwa for all? Why particularly for men? The answer is that the Rishi is already moving forward in thought to the idea of *aśanāyā mṛtyuḥ* with which he opens the second Brahmana of the Upanishad. Man, first and supreme type of terrestrial creatures, is most of all subject to this mystery of wasting and death which the Titans bear with difficulty and the gods and Gandharvas entirely overcome. For in man that characteristic of enjoyment which by enjoying devours and wastes both its object and itself is especially developed and he bears that consequent pressure of *aśanāyā mṛtyuḥ* which can only lighten and disappear when we rise upward in the scale of Being towards Brahman and become truly sons of immortality, *amṛtasya putrāḥ*. That form of force in matter that is self-destroying[2] because it wastes or preys upon others is humanity's *vāhana*.

Finally, there comes a consummation to the parable in which the thought of the Upanishad opens out to that ultimate

---

[1] *The placement of this phrase is uncertain.*
[2] *Doubtful reading.*

idea for which the image of the Horse is only a *pratiṣṭhā* and a preface, — the liberation from *aśanāyā mṛtyuḥ*. Of this Horse of the Worlds, who bears up all beings, the sea is the brother and the sea is the birthplace. There can be no doubt of the meaning of this symbol. It is the upper Ocean of the Veda in which it imaged the superior and divine existence, these are the waters of supramaterial causality. From that this lower Ocean of our manifestation derives its waters, its flowing energies, *apaḥ*; from that, when the Vritras are slain and the firmaments opened, it is perpetually replenished, *prati samudram syanda-mānāḥ*, and of that it is the shadow and the reproduction of its circumstances under the conditions of mental illusion, — Avidya, mother of limitation and death. This image not only consumates this passage but opens a door of escape from that which is to follow. Deliverance from the dominion of *aśanāyā mṛtyuḥ* is possible because of this circumstance that this sea of divine being is *bandhu*, kin and friend to the Horse. The *aparārdha* proves to be of the same essential nature as the *parārdha*, our mortal part is kin to our unlimited and immortal part, because the Horse of the Worlds in his essence comes to us from that divine source and partakes of its nature, and from what other except this Ocean can the Horse of the Worlds, who is material yet supramaterial, be said to have derived his being? We, appearing bound, mortal and limited, are manifestations of a free and infinite reality and from that from which we were born comes friendship and assistance for that which we are, towards making us that which we shall be. From our kindred heavens the Love[1] descends always that works to raise up the lower to its brother, the higher.[2]

---

[1] *Or,* force.

[2] *The placement of some of the phrases in these last three sentences is uncertain.*

CHHANDOGYA UPANISHAD

Chapter One, Sections 1, 2 and 3

Chhandogya Upanishad

CHAPTER ONE: SECTION 1

ओमित्येतदक्षरमुद्गीथमुपासीत । ओमिति ह्युद्गायति तस्योप-
व्याख्यानम् ॥१॥

1. Worship ye OM, the eternal syllable, OM is Udgitha, the chant of Sama-veda; for with OM they begin the chant of Sama. And this is the exposition of OM.

एषां भूतानां पृथिवी रसः पृथिव्या आपो रसः । अपामोषधयो
रस ओषधीनां पुरुषो रसः पुरुषस्य वाग्रसो वाच ऋग्रस ऋचः साम
रसः साम्न उद्गीथो रसः ॥२॥

2. Earth is the substantial essence of all these creatures and the waters are the essence of earth; herbs of the field are the essence of the waters; man is the essence of the herbs. Speech is the essence of man, Rig-veda the essence of Speech, Sama the essence of Rik. Of Sama OM is the essence.

स एष रसानाꣳरसतमः परमः पराध्योंऽष्टमो यदुद्गीथः ॥३॥

3. This is the eighth essence of the essences and the really essential, the highest and it belongeth to the upper hemisphere of things.

कतमा कतमर्क् कतमत् कतमत्साम कतमः कतम उद्गीथ इति
विमृष्टं भवति ॥४॥

4. Which among things and which again is Rik; which among things and which again is Sama; which among things and which again is OM of the Udgitha — this is now pondered.

वागेवर्क् प्राणः सामोमित्येतदक्षरमुद्गीथः । तद्धा एतन्मिथुनं यद्वाक्च
प्राणश्चर्क् च साम च ॥५॥

5.   Speech is Rik, Breath is Sama; the Imperishable is OM of Udgitha. These are the divine lovers, Speech and Breath, Rik and Sama.

तदेतन्मिथुनमोमित्येतस्मिन्नक्षरे संसृज्यते यदा वै मिथुनौ समागच्छत
आपयतो वै तावन्योन्यस्य कामम् ॥६॥

6.   As a pair of lovers are these and they cling together in OM the eternal syllable; now when the beloved and her lover meet, verily they gratify each the desire of the other.

आपयिता ह वै कामानां भवति य एतदेवं विद्वानक्षरमुद्गीथ-
मुपास्ते ॥७॥

7.   He becometh a gratifier of the desires of men who with this knowledge worshippeth OM the eternal syllable.

तद्वा एतदनुज्ञाक्षरं यद्धि किं चानुजानात्योमित्येव तदाह् एषा एव
समृद्धिर्यदनुज्ञा । समर्धयिता ह वै कामानां भवति य एतदेवं विद्वा-
नक्षरमुद्गीथमुपास्ते ॥८॥

8.   Now this OM is the syllable of Assent; for to whatsoever one assenteth, one sayeth OM; and assent is blessing of increase. Verily he becometh a blesser and increaser of the desires of men who with this knowledge worshippeth OM the eternal syllable.

तेनेयं त्रयी विद्या वर्तंत ओमित्याश्रावयत्योमिति शंसत्योमित्युद्-
गायत्येतस्यैवाक्षरस्यापचित्यै महिम्ना रसेन ॥९॥

9.   By OM the triple knowledge proceedeth; with OM the priest reciteth the Rik, with OM he pronounceth the Yajur, with OM he chanteth the Sama. And all this is for the heaping up of the Imperishable and by the greatness of It and the delightfulness.

तेनोभौ कुरुतो यश्चैतदेवं वेद यश्च न वेद । नाना तु विद्या

चाविद्या च यदेव विद्यया करोति श्रद्धयोपनिषदा तदेव वीर्यवत्तरं
भवतीति खल्वेतस्यैवाक्षरस्योपव्याख्यानं भवति ॥१०॥

10. He doeth works by OM who hath the knowledge, and he
also who hath it not; but these are diverse, the Knowledge
and the Ignorance. Whatso work one doeth with knowledge, with faith and with the secret of Veda, it becometh
to him more virile and mighty. This is the exposition of the
eternal letters.

CHAPTER ONE: SECTION 2

देवासुरा ह वै यत्र संयेतिर उभये प्राजापत्यास्तद्ध देवा उद्गीथ-
माजह्रुरनेनैनानभिभविष्याम इति ॥१॥

1. The Gods and the Demons strove together and both were
children of the Almighty Father. Then the Gods took up
for weapon OM of Udgitha, for they said, "With this we
shall overcome these Titans."

ते ह नासिक्यं प्राणमुद्गीथमुपासांचक्रिरे। तꣳहासुराः पाप्मना
विविधुस्तस्मात्तेनोभयं जिघ्रति सुरभि च दुर्गन्धि च पाप्मना ह्येष
विद्धः ॥२॥

2. The Gods worshipped OM as Breath in the nostrils; but the
Demons came and smote it with the arrow of Evil; therefore
it smelleth both alike, the sweet scent and the evil odour.
For it is smitten through and through with Evil.

अथ ह वाचमुद्गीथमुपासांचक्रिरे। ताꣳहासुराः पाप्मना विविधु-
स्तस्मात्तेयोभयं वदति सत्यं चानृतं च पाप्मना ह्येषा विद्धा ॥३॥

3. Then the Gods worshipped OM as Speech; but the Demons
came and smote it with the arrow of Evil; therefore it speaketh
both alike, Truth and Falsehood. For it is smitten through
and through with Evil.

अथ ह चक्षुरुद्गीथमुपासांचक्रिरे । तद्धासुराः पाप्मना विविधु-
स्तस्मात्तेनोभयं पश्यति दर्शनीयं चादर्शनीयं च पाप्मना ह्येतद्
विद्धम् ॥४॥

4.   Then the Gods worshipped OM as the Eye; but the Demons
     came and smote it with the arrow of Evil; therefore it be-
     holdeth both alike, the fair to see and the foul of favour.
     For it is smitten through and through with Evil.

अथ ह श्रोत्रमुद्गीथमुपासांचक्रिरे । तद्धासुराः पाप्मना विविधु-
स्तस्मात्तेनोभयꣳ शृणोति श्रवणीयं चाश्रवणीयं च पाप्मना ह्येत-
द्विद्धम् ॥५॥

5.   Then the Gods worshipped OM as the Ear; but the Demons
     came and smote it with the arrow of Evil; therefore it heareth
     both alike, that which is well to hear and that which is harsh
     and unseemly. For it is smitten through and through with
     Evil.

अथ ह मन उद्गीथमुपासांचक्रिरे । तद्धासुराः पाप्मना विविधु-
स्तस्मात्तेनोभयꣳसंकल्पयते संकल्पनीयं चासंकल्पनीयं च पाप्मना
ह्येतद्विद्धम् ॥६॥

6.   Then the Gods worshipped Udgitha as Mind; but the De-
     mons came and smote it with the arrow of Evil; therefore it
     conceiveth both alike, right thoughts and unlawful imagi-
     nations. For it is smitten through and through with Evil.

अथ ह य एवायं मुख्यः प्राणस्तमुद्गीथमुपासांचक्रिरे । तꣳहासुरा
ऋत्वा विदध्वꣳसुर्यथाश्मानमाखणमृत्वा विध्वंसेत ॥७॥

7.   Then the Gods worshipped OM as this which is Breath in
     the mouth and the Demons rushing against it dashed them-
     selves to pieces; as when an object striketh against firm and
     solid rock, it dasheth to pieces upon the rock.

एवं यथाऽश्मानमाखणमृत्वा विध्वꣳसत एवꣳहैव स विध्वꣳसते य
एवंविदि पापं कामयते यश्चैनमभिदासति स एषोऽश्माखणः ॥८॥

8. And even as an object hurling against firm and solid rock dasheth itself to pieces, so he hurleth himself upon destruction whoso desireth evil against the Knower or whoso doeth him hurt; for the Knower is as that firm and solid rock.

नैवैतेन सुरभि न दुर्गन्धि विजानात्यपहतपाप्मा ह्येष तेन यदश्नाति
यत्पिबति तेनेतरान्प्राणानवति । एतमु एवान्ततोऽवित्त्वोत्क्रामति
व्याददात्येवान्तत इति ॥९॥

9. With this Breath one cogniseth neither sweet scent nor ill odour, for it hath flung Evil from it. Whatsoever one eateth with this or drinketh, thereby it cherisheth the other breaths. At the end and last when he findeth not the breath, the Spirit goeth out from the body; verily he openeth wide the mouth as he goeth.

तश्हाङ्गिरा उद्गीथमुपासांचक्र एतमु एवाङ्गिरसं मन्यन्तेऽङ्गानां
यद्रसः ॥१०॥

10. Angiras worshipped OM of Udgitha as Breath in the mouth and men think of Breath in the mouth as Angiras because it is essence of the members of the body.

तेन तश्ह बृहस्पतिरुद्गीथमुपासांचक्र एतमु एव बृहस्पतिं मन्यन्ते
वाग्घि बृहती तस्या एष पतिः ॥११॥

11. By the strength of Angiras, Brihaspati worshipped OM as Breath in the mouth, and men think of the Breath as Brihaspati, because Speech is the great goddess and Breath is the lord of Speech.

तेन तश्हायास्य उद्गीथमुपासांचक्र एतमु एवायास्यं मन्यन्त आस्या-
द्ययते ॥१२॥

12. By the strength of Brihaspati, Ayasya worshipped OM as Breath in the mouth and men think of the Breath as Ayasya, because 'tis from the mouth it cometh.

तेन तश्ह बको दाल्भ्यो विदांचकार। स ह नैमिशीयानामुद्गाता
बभूव स ह स्मैभ्यः कामानागायति ॥१३॥

13. By the strength of Ayasya, Baka the son of Dalbha knew the
Breath. And he became the Chanter of the Sama among the
Naimishiyas and he chanteth their desires for them unto
fulfilment.

आगाता ह वै कामानां भवति य एतदेवं विद्वानक्षरमुद्गीथमुपास्त
इत्यध्यात्मम् ॥१४॥

14. Verily he becometh a chanter unto fulfilment of the desires of
men who with this knowledge worshippeth OM of Udgitha,
the eternal syllable. Thus far concerning Self is the exposition.

CHAPTER ONE: SECTION 3

अथाधिदैवतं य एवासौ तपति तमुद्गीथमुपासीतोद्यन्वा एष प्रजाभ्य
उद्गायति। उद्यँस्तमोभयमपहन्त्यपहन्ता ह वै भयस्य तमसो
भवति य एवं वेद ॥१॥

1. Thereafter concerning the Gods. Lo yonder burning fire in the
heavens, worship ye Him as the Udgitha; for the Sun riseth
and singeth his bright hymn unto the peoples. Yea he riseth,
and darkness is slain and its terror — therefore shall he be a
slayer of the terror and the darkness, he who thus knoweth.

समान उ एवायं चासौ चोष्णोऽयमुष्णोऽसौ स्वर इतीममाचक्षते
स्वर इति प्रत्यास्वर इत्यमुं तस्माद्वा एतमिममुं चोद्गीथमुपा-
सीत ॥२॥

2. Breath and the Sun are one and alike — for the one is heat and
the other is heat, and they call Breath the mover and the Sun
too they call the mover and also the mover that returneth
upon his paths they call him — therefore ye shall worship both
the one and the other as Udgitha.

अथ खलु व्यानमेवोद्गीथमुपासीत यद्वै प्राणिति स प्राणो यदपानिति
सोऽपानः । अथ यः प्राणापानयोः सन्धिः स व्यानो यो व्यानः
सा वाक् । तस्मादप्राणन्ननपानन्वाचमभिव्याहरति ॥३॥

3. Thereafter verily ye shall worship Vyana the middle breath as Udgitha. For when one breathes forth it is Prana, the Main Breath, and when one breathes down it is Apana, the lower breath. Now this which is the joint and linking of the main breath and the lower breath, is Vyana — and Vyana, it is Speech. Therefore 'tis when one neither breatheth forth nor breatheth down that one giveth utterance to Speech.

या वाक्सक्तेस्मादप्राणन्ननपानन्नृचमभिव्याहरति यर्क् तत्साम तस्मा-
दप्राणन्ननपानन्साम गायति यत्साम स उद्गीथस्तस्मादप्राणन्ननपान-
न्नुद्गायति ॥४॥

4. But Speech is the Rik — therefore 'tis when one neither breatheth out nor breatheth in that one uttereth the Rik. And Rik it is Sama — therefore 'tis when one neither breatheth out nor breatheth in that one chanteth the Sama. But Sama it is Udgitha — therefore 'tis when one neither breatheth out nor breatheth in that one singeth Udgitha.

अतो यान्यन्यानि वीर्यवन्ति कर्माणि यथाग्नेर्मंन्थनमाजेः सरणं दृढस्य
धनुष आयमनमप्राणन्ननपानन् स्तानि करोत्येतस्य हेतोर्व्यानमेवोद्गीथ-
मुपासीत ॥५॥

5. Hence whatsoever actions there be that are of might and forcefulness as smiting out fire from the tinder or leaping a great barrier or the bending a stark and mighty bow, it is when one neither breatheth out nor breatheth in that one doeth these. And for this cause ye shall worship the middle breath as Udgitha.

अथ खलूद्गीथाक्षराण्युपासीतोद्गीथ इति प्राण एवोत्प्राणेन ह्युत्तिष्ठ-
ति वाग्गीर्वाचो ह गिर इत्याचक्षतेऽन्नं थमन्ने ह्येद सर्वं स्थितम् ॥६॥

6. Thereafter verily ye shall worship the syllables of the Udgitha

saying Udgitha and Prana is the first syllable, because one riseth up with the main breath and Speech is the second syllable, because they call Speech that which goeth forth and food is the third syllable, because in food all this Universe is established.

द्यौरेवोदन्तरिक्षं गीः पृथिवी थमादित्य एवोद्वायुर्गोरग्निस्थं सामवेद
एवोद्यजुर्वेदो गीर्ऋग्वेदस्थं दुग्धेऽस्मे वाग्दोहं यो वाचो दोहोऽन्न-
वानन्नादो भवति य एतान्येवं विद्वानुद्गीथाक्षराण्युपास्त उद्गीथ
इति ॥७॥

7. Heaven is the first syllable, the middle air is the second syllable, earth is the third syllable. The Sun is the first syllable, Air is the second syllable, Fire is the third syllable. The Samaveda is the first syllable, Yajurveda is the second syllable, Rigveda is the third syllable. To him Speech is a cow that yieldeth sweet milk — and what is this milking of Speech? — even that he becometh rich in food and the eater of food who knoweth these and worshippeth the syllables of Udgitha saying lo even this is Udgitha.

Incomplete

Notes on the Chhandogya Upanishad

THE INITIAL SENTENCE

ओमित्येतदक्षरमुद्गीथमुपासीत । ओमिति ह्युद्गायति तस्योपव्याख्यानम् ॥१॥

OM is the syllable (the Imperishable One); one should follow after it as the upward Song (movement); for with OM one sings (goes) upwards; of which this is the analytical explanation.

So, literally translated in its double meaning, both its exoteric, physical and symbolic sense and its esoteric symbolised reality, runs the initial sentence of the Upanishad. These opening lines or passages of the Vedanta are always of great importance; they are always so designed as to suggest or even sum up, if not all that comes afterwards, yet the central and pervading idea of the Upanishad. The *iśā vāsyam* of the Vajasaneyi, the *kenesitaṁ ... manas* of the Talavakara, the Sacrificial Horse of the Brihadaranyaka, the solitary Atman with its hint of the future world-vibrations in the Aitareya are of this type. The Chhandogya, we see from its first and introductory sentence, is to be a work on the right and perfect way of devoting oneself to the Brahman; the spirit, the methods, the formulae are to be given to us. Its subject is the Brahman, but the Brahman as symbolised in the OM, the sacred syllable of the Veda; not, therefore, the pure state of the Universal Existence only, but that Existence in all its parts, the waking world and the dream self and the sleeping, the manifest, half-manifest and hidden, Bhurloka, Bhuvar and Swar, — the right means to win all of them, enjoy all of them, transcend all of them, is the subject of the Chhandogya. OM is the symbol and the thing symbolised. It is the symbol, *akṣaram*; the syllable in which all sound of speech is brought back to its wide, pure indeterminate state; it is the symbolised, *akṣaram*, the changeless, undiminishing, unincreasing, unappearing, undying Reality which shows itself to experience in all this change, increase, diminution, appearance, departure which in a particular sum and harmony of them we call the world, just as OM, the pure eternal sound-basis of speech shows itself to the ear in the variations and combinations of impure sound which in a particular sum and harmony of them we call the Veda. We are to follow after this OM with all our souls, *upāsita,* — to apply ourselves to it and devote ourselves to its knowledge and possession, but always to OM as the Udgitha. Again in this word we have the symbolic sense and the truth symbolised expressed, as in *akṣaram* and OM, in a single vocable with a double function and significance.

The Sanskrit has always been a language in which one word is naturally capable of several meanings and therefore carries with it a number of varied associations. It lends itself, therefore, with peculiar ease and naturalness to the figure called *śleṣa* or embrace, the marriage of different meanings in a single form of words. Paronomasia in English is mere punning, a tour de force, an incongruity, a grotesque and artificial play of humour. Paronomasia, *śleṣa* in Sanskrit, though in form precisely the same thing, is not punning, not incongruous but easily appropriate, not incongruous or artificial, but natural and often inevitable, not used for intellectual horseplay, but with a serious, often a high and worthy purpose. It has been abused by rhetorical writers; yet great and noble poetical effects have been obtained by its aid, as, for instance, when the same form of words has been used to convey open blame and cover secret praise. Nevertheless in classical Sanskrit, the language has become a little too rigid for the perfect use of the figure; it is too literary, too minutely grammatised; it has lost the memory of its origins. A sense of cleverness and artifice suggests itself to us because meanings known to be distinct and widely separate are brought together in a single activity of the word which usually suggests them only in different contexts. But in the Vedic *śleṣa* we have no sense of cleverness or artifice, because the writers themselves had none. The language was still near to its origins and had, not perhaps an intellectual, but still an instinctive memory of them. With less grammatical and as little etymological knowledge as Panini and the other classical grammarians, the Rishis had better possession of the soul of Sanskrit speech. The different meanings of a word, though distinct, were not yet entirely separate; many links yet survived between them which were afterwards lost; the gradations of sense remained, the hint of the word's history, the shading off from one sense to another. *Ardha* now means half and it means nothing else. To the Vedic man it carried other associations. Derived from the root *ṛdh* which meant originally to go and join, then to add, to increase, to prosper, it bore the sense of place of destination, the person to whom I direct myself, or simply place; also increase, addition, a part added and so simply a part or half. To have used it in any other sense than "place of destination" or as at once "half, part" and "a place of destination" would not be a violence to the Vedic mind, but a natural association of ideas. So when they spoke of the higher worlds of Sachchidananda as Parardha, they meant at once the higher half of man's inner existence and the *param dhāma* or high seat of Vishnu in other worlds and, in addition, thought of that high seat as the destination of our upward movement. All this rose at once to their mind when the word was uttered, naturally, easily and, by long association, inevitably.

OM is a word in instance. When the word was spoken as a solemn affirmation, everyone thought of the Pranava in the Veda, but no one could listen to the word OM without thinking also of the Brahman in Its triple manifestation and in Its transcendent being. The word, *akṣaram*, meaning both syllable and unshifting, when coupled with OM, is a word in instance; "OM the syllable" meant also, inevitably, to the Vedic mind "Brahman, who changes not nor perishes". The words *udgītha* and *udgāyati* are words in instance. In classical Sanskrit the prepositional prefix to the verb was dead and bore only a conventional significance or had no force at all; *udgāyati* or *pragāyati* is not very different from the simple *gāyati*; all mean merely sing or chant. But in Veda the preposition is still living and joins its verb or separates itself as it pleases; therefore it keeps its full meaning always. In Vedanta the power of separation is lost, but the separate force remains. Again the roots *gī* and *gā* in classical Sanskrit mean to sing and have resigned the sense of going to their kinsman *gam*; but in Vedic times, the sense of going was still active and common. They meant also to express, to possess, to hold; but these meanings once common to the family are now entrusted to particular members of it, *gir*, for expression, *gṛh*, for holding. *Gāthā, gīthā, gāna, gāyati, gātā, gātu*, meant to the Vedic mind both going and singing, *udgītha* meant ascension as well as casting upward the voice or the soul in song. When the Vedic singer said *ud gāyāmi*, the physical idea was that, perhaps, of the song rising upward, but he had also the psychical idea of the soul rising up in song to the gods and fulfilling in its meeting with them and entering into them its expressed aspiration. To show that this idea is not a modern etymological fancy of my own, it is sufficient to cite the evidence of the Chhandogya Upanishad itself in this very chapter where Baka Dalbhya is spoken of as the Udgata of the Naimishiyas who obtained their desires for them by the Vedic chant, *ebhyaḥ āgāyati kāmān*; so, adds the Upanishad, shall everyone be a "singer to" and a "bringer to" of desires, *āgātā kāmānām*, who with this knowledge follows after OM, the Brahman, as the Udgitha.

This then is the meaning of the Upanishad that OM, the syllable, technically called the Udgitha, is to be meditated on as a symbol of the fourfold Brahman with two objects, the "singing to" of one's desires and aspirations in the triple manifestation and the spiritual ascension into the Brahman Itself so as to meet and enter into heaven after heaven and even into Its transcendent felicity. For, it says, with the syllable OM one begins the chant of the Sama-veda, or, in the esoteric sense, by means of the meditation on OM one makes this soul-ascension and becomes master of all the soul desires. It is in this aspect and to this end that the Upanishad will expound OM. To explain Brahman in Its nature and workings, to teach the right worship and meditation on Brahman, to establish what are the different means of attainment of different results and the formulae of the meditation and worship, is its purpose. All this work of explanation has to be done in reference to Veda and Vedic sacrifice and ritual of which OM is the substance. In a certain sense, therefore, the Upanishad is an explanation of the purpose and symbology of Vedic formulae and ritual; it sums up the results of the long travail of seeking by which the first founders and pioneers of Vedantism in an age when the secret and true sense of Veda had been largely submerged in the ceremonialism and formalism of the close of the Dwapara Yuga, attempted to recover their lost heritage partly by reference to the adepts who still remained in possession of it, partly by the traditions of the great seekers of the past Yuga, Janaka, Yajnavalkya, Krishna and others, partly by their own illuminations and spiritual experience. The Chhandogya Upanishad is thus the summary history of one of the greatest and most interesting ages of human thought.

SATYAKAMA JABALA

The story of Satyakama Jabala occupies five sections, the third to the eighth,[1] of the fourth chapter in the Chhandogya Upanishad. The Chhandogya seems to be the most ancient of the extant Upanishads. It speaks of Krishna, son of Devaki, and Dhritarashtra Vaichitravirya in a tone that would justify us in assuming that it regarded them not as ancient and far-off names but as men who had walked the earth in living memory. The movement of philosophic speculation of which the Upanishads are the extant record, was an attempt to pass from the old ritualistic *karma* to the freedom of the *jñānamārga.* According to the writer of the Gita, this was not a new movement, but a return to a past and lost discipline; for Srikrishna says to Arjuna of the true or *sajñāna karmamārga* he reveals to him, "This is the imperishable Yoga I declared unto Vivaswan, Vivaswan revealed it to Manu and Manu to Ikshvaku told it. Thus was it known to the royal sages by hereditary transmission, till by the great lapse of time this Yoga was lost, O scourge of thy foes. This is the same ancient Yoga that I have told unto [thee] today, because thou art my lover and my friend; for this is the highest of all the inner truths."

The Dwapara Yuga was the age of Kuru preeminence and the Kurus were a great practical, warlike, ritualistic, juristic race of the Roman type, with little of the speculative temper or moral enthusiasm of the eastern Coshalas, Videhas, Kashis, Chedis. The West of India has always been noted for its practical, soldierly, commercial bent of mind in comparison with the imaginative and idealistic Eastern races and the scholastic, logical and metaphysical South. According to the Hindu theory of the Yugas, it is in the Dwapara that everything is codified, ritualised, formalised. In the Satya Vishnu descends among men as Yajna. Yajna is the spirit of adoration and sacrifice, and in the Satya Yajna reigns in the hearts of men, and there is no need of external ritual, external sacrifices, elaborate law, government, castes, classes and creeds. Men follow the law by the necessity of their puri-

---

[1] *In most editions, the fourth to the ninth. [Ed.]*

fied nature and their complete knowledge. The kingdom of God
and the Veda are in the hearts of His people. In the Treta the
old perfect order begins to break and Vishnu descends as the
cakravartī rājā, the warrior and ruler, Kartavirya, Parasurama,
Rama, and the sword, the law, and the written Veda are insti-
tuted to govern men. But there is still great elasticity and freedom and within certain limits men follow the healthy impulse of
their nature, only slightly corrupted by the first descent from
purity. It is in the Dwapara that form and rule have to take the
place of the idea and the spirit as the true governors of religion,
ethics and society. Vishnu then descends as Vyasa, the great
codifier and systematiser of knowledge.

At the end of the Dwapara, when Srikrishna came, this
tendency had reached its extreme development, and the form
tended to take the place of the idea and the rule to take the place
of the spirit not only in the outward conduct but in the hearts
of men. Nevertheless an opposite tendency had already begun.
Dhritarashtra himself was an earnest inquirer into the inner
meaning of things. Great Vedantists were living and teaching,
such as the rishi Ghora to whom Srikrishna himself went for the
word of illumination. Srikrishna was the intellectual force that
took up all these scattered tendencies and, by breaking down the
strong formalism of the Dwapara, prepared the work of the
Kali. In the Gita he denounces those who will not go outside
the four corners of the Veda and philosophises the whole theory
of the sacrificial system; he contemptuously dismisses the guidance of the set ethical systems and establishes an inward and
spiritual rule of conduct. To many of his time he seems to have
appeared as a baneful and destructive portent; like all great revolutionary innovators, he is denounced by Bhurisravas as a well-
known misleader of men and corrupter of morals. It is the work
of the Kali Yuga to destroy everything by questioning everything
in order to establish after a struggle between the forces of purity
and impurity a new harmony of life and knowledge in another
Satya Yuga.

After the destruction of the conservative Kurus and Pan-
chalas at Kurukshetra, the development of the Vedanta com-
menced and went on progressing till in its turn it reached its ex-

treme and excessive development in the teachings of Buddha and Shankaracharya. But at the period of the Chhandogya it is in its early stage of development. The first sections of the Upanishad are taken up with an esoteric development of the inner meaning of certain parts of the sacrificial formulae, which in itself is sufficient to show that the work belongs to the first stratum of Vedantic formation.

The story of Satyakama is one of the most typical in the Upanishad. It is full of sidelights on early Vedantic teaching, Yogic *sādhanā* and that deep psychical knowledge which the writer took for granted in the hearers of his work. So much knowledge, indeed, is thus taken for granted that it is impossible for anyone not himself a practiser of Yoga, to understand anything but its broad conclusions. The modern commentators, Shankara included, have approached it in order to establish particular metaphysical doctrines, not to elucidate its entire significance. I shall take the side that has been neglected; for what to the European inquirer are merely "the babblings of children", bear to the Yogin an aspect of infinite truth, value and significance.

CHAPTER II

"Now Satyakama Jabala spoke unto his mother Jabala and said, 'Mother, I shall go and lead the life of the Brahmacharin; tell me what is my *gotra*.' But she answered him, 'This I know not, my son, of what *gotra* thou art; resorting to many as a serving-woman in my youth I got thee, therefore I know not of what *gotra* thou art. But Jabala is my name and Satyakama is thine, Satyakama Jabala therefore call thyself.' So he came to Haridrumata the Gautama and said, 'I would stay with my Lord as a Brahmacharin, let me therefore enter under thee.' And he said to him, 'My son, of what *gotra* art thou?' But the other answered, 'This, alas, I know not, of what *gotra* I am; I asked my mother and she answered me, "Resorting to many in my youth as a serving-woman I got thee, therefore I know not of what *gotra* thou art, but Jabala is my name and Satyakama is thine"; Satyakama Jabala therefore am I.' And he said to him,

'None who is not a Brahmin can be strong enough to say this; gather the firewood, my son, I will take thee under me, for thou didst not depart from the truth.' He admitted him and put forth four hundred cows weak and lean and said, 'These, my son, do thou follow as a herd,' and he set the cows in motion and said, 'Return not until they are a thousand.' And he fared abroad with them during the years till they were a thousand."

So the story opens, and simple as it seems, it already contains several points of capital importance in understanding the ideas of the time and the principles of the old Vedantic *sādhanā*. Satyakama, as we gather from other passages, was one of the great Vedantic teachers of the time immediately previous to the composition of the Chhandogya Upanishad. But his birth is the meanest possible. His mother is a serving-girl, not a *dāsī* attached to a permanent household whose son could have named his father and his *gotra*, but a *paricārikā*, serving for hire at various houses, "resorting to many" and therefore unable to name her son's father. Satyakama has, therefore, neither caste, nor *gotra*, nor any position in life. It appears from this story as from others that, although the system of the four castes was firmly established, it counted as no obstacle in the pursuit of knowledge and spiritual advancement. The Kshatriya could teach the Brahmin, the illegitimate and fatherless son of the serving-girl could be *guru* to the purest and highest blood in the land. This is nothing new or improbable, for it has been so throughout the history of Hinduism and the shutting out of anyone from spiritual truth and culture on the ground of caste is an invention of later times. In the nature of things the usual rule would be for the greater number of spiritual preceptors to be found in the higher castes, but this was the result of natural laws and not of a fixed prohibition. It is noticeable also from this and other instances that it was the father's position that fixed the son's, and the mother's seems to have been of very minor importance. The question about the *gotra* was of importance, probably, with regard to the rites and other circumstances of initiation. Satyakama must have known perfectly well that he was the illegitimate son of a serving-woman, but he wished to know his father's name and *gotra* because he would have to tell it to his *guru*. Even after knowing the worst, he persisted in his intention of taking up spiritual studies, so that he can have had no fear of being rejected on account of his base origin. His *guru*, impressed by his truthfulness, says, "None but a Brahmin would have the moral strength to make such an avowal." It can hardly be meant by this that Satyakama's father must have been a Brahmin, but that since he had the Brahmin qualities, he must be accepted as a Brahmin. Even the Kshatriya would have hesitated to speak so truthfully, because the Kshatriya is by nature a lover of honour and shuns dishonour, he has the sense of *māna* and *apamāna*; but the true Brahmin is *samo mānāpamānayoḥ*, he accepts indifferently worldly honour and dishonour and cares only for the truth and the right. In short the Gautama concludes that, whatever may be Satyakama's physical birth, spiritually he is of the highest order and especially fitted for a *sādhaka; na satyād agāḥ*, he did not depart from the truth.

The second point is the first action of the *guru* after the ceremony of initiation. Instead of beginning the instruction of this promising disciple he sends him out with four hundred miserable kine, more likely to die than prosper and increase, and forbids him to return till he has increased them to a thousand. Wherefore this singular arrangement? Was it a test? Was it a discipline? But Haridrumata had already seen that his new disciple had the high Brahmin qualities. What more did he require?

The perfect man is a fourfold being and one object of Vedantic discipline is to be the perfect man, *siddha*. When Christ said, "Be ye perfect as your Father in heaven is perfect," he was only repeating in popular language the Vedantic teaching of *sādharmya*, likeness to God.

Incomplete

SHWETASHWATARA UPANISHAD

Chapters 4-6

Shwetashwatara Upanishad

CHAPTER FOUR

य एकोऽवर्णो बहुधा शक्तियोगाद्वर्णाननेकान्निहितार्थो दधाति ।
वि चैंति चान्ते विश्वमादौ स देवः स नो बुद्धचा शुभया संयुनक्तु ॥१॥

1. He who is one and without hue, but has ordained manifoldly many hues by the Yoga of his Force and holds within
himself all objects, and in Him the universe dissolves in
the end, that Godhead was in the beginning. May He
yoke us with a good and bright understanding.

तदेवाग्निस्तदादित्यस्तद्वायुस्तदु चन्द्रमाः ।
तदेव शुक्रं तद् ब्रह्म तदापस्तत्प्रजापतिः ॥२॥

2. That alone is the fire and That the sun and That the wind
and That too the moon; That is the Luminous, That the
Brahman, That the waters, That the Father and Lord of
creatures.

त्वं स्त्री त्वं पुमानसि त्वं कुमार उत वा कुमारी ।
त्वं जीर्णो दण्डेन वञ्चसि त्वं जातो भवसि विश्वतोमुखः ॥३॥

3. Thou art the woman and Thou the man; Thou art a boy
and again a young virgin; Thou art yonder worn and aged
man that walkest bent with thy staff. Lo, Thou becomest
born and the world is full of thy faces.

नीलः पतङ्गो हरितो लोहिताक्षस्तडिद्गर्भ ऋतवः समुद्राः ।
अनादिमत्त्वं विभूत्वेन वर्तसे यतो जातानि भुवनानि विश्वा ॥४॥

4. Thou art the blue bird and the green and the scarlet-eyed,
the womb of lightning and the seasons and the oceans.
Thou art that which is without beginning and Thou movest
with Thy pervasive extension whence all the worlds are
born.

अजामेकां लोहितशुक्लकृष्णां बह्वीः प्रजाः सृजमानां सरूपाः ।
अजो ह्येको जुषमाणोऽनुशेते जहात्येनां भुक्तभोगामजोऽन्यः ॥५॥

5. There is One, unborn, white and black and red, who is
    ever bringing forth many creatures with forms and her one
    unborn loves and cleaves to and lies with her; another
    unborn abandons, when all her enjoyments have been
    enjoyed.

द्वा सुपर्णा सयुजा सखाया समानं वृक्षं परिषस्वजाते ।
तयोरन्यः पिप्पलं स्वाद्वत्त्यनश्नन्नन्यो अभिचाकशीति ॥६॥

6. Two winged birds cling about a common tree, comrades,
    yoke-fellows; and one eats the sweet fruit of the tree, the
    other eats not, but watches.

समाने वृक्षे पुरुषो निमग्नोऽनीशया शोचति मुह्यमानः ।
जुष्टं यदा पश्यत्यन्यमीशमस्य महिमानमिति वीतशोकः ॥७॥

7. The Soul upon a common tree is absorbed and because he
    is not lord, grieves and is bewildered; but when he sees
    and cleaves to that other who is the Lord, he knows that
    all is His greatness and his sorrow passes away from him.

ऋचो अक्षरे परमे व्योमन् यस्मिन्देवा अधि विश्वे निषेदुः ।
यस्तं न वेद किमृचा करिष्यति य इत्तद्विदुस्त इमे समासते ॥८॥

8. In the highest immutable Heaven where all the gods have
    taken up their session, there are the verses of the Rig-veda,
    and he who knows Him not, what shall he do with the
    Rik? They who know That, lo, it is they who thus are
    seated.

छन्दांसि यज्ञाः क्रतवो व्रतानि भूतं भव्यं यच्च वेदा वदन्ति ।
अस्मान्मायी सृजते विश्वमेतत्तस्मिंश्चान्यो मायया सन्निरुद्धः ॥९॥

9. Rhythms and sacrifices and ritual and vows, what has been
    and what is to be and what the Vedas declare, — the

Master of Maya brings forth from that all this that is and there is another whom within it his Maya holds imprisoned.

मायां तु प्रकृतिं विद्यान्मायिनं तु महेश्वरम् ।
तस्यावयवभूतैस्तु व्याप्तं सर्वमिदं जगत् ॥१०॥

10. Thou shalt know Maya to be Force of Nature and the Master of Maya to be the great Lord; this whole universe is occupied by His becomings that are His members.

यो योनिं योनिमधितिष्ठत्येको यस्मिन्निदं सं च वि चैति सर्वम् ।
तमीशानं वरदं देवमीड्यं निचाय्येमां शान्तिमत्यन्तमेति ॥११॥

11. He who being One enters every womb and in whom all this comes together and goes apart, the adorable God-head who rules as lord and gives us our desirable boons, one having seen comes exceedingly unto this peace.

यो देवानां प्रभवश्चोद्भवश्च विश्वाधिपो रुद्रो महर्षिः ।
हिरण्यगर्भं पश्यत जायमानं स नो बुद्ध्या शुभया संयुनक्तु ॥१२॥

12. He who is the coming to birth of the gods and the arising of their being, the master of the universe, the Violent One, the Great Seer beheld Hiranyagarbha born, — may he yoke us with a bright and good understanding.

यो देवानामधिपो यस्मिँल्लोका अधिश्रिताः ।
य ईशे अस्य द्विपदश्चतुष्पदः कस्मै देवाय हविषा विधेम ॥१३॥

13. He who is the master of the gods, in whom the worlds are lodged and who rules over this two-footed and four-footed, to what god should we offer the worship of our oblation?

सूक्ष्मातिसूक्ष्मं कलिलस्य मध्ये विश्वस्य स्रष्टारमनेकरूपम् ।
विश्वस्यैकं परिवेष्टितारं ज्ञात्वा शिवं शान्तिमत्यन्तमेति ॥१४॥

14. Subtle beyond the subtle in the midst of the hustling chaos, the creator of the universe who has many forms and being

one encompasses all, knowing as the Benign, one comes
exceedingly to the peace.

स एव काले भुवनस्य गोप्ता विश्वाधिपः सर्वभूतेषु गूढः ।
यस्मिन्युक्ता ब्रह्मर्षयो देवताश्च तमेवं ज्ञात्वा मृत्युपाशांश्छिनत्ति ॥१५॥

15. He in Time is the guardian of the world of existence and
the master of the universe secret in all existences, — in
whom have union of Yoga the holy sages and the gods;
thus knowing him one cuts asunder the snares of Death.

घृतात्परं मण्डमिवातिसूक्ष्मं ज्ञात्वा शिवं सर्वभूतेषु गूढम् ।
विश्वस्यैकं परिवेष्टितारं ज्ञात्वा देवं मुच्यते सर्वपाशैः ॥१६॥

16. Knowing him who is exceedingly subtle like the cream
above the clarified butter, the Benign secret in all existences, knowing the God who being one encompasses all,
one is released from every bondage.

एष देवो विश्वकर्मा महात्मा सदा जनानां हृदये संनिविष्टः ।
हृदा मनीषा मनसाभिक्लृप्तो य एतद्विदुरमृतास्ते भवन्ति ॥१७॥

17. This is the God, the mighty Soul, the Architect of all,
seated for ever in the hearts of creatures and he is realised
by the heart and the intellect and the mind; who know
this, they become immortal.

यदातमस्तन्न दिवा न रात्रिन सन्न चासञ्छिव एव केवलः ।
तदक्षरं तत्सवितुर्वरेण्यं प्रज्ञा च तस्मात्प्रसृता पुराणी ॥१८॥

18. When there is no darkness, that is neither day nor night,
nor being nor non-being, it is the absolute Benign alone;
That is the immutable, That the supreme light of the
Creating Sun and from it the Wisdom went forth that is
of old.

नैनमूर्ध्वं न तिर्यञ्चं न मध्ये परिजग्रभत् ।
न तस्य प्रतिमा अस्ति यस्य नाम महद्यशः ॥१९॥

19. Him one shall not seize as on high nor as one on a level plane nor in the middle; there is no image for him whose name is a mighty glory.

न संदृशे तिष्ठति रूपमस्य न चक्षुषा पश्यति कश्चनैनम् ।
हृदा हृदिस्थं मनसा य एनमेवं विदुरमृतास्ते भवन्ति ॥२०॥

20. The form of Him stands not within the vision and none beholds Him by the eye; but by the heart and the mind, for in the heart is His station; who thus know Him, they become immortal.

अजात इत्येवं कश्चिद्भीरुः प्रपद्यते ।
रुद्र यत्ते दक्षिणं मुखं तेन मां पाहि नित्यम् ॥२१॥

21. One here and there approaches Him with awe thinking of Him as the Unborn. O Violent One, that which is thy auspicious right-hand face, with that protect me ever.

मा नस्तोके तनये मा न आयुषि मा नो गोषु मा नो अश्वेषु रीरिषः ।
वीरान्मा नो रुद्र भामितो वधीर्हविष्मन्तः सदमित्त्वा हवामहे ॥२२॥

22. Do no hurt to our son nor our grandson nor our life nor our cattle nor our horses. O Violent One, slay not in thy anger our heroes; ever to Thee with the oblation we call.

CHAPTER FIVE

द्वे अक्षरे ब्रह्मपरे त्वनन्ते विद्याविद्ये निहिते यत्र गूढे ।
क्षरं त्वविद्या ह्यमृतं तु विद्या विद्याविद्ये ईशते यस्तु सोऽन्यः ॥१॥

1. Both of these in the Transcendent, the Knowledge and the
   Ignorance, yea, both have their hidden being in the Eternal
   and Infinite Who dwelleth beyond Brahman of the Veda,
   and are set in it for ever. But of these Ignorance dieth and
   Knowledge liveth for ever; and He who is master of both
   is other than they.

यो योनिं योनिमधितिष्ठत्येको विश्वानि रूपाणि योनीश्च सर्वाः ।
ऋषिं प्रसूतं कपिलं यस्तमग्रे ज्ञानैर्बिभर्ति जायमानं च पश्येत् ॥२॥

2. He being One entereth upon womb and womb, yea, upon
   all forms of being and upon all wombs of creatures. This
   was He that of old filled with many sorts of Knowledge
   Kapila, the seer, after his Mother bore him; yea, He saw
   Kapila shaping.[1]

एकैकं जालं बहुधा विकुर्वन्नस्मिन्क्षेत्रे संहरत्येष देवः ।
भूयः सृष्ट्वा यतयस्तथेशः सर्वाधिपत्यं कुरुते महात्मा ॥३॥

3. God weaveth Him one net or He weaveth Him another and
   He maketh it of manifold meshes and casteth it abroad in
   this field of the body; then He draweth it in again. Also
   He created Yatis, great Seekers, and thus the Mighty
   Mind wieldeth the sceptre of His universal Lordship.[2]

सर्वा दिश ऊर्ध्वमधश्च तिर्यक्प्रकाशयन्भ्राजते यद्बनड्वान् ।
एवं स देवो भगवान्वरेण्यो योनिस्वभावानधितिष्ठत्येकः ॥४॥

4. The Sun riseth and driveth the world's wain, then he

   [1] Or, He in the beginning filled with kinds of knowledge Kapila, the Seer of old when he
   was born from his Mother, yea, He saw Kapila in his shaping.
   [2] Or, and thus the Mighty Mind, the Master, exerciseth the sovereignty over all this creation (or, of all the Universe).

blazeth illumining all the regions and above and below and the level grow one lustre, even so this glorious and shining God, being One, entereth upon and ruleth nature that clingeth to the womb, to each womb its nature.[1]

यच्च स्वभावं पचति विश्वयोनिः पाच्यांश्च सर्वान्परिणामयेद्यः ।
सर्वमेतद्विश्वमधितिष्ठत्येको गुणांश्च सर्वान्विनियोजयेद्यः ॥५॥

5. For He who is the Womb of the World bringeth each nature to its perfection and He matureth all those that are yet to be perfected. He indwelleth and presideth over all this His world and setteth all the modes of Nature to their workings.

तद्वेदगुह्योपनिषत्सु गूढं तद् ब्रह्मा वेदते ब्रह्मयोनिम् ।
ये पूर्वेदेवा ऋषयश्च तद्विदुस्ते तन्मया अमृता वै बभूवुः ॥६॥

6. This is that secret mystery which is hidden in the Upanishads, for the Upanishad is the Secret of the Veda. This is that which Brahma knoweth for the Womb of the Eternal and the older Gods and the sages who knew of This, became This and were immortal.[2]

गुणान्वयो यः फलकर्मकर्ता कृतस्य तस्यैव स चोपभोक्ता ।
स विश्वरूपस्त्रिगुणस्त्रिवर्त्मा प्राणाधिपः संचरति स्वकर्मभिः ॥७॥

7. There is One who maketh works and their fruits to them, for the moods of Nature cleave to Him; this is He that enjoyeth the works He hath done; and the World is His body and He hath three modes of His natures and the roads of His travel are likewise three.[3] Lo, the Master of Life, by the momentum of His own works, He moveth in the centuries.

---

[1] *Or*, even so the Lord, the Shining and Glorious, being One, possesseth and ruleth the nature that cleaveth to the womb, to each kind its nature (*or*, possesseth various natures of wombs and ruleth over them).

[2] *Or*, and the Rishis knew It, therefore they became That and were immortal.

[3] *Or*, Who is the Maker of works and their fruits, because the mood-stuffs of Nature cleave to Him, He also reapeth from all work that He hath done and the World is His shape and the stuff of His working is threefold and three are the paths of His travel.

अङ्गुष्ठमात्रो रविवुल्यरूपः सङ्कल्पाहंकारसमन्वितो यः ।
बुद्धेर्गुणेनात्मगुणेन चैव आराग्रमात्रो ह्यपरोऽपि दृष्टः ॥८॥

8. His size is as the size of a man's thumb, but His aspect as
    the Sun in its glory; and He hath Volition and He hath
    Personality; but there is another whom we see by virtue
    of the Understanding and by virtue of the Spirit for the
    point of a cobbler's awl is not finer to vision.

बालाग्रशतभागस्य शतधा कल्पितस्य च ।
भागो जीवः स विज्ञेयः स चानन्त्याय कल्पते ॥९॥

9. Take thou the hundredth part of the point of a hair, divide
    it into a hundred parts again; then as is a part of that
    hundredth part of a hundredth, such shalt thou find this
    Spirit in man, if thou seek to separate Him; yet 'tis this
    in thee that availeth towards Infinity.

नैव स्त्री न पुमानेष न चैवायं नपुंसकः ।
यद्यच्छरीरमादत्ते तेन तेन स रक्ष्यते ॥१०॥

10. Not woman is He, nor man either, not yet sexless; but
    whatsoever body He take, that confineth and preserveth
    Him.

सङ्कल्पनस्पर्शनदृष्टिमोहैर्ग्रासाम्बुवृष्ट्या चात्मविवृद्धिजन्म ।
कर्मानुगान्यनुक्रमेण देही स्थानेषु रूपाण्यभिसम्प्रपद्यते ॥११॥

11. As body is born and groweth by food and drink and plenty,
    so also the Spirit in body progressively attaineth to succes-
    sive forms in their fit places — by the allurements of sight,
    by the witcheries of touch, by the magic of volition; accord-
    ing to his works he progresseth and his forms shape them-
    selves to his works.

स्थूलानि सूक्ष्माणि बहूनि चैव रूपाणि देही स्वगुणैर्वृणोति ।
क्रियागुणैरात्मगुणैश्च तेषां संयोगहेतुरपरोऽपि दृष्टः ॥१२॥

12. Forms gross and forms subtle, forms many, — the Spirit
    in the body evolveth them all by His own nature in its work-
    ing; by the law of action of His works and the law of ac-
    tion of the Spirit in man, by these he evolveth them. But
    there is Another in Whom we behold Cause whereby all
    these meet together.[1]

अनाद्यनन्तं कलिलस्य मध्ये विश्वस्य स्रष्टारमनेकरूपम् ।
विश्वस्यैकं परिवेष्टितारं ज्ञात्वा देवं मुच्यते सर्वपाशैः ॥१३॥

13. Without beginning, without end in the welter and the
    chaos, who createth the world by taking many figures and
    as the One girdeth and encompasseth it, He is the Lord and
    if thou know Him thou shalt break free from all kinds
    of bondage.

भावग्राह्यमनीडाख्यं भावाभावकरं शिवम् ।
कलासर्गकरं देवं ये विदुस्ते जहुस्तनुम् ॥१४॥

14. Shiva, the Master of all becomings and not-becomings
    and from Him this whole creation floweth and it is only
    one part of Shiva, but He is not named after any nest of the
    wingèd Spirit, and the heart alone can apprehend Him —
    they who know Shiva, the Blessed One, abandon body for
    ever.

---

[1] *Or*, But there is yet Another in Whom we see the cause wherefore all these stand as one
whole and have met together.

CHAPTER SIX

स्वभावमेके कवयो वदन्ति कालं तथान्ये परिमुह्यमानाः ।
देवस्यैष महिमा तु लोके येनेदं भ्राम्यते ब्रह्मचक्रम् ॥१॥

1. 'Tis Nature and Self-existence, say one school of the Seers.
Nay, 'tis Time, say another; both are deceived and bewildered. 'Tis the Majesty of the Lord in the world of
His creatures whereby this Wheel of the Eternal whirleth
about continually.

येनावृतं नित्यमिदं हि सर्वं ज्ञः कालकारो गुणी सर्वविद्यः ।
तेनेशितं कर्म विवर्तते ह पृथ्व्यप्तेजोऽनिलखानि चिन्त्यम् ॥२॥

2. He envelopeth this whole Universe with Himself for ever,
He that knoweth, Maker of Time, and the Modes of
Nature dwell in Him; yea, all things He discerneth. And
by His governance the Law of Works revolveth in its cycle.
Earth, water, fire, air, ether, of these thou shalt consider
(as the substance wherein it turneth).

तत्कर्म कृत्वा विनिवर्त्य भूयस्तत्त्वस्य तत्त्वेन समेत्य योगम् ।
एकेन द्वाभ्यां त्रिभिरष्टभिर्वा कालेन चैवात्मगुणैश्च सूक्ष्मैः ॥३॥

3. The Lord doeth works and resteth again from His works,
one or two or three or eight He yoketh Himself with the
Principle of things in their essence and with Time He yoketh
Himself and with Self in its subtle workings.

आरभ्य कर्माणि गुणान्वितानि भावांश्च सर्वान्विनियोजयेद्यः ।
तेषामभावे कृतकर्मनाशः कर्मक्षये याति स तत्त्वतोऽन्यः ॥४॥

4. So He beginneth works that are subject to the Modes of
Nature, and setteth all existences to their workings: and
when these things are not, thereby cometh annihilation of
work that hath been done; and with the perishing of work,
He departeth out of them; for in His final truth He is other
than they.

आदिः स संयोगनिमित्तहेतुः परस्त्रिकालादकलोऽपि दृष्टः ।
तं विश्वरूपं भवभूतमीडचं देवं स्वचित्तस्थमुपास्य पूर्वं ॥५॥

5. Lo, we have beheld Him and He is the Beginning and the
Cause of all Causes whereby these elements meet together
and form ariseth; the past, the present and the future are
this side of Him and Time hath no part in Him. Let us
worship the Ancient of Days in our own hearts who sitteth.
Let us wait upon God who must be adored, for the world
is His shape and the Universe is but His becoming.[1]

स वृक्षकालाकृतिभिः परोऽन्यो यस्मात्प्रपञ्चः परिवर्ततेऽयम् ।
धर्मावहं पापनुदं भगेशं ज्ञात्वात्मस्थममृतं विश्वधाम ॥६॥

6. Time and Form and the Tree of Things, none of these is
He for He is more than they and it is from Him that this
Cosmos beginneth. We will know this Master of grace
and glory, for He cometh to us carrying righteousness in
His hand and He driveth Sin from its strong places. We
will know Him for He is in our Self and immortal and the
world's foundation.[2]

तमीश्वराणां परमं महेश्वरं तं देवतानां परमं च दैवतम् ।
पतिं पतीनां परमं परस्ताद्विदाम देवं भुवनेशमीडचम् ॥७॥

7. We will know this Mightiest one who is far above all the
mighty — this summit of the gods and their godhead,
King of Kings and Lord of Lords, who towereth high above
all summits and greatnesses. Let us learn of God for He
is this World's Master and all shall adore Him.[3]

---

[1] *Or*, We see Him to be the beginning, the Informing Cause whereby all standeth together;
the past, the present and the future are this side of Him and Time hath no part in Him. Worship ye the Adorable whose shape is the whole Universe and who hath become in the Universe,
worship ye the Lord, the Ancient of Days, in your own hearts who sitteth.

[2] *Or*, He is other than Time and Form and the Tree of the Cosmos and He is greater than
they, from Whom this world of phenomena becometh and revolveth. Know ye the Master
of Grace who bringeth virtue and driveth away sin. He dwelleth in the Spirit of man, the
Immortal, in whom the whole world hath its (*or*, all things have their) home and dwelling-
place.

[3] *Or*, Him may we know, the Highest, Prince of Princes and King of Kings, the summit

न तस्य कार्यं करणं च विद्यते न तत्समश्चाभ्यधिकश्च दृश्यते ।
परास्य शक्तिर्विविधैव श्रूयते स्वाभाविकी ज्ञानबलक्रिया च ॥८॥

8. God needeth not to do anything neither hath He any organ of doing; there is none greater than He nor do we see any that is His equal — for His power is far over all, only men hear of it under a thousand names and various fashions.[1] Lo, the strength of Him and the works of Him and His Knowledge, they are self-efficient and their own cause and nature.

न तस्य कश्चित्पतिरस्ति लोके न चेशिता नैव च तस्य लिङ्गम् ।
स कारणं करणाधिपाधिपो न चास्य कश्चिज्जनिता न चाधिपः ॥९॥

9. He hath no master in all this world, there is none that shall rule over Him. Nor feature nor distinction hath He; for He is begetting cause and sovran over the lords of these natural organs, but Himself hath no begetter neither any sovran.[2]

यस्तन्तुनाभ इव तन्तुभिः प्रधानजैः स्वभावतो देव एकः स्वमावृणोत् ।
स नो दधाद् ब्रह्माप्ययम् ॥१०॥

10. Even as is the spider that out of himself fashioneth his own web, so is God One and nought else existeth, but by his own nature covereth Himself up in the threads He hath spun out of primal matter. May the One God ordain unto us departure into His Eternal.[3]

एको देवः सर्वभूतेषु गूढः सर्वव्यापी सर्वभूतान्तरात्मा ।
कर्माध्यक्षः सर्वभूताधिवासः साक्षी चेता केवलो निर्गुणश्च ॥११॥

and godhead of the gods, High Lord over lords above all highness, the Master of tne Worlds whom we must worship.

[1] *Or*, He hath nought that He must do nor any organ of His doing; there is none like Him seen nor any greater. His might is over all aud we hear of it in diverse fashions.

[2] *Or*, but there is none that is His father or His sovran.

[3] *Or*, As the spider fashioneth a web and its threads are from his own body, so of his own nature the One God than whom nought else existeth, wrapt Himself from sight in the web born of eternal Matter. May He ordain to us departure into the Eternal.

11. One God who alone is and He lurketh hidden in every creature, for He pervadeth and is the inmost Self of all beings, He presideth over all work and is the home of all things living. He is the Mighty Witness who relateth thought with thought and again He is the Absolute in whom mood is not nor any attribute.[1]

एको वशी निष्क्रियाणां बहूनामेकं बीजं बहुधा यः करोति ।
तमात्मस्थं येऽनुपश्यन्ति धीरास्तेषां सुखं शाश्वतं नेतरेषाम् ॥१२॥

12. One God and alone He controlleth the many who have themselves no separate work nor purpose; and He developeth one seed into many kinds of creatures; the strong-hearted behold God in their own Self, therefore for them is everlasting bliss and not for others.[2]

नित्योऽनित्यानां चेतनश्चेतनानामेको बहूनां यो विदधाति कामान् ।
तत्कारणं सांख्ययोगाधिगम्यं ज्ञात्वा देवं मुच्यते सर्वपाशैः ॥१३॥

13. One Eternal of all these that pass and are not, One conscious in all consciousnesses; He being One ordereth the desires of many; He alone is the great Source to which Sankhya and Yoga bring us. If thou know God thou shalt break free from every sort of bondage.

न तत्र सूर्यो भाति न चन्द्रतारकं नेमा विद्युतो भान्ति कुतोऽयमग्निः ।
तमेव भान्तमनुभाति सर्वं तस्य भासा सर्वमिदं विभाति ॥१४॥

14. There the sun cannot shine and the moon hath no splendour; the stars are blind; there our lightnings flash not neither any earthly fire; all that is bright is but the shadow of His brightness and by His shining all this shineth.

---

[1] *Or*, One God alone is hidden in all creatures; for He pervadeth all things and is the inner self of all beings, master of their works and home of all that liveth, the great Witness, the Well of conscious life, Absolute, without qualities.

[2] *Or*, the strong-hearted who behold Him in their own self where He sitteth, for them is the bliss that endureth for ever, and not for others.

एको हंसो भुवनस्यास्य मध्ये स एवाग्निः सलिले संनिविष्टः ।
तमेव विदित्वाति मृत्युमेति नान्यः पन्था विद्यतेऽयनाय ॥१५॥

15.   One Swan of Being in the heart of all this Universe and He
      is Fire that lieth deep in the heart of water. By Knowledge
      of Him, the soul passeth beyond the pursuit of Death and
      there is no other road for the great passage.

स विश्वकृद्विश्वविदात्मयोनिर्ज्ञः कालकारो गुणी सर्वविद्यः ।
प्रधानक्षेत्रज्ञपतिर्गुणेशः संसारमोक्षस्थितिबन्धहेतुः ॥१६॥

16.   He hath made all and knoweth all; for He is the womb out
      of which Self ariseth, and being possessed of the Nature
      Moods, He becometh Time's Maker and discerneth all
      things. And Matter is subject to Him and the Spirit in
      man that cogniseth his field of matter and the modes of
      Nature are his servants. He therefore is the cause of this
      coming into phenomena and of the release from phenom-
      ena — and because of Him is their endurance and because
      of Him is their bondage.[1]

स तन्मयो ह्यमृत ईशसंस्थो ज्ञः सर्वगो भुवनस्यास्य गोप्ता ।
य ईशे अस्य जगतो नित्यमेव नान्यो हेतुर्विद्यत ईशनाय ॥१७॥

17.   Lo, He is Immortal because He is utter existence; but He
      houseth Himself in the Lord and is the Knower, the Omni-
      present that standeth on guard over this His universe,[2]
      yea, He ruleth all this moving world for ever and for ever,
      and there is no other source of greatness and lordship.

यो ब्रह्माणं विदधाति पूर्वं यो वै वेदांश्च प्रहिणोति तस्मै ।
तं ह देवमात्मबुद्धिप्रकाशं मुमुक्षुर्वै शरणमहं प्रपद्ये ॥१८॥

----

[1] *Or,* There is eternal Matter and there is the Spirit within that knoweth his field in
matter; He is lord of both, He ruleth over Nature and her workings (*or,* the modes of Nature).
The world and deliverance out of the world and the endurance of things and the bonds of their
endurance, of all these He is the one Cause and reason.

[2] *Or,* He is purely Himself, for He is the Immortal manifested in the Mighty One and becometh the Knower who reacheth everywhere and guardeth His cosmos,

18. To Him who ordained Brahma the Creator from of old and sent forth unto him the Veda, I will hasten unto God who standeth self-revealed in the Spirit and in the Understanding. I will take refuge in the Lord for my salvation;[1]

निष्कलं निष्क्रियं शान्तं निरवद्यं निरञ्जनम् ।
अमृतस्य परं सेतुं दग्धेन्धनमिवानलम् ॥१९॥

19. Who hath neither parts nor works, for He is utterly tranquil, faultless, stainless, therefore He is the one great bridge that carrieth us over to Immortality, even as when a fire hath burnt up all its fuel.

यदा चर्मवदाकाशं वेष्टयिष्यन्ति मानवाः ।
तदा देवमविज्ञाय दुःखस्यान्तो भविष्यति ॥२०॥

20. When the sons of men shall fold up ether like a skin and wrap the heavens round them like a garment, then alone without knowledge of the Lord our God shall the misery of the World have an ending.

तपःप्रभावाद्देवप्रसादाच्च ब्रह्म ह श्वेताश्वतरोऽथ विद्वान् ।
अत्याश्रमिभ्यः परमं पवित्रं प्रोवाच सम्यगृषिसंघजुष्टम् ॥२१॥

21. By the might of his devotion and the grace of God in his being,[2] Shwetashwatara hereafter knew the Eternal and he came to the renouncers of the worldly life and truly declared unto them the Most High and Pure God, to whom the companies of seers resort for ever.

वेदान्ते परमं गुह्यं पुराकल्पे प्रचोदितम् ।
नाप्रशान्ताय दातव्यं नापुत्रायाशिष्याय वा पुनः ॥२२॥

22. This is the great secret of the Vedanta which was declared

---

[1] *Or*, To him who ordaineth Brahma of old and casteth out unto Him the Veda, God in whom the understanding of the Self findeth illumination, I desiring liberation make haste for refuge;

[2] *Or*, By the grace of the Lord, by the energy of his askesis,

in a former time, not on hearts untranquilled to be squan-
dered nor men sonless nor on one who hath no disciples.[1]

यस्य देवे परा भक्तिर्यथा देवे तथा गुरौ ।
तस्यैते कथिता ह्यर्थाः प्रकाशन्ते महात्मनः प्रकाशन्ते महात्मनः ॥२३॥

23. But whosoever hath supreme love and adoration for the
     Lord and as for the Lord, so likewise for the Master, to
     that Mighty Soul these great matters when they are told
     become clear of themselves, yea, to the Great Soul of him
     they are manifest.

---

[1] *Or,* Thou shalt not bestow it on a soul untranquillized, nor on the sonless man nor on
one who hath no disciple.

KAIVALYA UPANISHAD

The First Mantra

Kaivalya Upanishad

ॐ अथाश्वलायनो भगवन्तं परमेष्ठिनमुपसमेत्योवाच । अधीहि भगवन्
ब्रह्मविद्यां वरिष्ठां सदा सद्भिः सेव्यमानां निगूढाम् । यथाऽचिरा-
त्सर्वपापं व्यपोह्य परात्परं पुरुषं याति विद्वान् ॥१॥

OM. Ashwalayana to the Lord Parameshthi came and said,
"Teach me, Lord, the highest knowledge of Brahman, the
secret knowledge ever followed by the saints, how the wise
man swiftly putting from him all evil goeth to the Purusha
who is higher than the highest."

Nama
RUPA

Commentary

THE Lord Parameshthi is Brahma — not the Creator Hiranyagarbha, but the soul who in this *kalpa* has climbed up to be the instrument of Creation, the first in time of the Gods, the Pitamaha or original and general Prajapati; the Pitamaha, because all the fathers or special Prajapatis, Daksha and others, are his mind-born children. The confusion between the Grandsire and the Creator, who is also called Brahma, is common; but the distinction is clear. Thus in the Mundaka Upanishad, *brahmā devānām prathamaḥ sambabhūva*, it is the first of Gods, the earliest birth of Time, the father of Atharva, and not the unborn eternal Hiranyagarbha. In the Puranas Brahma is described as in fear of his life from Madhu and Kaitabha, and cannot be the fearless and immortal Hiranyagarbha. Nor would it be possible for Ashwalayana to come to Hiranyagarbha and say, "Teach me, Lord," for Hiranyagarbha has no form nor is He approachable nor does He manifest Himself to men as Shiva and Vishnu do. He is millionfold, Protean, intangible, and for that reason He places in each cycle a Brahma or divine Man between Him and the search and worship of men. It is Brahma or divine Man who is called Parameshthi or the one full of Parameshtham, that which is superlative and highest, — Hiranyagarbha. The power of Hiranyagarbha is in Brahma and creates through him the *nāma* and *rūpa* of things in this cycle.

To Brahma Parameshthi Ashwalayana comes as a disciple to a master and says to him, "Lord, teach me the Brahmavidya." He specifies the kind of knowledge he requires. It is *variṣṭha*, the best or highest, because it goes beyond the triple Brahman to the Purushottama or Most High God; it is secret, because even in the ordinary teaching of Vedanta, Purana and Tantra it is not expressed, it is always followed by the saints, the initiates. The *santaḥ* or saints are those who are pure of desire and full of knowledge, and it is to these that the secret knowledge has been given *sadā*, from the beginning. He makes his meaning yet clearer by stating the substance of the knowledge — *yathā*, how, by what means won by knowledge, *vidvān*, one can swiftly put sin from him and reach Purushottama.

There are three necessary elements of the path to Kaivalya, — first, the starting-point, *vidyā*, right knowledge, implying the escape from ignorance, non-knowledge and false knowledge; next, the process or means, escape from *sarvapāpam*, all evil, i.e. sin, pain and grief; last, the goal, Purushottama, the Being who is beyond the highest, that is, beyond Turiya being the Highest. By the escape from sin, pain and grief one attains absolute *ānanda*, and by *ānanda*, the last term of existence, we reach that in which *ānanda* exists. What is that? It is not Turiya who is *śivam*, *śāntam*, *advaitam*, *saccidānandam*, but that which is beyond *śivam* and *aśivam*, good and evil, *śāntam* and *kalilam*, calm and chaos, *dvaitam* and *advaitam*, duality and unity. Sat, Chit and Ananda are in this Highest, but He is neither Sat, Chit nor Ananda nor any combination of these. He is All and yet He is *neti, neti*. He is One and yet He is many. He is Parabrahman and He is Parameshwara. He is Male and He is Female. He is Tat and He is Sa. This is the Higher than the Highest. He is the Purusha, the Being in whose image the world and all the Jivas are made, who pervades all and underlies all the workings of Prakriti as its reality and self. It is this Purusha that Ashwalayana seeks.

NILARUDRA UPANISHAD

First Part

Nilarudra Upanishad

FIRST PART

ॐ अपश्यं त्वावरोहन्तं दिवितः पृथिवीमवः ।
अपश्यमस्यन्तं रुद्रं नीलग्रीवं शिखण्डिनम् ॥१॥

1. OM. Thee I beheld in thy descending down from the heavens
   to the earth, I saw Rudra, the Terrible, the azure-throated,
   the peacock-feathered, as he hurled.

दिव उग्रो अवारक्षत्प्रत्यष्ठाद् भूम्यामधि ।
जनासः पश्यते महं नीलग्रीवं विलोहितम् ॥२॥

2. Fierce he came down from the sky, he stood facing me on
   the earth as its lord, — the people behold a mass of strength,
   azure-throated, scarlet-hued.

एष एत्यवीरहा रुद्रो जलासभेषजाः ।
यत्तेक्ष्मेममनीनशद्व्यातीकारोऽप्येतु ते ॥३॥

3. This that cometh is he that destroyeth evil, Rudra the
   Terrible, born of the tree that dwelleth in the waters; let the
   globe of the storm winds come too, that destroyeth for thee
   all things of evil omen.

नमस्ते भवभावाय नमस्ते भाममन्यवे ।
नमस्ते अस्तु बाहुभ्यामुतो त इषवे नमः ॥४॥

4. Salutation to thee who bringeth the world into being, salutation to thee, the passionate with mighty wrath. Salutation
   be to thy arms of might, salutation be to thy angry shaft.

यामिषुं गिरिशन्त हस्ते बिभर्ष्यस्तवे ।
शिवां गिरित्र तां कृणु मा हिꣳसीत् पुरुषान्मम ॥५॥

5. The arrow thou bearest in thy hand for the hurling, O thou

that liest on the mountains, make an arrow of blessing, O
keeper of the hills, let it not slay my armed men.

शिवेन वचसा त्वा गिरिशाच्छावदामसि ।
यथा नः सर्वमिज्जगदयक्ष्मं सुमना असत् ॥६॥

6. With fair speech, O mountain-dweller, we sue to thee in the
    assembly of the folk, that the whole world may be for us a
    friendly and sinless place.

या ते इषुः शिवतमा शिवं बभूव ते धनुः ।
शिवा शरव्या या तव तया नो मृड जीवसे ॥७॥

7. That thy arrow which is the kindliest of all and thy bow
    which is well-omened and that thy quiver which beareth
    blessing, by that thou livest for us, O lord of slaughter.

या ते रुद्र शिवा तनूरघोरा पापकाशिनी ।
तया नस्तन्वा शन्तमया गिरिश त्वाभिचाकशत् ॥८॥

8. That thy body, O terrible One, which is fair and full of
    kindness and destroyeth sin, not thy shape of terrors, in that
    thy body full of peace, O mountaineer, thou art wont to be
    seen among our folk.

असौ यस्ताम्रो अरुण उत बभ्रुर्विलोहितः ।
ये चेमे अभितो रुद्रा दिक्षु श्रिताः सहस्रशो वैषां हेड ईमहे ॥९॥

9. This Aruna of the dawn that is tawny and copper-red and
    scarlet-hued, and these thy Violent Ones round about that
    dwell in the regions in their thousands, verily, it is these
    whom we desire.

Commentary

1. *Apaśyam*, I beheld. The speaker is the author of the Upanishad, a prince of the Aryan people, as we see from the fifth verse. He records a vision of Rudra descending from the heavens to the earth. *Avaḥ*, down, is repeated for the sake of vividness. In the second half of the *śloka* the *mūrti* or image in which he beheld the Divine Manifestation is described, Rudra, the God of might and wrath, the neck and throat blue, a peacock's feather as a crest, in the act of hurling a shaft.

2. He proceeds to describe the descent. He descended fiercely, that is, with wrath in his face, gesture and motion and stood facing the seer, *pratyaṣṭhāt*, on the earth and over it, *adhi*, in a way expressive of command or control. This image of Divine Power, seen by the prince in Yoga, becomes visible to the people in general as a mass of strength, *maha*, scarlet in colour, deep blue in the neck and throat. *Maha* is strength, bulk, greatness. The manifestation is that of wrath and might. The people see Rudra as a mass of brilliance, scarlet-ringed and crested with blue, the scarlet in Yoga denoting violent passion of anger or desire, the blue *śraddhā*, *bhakti*, piety or religion.

3. Rudra, whom we know as the slayer of evil, comes. The Rajarshi describes him as born of the tree that is in the waters. *Bheṣa* is by philology identical with the Latin *ficus* or fig-tree, *aśvattha*. The *aśvattha* is the Yogic emblem of the manifested world, as in the Gita, the tree of the two birds in the Shwetashwatara Upanishad, the single tree in the blue expanse of the Song of Liberation. The *jala* is the *āpaḥ* or waters from which the world rises. The Rishi then prays that the *vātikāraḥ*, mass of winds of which Rudra is lord and which in the tempest of their course blow away all calamity, such as pestilence etc., may come with him.

4. In the fourth verse he salutes the God. Rudra is the Supreme Ishwara, Creator of the World, He is the dreadful, wrathful and destroying Lord, swift to slay and punish. *Bhāma* is passionate anger, and the word *manyu* denotes a violent disturbed state of mind, passion, either of grief or of anger. *Bhāmamanyave* therefore means, one who is full of the passion of violent anger. Rudra is being saluted as a God of might and wrath, it is therefore to the arms as the seat of strength and the arrow as the weapon of destruction that salutation is made.

5. Rudra is coming in a new form of wrath and destruction in which the Aryans are not accustomed to see him. Apprehensive of the meaning of this vision, the King summons the people and in assembly prayer is offered to Rudra to avert possible calamity. The shaft is lifted to be hurled from the bow; it is prayed that it may be turned into a shaft of blessing, not of wrath. In this verse the Prince prays the God not to slay his men, meaning evidently, the armed warriors of the clan.

Incomplete

EARLY TRANSLATIONS FROM SOME
VEDANTIC TEXTS

The Karikas of Gaudapada

THE Karikas of Gaudapada are a body of authoritative verse maxims and reasonings setting forth in a brief and closely-argued manual the position of the extreme Monistic School of Vedanta philosophy. The monumental aphorisms of the Vedantasutra are meant rather for the master than the learner. Gaudapada's clear, brief and businesslike verses are of a wider utility; they presuppose only an elementary knowledge of philosophic terminology and the general trend of Monistic and Dualistic discussion. This preliminary knowledge granted, they provide the student with an admirably lucid and pregnant nucleus of reasoning which enables him at once to follow the Monistic train of thought and to keep in memory its most notable positions. It has also had the advantage, due no doubt to its pre-eminent merit and the long possession of authority and general use, of a full and powerful commentary by the great Master himself and a farther exposition by the Master's disciple, the clear-minded and often suggestive Anandagiri. To modern students there can be no better introduction to Vedanta philosophy — after some brooding over the sense of the Upanishads — than a study of Gaudapada's Karikas and Shankara's commentary with Deussen's *System of the Vedanta* in one hand and any brief and popular exposition of the Six Darshanas in the other. It is only after the Monistic School has been thoroughly understood that the Modified-Monistic and Dualistic-Monistic with their intermediary shades can be profitably studied. When the Vedantic theory has been mastered, the Sankhya, Yoga, Nyaya and Vaisheshika can in its light be easily mastered in succession with Vijnanabhikshu's work and the great synthesis of the Bhagavadgita to crown the whole structure. The philosophical basis will then be properly laid and the Upanishads can be studied with new interest, verifying or modifying as one goes one's original interpretation of the Sacred Books. This will bring to a close the theoretical side of the Jnanakanda; its practical and more valuable side can only be mastered in the path of Yoga and under the guidance of a Sadguru.

Gaudapada begins his work by a short exposition in clear philosophic terms of the poetical and rhythmic phraseology of the Upanishad. He first defines precisely the essential character of the Triune nature of the Self as manifested in the macrocosm and the microcosm, the Waker, the Dreamer and the Sleeper, who all meet and disappear in the Absolute.

बहिःप्रज्ञो विभुर्विश्वो ह्यन्तःप्रज्ञस्तु तेजसः ।
घनप्रज्ञस्तथा प्राज्ञ एक एव त्रिधा स्थितः ॥१॥

1. The Vishwa being the Lord who pervades and is conscious of the external, Taijasa he who is conscious of the internal, Prajna he in whom consciousness is (densified and) drawn into itself, the Self presents himself to the memory as One under three conditions.

अत्र एतस्मिन्नर्थोक्तेऽर्थे एते श्लोका भवन्ति — बहिःप्रज्ञ इति । पर्यायेण त्रिस्थानत्वात्
सोऽहमिति स्मृत्या प्रतिसंधानाच्च स्थानत्रयव्यतिरिक्तत्वमेकत्वं शुद्धत्वमसङ्गत्वं च सिद्धमित्य-
भिप्रायः, महामत्स्यादिदृष्टान्तश्रुतेः ॥

Shankara: The position taken is this, as *the entity which cognizes* enters into three conditions one after another *and not simulta-neously*, and is moreover *in all three* connected by the memory which *persists in feeling* "This is I" "This is I" "This is I", it is obvious that it is something beyond and above the three condi-tions, and therefore one, absolute and without attachment to its conditions. And this is supported by the illustrations like that of the large fish given in the Scripture.

दक्षिणाक्षिमुखे विश्वो मनस्यन्तस्तु तेजसः ।
आकाशे च हृदि प्राज्ञस्त्रिधा देहे व्यवस्थितः ॥२॥

2. Vishwa in the gate of the right eye, Taijasa within the mind, Prajna in the ether, the heart, this is its threefold station in the body.

जागरितावस्थायामेव विश्ववादीनां त्रयाणामनुभवप्रदर्शनार्थोऽयं श्लोक: —— दक्षिणाक्षीति ।
दक्षिणमक्ष्येव मुखम्, तस्मिन्प्राधान्येन द्रष्टा स्थूलानां विश्व: अनुभूयते, 'इन्धो ह वै नामैष
योऽयं दक्षिणेऽक्षन्पुरुष:' इति श्रुते: । इन्धो दीप्तिगुणो वैश्वानर आदित्यान्तर्गतो वैराज आत्मा
चक्षुषि च द्रष्टक: । नन्वन्यो हिरण्यगर्भ:, क्षेत्रज्ञो दक्षिणेऽक्षिण्यक्ष्णोनियन्ता द्रष्टा चान्यो
देहस्वामी; न, स्वतो भेदानभ्युपगमात्; 'एको देव: सर्वभूतेषु गूढ:' इति श्रुते:, 'क्षेत्रज्ञं चापि
मां विद्धि सर्वक्षेत्रेषु भारत', 'अविभक्तं च भूतेषु विभक्तमिव च स्थितम्' इति स्मृतेश्च; सर्वेषु
करणेष्वविशेषेष्वपि दक्षिणाक्षिण्युपलब्धिपाटवदर्शनात्तत्र विशेषेण निर्देशोऽस्य विश्वस्य । दक्षि-
णाक्षिगतो दृष्ट्वा रूपं निमीलिताक्षस्तदेव स्मरन्मनस्यन्त: स्वप्न इव तदेव वासनारूपाभिव्यक्तं
पश्यति । यथा तत्र तथा स्वप्ने; अत: मनसि अन्तस्तु तैजसोऽपि विश्व एव । आकाशे च
हृदि स्मरणाख्यव्यापारोपरमे प्राज्ञ एकीभूतो घनप्रज्ञ एव भवति, मनोव्यापाराभावात् । दर्शन-
स्मरणे एव हि मन:स्पन्दितम्; तदभावे हृदेवाविशेषेण प्राणात्मनावस्थानम्, 'प्राणो ह्येवैतान्
सर्वान्संवृङ्क्ते' इति श्रुते: । तैजस: हिरण्यगर्भ:, मन:स्थत्वात्; 'लिङ्गं मन:', 'मनोमयोऽयं
पुरुष:' इत्यादिश्रुतिभ्य: । ननु, व्याकृत: प्राण: सुषुप्ते; तदात्मकानि करणानि भवन्ति; कथ-
मव्याकृतता ? नैष दोष:, अव्याकृतस्य देशकालविशेषाभावात् । यद्यपि प्राणाभिमाने सति व्य-
कृततैव प्राणस्य; तथापि पिण्डपरिच्छिन्नविशेषाभिमाननिरोध: प्राणे भवतीत्यव्याकृत एव प्राण:
सुषुप्ते परिच्छिन्नाभिमानवताम् । यथा प्राणलये परिच्छिन्नाभिमानिनां प्राणोऽव्याकृत:, तथा
प्राणाभिमानिनोऽप्यविशेषापत्तावव्याकृतता समाना, प्रसवबीजात्मकत्वं च । तदध्यक्षश्चैको-
ऽव्याकृतावस्थ: । परिच्छिन्नाभिमानिनामध्यक्षाणां च तेनैकत्वमिति पूर्वोक्तं विशेषणमेकीभूत:
प्रज्ञानघन इत्याद्युपपन्नम् । तस्मिन्नेतस्मिन्नुक्तहेतुसत्त्वाच्च । कथं प्राणशब्दत्वमव्याकृतस्य ?
'प्राणबन्धनं हि सोम्य मन:' इति श्रुते: । ननु, तत्र 'सदेव सोम्य' इति प्रकृतं सद् ब्रह्म
प्राणशब्दवाच्यम्; नैष दोष:, बीजात्मकत्वाभ्युपगमात्सत: । यद्यपि सद्ब्रह्म प्राणशब्दवाच्यं
तत्र, तथापि जीवप्रसवबीजात्मकत्वमपरित्यज्यैव प्राणशब्दत्वं सत: सच्छब्दवाच्यता च । यदि हि
निर्बीजरूपं विवक्षितं ब्रह्माभविष्यत्, 'नेति नेति', 'यतो वाचो निवर्तन्ते', 'अन्यदेव तद्विदितादथो
अविदितादधि' इत्यवक्ष्यत्; 'न सत्तन्नासदुच्यते' इति स्मृते: । निर्बीजतयैव चेत्, सति प्रलीनानां
संपन्नानां सुषुप्तिप्रलययो: पुनरुत्थानानुपपत्ति: स्यात्; मुक्तानां च पुनरुत्पत्तिप्रसङ्ग:, बीजाभावा-
विशेषात्, ज्ञानदाह्यबीजाभावे च ज्ञानार्थक्यक्यप्रसङ्ग:; तस्मात्सबीजत्वमभ्युपगमेनैव सत: प्राणत्व-
व्यपदेश:, सर्वश्रुतिषु च कारणत्वव्यपदेश: । अत एव 'अक्षरात्परत: पर:', 'सबाह्याभ्यन्तरो
ह्यज:', 'यतो वाचो निवर्तन्ते', 'नेति नेति' इत्यादिना बीजत्वापनयनेन व्यपदेश: । तामबीजा-
वस्थां तस्यैव प्राज्ञशब्दवाच्यस्य तुरीयत्वेन देहादिसंबन्धजाप्रदादिरहितां पारमार्थिकीं पृथग्वक्ष्यति ।
बीजावस्थापि 'न किञ्चिदवेदिषम्' इत्युत्थितस्य प्रत्ययदर्शनाद्धेहेऽनुभूयत एवेति त्रिधा देहे
व्यवस्थित इत्युच्यते ॥

Shankara: 1. The object of this verse is to show that these three, Vishwa, Taijasa and Prajna, are experienced even in the waking state. The right eye is the door, *the means*, through which especially Vishwa, the seer of gross objects, becomes subject to experience. The Sruti saith, "Verily and of a truth Indha is he, even this Being as he standeth here in the right eye." Vaishwanara is

Indha, because his essential principle is light and is at once the macrocosmic Self within the Sun and the seer in the eye.

2. "But," it will be objected, "Hiranyagarbha is one and the cognizer of the material field, the guide and seer in the right eye is quite another, the master of the body." Not so; for in itself — *if we look into the real nature of our perceptions* — we do not realise any difference between them. And the Scripture saith, "One God hidden in all creatures" and the Smriti also:

"Know me, O son of Bharata, for the knower of the body in all bodies. I stand undivided in all creatures and only seem to be divided."

3. *Be it noted that* though Vishwa works indeed in all the organs of sense without distinction, yet because the perceptions of the right eye are noticed to be superior in acuteness and clearness it is for that reason only specifically mentioned as his abiding-place. After this Vishwa then dwelling in the right eye has seen a shape or appearance, if he remembers it when he has closed his eyes, he still sees within in the mind, as if in a dream, the same shape or appearance as manifested in the form of the idea or impression it has left. And it is just the same in a dream, *the impression or idea preserved by memory reproduces in sleep the same shape or appearance that was seen in waking.* It follows that this Taijasa who is within in the mind is no other than Vishwa himself.

4. Then by cessation of the process called memory Prajna in the ether or heart becomes unified or as it is said densified consciousness drawn into itself. And this happens because the processes of the mind are absent; for sight and memory are vibrations of the mind and in their absence the Self in the form of Prana takes its abode in the ether or heart without possibility of separation or distinction. For the Scripture saith, "It is Prana that swalloweth up all these into itself." Taijasa is the same as Hiranyagarbha because it has its abode in the mind, and the mind is the subtle part of the body, as is clear from the verse, "This *purusa* is all mind," and from other like sayings of Scripture.

5. It may be objected that Prana in the state of Sleep is

really differenced and manifest and the senses become one with Prana, so how do you predicate of it absence of manifestation and differentia *by saying it becomes One?* But there is no real fault in the reasoning; since in the undifferenced the particularising conditions of space and time are absent *and the same is the case with Prana in the state of Sleep.* Although indeed the Prana is *in a sense* differenced because the idea of separate existence as Prana remains, yet the more special sense of separate existence as circumscribed by the body is brought to a stop in Prana and Prana is therefore undifferenced and unmanifest in the Sleep in relation *at least* to the possessors of this circumscribed egoism. And just as the Prana of those who have the circumscribed bodily egoism becomes undifferenced when it is absorbed *at the end of the world,* so it is with him who has the sense of existence as Prana only in the condition *of Sleep* which is *in reality* precisely the same *as that of the temporary disappearance of phenomena at the end of a world*; both states alike are void of differentia and manifestation and *both alike* are pregnant with the seeds of *future* birth. The *Self* governing either state is one and the same, it is *Self* in an undifferenced and unmanifest condition. It follows that the governing Self in each case and the experiences of the circumscribed bodily egoism are one and the same; therefore the descriptions previously given of Prajna become One or become densified and self-concentrated consciousness etc. are quite applicable; and the arguments already advanced support the same conclusion.

6. "But," you will say, "why is the name Prana given to the Undifferenced?" On the ground of the Scripture, "For, O fair son, the cord and fastening of the mind is Prana." "O but," you answer, "there the words 'O fair son, Existence itself *is Prana*' show that it is Brahman Existent which being the subject of the verses must be intended by the word Prana." However, my reasoning is not thereby vitiated, because we all understand the Existent to be pregnant with the seed *of future birth.* Although, then, it is Brahman Existent which is meant by Prana, all the same the name Prana is given to the Existent because the idea of pregnancy with the seed from which the Jiva or life-conditioned human spirit is to be born, has not been eliminated from it and

indeed it is only when this idea is not eliminated from the idea of Brahman that he can be called Brahman Existent. For if it were the absolute seedless Brahman of which the Scripture had meant to speak, it would have used such expressions as: "He is not this, not that nor anything which we can call him"; "From whom words return baffled"; "He is other than the known and different from the Unknown." The Smriti also says, "He (the Absolute) is called neither Existent nor non-Existent." Besides if the Existent be seedless, then there would be no ground for supposing that those who have coalesced with and become absorbed into the Existent in the state of Sleep or the destruction of a world can again awake *out of either of these conditions.* Or if they can, then we should immediately have the contingency of liberated souls again coming into phenomenal existence; for *on this hypothesis* the condition *of souls liberated into the Absolute and those absorbed into the Existent* would be alike, neither having seed *or cause of future phenomenal existence. And if to remove this objection you say that* it is the seed *of ignorance* which has to be burnt away in the fire of Knowledge *that is absent in the case of liberated souls and some other seed of things in the other case,* you are in danger of proving that Knowledge (*of the Eternal*) is without use or unnecessary *as a means of salvation.*

7. It is clear then that it is on the understanding that the Existent is pregnant with the seed of phenomenal life that in all the Scripture it is represented as Prana and the cause of things. Consequently it is by elimination of this idea of the seed that it is designated by such phrases as "He is the unborn in whom the objective and subjective are One"; "From whom words return baffled"; "He is not this nor that nor anything we can call him" and the rest. Our author will speak separately of this seedless condition of the Same Self which has been designated by the term Prajna. This condition by its being the Fourth or Absolute is devoid of all relations such as body, *prāṇa* etc. and is alone finally and transcendentally true. Now the condition of undifferenced seedfulness also is *like the two others* experienced in this body in the form of the idea of the awakened man which tells him, "*For so long* I felt and knew nothing." Thus then the Self is said to have a threefold station in the body.

विश्वो हि स्थूलभुङ्ग नित्यं तैजसः प्रविविक्तभुक् ।
आनन्दभुक्तथा प्राज्ञस्त्रिधा भोगं निबोधत ॥३॥

3. Vishwa is the enjoyer of gross objects, Taijasa of subtle, and
   Prajna of pure (unrelated) pleasure; thus shall ye understand the threefold enjoyment *of the Self in the body.*

स्थूलं तर्पयते विश्वं प्रविविक्तं तु तैजसम् ।
आनन्दश्च तथा प्राज्ञं त्रिधा तृप्तिं निबोधत ॥४॥

4. The gross utterly satisfieth Vishwa, but the subtle Taijasa
   and pure pleasure satisfieth Prajna, thus shall ye understand
   the threefold satisfaction *of the Self in the body.*

उक्तार्थौ हि श्लोकौ ॥

Shankara: The meaning of these two verses has been explained.

त्रिषु धामसु यद्भोज्यं भोक्ता यश्च प्रकीर्तितः ।
वेदैतदुभयं यस्तु स भुञ्जानो न लिप्यते ॥५॥

5. That which is enjoyed in the three conditions and that
   which is the enjoyer, he who knoweth both these as one enjoyeth and receiveth no stain.

त्रिषु धामसु जाग्रदादिषु स्थूलप्रविविक्तानन्दाख्यं यद्भोज्यमेकं त्रिधाभूतम्; यश्च विश्व-
तैजसप्राज्ञाख्यो भोक्तैकः 'सोऽहम्' इत्येकत्वेन प्रतिसंधानात् द्रष्टृत्वाविशेषाच्च प्रकीर्तितः; यो
वेद एतदुभयं भोज्यभोक्तृतया अनेकधा भिन्नम्, स भुञ्जानः न लिप्यते, भोज्यस्य सर्वस्यैक-
भोक्तृभोज्यत्वात् । न हि यस्य यो विषयः, स तेन हीयते वर्धते वा । न हानिः स्वविषयं
दग्ध्वा काष्ठादि, तद्वत् ॥

Shankara: That which is enjoyed under the names of gross objects,
subtle objects and pure pleasure in the three conditions, waking,
dream and sleep is one and the same thing although it has taken
a threefold aspect. And that which enjoys under the names of
Vishwa, Taijasa and Prajna, has been declared to be one because
they are connected by the sense of oneness expressed in the continual feeling "This is I, This is I" and because the nature of cognition is one and without difference throughout. Whoever knows
both these to be one though split up into multiplicity by the

sense of being enjoyer or enjoyed, does not receive any stain from enjoyment, because the subject of enjoyment is the One universal and the enjoyer too is not different from the enjoyed. For *note that* whoever be the enjoyer or whatever his object of enjoyment, he does not increase with it or diminish with it, just as in the case of fire when it has burnt up its object in the shape of wood or other fuel, *it remains no less or greater than it was before.*

प्रभवः सर्वभावानां सतामिति विनिश्चयः ।
सर्वं जनयति प्राणश्चेतोंशून्पुरुषः पृथक् ॥६॥

6. It is a certain conclusion that all existences which take birth are already in being; Prana brings the All into phenomenal being, it is this *Prana or* Purusha which *sends* its separate rays of consciousness abroad.

सतां विद्यमानानां स्वेन अविद्याकृतनामरूपमायास्वरूपेण सर्वभावानां विश्वतैजसप्राज्ञभेदानां प्रभवः उत्पत्तिः । वक्ष्यति च — 'वन्ध्यापुत्रो न तत्त्वेन मायया वापि जायते' इति । यदि ह्यसतामेव जन्म स्यात्, ब्रह्मणोऽव्यवहार्यस्य ग्रहणद्वाराभावादसत्त्वप्रसङ्गः । दृष्टं च रज्जु-सर्पादीनामविद्याकृतमायाबीजोत्पन्नानां रज्ज्वाद्यात्मना सत्त्वम् । न हि निरास्पदा रज्जुसर्प-मृगतृष्णिकादयः क्वचिदुपलभ्यन्ते केनचित् । यथा रज्ज्वां प्राक्सर्पोत्पत्तेः रज्ज्वात्मना सर्पः सन्नेवासीत्, एवं सर्वभावानामुत्पत्तेः प्राक्प्राणबीजात्मनैव सत्त्वमिति । श्रुतिरपि वक्ति 'ब्रह्मैवेदम्,' 'आत्मैवेदमग्र आसीत्' इति । अतः सर्वं जनयति प्राणः चेतोंशून्, अंशव इव रवेश्चिदात्म-कस्य पुरुषस्य चेतोरूपा जलार्कसमाः प्राज्ञतैजसविश्वभेदेन देवमनुष्यतिर्यगादिदेहमेदेषु विभाव्य-मानाश्चेतोंईश्वरो ये, तान् पुरुषः पृथक् सृजति विषयभावविलक्षणानग्निनिर्विस्फुलिङ्गवत्सलक्षणान् जलार्कवच्च जीवलक्षणांस्त्वितरान्सर्वभावान् प्राणो बीजात्मा जनयति, 'यथोर्णनाभिः,' 'यथाग्नेः क्षुद्रा विस्फुलिङ्गाः' इत्यादिश्रुतेः ॥

Shankara: All existences (divided as Vishwa, Taijasa and Prajna) are already in being, that is, they existed before and it is only by their own species and nature and illusion of name and form created by Ignorance that they take birth or in other words put forth into phenomenal existences. As indeed the writer says later on, "A son from a barren woman is not born either in reality or by illusion." For if birth of the non-existent — *that is something coming out of nothing* — were possible, then there would be no means of grasping this world of usage and experience and the Eternal itself would become an unreality. Moreover we have

seen that the snake in the rope and other appearances born of the
seed of illusion created by Ignorance do really exist as the self of
the rope *or other substratum in the case.* For the snake in the
rope, the mirage and other *hallucinations of the sort* are never
experienced by anybody unless there is some substratum. Just as
before the coming into phenomenal being of the snake it existed
already in the rope as the rope's self, so before the coming to birth
of all phenomenal existences, they already existed as the self of the
seed of things called Prana. And the Scripture also saith, "This universe is the Eternal", "In the beginning all this was the Spirit." The
Prana gives birth to the All as separate rays of consciousness; —
just as the rays of the Sun, so are these consciousness-rays of the
Purusha who is Chit or conscious existences and they are clearly
distinguished in different bodies of gods, animals, etc. under
three different lights as Vishwa, Taijasa and Prajna, in the same
way as reflections of the sun are clearly seen in different pieces of
water; they are thrown from the Purusha and though they differ
according to the separate existences which are their field of action
and enjoyment, yet they are all alike like sparks from a fire being
all Jiva or conditioned Self. Thus the Prana or causal Self gives
phenomenal birth to all other existences as the spider to his web.
Compare the Scripture, "As a fire sendeth forth sparks."

विभूतिं प्रसवं त्वन्ये मन्यन्ते सृष्टिचिन्तकाः ।
स्वप्नमायासरूपेति सृष्टिरन्यैर्विकल्पिता ॥७॥

7. Some who concern themselves with the *cause of* creation
   think that Almighty Power is the origin of things and by
   others creation is imagined as like to illusion or a dream.

विभूतिर्विस्तार ईश्वरस्य सृष्टिरिति सृष्टिचिन्तका मन्यन्ते; न तु परमार्थचिन्तकानां
सृष्टावादर इत्यर्थः; 'इन्द्रो मायाभिः पुरुरूप ईयते' इति श्रुतेः । न हि मायाविनं सूत्रमाकाशे
निःक्षिप्य तेन सायुधमारुह्य चक्षुर्गोचरतामतीत्य युद्धेन खण्डशश्छिन्नं पतितं पुनरुत्थितं च
पश्यतां तत्कृतमायादिसतत्त्वचिन्तायामादरो भवति । तथैवायं मायाविनः सूत्रप्रसारणसमः
सुषुप्तस्वप्नादिविकासः; तदारूढमायाविसमश्च तत्स्थप्राज्ञतैजसादिः; सूत्रतदारूढाभ्यामन्यः परमार्थ-
मायावी । स एव भूमिष्ठो मायाच्छन्नः अदृश्यमान एव स्थितो यथा, तथा तुरीयाख्यं पर-
मार्थतत्त्वम् । अतस्तच्चिन्तायामेवादरो मुमुक्षूणामार्याणाम्, न निष्प्रयोजनायां सृष्टावादर इत्यतः
सृष्टिचिन्तकानामेवैते विकल्पा इत्याह — स्वप्नमायासरूपेति । स्वप्नसरूपा मायासरूपा चेति ॥

Shankara: Those who concern themselves with creation think that creation is the pervading Power, the extension, so to speak, of God; but it is implied, those who concern themselves with final and transcendental truth do not care about speculations on creation. For when men see a conjurer throw a rope into the air and ascend it armed and accoutred and then after he has climbed out of sight fall hewn to pieces in battle and rise again *whole*, they do not care about inquiring into the illusion he has created with all its properties and origins. Just so this evolution of the Sleep, Dream and Waking conditions is just like the self-lengthening of the juggler's rope and the Prajna, Taijasa and Vishwa self-abiding in the three conditions is like the conjurer climbing up the rope, but the real conjurer is other than the rope or its climber. Just as he stands on the ground invisible and hidden in illusion, so is it with the real and transcendental fact called the Fourth. Therefore it is for Him that the Aryan-minded care, those who follow after salvation, and they do not care for speculations about creation which are of no importance to them. Accordingly the writer implies that all these theories are only imaginations of those who concern themselves with the origin of creation and then goes on to say that by others creation is imagined as like to an illusion or again as like to a dream.

इच्छामात्रं प्रभोः सृष्टिरिति सृष्टौ विनिश्चिताः ।
कालात्प्रसूति भूतानां मन्यन्ते कालचिन्तकाः ॥८॥

8. Those who have made up their minds on the subject of creation say it is merely the Will of the Lord; those who concern themselves about Time think that from Time is the birth of creatures.

इच्छामात्रं प्रभोः सत्यसंकल्पत्वात् सृष्टिः घटादीनां संकल्पनामात्रम्, न संकल्पनातिरिक्तम् ।
कालादेव सृष्टिरिति केचित् ॥

Shankara: Creation is the Will of the Lord because the divine ideas must be true facts — pots etc. are ideas only and nothing more than ideas. Some say that creation is the result of Time.

भोगार्थं सृष्टिरित्यन्ये क्रीडार्थमिति चापरे ।
देवस्यैष स्वभावोऽयमाप्तकामस्य का स्पृहा ॥९॥
इति ।

9. Others say that creation is for the sake of enjoyment, yet others say it is for play. *Really,* this is the very nature of the Lord; *as for other theories, well,* He has all He can desire and why should He crave for anything?

भोगार्थम् क्रीडार्थमिति च अन्ये सृष्टि मन्यन्ते । अनयोः पक्षयोर्दूषणं देवस्यैष स्वभावो-ऽयमिति देवस्य स्वभावपक्षमाश्रित्य, सर्वेषां वा पक्षाणाम् — आप्तकामस्य का स्पृहेति । न हि रज्ज्वादीनामविद्यास्वभावव्यतिरेकेण सर्पाद्याभासत्वे कारणं शक्यं वक्तुम् ॥

Shankara: Others think creation *was made* for enjoyment or for play. These two theories are criticised by the line "This is the very nature of the Lord." Or, it may be, that the theory of Divine Nature is resorted to in order to criticise all *other* theories *by the argument* He has all He can desire and why should He crave for anything? For no cause can be alleged for the appearance of the snake etc. in the rope and other substrata except the very nature of Ignorance.

निवृत्तेः सर्वदुःखानामीशानः प्रभुरव्ययः ।
अद्वैतः सर्वभावानां देवस्तुर्यो विभुः स्मृतः ॥१०॥

10. He who is called the Fourth is the Master of the cessation of all ills, the Strong Lord and undecaying, the One without Second of all existences, the Shining One who pervadeth.

अत्रैते श्लोका भवन्ति । प्राज्ञतैजसविश्वलक्षणानां सर्वदुःखानां निवृत्तेः ईशानः तुरीय आत्मा । ईशान इत्यस्य पदस्य व्याख्यानं प्रभुरिति; दुःखनिवृत्ति प्रति प्रभुर्भवतीत्यर्थः, तद्विज्ञाननिमित्तत्वाद् दुःखनिवृत्तेः । अव्ययः न व्येति, स्वरूपान्न व्यभिचरति न च्यवत इत्येतत् । कुतः ? यस्मात् अद्वैतः, सर्व-भावानाम् — सर्पादीनां रज्जुरद्वया सत्या च; एवं तुरीयः, 'न हि द्रष्टुर्दृष्टेर्विपरिलोपो विद्यते' इति श्रुतेः — अतो रज्जुसर्पवन्मृषात्वात् । स एष देवः द्योतनात् तुर्यं; चतुर्थं; विभुः व्यापी स्मृतः ॥

Shankara: The Fourth Self *or transcendental* is the master of the cessation of all ills, which belong to the conditions of Prajna, Taijasa and Vishwa. The expression Strong Lord is an explanation of the word Master; it is implied that His strength and lordship are in relation to the cessation of ills, because the cessation of ills results from the knowledge of Him. Undecaying, because He does not pass away, swerve or depart, i.e., from his essential nature. How is this? Because He is the One without a second owing to the vanity[1] of all phenomenal existences. He is also called God, the Shining One, because of effulgence, the Fourth and He who pervades, exists everywhere.

कार्यकारणबद्धौ ताविष्येते विश्वतैजसौ ।
प्राज्ञः कारणबद्धस्तु द्वौ तौ तुर्ये न सिध्यतः ॥११॥

11. Vishwa and Taijasa are acknowledged to be bound by cause and effect, Prajna is bound by cause only; both of these are held not to exist in the Fourth.

विश्ववादीनां सामान्यविशेषभावो निरूप्यते तुर्ययाथात्म्यावधारणार्थम् — कार्यं क्रियत इति फलभावः, कारणं करोतीति बीजभावः । तत्त्वाग्रहणान्यथाग्रहणाभ्यां बीजफलभावाभ्यां तौ यथोक्तौ विश्वतैजसौ बद्धौ संगृहीतौ इष्येते । प्राज्ञस्तु बीजभावेनैव बद्धः । तत्त्वाप्रतिबोधमात्र-मेव हि बीजं प्राज्ञत्वे निमित्तम् । ततः द्वौ तौ बीजफलभावौ तत्त्वाग्रहणान्यथाग्रहणे तुरीये न सिध्यतः न विद्येते, न संभवत इत्यर्थः ॥

Shankara: The common and particular characteristics of Vishwa and the two others are now determined in order that the real self of the Fourth may become clear. Effect, that which is made or done, is existence as result. Cause, that which makes or does, is existence as seed. By inapprehension and misapprehension of the Truth the aforesaid Vishwa and Taijasa are, it is agreed, bound or imprisoned by existence as result and seed. But Prajna is bound by existence as seed only. For the seed state which lies in unawakening to the Truth alone *and not in misreading of Him* is the reason of the state of Prajna. Therefore both of these, existence as cause and existence as effect, inapprehension and misapprehension of the Truth are held not to apply to the Fourth, i.e., do not exist and cannot happen in Him.

नात्मानं न परं चैव न सत्यं नापि चानृतम् ।
प्राज्ञः किंचन संवेत्ति तुर्यं तत्सर्वदृक्सदा ॥१२॥

12. Prajna cogniseth nought, neither self nor others, neither

---

[1] *Or*, falseness.

truth nor falsehood; theFourth seeth all things for ever.

कथं पुनः कारणबद्धत्वं प्राज्ञस्य तुरीये वा तत्त्वाग्रहणान्यथाग्रहणलक्षणौ बन्धौ न सिध्यत इति ? यस्मात् — आत्मविलक्षणम्, अविद्याबीजप्रसूतं वेद्यं बाह्यं द्वैतम् — प्राज्ञो न किंचन संवेत्ति, यथा विश्वतैजसौ; ततश्चासौ तत्त्वाग्रहणेन तमसा अन्यथाग्रहणबीजभूतेन बद्धो भवति । यस्मात् तुर्यं तत्सर्वदृक्सदा तुरीयादन्यस्याभावात् सर्वदा सदैव भवति, सर्वं च तद्दृक्चेति सर्वदृक्; तस्मात् तत्त्वाग्रहणलक्षणं बीजम् । तत्र तत्प्रसूतस्यान्यथाग्रहणस्याप्यत एवाभावः । न हि सवितरि सदाप्रकाशात्मके तद्विरुद्धमप्रकाशनमन्यथाप्रकाशनं वा संभवति, 'न हि द्रष्टुर्दृष्टेर्विपरिलोपो विद्यते' इति श्रुतेः । अथवा, जाग्रत्स्वप्नयोः सर्वभूतावस्थः सर्ववस्तुदृगाभासस्तुरीय एवेति सर्वदृक्सदा, 'नान्यदतोऽस्ति द्रष्टृ' इत्यादिश्रुतेः ॥

Shankara: But how then is Prajna bound by Cause, while in the Fourth the two kinds of bondage conditioned by inapprehension and misapprehension of the Truth is said to be impossible? Because Prajna does not cognize at all this duality of an outside universe born from Ignorance and conditioned as distinct from Self, so that like Vishwa and Taijasa he also is bound by inapprehension of the Truth, by that blind darkness which becomes the seed of misapprehension; and because the Fourth seeth all things for ever. That is to say, since nothing *really* exists except the Fourth, He is necessarily seer of all that is, Omniscient and all-cognizant at all times and for ever; in him therefore the seed state of which the conditioning feature is inapprehension of the Truth, cannot possibly exist. Absence of the misapprehension which arises out of inapprehension naturally follows. The Sun is for ever illuminative by its nature and non-illumination or mis-illumination as contrary to its nature cannot happen to it; *and the same train of reasoning applies to the Omniscience of the* [...].[1] The Scripture also says, "For of the Sight of the Seer there is no annihilation." Or indeed, since it is the Fourth that in the Waking and Dream State dwelling in all creatures is the light or reflection in them to which all objects *present themselves as* visible, *cognizable* objects, it is *in this way too* the seer of all things for ever. The Scripture says, "There is nought else than This that seeth."

Incomplete

---

[1] *This sentence was left incomplete.*

Sadananda's Essence of Vedanta

INVOCATION

To the Absolute

अखण्डं सच्चिदानन्दम् अवाङ्मनसगोचरम् ।
आत्मानमखिलाधारम् आश्रयेऽभीष्टसिद्धये ॥१॥

1. I take refuge with Him who is *sheer* Existence, Intelligence and Bliss, impartible, beyond the purview of speech and mind, the Self in whom the whole Universe exists — may my desire and purpose attain fulfilment.

To the Masters

अर्थतोऽप्यद्वयानन्दान् अतीतद्वैतभानतः ।
गुरूनाराध्य वेदान्तसारं वक्ष्ये यथामति ॥२॥

2. After homage to the Masters who in deed as well as word delight in the One without second and from whom the seemings of duality have passed away, I will declare the Essence of Vedanta according to my intellectual capacity.

PRELIMINARY STATEMENT

The Training of the Vedantin

वेदान्तो नाम उपनिषत्प्रमाणम्, तदुपकारीणि शारीरक-सूत्रादीनि च ॥३॥

3. By Vedanta is meant the Upanishads as authoritative basis of the philosophy and as useful supplementary inquiries the Aphoristic Books that treat of the Embodied Soul.

अस्य वेदान्तप्रकरणत्वात् तदीयैरेवानुबन्धैस्तद्गतासिद्धेनं ते पृथगालोचनीयाः ॥४॥

4. Now since Vedanta is the subject of this work, its circum-

stantiae — the conclusions sought to be established being similar in both, — are the same as those of the Vedanta and need not be separately discussed.

तत्र अनुबन्धो नाम अधिकारिविषयसम्बन्धप्रयोजनानि ॥५॥

5. In circumstantiae we include four things, the fit hearer, the subject, the logical relation, the object of the work.

अधिकारी तु विधिवदधीतवेदवेदाङ्गत्वेन आपाततोऽधिगताखिलवेदार्थः अस्मिन् जन्मनि जन्मान्तरे वा काम्यनिषिद्धवर्जनपुरःसरं नित्य-नैमित्तिकप्रायश्चित्तो-पासनानुष्ठानेन निर्गत-निखिल-कल्मषतया नितान्त-निर्मलस्वान्तः-साधनचतुष्टय-सम्पन्नः प्रमाता ॥६॥

6. Now the fit hearer of Vedanta must be one who is competent to form a right judgment of it. He must therefore have mastered [...][1] by proper study of Veda and its accessory sciences the entire meaning of Veda; he must in this life or another have begun by abandoning forbidden actions and actions prompted by desire and then by the performance of daily observances, occasional observances, penance and adoration freed himself from all sin and stain and attained to perfect purity of the mind and heart; and he must be in possession of the four Ways and Means.

काम्यानि स्वर्गादीष्टसाधनानि ज्योतिष्टोमादीनि ॥७॥

7. By actions of desire is understood all ways and means by which we pursue various kinds of happiness from Paradise downward — the Jyotishtoma sacrifice for example.

निषिद्धानि नरकाद्यनिष्टसाधनानि ब्रह्म-हननादीनि ॥८॥

8. By forbidden actions is meant all ways and means by which we compass all our ills from the torments of Hell downward, — Brahminicide for example and other sins and disobediences.

---

[1] *Blank in manuscript.*

नित्यानि अकरणे प्रत्यवायसाधनानि सन्ध्यावन्दनादीनि ॥९॥

9. By regular observances is meant ceremonies like the evening prayer etc., the non-performance of which turns them into means of offence and stumbling-blocks.

नैमित्तिकानि पुत्रजन्माद्यनुबन्धीनि जातेष्टचादीनि ॥१०॥

10. By occasional observances is understood ceremonies circumstantial to particular occasions, such as the Blessing of the New-born attendant on the birth of a son.

प्रायश्चित्तानि पापक्षयमात्रसाधनानि चान्द्रायणादीनि ॥११॥

11. By penances is understood vows and forms of self-discipline such as the Chandrayan vow which are means *only* towards the purging away of sin.

उपासनानि सगुणब्रह्मविषयक-मानसव्यापाररूपाणि शाण्डिल्यविद्यादीनि ॥१२॥

12. By adoration is understood the various forms of mental working which have for their whole subject and purpose the Eternal in His aspect as a Personal Deity — Shandilya's Art of Divine Love, for example.

एतेषां नित्यादीनां बुद्धिशुद्धिः परं प्रयोजनम्, उपासनानान्तु चित्तैकाग्र्यम् ।
तमेतमात्मानं वेदानुवचनेन ब्राह्मणा विविदिषन्ति यज्ञेनेत्यादिश्रुतेः, तपसा
कल्मषं हन्ति इत्यादिस्मृतेश्च ॥१३॥

13. The main object of the first three, observances regular and occasional and penance, is the purification of the Understanding; but the main object of adoration is singleness of heart and mind towards one object. This is proved by such passages as these from Revealed Scripture, "This is that Self of whom the Brahmins shall seek to know by exposition of Veda and by Sacrifice shall they seek to know Him" — and by other passages from the Unrevealed Scripture such as, "By Tapasya (energism of will) one slayeth sin."

नित्यनैमित्तिकयोरुपासनानाञ्च अवान्तरफलं पितृलोकसत्यलोकप्राप्ति: । कर्मणा पितृलोको विद्यते देवलोक: इत्यादिश्रुते: ॥१४॥

14. A secondary result of observances regular and occasional and of adoration and worship is attainment to the world of the fathers and to the world of the Living Truth. For so the Scripture says, "By action the World of the Fathers is found and the World of the Gods also."

साधनानि नित्यानित्यवस्तु-विवेकेह्यामुत्रफलभोगविराग-शमदमादिसम्पत्तिमुमुक्षु-त्वानि ॥१५॥

15. By Ways and Means we understand Discrimination of eternal objects from the transient; Disattachment from enjoyment in this world or another; Calm, Self-Conquest and the other moral excellences; and Desire of Salvation.

नित्यानित्यवस्तु-विवेकस्तावत् ब्रह्मैव नित्यं वस्तु ततोऽन्यदखिलमनित्यमिति विवेचनम् ॥१६॥

16. By Discrimination of eternal objects from the transient we understand the discernment of Brahman as the one thing eternal and of everything other than Brahman as transient and perishable.

Incomplete

APPENDIX

APPENDIX

Upanishadic Citations from
The Life Divine

Brihadaranyaka Upanishad

पृथिवी पाजस्यम् ।

Earth is His footing.   I.1.1. (*The Life Divine, p, 11*)

नैवेह किञ्चनाग्र आसीन्मृत्युनैवेदमावृतमासीत् । अशनाययाऽशनाया हि
मृत्युस्तन्मनोऽकुरुतात्मन्वी स्यामिति ॥

In the beginning all was covered by Hunger that is Death;
that made for itself Mind so that it might attain to possession of
self.   I.2.1. (*p. 188*)

असतो मा सद्गमय तमसो मा ज्योतिर्गमय मृत्योर्मामृतं गमयेति ।

From the non-being to true being, from the darkness to the
Light, from death to Immortality.   I.3.28. (*p. 824*)

य एवं वेदाऽहं ब्रह्मास्मीति स इदꣳ सर्वं भवति... अथ योऽन्यां
देवतामुपास्तेऽन्योऽसावन्योऽहमस्मीति न स वेद ॥

He who has the knowledge "I am Brahman" becomes all
this that is; but whoever worships another divinity than the
One Self and thinks, "Other is he and I am other", he knows
not.   I.4.10. (*p. 553*)

आत्मेति योऽयं विज्ञानमयः... हृदन्तर्ज्योतिः पुरुषः स समानः सन्नुभौ
लोकावनुसञ्चरति... स हि स्वप्नो भूत्वेमं लोकमतिक्रामति मृत्यो रूपाणि ॥
तस्य वा एतस्य पुरुषस्य द्वे एव स्थाने भवत इदं च परलोकस्थानं च सन्ध्यं
तृतीयꣳ स्वप्नस्थानं तस्मिन् सन्ध्ये स्थाने तिष्ठन्नेते उभे स्थाने पश्यतीदं च
परलोकस्थानं च... स यत्र प्रस्वपित्यस्य लोकस्य सर्वावतो मात्रामुपादाय स्वयं
विहत्य स्वयं निर्माय स्वेन भासा स्वेन ज्योतिषा प्रस्वपित्यत्रायं पुरुषः
स्वयंज्योतिर्भवति ॥ न तत्र रथा न... पन्थानो भवन्ति... न तत्रानन्दा

मुदः प्रमुदो भवन्ति...न तत्र वेशान्ताः पुष्करिण्यः स्रवन्त्यो भवन्त्यथ...
सृजते स हि कर्ता॥...

स्वप्नेन शारीरमभिप्रहृत्याऽऽसुप्तः सुप्तानभिचाकशीति॥
प्राणेन रक्षन्नवरं कुलायं बहिष्कुलायादमृतश्चरित्वा।
स ईयतेऽमृतो यत्र कामꣳ हिरण्मयः पुरुष एकहꣳसः॥
...अथो खल्वाहुर्जागरितदेश एवास्यैष इति यानि ह्येव जाग्रत्पश्यति
तानि सुप्त इत्यत्रायं पुरुषः स्वयंज्योतिर्भवति॥

This Self is a self of Knowledge, an inner light in the heart;
he is the conscious being common to all the states of being and
moves in both worlds. He becomes a dream-self and passes
beyond this world and its forms of death.... There are two planes
of this conscious being, this and the other worlds; a third state
is their place of joining, the state of dream, and when he stands
in this place of their joining, he sees both planes of his existence,
this world and the other world. When he sleeps, he takes the
substance of this world in which all is and himself undoes and
himself builds by his own illumination, his own light; when
this conscious being sleeps, he becomes luminous with his self-
light.... There are no roads nor chariots, nor joys nor pleasures,
nor tanks nor ponds nor rivers, but he creates them by his own
light, for he is the maker. By sleep he casts off his body and un-
sleeping sees those that sleep; he preserves by his life-breath
this lower nest and goes forth, immortal, from his nest; immortal, he goes where he wills, the golden Purusha, the solitary
Swan. They say, "the country of waking only is his, for the
things which he sees when awake, these only he sees when
asleep"; but there he is his own self-light.

IV.3.7,9-12,14. (*p. 412*)

न हि द्रष्टुर्दृष्टेर्विपरिलोपो विद्यते...। न हि वक्तुर्वक्तेः। ...न हि
श्रोतुः श्रुतेः...न हि विज्ञातुर्विज्ञातेर्विपरिलोपो विद्यतेऽविनाशित्वात्, न तु तद्
द्वितीयमस्ति ततोऽन्यद्विभक्तं...यत्पश्येत्...,यद्वदेत्...,यच्छृणुयात्...,
यद्विजानीयात्॥

There is no annihilation of the seeing of the seer, the speaking of the speaker...the hearing of the hearer...the knowing
of the knower, for they are indestructible; but it is not a second

or other than and separate from himself that he sees, speaks to, hears, knows. IV.3.23,26,30. (*p. 524*)

अथो खल्वाहुः काममय एवायं पुरुष इति, स यथाकामो भवति
तत्क्रतुर्भवति, यत्क्रतुर्भवति तत्कर्म कुरुते, यत्कर्म कुरुते तदभिसम्पद्यते ॥ ...
तदेव सक्तः सह कर्मणैति लिङ्गं मनो यत्र निषक्तमस्य ।
प्राप्यान्तं कर्मणस्तस्य यत्किञ्चेह करोत्ययम् ।
तस्माल्लोकात्पुनरेत्यस्मै लोकाय कर्मणे ॥

They say indeed that the conscious being is made of desire. But of whatsoever desire he comes to be, he comes to be of that will, and of whatever will he comes to be, he does that action, and whatever his action, to (the result of) that he reaches.... Adhered to by his Karma,[1] he goes in his subtle body to wherever his mind cleaves, then, coming to the end of his Karma, even of whatsoever action he does here, he returns from that world to this world for Karma. IV.4.5,6. (*p. 792*)

ब्रह्मैव सन्ब्रह्माप्येति ॥

He becomes the Eternal and departs into the Eternal.
IV.4.6. (*p. 657*)

अथायमशरीरोऽमृतः प्राणो ब्रह्मैव तेज एव ।

This bodiless and immortal Life and Light is the Brahman.
IV.4.7. (*p. 657*)

अणुः पन्था विततः पुराणो माꣳस्पृष्टोऽनुवित्तो मयैव ।
तेन धीरा अपियन्ति ब्रह्मविदः स्वर्गं लोकमित ऊर्ध्वं विमुक्ताः ॥

Long and narrow is the ancient Path, — I have touched it, I have found it, — the Path by which the wise, knowers of the Eternal, attaining to salvation, depart hence to the high world of Paradise. IV.4.8. (*p. 657*)

---

[1] Action, *karma*. In the view expressed in this verse of the Upanishad the Karma or action of this life is exhausted by the life in the world beyond in which its results are fulfilled and the soul returns to earth for fresh Karma. The cause of birth in this world, of Karma, of the soul's passage to other-world existence and its return here is, throughout, the soul's own consciousness, will and desire.

यत्र हि द्वैतमिव भवति तदितर इतरं पश्यति, . . . तदितर इतरꣳ शृणोति,
तदितर इतरं मनुते, तदितर इतरꣳ स्पृशति, तदितर इतरं विजानाति ।
यत्र त्वस्य सर्वमात्मैवाभूत्तत्केन कं . . . विजानीयाद्येनेदꣳ सर्वं विजानाति. . . ॥
सर्वं तं परादाद्योऽन्यत्रात्मनः सर्वं वेद; इदं ब्रह्म, . . . इमानि भूतानीद
सर्वं यदयमात्मा ॥

Where there is duality, there other sees other, other hears,
touches, thinks of, knows other. But when one sees all as the
Self, by what shall one know it? it is by the Self that one knows
all this that is. . . . All betrays him who sees all elsewhere than in
the Self; for all this that is is the Brahman, all beings and all
this that is are this Self.　　IV.5.15,7. (*p. 524*)

प्रथमोत्तमे . . . सत्यं मध्यतोऽनृतं तदेतदनृतमुभयतः सत्येन परिगृहीतꣳ
सत्यभूयमेव भवति ॥

The first and the highest are truth; in the middle there is
falsehood, but it is taken between the truth on both sides of it
and it draws its being from the truth.[1]　　V.5.1. (*p. 596*)

Chhandogya Upanishad

सदेव . . . इदमग्र आसीदेकमेवाद्वितीयम् ।

In the beginning was the one Existence without a second.
　　　　　　　　　　　　　　　　　　　　VI.2.1. (*p. 128*)

सदेव . . . . एकमेवाद्वितीयम् ।

One indivisible that is pure existence.　　VI.2.1. (*p. 71*)

तत्त्वमसि, श्वेतकेतो !

---

[1] The truth of the physical reality and the truth of the spiritual and superconscient reality.
Into the intermediate subjective and mental realities which stand between them, falsehood can
enter, but it takes either truth from above or truth from below as the substance out of which
it builds itself and both are pressing upon it to turn its misconstructions into truth of life and
truth of spirit.

Thou art That, O Shwetaketu.   VI.8.7. (*p. 683*)

स्मरो ... भूयः ... न स्मरन्तो नैव ते कञ्चन ... मन्वीरन्न विजानीरन् ...
यावत् स्मरस्य गतं तत्रास्य यथाकामचारो भवति ... ॥

Memory is greater: without memory men could think and
know nothing.... As far as goes the movement of Memory, there
he ranges at will.   VII.13.1,2. (*p. 501*)

Isha Upanishad

यस्मिन्सर्वाणि भूतान्यात्मेवाभूद्विजानतः ।
तत्र को मोहः कः शोक एकत्वमनुपश्यतः ॥

He whose self has become all existences, for he has the knowledge, how shall he be deluded, whence shall he have grief, he who
sees everywhere oneness?   Verse 7. (*p. 150*)

तत्र को मोहः कः शोक एकत्वमनुपश्यतः ॥

Whence shall he have grief, how shall he be deluded who
sees everywhere the Oneness?   Verse 7. (*p. 218*)

कविर्मनीषी परिभूः स्वयंभूर्याथातथ्यतोऽर्थान्व्यदधाच्छाश्वतीभ्यः समाभ्यः ॥

The Seer, the Thinker, the Self-existent who becomes everywhere has ordered perfectly all things from years sempiternal.
                                                Verse 8. (*p. 388*)

अविद्यया मृत्युं तीर्त्वा विद्ययामृतमश्नुते ।
विनाशेन मृत्युं तीर्त्वा सम्भूत्यामृतमश्नुते ।

By the Ignorance they cross beyond Death and by the
Knowledge enjoy Immortality.... By the Non-Birth they cross
beyond Death and by the Birth enjoy Immortality.
                                                Verses 11,14. (*p. 33*)

हिरण्मयेन पात्रेण सत्यस्यापिहितं मुखम् ।
तत् त्वं पूषन्नपावृणु सत्यधर्माय दृष्टये ॥
पूषन्नेकर्षे... व्यूह रश्मीन्समूह ।
...यत्ते रूपं कल्याणतमं तत्ते पश्यामि
योऽसावसौ पुरुषः सोऽहमस्मि ॥

The face of Truth is hidden by a golden lid; that remove, O Fostering Sun, for the Law of the Truth, for sight. O Sun, O sole Seer, marshal thy rays, gather them together, — let me see of thee thy happiest form of all; that Conscious Being everywhere, He am I.

Verses 15,16. (p. 271)

सोऽहमस्मि ।

He am I.

Verse 16. (p. 365)

Katha Upanishad

अर्यं लोको नास्ति पर इति मानी...॥

One who thinks there is this world and no other...

I.2.6. (p. 553)

...बुद्धेरात्मा महान्परः ॥
महतः परमव्यक्तमव्यक्तात्पुरुषः परः ।
पुरुषान्न परं किञ्चित् सा काष्ठा सा परा गतिः ॥

High beyond the Intelligence is the Great Self, beyond the Great Self is the Unmanifest, beyond the Unmanifest is the Conscious Being. There is nothing beyond the Being, — that is the extreme ultimate, that the supreme goal.

I.3.10,11. (p. 295)

एष सर्वेषु भूतेषु गूढोत्मा न प्रकाशते ।
दृश्यते त्वग्र्यया बुद्ध्या सूक्ष्मया सूक्ष्मदर्शिभिः ॥

This secret Self in all beings is not apparent, but it is seen by means of the supreme reason, the subtle, by those who have the subtle vision. I.3.12. (*p. 60*)

परांञ्चि खानि व्यतृणत्स्वयंभूस्तस्मात्पराङ् पश्यति नान्तरात्मन् ।
कश्चिद्धीरः प्रत्यगात्मानमैक्षदावृत्तचक्षुरमृतत्वमिच्छन् ॥

The Self-Existent has pierced the doors of sense outward, therefore one sees things outwardly and sees not in one's inner being. Rarely a sage desiring immortality, his sight turned inward, sees the Self face to face. II.1.1. (*p. 524*)

य इमं मध्वदं वेद आत्मानं जीवमन्तिकात् ।
ईशानं भूतभव्यस्य न ततो विजुगुप्सते . . . ॥

He who knows this Self who is the eater of the honey of existence and the lord of what is and shall be, has thenceforward no shrinking. II.1.5. (*p. 218*)

अङ्गुष्ठमात्रः पुरुषः . . . . ।

The Purusha, the inner Self, no larger than the size of a man's thumb. II.1.12,13. (*p. 218*)

अङ्गुष्ठमात्रः पुरुषो मध्य आत्मनि तिष्ठति ।
ईशानो भूतभव्यस्य . . . स एवाद्य स उ श्वः . . . ॥

A conscious being, no larger than a man's thumb, stands in the centre of our self; he is master of the past and the present ... he is today and he is tomorrow. II.1.12,13. (*p. 553*)

पुरुषो मध्य आत्मनि तिष्ठति । ईशानो भूतभव्यस्य . . . ॥
. . . ज्योतिरिवाधूमकः ॥ . . .

A conscious being is in the centre of the self, who rules past and future; he is like a fire without smoke.
II.1.12,13. (*p. 889*)

हृꣳसः शुचिषत् . . . ऋतजाः . . . ऋतं बृहत् ॥

The Swan that settles in the purity ... born of the Truth, — itself the Truth, the Vast.

II.2.2. (*p. 889*)

य एष सुप्तेषु जागर्ति ... ।

This is he that is awake in those who sleep.

II.2.8. (*p. 80*)

एको वशी सर्वभूतान्तरात्मा ।
सूर्यो यथा सर्वलोकस्य चक्षुर्न लिप्यते ...

One controlling inner Self of all beings.... As the Sun, the eye of the world, is not touched by the external faults of vision, so this inner Self in beings is not touched by the sorrow of the world.

II.2.12,11. (*p. 388*)

एकं रूपं बहुधा यः करोति ।

He fashions one form of things in many ways.

II.2.12. (*p. 824*)

ऊर्ध्वमूलोऽवाक्शाख एषोऽश्वत्थः सनातनः ।
तदेव शुक्रं तद्ब्रह्म तदेवामृतमुच्यते ।
तस्मिँल्लोकाः श्रिताः सर्वे तदु नात्येति कश्चन । एतद्वै तत् ॥

This is the eternal Tree with its root above and its branches downward; this is Brahman, this is the Immortal; in it are lodged all the worlds and none goes beyond it. This and That are one.

II.3.1. (*p. 765*)

अङ्गुष्ठमात्रः पुरुषोऽन्तरात्मा ... ।

The Purusha, the inner Self, no larger than the size of a man's thumb.

II.3.17. (*p. 218*)

तं स्वाच्छरीरात् प्रबृहेत् ... धैर्येण ॥

That, one must disengage with patience from one's own body.

II.3.17. (*p. 889*)

Kena Upanishad

न वाग्गच्छति नो मनः ।

Mind attains not there, nor speech. I.3. *(p. 12)*

अन्यदेव तद्विदितादथो अविदितादधि ।

Other is That than the known; also it is above the Unknown. I.3. *(p. 13)*

तदेव ब्रह्म त्वं विद्धि नेदं यदिदमुपासते ॥

Know That for the Brahman and not this which men cherish here. I.4. *(p. 388)*

तद्ध तद्वनं नाम तद्वनमित्युपासितव्यम् ... ।

The name of That is the Delight; as the Delight we must worship and seek after It. IV.6. *(p. 100)*

Mandukya Upanishad

सोऽयमात्मा चतुष्पात् । जागरितस्थानो बहिःप्रज्ञः ... स्थूलभुक् ... प्रथमः
पादः । स्वप्नस्थानोऽन्तःप्रज्ञः ... प्रविविक्तभुक् ... द्वितीयः पादः । ... सुषुप्त-
स्थान एकीभूतः प्रज्ञानघन एवानन्दमयो ह्यानन्दभुक् ... तृतीयः पादः । एष
सर्वेश्वर एष सर्वज्ञ एषोऽन्तर्यामी ... । अदृष्टम् ... अलक्षणम् ... एकात्म-
प्रत्ययसारम् ... चतुर्थम् ... स आत्मा स विज्ञेयः ॥

This Self is fourfold, — the Self of Waking who has the outer intelligence and enjoys external things, is its first part; the Self of Dream who has the inner intelligence and enjoys things subtle, is its second part; the Self of Sleep, unified, a massed intelligence, blissful and enjoying bliss, is the third part ... the lord of all, the omniscient, the inner Control. That which is unseen, indefinable, self-evident in its one selfhood, is the fourth part:

this is the Self, this is that which has to be known.

Verses 2-7. (p. 553)

सर्वं ह्येतद् ब्रह्मायमात्मा ब्रह्म सोऽयमात्मा चतुष्पात् ॥ अव्यवहार्यम् ...
अलक्षणमचिन्त्यम् ... प्रपञ्चोपशमम् ॥

All this is the Brahman; this Self is the Brahman and the
Self is fourfold. Beyond relation, featureless, unthinkable, in
which all is still.

Verses 2,7. (p. 17)

सुषुप्तस्थान एकीभूतः प्रज्ञानघन एवानन्दमयो ह्यानन्दभुक् ... एष सर्वेश्वर
एष सर्वज्ञ एषोऽन्तर्याम्येष योनिः सर्वस्य ।

One seated in the sleep of Superconscience, a massed Intelligence, blissful and the enjoyer of Bliss.... This is the omnipotent, this is the omniscient, this is the inner control, this is the
source of all.

Verses 5,6. (p. 132)

अदृष्टमव्यवहार्यमग्राह्यमलक्षणमचिन्त्यमव्यपदेश्यमेकात्मप्रत्ययसारं प्रपञ्चोपशमं
शान्तं शिवम् ... स आत्मा स विज्ञेयः ॥

The Unseen with whom there can be no pragmatic relations,
unseizable, featureless, unthinkable, undesignable by name,
whose substance is the certitude of One Self, in whom world-
existence is stilled, who is all peace and bliss — that is the Self,
that is what must be known.

Verse 7. (p. 295)

Mahopanishad

अज्ञानभूः सप्तपदा ज्ञभूः सप्तपदैव हि ॥

Seven steps has the ground of the Ignorance, seven steps
has the ground of the Knowledge.

V.1. (p. 726)

स्वरूपावस्थितिर्मुक्तिस्तद्भ्रंशोऽहन्त्ववेदनम् ॥

To dwell in our true being is liberation; the sense of ego is a fall from the truth of our being.   V.2. (*p. 511*)

Maitrayani Upanishad

द्वे वाव ब्रह्मणो रूपे कालश्चाकालश्च ।

Two are the forms of Brahman, Time and the Timeless.

VI.15. (*p. 501*)

अमन्यतान्यतात्मानो वे ते ... तदिमे मूढा उपजीवन्त्यभिष्वङ्गणस्तयार्याभि-
घातिनोऽनृताभिशंसिनः सत्यमिवानृतं पश्यन्ति ।

They live according to another idea of self than the reality, deluded, attached, expressing a falsehood, — as if by an enchantment they see the false as the true.

VII.10. (*p. 596*)

Mundaka Upanishad

तपसा चीयते ब्रह्म ततोऽन्नमभिजायते ।
अन्नात्प्राणो मनः सत्यं लोकाः कर्मसु चामृतम् ॥

By energism of consciousness[1] Brahman is massed; from that Matter is born and from Matter Life and Mind and the worlds.   I.1.8. (*p. 566*)

अविद्यायामन्तरे वर्तमानाः ...
जङ्घन्यमानाः परियन्ति मूढा अन्धेनैव नीयमाना यथान्धाः ॥

They live and move in the Ignorance and go round and round, battered and stumbling, like blind men led by one who is blind.   I.2.8. (*p. 596*)

[1] Tapas.

पद्भ्यां पृथिवी ।

Earth is His footing. II.1.4. (*p. 11*)

सप्त इमे लोका येषु चरन्ति प्राणा गुहाशया निहिताः सप्त सप्त ॥

Seven are these worlds in which move the life-forces that are hidden within the secret heart as their dwelling-place seven by seven. II.1.8. (*p. 765*)

सत्येन लभ्यस्तपसा ह्येष आत्मा सम्यग्ज्ञानेन... ।

This Self is to be won by the Truth and by an integral knowledge. III.1.5. (*p. 633*)

एतैरुपायैर्यंतते यस्तु विद्वांस्तस्यैष आत्मा विशते ब्रह्मधाम ॥
... ज्ञानतृप्ताः कृतात्मानः... ।
ते सर्वगं सर्वतः प्राप्य धीरा युक्तात्मानः सर्वमेवाविशन्ति ॥

He strives by these means and has the knowledge: in him this spirit enters into its supreme status.... Satisfied in knowledge, having built up their spiritual being, the Wise, in union with the spiritual self, reach the Omnipresent everywhere and enter into the All. III.2.4,5. (*p. 848*)

वेदान्तविज्ञानसुनिश्चितार्थाः... शुद्धसत्वाः ।

Made certain of the meaning of the highest spiritual knowledge, purified in their being. III.2.6. (*p. 848*)

Prashna Upanishad

अत्रैष देवः स्वप्ने... प्रत्यनुभूतं पुनः पुनः प्रत्यनुभवति दृष्टं चादृष्टं च श्रुतं चाश्रुतं चानुभूतं चाननुभूतं च सच्चासच्च सर्वं पश्यति, सर्वः पश्यति ॥

Here this God, the Mind, in its dream experiences again and

again what once was experienced, what has been seen and what
has not been seen, what has been heard and what has not been
heard; what has been experienced and what has not been experienced, what is and what is not, all it sees, it is all and sees.

IV.5. (*p. 511*)

... दृष्टं चादृष्टं च ... अनुभूतं चाननुभूतं च सच्चासच्च सर्वं पश्यति सर्वः
पश्यति ॥

What is seen and what is not seen, what is experienced and
what is not experienced, what is and what is not, — all it sees,
it is all and sees. IV.5. (*p. 412*)

एष हि द्रष्टा, स्प्रष्टा, श्रोता, घ्राता, रसयिता, मन्ता, बोद्धा, कर्ता,
विज्ञानात्मा पुरुषः ।

This is he who is that which sees, touches, hears, smells,
tastes, thinks, understands, acts in us, a conscious being, a self
of knowledge. IV.9. (*p. 501*)

Shwetashwatara Upanishad

ते ध्यानयोगानुगता अपश्यन् देवात्मशक्ति स्वगुणैर्निगूढाम् ।

They beheld the self-force of the Divine Being deep hidden
by its own conscious modes of working. I.3. (*p. 80*)

सर्वाजीवे सर्वसंस्थे बृहन्ते अस्मिन् हंसो भ्राम्यते ब्रह्मचक्रे ।
पृथगात्मानं प्रेरितारं च मत्वा जुष्टस्ततस्तेनामृतत्वमेति ॥

The Soul of man, a traveller, wanders in this cycle of
Brahman, huge, a totality of lives, a totality of states, thinking
itself different from the Impeller of the journey. Accepted by
Him, it attains its goal of Immortality. I.6. (*p. 42*)

ज्ञाज्ञौ द्वावजावीशनीशावजा ह्येका भोक्तृभोग्यार्थयुक्ता ।

Two Unborn, the Knower and one who knows not, the Lord
and one who has not mastery: one Unborn and in her are the
object of enjoyment and the enjoyer.   I.9. (*p. 482*)

अङ्गुष्ठमात्रः पुरुषोऽन्तरात्मा . . . ।

The Purusha, the inner Self, no larger than the size of a
man's thumb.   III.13. (*p. 218*)

पुरुष एवेद॰ सर्वं यद् भूतं यच्च भव्यम् ।
उतामृतत्वस्येशानो यदन्नेनातिरोहति ॥

The Purusha is all this that is, what has been and what is
yet to be; he is the master of Immortality and he is whatever
grows by food.   III.15. (*p. 439*)

त्वं स्त्री त्वं पुमानसि त्वं कुमार उत वा कुमारी ।
त्वं जीर्णो दण्डेन वञ्चसि . . . ॥
नीलः पतङ्गो हरितो लोहिताक्षः . . . ॥

Thou art man and woman, boy and girl; old and worn thou
walkest bent over a staff; thou art the blue bird and the green
and the scarlet-eyed. . . .   IV.3,4. (*p. 683*)

समाने वृक्षे पुरुषो निमग्नोऽनीशया शोचति मुह्यमानः ।
जुष्टं यदा पश्यत्यन्यमीशमस्य महिमानमिति वीतशोकः ॥

The soul seated on the same tree of Nature is absorbed and
deluded and has sorrow because it is not the Lord, but when it
sees and is in union with that other self and greatness of it which
is the Lord, then sorrow passes away from it.   IV.7. (*p. 51*)

अस्मान्मायी सृजते विश्वमेतत् तस्मिंश्चान्यो मायया संनिरुद्धः ॥
मायां तु प्रकृतिं विद्यान्मायिनं तु महेश्वरम् . . . ।

The Master of Maya creates this world by his Maya and
within it is confined another; one should know his Maya as
Nature and the Master of Maya as the great Lord of all.
                                                  IV.9,10. (*p. 439*)

मायां तु प्रकृतिं विद्यान्मायिनं तु महेश्वरम् ॥

One must know Maya as Prakriti and the Master of Maya
as the great Lord of all. IV.10. (*p. 322*)

तस्यावयवभूतैस्तु व्याप्तं सर्वमिदं जगत् ॥

This whole world is filled with beings who are His members.
IV.10. (*p. 683*)

द्वे अक्षरे ब्रह्मपरे त्वनन्ते विद्याविद्ये निहिते यत्र गूढे ।
क्षरं त्वविद्या ह्यमृतं तु विद्या विद्याविद्ये ईशते यस्तु सोऽन्यः ॥

Two are there, hidden in the secrecy of the Infinite, the
Knowledge and the Ignorance; but perishable is the Ignorance,
immortal is the Knowledge; another than they is He who rules
over both the Knowledge and the Ignorance. V.1. (*p. 482*)

एकैकं जालं बहुधा विकुर्वन्नस्मिन्क्षेत्रे संचरत्येष देवः. . . ॥
योनिस्वभावानधितिष्ठत्येकः ॥
यच्च स्वभावं पचति विश्वयोनिः पाच्यांश्च सर्वान्परिणामयेद्यः ।
. . . गुणांश्च सर्वान्विनियोजयेद्यः ॥

The Godhead moves in this Field modifying each web of
things separately in many ways.... One, he presides over all
wombs and natures; himself the womb of all, he is that which
brings to ripeness the nature of the being and he gives to all who
have to be matured their result of development and appoints
all qualities to their workings. V.3-5. (*p. 824*)

बुद्धेर्गुणेनात्मगुणेन चैव . . . दृष्टः ॥
बालाग्रशतभागस्य शतधा कल्पितस्य च ।
भागो जीवः स विज्ञेयः स चानन्त्याय कल्पते ॥
नैव स्त्री न पुमानेष न चैवायं नपुंसकः ।
यच्छरीरमादत्ते तेन तेन स युज्यते ॥

Equipped with qualities, a doer of works and creator of their
consequences, he reaps the result of his actions; he is the ruler

of the life and he moves in his journey according to his own acts; he has idea and ego and is to be known by the qualities of his intelligence and his quality of self. Smaller than the hundredth part of the tip of a hair, the soul of the living being is capable of infinity. Male is he not nor female nor neuter, but is joined to whatever body he takes as his own.　　　　V.7-10. (*p. 792*)

... आत्मविवृद्धिजन्म ।
कर्मानुगान्यनुक्रमेण देही स्थानेषु रूपाण्यभिसंप्रपद्यते ॥
स्थूलानि सूक्ष्माणि बहूनि चैव रूपाणि देही स्वगुणैर्वृणोति ॥

There is a birth and growth of the self. According to his actions the embodied being assumes forms successively in many places; many forms gross and subtle he assumes by force of his own qualities of nature.　　　　V.11,12. (*p. 742*)

स्वभावमेके ... वदन्ति कालं तथान्ये ।

Some speak of the self-nature of things, others say that it is Time.　　　　VI.1. (*p. 501*)

देवस्यैष महिमा तु लोके येनेदं भ्राम्यते ब्रह्मचक्रम् ॥
तमीश्वराणां परमं महेश्वरं तं देवतानां परमं च दैवतम् ।
... विदाम देवं भुवनेशमीड्यम् ॥
... परास्य शक्तिर्विविधैव श्रूयते स्वाभाविकी ज्ञानबलक्रिया च ॥
एको देवः सर्वभूतेषु गूढः सर्वव्यापी सर्वभूतान्तरात्मा ।
कर्माध्यक्षः सर्वभूताधिवासः साक्षी चेता केवलो निर्गुणश्च ॥

It is the might of the Godhead in the world that turns the wheel of Brahman. Him one must know, the supreme Lord of all lords, the supreme Godhead above all godheads. Supreme too is his Shakti and manifold the natural working of her knowledge and her force. One Godhead, occult in all beings, the inner Self of all beings, the all-pervading, absolute without qualities, the overseer of all actions, the witness, the knower.

VI.1,7,8,11. (*p. 322*)

एको देवः सर्वभूतेषु गूढः सर्वव्यापी सर्वभूतान्तरात्मा ।
कर्माध्यक्षः... साक्षी चेता केवलः... ॥
एको वशी निष्क्रियाणां बहूनामेकं बीजं बहुधा यः करोति ॥

The one Godhead secret in all beings, all-pervading, the
inner Self of all, presiding over all action, witness, conscious
knower and absolute... the One in control over the many who
are passive to Nature, fashions one seed in many ways.

VI.11,12. (*p. 824*)

Taittiriya Upanishad

सत्यं ज्ञानमनन्तं ब्रह्म ।

Brahman, the Truth, the Knowledge, the Infinite.

II.1. (*p. 322*)

सत्यं ज्ञानमनन्तं ब्रह्म । यो वेद... सोऽश्नुते सर्वान् कामान् सह ब्रह्मणा
विपश्चिता ॥

He who knows the Truth, the Knowledge, the Infinity that
is Brahman shall enjoy with the all-wise Brahman all objects of
desire.

II.1. (*p. 207*)

स वा एष पुरुषोऽन्नरसमयः ।... तस्माद्वा एतस्मादन्नरसमयात् । अन्योऽन्तर
आत्मा प्राणमयः । तेनैष पूर्णः ।... अन्योऽन्तर आत्मा मनोमयः ।... अन्योऽन्तर
आत्मा विज्ञानमयः ।... अन्योऽन्तर आत्मानन्दमयः । तेनैष पूर्णः ॥

There is a self that is of the essence of Matter — there is
another inner self of Life that fills the other — there is another
inner self of Mind — there is another inner self of Truth-Know-
ledge — there is another inner self of Bliss.

II.1-5. (*p. 252*)

प्राणो हि भूतानामायुः । तस्मात्सर्वायुषमुच्यते ॥

Pranic energy is the life of creatures; for that is said to be
the universal principal of life.

II.3. (*p. 173*)

तस्मात्सर्वायुषमुच्यत इति ।

This it is that is called the universal life. II.3. (*p. 207*)

असन्नेव स भवति । असद्ब्रह्मेति वेद चेत् । अस्ति ब्रह्मेति चेद्वेद ।
सन्तमेनं ततो विदुः ॥

If one knows Him as Brahman the Non-Being, he becomes
merely the non-existent. If one knows that Brahman Is, then
is he known as the real in existence. II.6. (*p. 25*)

सोऽकामयत । बहु स्यां प्रजायेयेति । स तपोऽतप्यत । स तपस्तप्त्वा
इदꣳ सर्वमसृजत यदिदं किञ्च । तत्सृष्ट्वा तदेवानुप्राविशत् । तदनुप्रविश्य
सच्च त्यच्चाभवत् । निरुक्तं चानिरुक्तं च । निलयनं चानिलयनं च । विज्ञानं
चाविज्ञानं च । सत्यं चानृतञ्च सत्यमभवत् । यदिदं किञ्च । तत्सत्यमित्या-
चक्षते ॥

He desired, "May I be Many", he concentrated in Tapas,
by Tapas he created the world; creating, he entered into it;
entering, he became the existent and the beyond-existence, he
became the expressed and the unexpressed, he became knowledge and ignorance, he became the truth and the falsehood:
he became the truth, even all this whatsoever that is. "That
Truth" they call him. II.6. (*p. 566*)

अभवत् ... सत्यं चानृतं च सत्यमभवत् । यदिदं किञ्च ॥

It became both truth and falsehood. It became the Truth,
even all this that is. II.6. (*p. 271*)

असद्वा इदमग्र आसीत् । ततो वै सदजायत ॥

In the beginning all this was the Non-Being. It was thence
that Being was born. II.7. (*p. 27*)

को ह्येवान्यात्कः प्राण्यात् यदेष आकाश आनन्दो न स्यात् ।

For who could live or breathe if there were not this delight of existence as the ether in which we dwell?   II.7. (*p. 91*)

आनन्दं ब्रह्मणो विद्वान् न बिभेति कुतश्चन ।

He who has found the bliss of the Eternal has no fear from any quarter.   II.9. (*p. 218*)

आनन्दं ब्रह्मणो विद्वान् ... एत ह॒ वाव न तपति किमह॒ साधु नाकरवम् । किमहं पापमकरवमिति । स य एवं विद्वान् ... उभे ह्येवैष एते आत्मान॒ स्पृणुते ॥

He who has found the bliss of the Eternal is afflicted no more by the thought, "Why have I not done the good? Why have I done evil?" One who knows the self extricates himself from both these things.   II.9. (*p. 596*)

स तपोऽतप्यत । स तपस्तप्त्वा ॥ अन्नं ब्रह्मेति व्यजानात् । अन्नाद्ध्येव खल्विमानि भूतानि जायन्ते । अन्नेन जातानि जीवन्ति । अन्नं प्रयन्त्यभिसं-विशन्तीति । तद्विज्ञाय । पुनरेव वरुणं पितरमुपससार । अधीहि भगवो ब्रह्मेति । त॒ होवाच । तपसा ब्रह्म विजिज्ञासस्व । तपो ब्रह्मेति ॥ ...

He energised conscious-force (in the austerity of thought) and came to the knowledge that Matter is the Brahman. For from Matter all existences are born; born, by Matter they increase and enter into Matter in their passing hence. Then he went to Varuna, his father, and said, "Lord, teach me of the Brahman." But he said to him: "Energise (again) the conscious-energy in thee; for the Energy is Brahman."   III.1,2. (*p. 6.*)

अन्नं ब्रह्मेति व्यजानात् ।

He arrived at the knowledge that Matter is Brahman.

III.2. (*p. 231*)

तपो ब्रह्मेति ॥

Energism of consciousness[1] is Brahman.   III.2-5. (*p. 566*)

---

[1] Tapas.

मनो ब्रह्मेति व्यजानात् ।

He discovered that Mind was the Brahman.   III.4. (*p. 159*)

आनन्दाद्धयेव खल्विमानि भूतानि जायन्ते ।   आनन्देन जातानि जीवन्ति ।
आनन्दं प्रयन्त्यभिसंविशन्तीति ॥

From Delight all these beings are born, by Delight they exist
and grow, to Delight they return.   III.6. (*p. 91*)

अस्माल्लोकात्प्रेत्य एतमन्नमयमात्मानमुपसंक्रम्य;   एतं प्राणमयमात्मानमुप-
संक्रम्य;   एतं   मनोमयमात्मानमुपसंक्रम्य;   एतं   विज्ञानमयमात्मानमुपसंक्रम्य;
एतमानन्दमयमात्मानमुपसंक्रम्य;   इमाँल्लोकान्कामान्नी कामरूप्यनुसञ्चरन् ॥

He passes in his departure from this world to the physical
Self; he passes to the Self of life; he passes to the Self of mind;
he passes to the Self of knowledge; he passes to the Self of bliss;
he moves through these worlds at will.

III.10. (*p. 792*)

Peace Recitations

(Sanskrit texts preceding six Upanishads translated by Sri Aurobindo in Baroda)

Isha Upanishad

ॐ पूर्णमदः पूर्णमिदं पूर्णात्पूर्णमुदच्यते ।
पूर्णस्य पूर्णमादाय पूर्णमेवावशिष्यते ॥
ॐ शान्तिः शान्तिः शान्तिः ॥

OM. Complete in itself is that yonder and complete in itself is that which is here and the complete ariseth from the complete: but when thou takest the complete from its fullness, that which remaineth is also complete. OM. Peace! Peace! Peace!

*

Kena Upanishad

ॐ आप्यायन्तु ममाङ्गानि वाक्प्राणश्चक्षुः श्रोत्रमथो बलमिन्द्रियाणि च
सर्वाणि सर्वं ब्रह्मोपनिषदं माहं ब्रह्म निराकुर्यां मा मा ब्रह्म निराकरोदनिरा-
करणमस्त्वनिराकरणं मेऽस्तु तदात्मनि निरते य उपनिषत्सु धर्मास्ते मयि सन्तु
ते मयि सन्तु ॥
ॐ शान्तिः शान्तिः शान्तिः ॥

OM. May my members increase unto me, speech and breath and vision and hearing and the strength of me and all my organs. All is the Eternal of the Upanishad: May I never reject the Eternal; me may He never reject; let rejection be far from me, let rejection be far. Then when I have found the delight of the Self as my possession, may it be my possession. May the law that is declared in the Upanishad be in me. OM. Peace! Peace! Peace!

*

Katha Upanishad

ॐ सह नाववतु। सह नौ भुनक्तु। सह वीर्यं करवावहै। तेजस्वि
नावधीतमस्तु। मा विद्विषावहै॥
ॐ शान्तिः शान्तिः शान्तिः॥

OM. Together may He protect us: together may He pos-
sess us: together may we make unto us strength and virility!
May what we have studied be full to us of light and power!
May we never hate! OM. Peace! Peace! Peace!

*

Mundaka, Prashna and Mandukya Upanishads

ॐ भद्रं कर्णेभिः शृणुयाम देवा
भद्रं पश्येमाक्षभिर्यजत्राः।
स्थिरैरङ्गैस्तुष्टुवाꣳसस्तनूभि-
र्व्यशेम देवहितं यदायुः॥
स्वस्ति न इन्द्रो वृद्धश्रवाः
स्वस्ति नः पूषा विश्ववेदाः।
स्वस्ति नस्ताक्ष्र्यो अरिष्टनेमिः
स्वस्ति नो बृहस्पतिर्दधातु॥
ॐ शान्तिः शान्तिः शान्तिः॥

OM. May we hear what is auspicious with our ears, O ye
Gods: May we see what is auspicious with our eyes, O ye of the
sacrifice: giving praise with steady limbs, with motionless bodies,
may we enter into that life which is founded in the Gods.

Ordain weal unto us Indra of high-heaped glories: ordain
weal unto us Pushan, the all-knowing Sun: ordain weal unto us
Tarkshya Arishtanemi: Brihaspati ordain weal unto us. OM.
Peace! Peace! Peace!

GLOSSARY AND INDEX

GLOSSARY OF SANSKRIT TERMS

Most Sanskrit words and phrases occurring in this book are defined below. Exceptions are most words used in translations or in word by word analyses (as in the commentary on the Nilarudra Upanishad). Words used as philological examples and most names of personages etc. are also excluded. As far as possible the definitions have been made using Sri Aurobindo's own words. All the terms have been transliterated here according to the international system; where this transliteration differs significantly from the easier transliteration sometimes used by Sri Aurobindo, the easier spelling is given within marks of parenthesis and a cross-reference is provided.

acalaḥ sanātanaḥ — motionless, sempiternal.

adhibhūta — the elemental; the objective phenomenon of being.

adhidaiva — that which pertains to the Gods (non-material powers); the subjective phenomenon of being.

adhyātma — the spiritual, everything that has to do with the highest existence in us (*ātman*).

advaita(m) — non-duality, unity.

āgāta kāmānām — a chanter unto fulfilment of the desires (of men).

agni — Fire; the divine force.

agni vaiśvānara — Agni as the universal in Man or universal Power.

ahaṁkāra — ego-sense.

ājñāna — Knowledge-Will; the operation by which the consciousness dwells on an image of things so as to govern and possess it in power.

ajñeyam atarkyam — unknowable and that which logic cannot reach.

akṛta — not constructed or put together.

akṣara — unmoving, unshifting, immutable; syllable.

akṣara puruṣa (Akshara Purusha) — the Self standing back from the changes and movements of Nature.

akṣitaṁ śravaḥ — inexhaustible store of memory.

amṛtam — Immortality.

amṛtasya putrāḥ — sons of Immortality.

ānanda — bliss, beatitude, self-delight.

ānandamaya puruṣa — Bliss-Self, the all-blissful being or all-enjoying and all-productive Soul.

anilam amṛtam — immortal Breath.

aniś — not lord, subject.

anna(m) — food; gross visible matter.

annakoṣa — the material or food sheath.

annamayaṁ jagat — gross material world.

annamaya puruṣa — material being.

antarikṣam — the mid-region, intermediate or connecting level of the vital or nervous consciousness.

anu ajāyata — was born.

anyadeva — other verily.

āpaḥ — waters.

apamāna — disgrace.

apāna — one of the five *prāṇas*, situated in the lower part of the trunk; it presides over the lower functions and is the breath of death, for it gives away the vital force out of the body.

aparā prakṛti — the lower Nature.

aparārdha — the lower half of universal existence.

apas — waters.

arthān — objects.

arvan — (war-)horse.

aśanāyā mṛtyuḥ — hunger that is death.

āsanya — breath of the mouth.

Ashwa (etc.) — see *aśva*.

aśivam — evil.

aśnute saha brahmaṇā — enjoyeth ... along with the *brahman*.

asuryāḥ — titanic or undivine.

asūryāḥ — sunless.

aśva (Ashwa) — Horse, a figure of the *prāṇa*, the dynamic force of Life.

aśvamedha — the Horse-Sacrifice.

aśvattha — fig-tree (symbolises the cosmic manifestation).

ātman — 1. Self, Spirit, immutable existence; 2. substance, body.

ātmavān — in possession of Self.

AUM — the sacred syllable OM (which see), with its three constituent letters shown separately.

avatāra — Incarnation, the Divine manifest in a human appearance.

avedit — one comes to (that) knowledge.

avidyā — the Ignorance, the consciousness of Multiplicity.

avidyāyām antare vartamānāḥ — living and moving within the Ignorance; in *avidyā* and enclosed within it.

avyākṛta prakṛti — undifferentiated Nature.

avyakta — the Unmanifest.

avyavahāryam — without relations.

bandhu — kin, friend.

bhakti — devotion.

bhāva — becoming.

bhūmā — the Large.

bhūr — the material world.

bhūrloka — the material world, the world of formal becoming.

bhūtāni abhūt — became the Becomings.

bhūtāni ... ātmānam — existences ... the Self (reference to Isha Upanishad 6, translated thus: but he who sees everywhere the Self in all existences and all existences in the Self ...).

bhuvana(m) — becoming, world.

bhuvar — world of various becoming (the intermediate dynamic, vital or nervous consciousness).

bhuvarloka — world of free vital becoming in form.

brahmā — the creative deity; the Power of the Divine which creates the worlds by the Word.

brahmacārin — a student practising celibacy.

Brahmā devānāṁ prathamaḥ sambabhūva — Brahmā first of the Gods was born.

brahmaloka — world of the *brahman*.

brahman — the Reality, the Eternal, the Absolute.

brāhmaṇas — that portion of the Veda which contains rules for the employment of hymns, old legends, etc., in prose.

brahmaṇā vipaścitā — with the wise-thinking *brahman*.

brahmaṇo rūpam — the form of the *brahman*.

brahmavid āpnoti — the knower of *brahman* reacheth.

brahmavid āpurti param — the knower of *brahman* reacheth the highest.

brahmavidyā — the knowledge of the *brahman*.

bṛhat — the Large.

caitanya — consciousness.

caitanya puruṣa — conscious being; the all-conscious Soul.

cakras — ganglionic centres in the nervous system, subtle centres.

cakravartī rājā — universal sovereign.

Chaitanya, etc. — see *caitanya* etc.

Chakras — see *cakras*.

Chit etc. — see *cit* etc.

cit — consciousness; the free and all-creative self-awareness of the Absolute.

cit-śakti — consciousness-force, the divine Energy.

cit-tapas — pure energy of Consciousness.

darśanas — the (six) systems of orthodox Indian philosophy.

dāsī — a female slave or servant, especially one attached to a permanent household.

deva — god.

devātmaśaktiṁ svaguṇair nigūḍhām — the self-power of the divine Existent hidden by its own modes.

dharma — law of being, rule or law of action; the collective Indian conception of the religious, social and moral rule and conduct.

dhīra — the strong and wise soul.

dhīrāḥ — plural of above.

dṛṣṭi — seeing.

duritāni — uneven tracts.

dvaitam — duality.

dvāpara yuga — the third of the four ages.

ebhyaḥ āgāyati kāmān — he chants their desires for them unto fulfilment.

ekatvam anupaśyataḥ — seeing everywhere oneness.

etau vai mahimānau — these two are his greatnesses.

eva — verily.

gandha — odour.

gandharvas — celestial musicians.

girām upaśrutiṁ cara, stomān abhi svara, abhi gṛṇīhi, ā ruva — respond with the *śruti* to our words, come, vibrate to (answer) our songs of praise, speak them out as they rise, cry out thy response.

gotra — family, tribe.

guhāhitam — established in our secret being.

guru — preceptor, spiritual teacher.

haya — horse.

hṛdya samudra — Ocean of the Heart.

ihaiva — here, in this mortal life and body.

Indra — a god, Master of the World of Light and Immortality, Power of divine Mind.

iś (Ish) — the Lord.

iśā vāsyam — for habitation by the Lord.

iśvara (Ishwara) — the Lord.

jagat — the perpetual movement, the world.

jagatī — the movement, the world.

jagatyāṁ jagat — universe of movement in the universal motion.

jala — water.

janaloka — world of creative Delight.

Jātavedas — the knower of all births.

jīvātman — individual self in the living creature.

jñāna — pure knowledge.

jñānakāṇḍa — the section of knowledge of the Veda, identified with the Upanishads.

jñānamārga — the path of knowledge.

jugupsā — shrinking, contraction, self-protecting recoil.

kaivalya — absolute unity.

kāla — Time in its essentiality.

kali yuga — the last of the four ages: the Age of Iron.

kalilam — chaos.

kalpa — aeon.

karma — action, work; ritual works; the principle of Action in the universe with its stream of cause and infallible effect, for man the sum of his past actions whose results reveal themselves not at once, but in the dispensation of Time, partly in this life, mostly in lives to come.

karmāṇi — works.

kārikā — a concise statement of doctrine in verse.

kavi — seer.

kavir manīṣī paribhūḥ svayambhūḥ — the Seer, the Thinker, the One who becomes everywhere, the Self-existent.

kena — by whom or what.

keneṣitaṁ . . . manas — by whom . . . the mind. (Kena Upanishad 1.1).

kiṁnara — being of superhuman beauty, unearthly sweetness of voice and wild freedom.

ko devaḥ — what Godhead?

kratu — mental will.

kṣara — moving or mutable.

kṣara puruṣa — the Self reflecting the changes and movements of Nature.

kṣatriya — a member of the second of the four social orders, the warrior and leader.

kṣatratejas — the power of the *kṣatriya*.

kṣobha — disturbance.

kurvanneva — doing verily.

lilā — play.

maharloka — world of large consciousness.

mahas — "the Large"; the great world, the world of Truth.

mahat ātman — the great Soul or Vast Self.

māna — honour.

manaḥkoṣa — mental sheath.

manas — (sense-)mind.

manīṣī — the thinker.

manomaya puruṣa — the mental being.

mantra — inspired verse of the Veda; sacred syllable, name or mystic formula.

manu — the mental being in a terrestrial body.

Maruts — nervous forces of Life that become forces of thought.

Mātariśvan — "he who extends himself in the Mother or the Container"; Master of life.

māyā — signified originally in the Veda comprehensive and creative knowledge, wisdom that is from of old; afterwards taken in its second and derivative sense, cunning, magic, Illusion.

meghadhvani — the sound of thunder.

moha — delusion.

mṛtyu — death.

mukhya — chief Breath or Breath of the mouth.

mūrti — image.

na abhāvo vidyate sataḥ — that which is cannot go out of existence.

nabhas — sky, ether; heaven (the mental principle).

na karma lipyate nare — action cleaves not to a man.

na lipyate — receives not their impression.

nāma — name.

namas — obeisance.

na satyād agāḥ — you have not deviated from truth.

nirukta — etymological interpretation.

nirvāṇa — extinction (of the ego-limitations, but not of all possibility of manifestation).

nyāya — the science of logic.

oṁ — the *mantra* or expressive sound symbol of the *brahman* in its four domains from the *turīya* to the external or material plane (i.e. the outward looking, the inward or subtle, and the superconscient causal — each letter A, U, M indicating one of these three in ascending order and the whole bringing out the fourth state, *turīya*); used as an initiating syllable pronounced as a benedictory prelude and sanction.

pājasyam — footing.

para — supreme or highest.

parabrahman — the supreme Unknowable; the Divine.

paramārtha — the highest spiritual truth; essential fact.

paraṁ dhāma — a supreme plane; supreme status.

parameṣṭham — that which is superlative and highest.

parameśvara — Supreme Lord.

parā prakṛti — the higher Nature.

parapuruṣa — supreme Soul; God.

parārdha — the upper half of universal existence.

paribhū — the One who becomes everywhere, God as the formal becoming.

paricārikā — a female servant, especially one serving for hire at various houses.

pariṇāma — evolutionary change (out of the original substance or energy).

pitāmaha — grandsire.

praiti — goes forward.

Prajāpati — the father of creatures.

prajāpatis — the original progenitors.

Prājña — the Lord of Wisdom.

prajñāna — apprehending consciousness.

prakṛti — Nature.

prāṇa — 1. the life-force, vital energy; 2. the five *prāṇas*: the five workings of the life-force: *prāṇa* (see definition 3 below), *apāna, vyāna, samāna, udāna* (all of which see); 3. one of the five *prāṇas*, it moves in the upper part of the body and is preeminently the breath of life, because it brings the universal force into the physical system and gives it there to be distributed.

prāṇakoṣa — the vital or nervous sheath.

prāṇamaya puruṣa — the vital or dynamic being.

pranava — the basic syllable *oṁ* (which see), foundation of all the creative sounds of the revealed word.

prāṇāyāma — the government and control of the respiration.

prasava — (self-)production.

prati samudraṁ syandamānāḥ — flowing towards the ocean.

pratiṣṭhā — support, foundation, pedestal.

pṛthivī — the Earth-Principle.

purāṇa — one of a class of sacred writings written in an easy form of Sanskrit, composed of legends, apologues, etc.

puruṣa — the conscious Soul, the Divine Being.

puruṣottama — the supreme divine Person.

Pūṣan — the Fosterer or Increaser, a form of the sun-god.

rājarṣi — a royal *ṛṣi*.

rasa — sap, essence, the essential delight-giving quality of things.

rāye — to the felicity.

rayi — movement, matter.

ṛjuḥ panthāḥ — the straight road

ṛṣi (Rishi) — Seer.

ṛtasya panthāḥ — the path of the Truth.

Rudra — the Terrible one, the God of might and wrath.

rūpa — form.

sa, saḥ — he.

śabda — sound.

saccidānanda(m) — the Divine Being, a trinity of Existence (*sat*), Consciousness (*cit*) and Delight (*ānanda*).

sadguru — a good or true *guru* (spiritual preceptor).

sādhaka — one who practises *sādhanā*.

sādhanā — the practice by which perfection is reached.

sādharmya — becoming of one law of being and action with the Divine.

saḥ — see *sa*.

sajñāna karmamārga — the path of works inclusive of knowledge.

sākṣī — witness.

śakti (Shakti) — Energy, Force, Will; the self-existent, self-cognitive, self-effective Power of the Lord.

samabhāvena — without respect to differences.

samamānāpamānayoḥ — equal in honour and disgrace.

samam brahma — the equal *brahman*.

samam hi brahma — for the *brahman* is equal.

samāna — one of the five *prāṇas*, it regulates the interchange of the *prāṇa* and *apāna* at their meeting-place, equalises them and is the most important agent in maintaining the equilibrium of the vital forces and their functions.

samatva — equality of soul.

sambhava — birth.

sambhūti — becoming, the Birth.

saṁjñāna — the contact of consciousness with an image of things by which there is a sensible possession of it in its substance.

saṁsāra — a cyclic movement; the ordinary life of the Ignorance.

saṁvatsara — Time in its periods determined by movement in Space.

sanātanaḥ — sempiternal, without end or beginning.

sāṅkhya — the analysis, the enumeration and discriminative setting forth of the principles of our being.

santaḥ — saints.

śāntam — calm.

sa paryagāt — it is He who has moved out everywhere.

sarvāṇi bhūtāni — literally "all things that have become", all becomings.

sarvāṇi bhūtāni ātmaiva abhūt — the Self-Being became all Becomings.

sarvāṇi vijñāna-vijṛmbhitāni — all things are self-deployings of the Divine Knowledge.

śāśvatībhyaḥ samābhyaḥ — from years sempiternal.

sat — pure existence.

sat puruṣa — the pure divine Self.

satyadharma — the Law of the Truth.

satyaloka — world of true existence.

satyam — truth of existence.

satyam ṛtam — Truth and Law.

satyam ṛtam bṛhat — the True, the Right, the Vast.

satya yuga — the first of the four ages: the Age of Truth.

Savitṛ — the Creator or Manifester.

Shakti — *see śakti*.

siddha — the perfect man.

śivam — good.

śleṣa — embrace; the rhetorical device of *double entendre*.

śloka — a type of Sanskrit metre; a verse.

smṛti — traditional or man-made law or scripture.

so'ham — He am I.

so'ham asmi — He am I.

śraddhā — faith.

sṛṣṭi — creation, projection into form.

śruti — spiritual audience; an inspired Scripture.

Sūrya — the Sun-God, represents the divine Illumination.

sūryadvāreṇa — the Sun as a door or gate.

suvar = svar.

svar (swar) — the luminous heaven, the world of the Sun or the Truth.

svarga (Swarga) — paradise, Brahman-world.

svargaloka (Swargaloka) — heavenly world.

svarloka — the world of free, pure and luminous mentality.

svayambhū — the Self-becoming.

tad vanam — "that Delight".

taijāsa — the Inhabitant in Lumious Mind, the Self that supports the Dream-State.

Talavakāra — another name for the Kena Upanishad.

tantra — a synthetical yogic system which starts from the Nature-Soul (*prakṛti*) and pursues as aims mastery, perfection, liberation and beatitude

tapas — force or energy.

tapoloka — world of energy of self-conscience.

tat — That.

tretā — the second of the four ages.

turīya — the fourth plane of our consciousness; the Superconscient.

udāna — one of the five *prāṇas*, it moves upward from the body to the crown of the head and is a regular channel of communication between the physical life and the greater life of the Spirit.

udgayati — one sings (goes) upwards.

udgītha — the upward song (movement).

Umā — name of a goddess, represents the supreme Nature.

Umā Haimavatī — *Umā* daughter of the snowy summits.

upaniṣad — the secret teaching that enters into the ultimate truth.

uṣas — Dawn.

uttama — supreme or highest.

uttama puruṣa — the supreme Being, the Lord.

vāgevāsya vāk — speech verily is the voice of him.

vāhana — vehicle.

vaiśeṣika — a system of philosophy whose characteristic doctrine is the eternally distinct nature of nine substances (air, fire, water, earth, mind, ether, time, space and soul), of which the first five, mind included, are held to be atomic.

vaiśvānara — the Universal Male, the Self that supports the waking state.

Vājasaneyi — another name for the Isha Upanishad.

vājin — horse.

vana — Vedic word for delight or delightful.

vāsyam — to be clothed; to be worn as garment; to be inhabited.

Vāyu — the Wind-God who in the Vedic system is Master of Life.

veda — Knowledge; one of the four most ancient Indian scriptures.

vedānta — the end or culmination of the *vedas*, i.e. the *upaniṣads*; a system of philosophy based on the *upaniṣads* teaching the culminating knowledge of the Absolute.

vibhavati — manifests its power (its full power and pervading presence).

vicacakṣire — revealed that to our understanding.

viddhi — Know (imperative).

vidhema — we would dispose.

vidhūnute — shakes (himself); throws (himself) out in energy.

vidmaḥ — we know.

vidvān — the wise man.

vidyā — the Knowledge, the consciousness of Unity.

vidyutas — electricity.

vijānataḥ — of one having the perfect knowledge.

vijñāna — Causal Idea or Supramental Knowledge-Will; the original comprehensive consciousness which holds an image of things in its essence, totality and parts and properties.

vijñānamaya puruṣa — the ideal being.

vijānīmaḥ — we can distinguish.

vijṛmbhate — stretches, extends (himself) in intensity.

vināśa — the Dissolution.

virāṭ puruṣa — the cosmic Spirit.

viśiṣṭagati — a peculiar and excelling kind of motion.

vitāni pṛṣṭhāni — the wide (straight open) levels.

vivarta — subjective evolution.

vṛjināni — involved windings.

Vṛtra — the Coverer, the demon who covers and holds back the Light.

vṛtras — coverers; powers of *Vṛtra* who intercept the waters and the light.

vyākaraṇa — grammar.

vyākṛta prakṛti — manifested nature.

vyakta — the manifest.

vyāna — one of the five *prāṇas*; pervasive, it distributes the vital energies throughout the body.

vyavahāra — practical relation.

yajña — sacrifice; the spirit of adoration and sacrifice.

yājñīya puruṣa — the sacrificial person; God expressing himself in the meterial universe.

yakṣa — Spirit, Daemon; one of the keepers of wealth.

Yama — Lord of Death, also the ordainer or controller who assures the law, the Dharma.

yāthātathyataḥ — according to their nature.

ye yathā mām prapadyante tāms tathaiva bhajāmyaham. Mama vartmānuvartante manuṣyāḥ pārtha sarvaśaḥ — As men approach Me (Krishna, the Divine), so I accept them to My love; men follow in every way My path, O son of Pritha.

yuga — an age.

yukta — yoked.

INDEX

A

Absolute, the, 37, 165, 166, 184
Action, 56, 86
   and freedom, 19, 32-33, 90-91,
     92-93
   See also Works
Adhibhūta, 114
Adhidaiva, 114
Adhyātma, 114
Agni,
   the divine Will, 88
   in the Isha Upanishad, 24n, 28,
     84-85
   in the Kena Upanishad, 173-74,
     175
   in the Rig-veda, 76-77, 85, 86
   and speech, 116, 173
   Vaishwanara, 85
Ahaṁkāra, 30
Aitareya Upanishad, 90, 357
   translation, 285-94
   citations, 131, 131n
Ajatashatru, 7, 12
Ajnana (*ājñāna*), 144, 145, 146
   vaster, 150
Akshara Brahman, 72
Akshara Purusha (*akṣara puruṣa*),
   43, 44
Amṛta(m), 41, 45
   See also Immortality
Ananda, 4, 32, 41, 49, 77, 92, 92n, 181
Anandagiri, 399
Anandamaya puruṣa, 45
Annakoṣa, 143
Annam, 41n, 327n
Annamaya puruṣa, 44
Antarikṣam, 340
Apana, 115
Aparārdha, 45
Aśanāyā mṛtyuḥ, 337, 346, 347
Asat, 63
Ashwa (*aśva*), 327n, 336-37
   See also Horse

Ashwamedha, 336
asura, 345
aśva, see Ashwa
Atman (*ātmā*), 43, 46, 114
   in Brihadaranyaka Upanishad,
     338
   see also Self
AUM, 127, 216n
   See also OM
Avidya, 30, 35, 37
   and mortality, 67-68
   and Vidya, 61-69, 95
   See also Ignorance

B

Beatitude,
   active, 49
   See also Bliss
Being and Becoming, 36, 93-94, 96
Bhagavadgita, *see* Gita
Bhūmā, 45n
Bhur, 340
Bhurloka, 79, 357
Bhuvar, 340, 357
Bhuvarloka, 79
Birth, 40
   and Immortality, 68-69
   and non-birth, 70-73, 96
Bliss, 113
   See also Ananda; Beatitude;
     Delight
Bliss-consciousness, 134
Body, 40, 86
   not real self, 120
Brahmaloka, 181
   of Mundaka Upanishad, 182
Brahman, 4, 28, 34, 36-37, 38-39,
     40, 43, 46, 61-62, 72, 93, 120,
     121-22, 124, 141, 142, 162,
     165, 169, 177, 184, 185,
     245-46, 357
   active, 56

BIBLIOGRAPHICAL NOTE

Sri Aurobindo first read the Upanishads (in English translation) in London in 1892. This was just before he returned to India after having spent fourteen years in England for his education. They were "the first Indian writings that took hold of me", he later wrote, and they "raised in me a strong enthusiasm". In India, at Baroda, Sri Aurobindo mastered Sanskrit, the study of which he had begun in England, and read the Upanishads in the original. Around the turn of the century he began writing translations of and commentaries on several of them, concentrating mostly on the Isha Upanishad. Translations "into simple and rhythmic English" of "six Upanishads namely the Isha, Kena, Katha, Mundaka, Prashna and Mandukya" were completed around 1906. (The typed manuscript of these translations, four of which were subsequently revised, is referred to as "typewritten MS" in the notes below.) About the same time Sri Aurobindo translated the Taittiriya, Aitareya and Shwetashwatara Upanishads and parts of other Upanishads and Vedantic works, began an extensive commentary on the Isha Upanishad entitled "The Karmayogin", and wrote several chapters of a large expository work known as *The Philosophy of the Upanishads*. Four of Sri Aurobindo's translations, those of the Isha, Kena, Katha and Mundaka Upanishads, were first published in his weekly journal *Karmayogin* (not to be confused with the commentary mentioned above) in 1909 and 1910.

During the first four years of Sri Aurobindo's stay in Pondicherry, that is between 1910 and 1914, he devoted much time to work on the Upanishads. In particular he wrote many pages of commentary on the Isha. In 1914 he launched the monthly review *Arya*, in which new translations of the Isha, Kena and Mundaka, the first two with new commentaries, appeared. Shortly after the *Arya* ceased publication in 1921, Sri Aurobindo's new translations began to appear in books. We give below detailed information on the writing and printing history of Sri Aurobindo's translations of (and commentaries on) each Upanishad appearing in the present volume.

ISHA. First translated in Baroda (i.e. before 1906); it forms part of typewritten MS. Several incomplete commentaries were also written in Baroda. A translation (a revision of typewritten MS) was published in the first issue of *Karmayogin* in June 1909. (This translation was reproduced in *Seven Upanishads*, published by Ashtekar & Co., Poona, in 1920.) A new translation with a new commentary ("Analysis") was published in the *Arya*, starting with its first issue (August 1914), and continuing until May 1915. The same translation and commentary were published as a book by Arya Publishing House, Calcutta, in 1921. A second, slightly revised, edition was brought out in 1924 and reprinted (as the third and fourth editions) in 1941 and 1945 by the same publishers. A fifth and a sixth edition were brought out by the Sri Aurobindo Ashram in 1951 and 1965. The translation without the commentary was included in *Eight Upanishads*, first published by the Sri Aurobindo Ashram in 1953. A second impression of the first edition of *Eight Upanishads* was issued in 1960; a second edition was printed by the same publishers in 1965.

KENA. First translated in Baroda; it forms part of typewritten MS. Some pages of commentary were written in Baroda. A translation (a revision of typewritten MS) was published in the *Karmayogin* in June 1909. (This translation was included in *Seven Upanishads*, Poona, in 1920.) A new translation with commentary was published in the *Arya* between June 1915 and July 1916. This translation was issued as a separate book by Sri Aurobindo Ashram, Pondicherry, in 1952. The translation without the commentary was included in *Eight Upanishads* in 1953 and subsequently. A revision, both of the translation and of the commentary, was made by Sri Aurobindo apparently during the 1920s. Titles were given to some, but not all of the chapters. The revised translation was first published in the second edition of the Ashram's *Kena Upanishad* in 1970. The revised commentary appears for the first time in the present volume.

KATHA. First translated in Baroda; it forms part of the typewritten MS. This translation, with a few revisions, was published in the *Karmayogin* in July and August 1909. The same translation was published in *Katha Upanishad* by Ashtekar & Co., Poona, in 1919. Sri Aurobindo began an extensive revision of his translation in Pondicherry. This revision, done on the pages of the old typewritten MS, was completed only through the first cycle of the Upanishad. When the translation was issued by the Sri Aurobindo Ashram in 1952 as the second edition of *Katha Upanishad*, this partially revised version was used. The same revised translation was used in *Eight Upanishads* in 1953 and subsequently.

MUNDAKA. First translated in Baroda; it forms part of typewritten MS. A revised version of this translation was published in the *Karmayogin* in February 1910. (This revised translation was included in *Seven Upanishads*, Poona, in 1920.) A further revised or new translation was published in the *Arya* in November and December 1920. Sri Aurobindo revised this *Arya* translation again thoroughly, apparently during the 1940s. This final revised version was used when the translation was published in *Eight Upanishads* in 1953 and subsequently.

TAITTIRIYA and AITAREYA. First translated in Baroda; not part of typewritten MS. First reproduced from handwritten and unrevised manuscripts as part of *Eight Upanishads* in 1953. The first part of *Readings in the Taittiriya Upanishad*, "The Knowledge of Brahman", was written just previous to its publication in the *Arya* in November 1918. The second part, "Truth, Knowledge, Infinity", seems to have been written for the next issue of the *Arya*, but was left incomplete and never published by Sri Aurobindo. It appears here for the first time.

MANDUKYA and PRASHNA. Translated in Baroda; they form part of typewritten MS. Neither translation was ever revised. Both were first published in *Eight Upanishads* in 1953.

BRIHADARANYAKA. In Pondicherry around 1912 Sri Aurobindo translated the first two sections and part of the third section of the first chapter of this Upanishad in the margins of his copy of the text. Immediately afterwards he began to write a commentary on the Upanishad which he entitled *The Great Aranyaka*. This commentary was not completed even to the extent of what had been translated. Some of the footnotes to the text were written by Sri Aurobindo as comments on Shankara's Sanskrit commentary, which was printed below the text in the edition used by him. Since these comments are not extensive enough to justify the printing of Shankara's commentary, a few of Sri Aurobindo's comments or parts of comments that deal directly with Shankara, none of them extensive or important, have been omitted. Sri Aurobindo's translation (with footnotes) is being printed in this volume for the first time.

CHHANDOGYA. The translation of parts of the first chapter of this Upanishad seems to have been done in Baroda. The two sections of *Notes on the Chhandogya Upanishad*, "The Initial Sentence" and "Satyakama Jabala", were written separately in Pondicherry around 1912. The first is entitled in the manuscript "Notes on the Chhandogya Upanishad/First Adhyaya" (but only the first sentence is treated). The manuscript title of the second is "Vedic Interpretations/Satyakama Jabala".

SHWETASHWATARA. Sri Aurobindo seems to have translated the fourth to sixth chapters of this Upanishad in Baroda. But he is recorded as saying, "I translated the Shwetashwatara Upanishad while I was in Bengal." (Nirodbaran, *Talks with Sri Aurobindo* Vol. II, p. 124). Perhaps Sri Aurobindo did the translation during one of his vacations from the Baroda College. The fourth chapter was retranslated in Pondicherry around 1917; it is being printed here for the first time. It is not known whether the first three chapters were ever translated.

KAIVALYA and NILARUDRA. These fragmentary translations with commentary were done in Pondicherry around 1912.

THE KARIKAS OF GAUDAPADA and SADANANDA'S ESSENCE OF VEDANTA (VEDANTASARA). These two early Vedantic texts were translated incompletely (the first with commentary) in Baroda.

The first collected edition of Sri Aurobindo's Upanishadic translations and commentaries was published as Volume 12 of the Sri Aurobindo Birth Centenary Library under the title *The Upanishads* in 1972. This volume included all material which had been published in books up to that time: viz. the translations of and commentaries on the Isha and the Kena Upanishads (taken from the 1965 edition of *Isha Upanishad* and the 1970 edition of *Kena Upanishad*) and the complete translations of the Katha, Mundaka, Mandukya, Prashna, Taittiriya and Aitareya Upanishads (taken from the second edition of *Eight Upanishads*). In the volume also appeared, for the first time in a book, certain incomplete or fragmentary translations of (and/or commentaries on) the Brihadaranyaka, Chhandogya, Shwetashwatara, Kaivalya and Nilarudra Upanishads and early Vedantic texts. In addition *The Upanishads* contained, for the first time in book form, several of Sri Aurobindo's early expository writings and commentaries. Both a de luxe and a popular edition of the Centenary Library volume were published in 1972. Later in the same year an impression in reduced facsimile was published. (In 1973 the Isha translation and commentary were issued separately in the same reduced format with new page numbers as a new edition of *Isha Upanishad*.)

The present volume is composed mainly of material selected from the Centenary Edition of *The Upanishads*. The early commentaries and expository writings of Sri Aurobindo that appeared in the 1972 volume, as well as similar writings published in 1973 in Volume 27 (*Supplement*) of the Centenary Library, and since 1977 in the semi-annual journal *Sri Aurobindo: Archives and Research*, and still others that are as yet unpublished, will be brought out in a separate volume. Apart from the omission of the earlier commentaries and expository writings, the present volume differs from the 1972 edition of *The Upanishads* in certain additions, in the rearrangement of the contents, and in editing. The additions are (1) as Introduction, a chapter from Sri Aurobindo's *Foundations of Indian Culture* ("Indian Literature – 2"), which was first published in the *Arya* in June 1920; (2) the incomplete translation of the Brihadaranyaka Upanishad, and the following articles: *Readings in the Taittiriya Upanishad*: "Truth, Knowledge, Infinity" and *Notes on the Chhandogya Upanishad*: "Satyakama Jabala"; (3) two Appendixes, one consisting of Sri Aurobindo's translations of Upanishadic passages cited in his work *The Life Divine* along with the Sanskrit texts of these passages, and the other of Sri Aurobindo's translations of the "peace recitations" which precede several of the Upanishads, along with their texts. Sri Aurobindo's translations of the recitations date from the Baroda period and are taken from the typewritten manuscript; (4) a glossary; and (5) an index. *Notes on the Chhandogya Upanishad*: "The Initial Sentence", published incompletely in the 1972 edition of *The Upanishads* is in the present volume given fully (to the extent of its handwritten manuscript). The later translation of Chapter 4 of the Shwetashwatara Upanishad is in the present volume substituted for the earlier one.

The material in this volume has been rearranged in three sections. Section One comprises translations and commentaries done (or, in the case of the *Katha Upanishad*, partially revised) by Sri Aurobindo after 1910, and thus constituting the real, finished corpus of his Upanishadic work. Section Two is made up of complete translations done before 1910. In Section Three are gathered incomplete and fragmentary writings done in Baroda (or Calcutta) and in Pondicherry, i.e. both before and after 1910.

The editors have checked every translation or commentary in the present volume against the last version seen by Sri Aurobindo. For the Isha Upanishad this final version is the last edition of *Isha Upanishad* published during his lifetime. For the Kena it is a set of pages from the *Arya* with Sri Aurobindo's revisions. These pages were found only recently. For the Mundaka it is the final revised version from *Eight Upanishads*. For each of the other writings Sri Aurobindo's manuscript was used for the checking. Some typographical and other errors have been corrected.

The present edition also reflects some modification of editorial policy. Archaic forms, which in the past were usually modernised, have in the present volume been allowed to stand. A uniform policy has been adopted in regard to footnotes. All footnotes set in roman type are Sri Aurobindo's; all those set in *italics* are the editors'. Where Sri Aurobindo has left two

alternative words or phrases in his manuscript, the one written first has been
given by the editors in a footnote after an italic *"Or"*. But alternatives
following a roman "Or" (as in the translations of the Kena, Mundaka and
Katha Upanishads) are footnotes written by Sri Aurobindo when the
passage concerned seemed by him to admit of two possible senses, both of
which he wanted to bring out. English words written in italics (or Sanskrit
words written in roman type) in the translations are words that were
underlined by Sri Aurobindo in his manuscripts. These are words that
correspond to no word in the texts, but were supplied by the translator to
better express the sense of the texts as he read them.

The present volume, new in editing and in form, is the second edition of
The Upanishads.